Natural Language Processing with ThoughtTreasure

Natural Language Processing with ThoughtTreasure

Erik T. Mueller

Reprinted June 30, 2012
Publisher: Erik T. Mueller

Although every effort has been made to ensure the accuracy and completeness of information contained in this book, the author and publisher assume no responsibility for errors, inaccuracies, omissions, or any inconsistency herein. Any slights of people, places, or organizations are unintentional.

ThoughtTreasure is a trademark of Erik T. Mueller.

All brand names and product names in this book are the trademarks or registered trademarks of their respective owners and/or manufacturers.

Mueller, Erik T.
Natural language processing with ThoughtTreasure / Erik T. Mueller
Library of Congress Catalog Card Number 97-91111

Contents

Preface

When the Dartmouth Summer Research Project on Artificial Intelligence was held in 1956, the creation of an intelligent computer seemed to be just around the corner. Since then, the number of researchers in the field has grown to over 10,000 and the number of pages in the biennial proceedings of the international joint conference on artificial intelligence to 2074. And here we are, over 40 years later, without computers that can truly understand and communicate. What went wrong?

In fact, significant progress has been made both in fundamental research (search, logic, machine learning, knowledge representation, computational linguistics, robotics) and in deployed applications (speech recognition, financial expert systems, chess-playing programs). We tend to forget these successes—as the cliché goes, once an aspect of human intelligence can be successfully simulated, it is no longer considered an AI problem.

But we have also come to see how complicated intelligence is. Perhaps this was always obvious to some, while to others it seemed just as obvious that one could walk up to a blank slate, the computer, and instruct it how to be intelligent, simply by writing the "right" program. Well it turns out not to be so simple. Our own intelligence, after all, is the result of billions of years of evolution.

We have also come to question our definition of intelligence. AI has classically viewed intelligence as a general, species-independent facility, an objective entity to be torn apart, reduced to its fundamental components. In fact, it may be more of a human artifact to be studied anthropologically.

The role and value of working in multiple paradigms has also become clear: We have branched out from symbolic models to subsymbolic models such as neural nets, cellular automata, genetic algorithms, and artificial life. We have also learned how to evaluate our programs quantitatively and how to speed the task of "writing the right program" by constructing rules and decision trees automatically.

Computers have also become more powerful and less expensive—a megabyte of semiconductor memory that cost $550,000 in 1970 now costs less than $10. This allows us to construct more layers of software or tools to help us build and debug programs, and to get rapid feedback from the larger and more complex systems we have created.

We have learned a lot in the last four decades. We have continued to advance as new problems and solutions come up daily. But some researchers have given up, considering artificial intelligence to be either misguided or impossible. I, and others, feel the idea is still workable and that despite various failures nothing has really changed—we still have ahead of us the monumental and exciting task of creating a truly thinking computer.

A few years having passed since my previous attempt at AI, the Daydreamer program (Mueller, 1990), I decided to try again. This time, instead of doing fundamental research on emotions and the stream of thought, I would draw on existing results from computational linguistics and AI. All techniques would be fair game. Beginning in April 1994, I worked full-time for two years on a new program called ThoughtTreasure. In April 1996, having gotten the program to the point where it could read some types of text and answer simple questions, I made the first version available on the Internet. Since then I have added more words and concepts, and worked on applications.

As you might have guessed, my objective of building a program that can understand arbitrary natural language remains unachieved. But I still think that by adding to ThoughtTreasure's set of "understanding agents", it will eventually be able to understand. This will take some time since it requires us painstakingly to identify, handle, and test a large number of possible input sentences. Over the coming years, let's add to ThoughtTreasure and similar programs, evolve them, run them on faster and faster machines, use more advanced debugging environments, and make AI happen!

I would like to thank those who responded to the ThoughtTreasure web site and Scott Turner for suggesting improvements to the manuscript. I especially thank my sister Rachel Mueller-Lust, my brother-in-law Andy Mueller-Lust, my father Robert Mueller, my mother Diana Mueller, and my wife Susanna Fischer.

Chapter 1: Introduction

Anyone who has tried typing a plain-English question into the Microsoft Office Assistant or the Infoseek search engine knows that computer programs have great difficulty understanding natural language. Instead of locating an answer to the question, the programs often return long lists of irrelevant responses. The problem is that unlike people, computers are unable to pinpoint what is being asked. Why is this?

An important reason is that natural language is highly ambiguous. Consider the text "I am". The "I" could be a subject pronoun, a Roman numeral, or the symbol for electric current. The "am" could be a verb, an abbreviation for before noon, or the symbol for americium. Now consider a 5-word sentence, where each word has 4 meanings. This sentence could conceivably have $4 \cdot 4 \cdot 4 \cdot 4 \cdot 4 = 1024$ meanings! Assuming the computer can generate all these meanings, it is then difficult for it to figure out which one was intended.

Natural language processing is in its infancy. Computational linguists are only starting to learn how to capture word meanings in a computer and how to build programs that track the meanings of sentences. Current computer hardware is not up to the task, even given the best available software. Still, it seems likely that if we want them to, computers will eventually be able to understand and communicate in natural language as easily as we can.

The ThoughtTreasure platform was created with the long-term goal of human-level comprehension in mind. It brings together much of the research and experience in linguistics and artificial intelligence to date, serving as a foundation for future work. The platform contains 135,000 lines of ANSI C code and concise-format database entries representing over 20,000 concepts associated with over 50,000 English and French words and phrases. It includes a syntactic and semantic parser, an English and French generator, and a chatterbot front end enabling the user to converse with the program.

What does ThoughtTreasure do?

ThoughtTreasure can answer simple questions relating to information stored in its database:

```
> What is your name?
Thomas.
```

```
> What time is it?
It is quarter past ten am.
> Are elephants purple?
No, they are not purple. Elephants are gray.
> What is the circumference of the Earth?
40003236 meters is its circumference.
> Who assassinated Henri IV?
François Ravaillac assassinated him.
```

ThoughtTreasure can make sense of simple sentences describing interpersonal relationships and emotional responses:

```
> Jacques is an enemy of François.
> He hates François.
Right, he is an enemy of François.
> Jacques succeeded at being elected President of
France.
> He is happy.
Right, he succeeds at being the president of France.
> François is happy for Jacques.
True, he succeeds at being the president of France.
But I thought that he was an enemy of François.
```

ThoughtTreasure can translate from English to French or French to English. It produces the following translation of the above exchange:

```
) Jacques est un ennemi de François.
) Il déteste François.
Effectivement, Jacques est son ennemi.
) Jacques réussit à être le président de la France.
) Il est heureux.
Effectivement, Jacques réussit à être le président de
la France.
) François est heureux pour Jacques.
Oui, Jacques réussit à être le président de la France.
Mais je croyais que Jacques était un ennemi de
François.
```

ThoughtTreasure can keep a calendar up-to-date based on input sentences such as:

```
> I have an appointment with Amy Newton on March 21,
1996 at eight pm.
> I canceled the appointment with Amy.
```

ThoughtTreasure can use grids to reason about objects in space. The following grid represents a corner grocery store:

```
VVVVVSSSwwwwwwwwwwwwwwwwwwwwwwwwwwwwwwwwwwwwwwwwwwwwwwwww
VVVVVSSSw                                          fnffw
VVVVVSS2q                                          ffffw
VVVVVSSSq                                          fxffw
VVVVVSSSw                                          ffffw
VVVVVSSSw    ttt           ffffmffff               ffffw
VVVVVSSSw    tttB     sssssssssssssssssssssssssssss ffffw
VVVVVSSSw cArtt       sssssssssssssssssssssssssssss fuffw
VVVVVSSSw    ttt           z         y             ffffw
VVVVVSSSw                                          fvffw
VVVVVSSSw                                          ffffw
VVVVVSSSw                                          ffffw
VVVVVSSSwl                                         fpffw
VVVVVSSSwwwwwwwwwwwwwwwwwwwwwwwwwwwwwwwwwwwwwwwwwwwwwwwww
```

The character "r" represents a cash register, "w" represents a wall, "V" represents the street, and so on. ThoughtTreasure tracks the locations of characters in the grid when parsing a simple story:

```
>>>>> Mrs. Jeanne Püchl was a grocer.
> What is her occupation?
She is a grocer.
> Jeanne Püchl was where?
She was in the corner grocery.
> She was near what salamis?
She is near the Danish salami.
> She was near what electronic devices?
She is near the cash register.
>>>>> At seven am she stepped out into the street.
> She stepped out into the street at what time?
She walked to the street from the corner grocery at
seven am.
> Where was her left foot?
Her left foot was in the corner grocery. Her left foot
was on the street.
```

ThoughtTreasure can identify names, places, products, and other tokens in text. Given the following email message from Jim to Karen:

```
Date: Mon, 11 Mar 1996 09:35:17-0500
From: jim@trollope.com (Jim Garnier)
To: karen@netabulous
Subject: Re: What's up?

On Mar 8, 11:53am, Karen Garnier wrote:
>What's up?
Not much. I saw the film "Horizons lointains" in Saumur
(Maine-et-Loire).

BTW, my new phone number is 212-555-3845.
Jim
P.S. I sold my 1977 Fiat Spider for $600. 8-)
```

ThoughtTreasure recognizes tokens such as the following:

```
[EMAILHEADER <standard-email-header><string-message-ID>
  <19960311093500>FROM<Jim><jim@trollope.com>TO<human2342>
  SUBJ<What's up?>]
[ATTRIBUTION <19940308115300>SPEAKER<Karen>]
[NAME:N <Karen Garnier>]
[NAME:N <Jim>]
[MEDIA_OBJ:N Horizons-lointains]
[POLITY:N Saumur]
[TELNO:N <212-555-3845>]
[TSRANGE:B @19770101000000:19770101000000]
[PRODUCT:N 1977-Fiat-1800-Spider]
[NUMBER:N NUMBER:USD:600]
[COMMUNICON [smile Jim]]
```

ThoughtTreasure can parse and answer simple questions about classified ads:

```
From: toddspi@quapaw.astate.edu (Todd Spires)
FS: 1978 Fiat 124 Spyder. Asking $3000.

> I want to buy a Fiat Spyder.
A 124, a 2000, or a 1800?
> A 124.
A 1978 Fiat 124 was for sale for 3000 dollars by Todd
Spire at "toddspi@quapaw.astate.edu".
```

ThoughtTreasure can learn from tables. Given the following table of telephone country codes:

```
Australia 61
Cameroon 237
Canada     1
Guyana    592
India      91
Italy     390
```

ThoughtTreasure automatically determines the locations of the fields, what type of information they contain (in this case country and telephone country code), and makes any necessary updates to its database of country codes.

ThoughtTreasure and this book

ThoughtTreasure is organized into linguistic modules called *components* (after Chomsky, 1965) and AI modules called *agencies* (after Minsky, 1986) composed of *agents*. These modules are:

- the lexical component,
- the syntactic component,
- the semantic component,
- the representation agency,
- the text agency,
- the planning agency, and
- the understanding agency.

This book is a complete handbook on ThoughtTreasure for the user, programmer, and researcher. It is organized by ThoughtTreasure module. Each chapter begins with an example, showing how the module addressed in the chapter applies to the construction of a new application, namely a program to parse and understand movie reviews. The interior of a chapter discusses the module in detail, provides reference material, and discusses further examples. The end of each chapter consists of a list of exercises and sample projects.

The representation agency is discussed in Chapter 2. This agency contains a database of concepts organized into a hierarchy, and assertions about concepts. It also contains the basic data structures and routines for representing and manipulating space, time, actors, objects, assertions, contexts, numbers, strings, and input/output channels.

The lexical component, which contains the English and French lexicon, is discussed in Chapter 3. Lexical entries and concepts are entered together using a concise language that speeds entry and enables the presentation of as much information as possible on the screen while coding.

ThoughtTreasure contains a detailed bilingual taxonomy of adverbs, pronouns, prepositions, interjections, logical relations, temporal relations, and speech acts. For example, the adverbs category is broken down into disjuncts, conjuncts, hedges, discourse markers, temporal adverbs, intensifiers, and downtoners.

The text agency is discussed in Chapter 4. This agency is responsible for converting input text into a set of parse nodes to be used by the syntactic parser. It includes text agents for various entities such as words, phrases, names, email addresses, dates, phone numbers, book titles, and product names.

The syntactic component—roughly the level described by Chomsky (1965; 1982)—is discussed in Chapter 5. This component consists of base rules, filters or constraints on when base rules can apply, and a syntactic parser. Transformations improve the output of the natural language generator. A generator of examples facilitates the coding of subcategorization restrictions.

The semantic component—roughly the level described by Lyons (1977) or Jackendoff (1972)—is discussed in Chapter 6. This component contains a semantic parser responsible for converting a syntactic parse tree into a ThoughtTreasure assertion. This is accomplished using what are basically compositional projection rules (see Katz and Fodor, 1963; Montague, 1974). Various grammatical constructs are handled: adjuncts, copulas, relative clauses, attachments (such as occupations and nationalities), relations and roles (such as *advisor* and *advisee*), appositives, genitives, and nominalizations.

The semantic component contains an anaphoric parser which resolves *intensions* produced by the semantic parser (such as "his sister who lives in Chicago") into *extensions* (such as a particular person). The anaphoric parser also resolves pronouns, articles, and determiners.

The semantic component contains a model of English and French verb tenses, a model of aspect designed expressly for English and French (Boulle, 1988), and a bilingual generator that converts ThoughtTreasure assertions into natural language.

The planning agency is discussed in Chapter 7. It consists of planning agents to achieve various human goals:

- *Planning agents for graspers and containers*: move hand, grasp, release, hand object to someone, open and close container, pour, connect objects together, turn switch.
- *Planning agents for transfer of location* (Ptrans; Schank, 1975): walk, stand, sit, lie down, drive, plan a trip using various modes of transportation.
- *Planning agents for transfer of possession* (Atrans): purchase ticket, pay, collect payment, work box office, work grocery store.
- *Planning agents for transfer of information* (Mtrans): speak, carry on conversation, obtain permission, handle proposal.
- *Planning agents for using devices*: place/handle phone call, take shower.
- *Planning agents for entertainment*: watch TV, attend performance.
- *Planning agents for interpersonal relationships*: maintain friends, meet with someone.
- *Other planning agents*: sleep, dress, appointment.

Planning agents are used to simulate household devices:

- *Telephone* (switching system): Receive dialed digits, provide audible dialtone/ringback/busy signal, ring phone, provide voice path between two phones.
- *TV set*: TV is on/off, what program is on what channel.
- *Shower*.
- *Motor vehicle*.

The hardest problem—one far from being solved—is contained in the understanding agency, discussed in Chapter 8. Its purpose is to take representations passed to it from the semantic component and appropriately adjust the states of all active planning agents. This is, its purpose is to adjust ThoughtTreasure's model of the world in order to account for the input. Previous research in this area is the work done on "scripts" (Schank and Abelson, 1977), "in-depth understanding" (Dyer, 1983), "commonsense knowledge" (Lenat and Guha, 1990), and "abduction" (Hobbs, Stickel, Appelt, and Martin, 1993).

The understanding agency includes understanding agents dedicated to specific domains and tasks (such as time, space, emotions and goals, interpersonal relationships, weather, answering questions, asking clarifying questions) and to steering particular planning agents. The agency includes a mechanism for setting up a simulated person's environment in a grid by analogy to known environments.

Learning by ThoughtTreasure is discussed in Chapter 9. The table text agent parses and learns from free-format tables. An inflectional morphology mechanism —using both hardcoded and automatically learned rules—generates inflections of English and French verbs, adjectives, and nouns. A derivational morphology mechanism learns new words and their approximate meanings using a database of 152 known affixes, and learns new derivational rules.

Applications of ThoughtTreasure—in addition to those presented elsewhere—and the ThoughtTreasure shell are discussed in Chapter 10. The shell allows the user to start applications such as the chatterbot and conduct tests of various program components.

Various experiences and unexpected events in the development of ThoughtTreasure are described in Chapter 11.

Conclusions and suggestions for further work are presented in Chapter 12.

Size comparison with other systems

Here is comparison of ThoughtTreasure's database with that of WordNet (Miller, 1995b), Cyc (Lenat, 1995), EDR (Yokoi, 1995), and LADL's electronic dictionary (Courtois and Silberztein, 1990).

	TT	WordNet	Cyc	EDR	LADL
languages	E,F	E	E	E,J	F
le	50,133	118,000		600,000	170,000
infl	32,802				600,000
obj	21,521	90,000	100,000	400,000	
<le, obj>	45,739	166,000			
polysemy	6.1%	17%			
assertions	37,162	116,000	1,000,000		
effort	2		100		

languages
The languages addressed by the system. (E = English, F = French, J = Japanese.)
le
The number of lexical entries, including words and phrases. For bilingual systems such as ThoughtTreasure and EDR, the numbers shown are the total for the two

languages. 60 percent of the lexical entries in ThoughtTreasure are for English. 37 percent of the lexical entries in ThoughtTreasure are phrases. (53 percent of the LADL lexical entries are phrases.)

infl

The number of validated inflections. ThoughtTreasure contains 127,448 automatically generated inflections (100,722 unique forms) of which only 32,802 have been checked for correctness by a human.

obj

The number of atomic concepts or objects.

<le, obj>

The number of links between lexical entries and objects. (14.8 percent of the lexical entries in ThoughtTreasure are not linked to any object, due to the presence in phrases of words which are not defined in isolation.)

polysemy

The percentage of lexical entries linked to more than one object. (Excluding those lexical entries not linked to any object, 7.4% of the lexical entries in ThoughtTreasure are polysemous.)

assertions

The number of assertions (facts containing atomic concepts) in the system. Assertions of ThoughtTreasure hardcoded in C are not included in this figure. 23,335 of ThoughtTreasure's assertions are hierarchical links.

effort

The number of person-years spent developing the system.

The ThoughtTreasure paradigm

ThoughtTreasure treats the problem of creating a computer which can understand natural language as largely an engineering one, along the lines of Lenat and Guha's (1990) large-scale knowledge base Cyc, and Minsky's (1986) view of intelligence as a giant society of interacting simple processes. The development of ThoughtTreasure was guided by a philosophy which can be summed up by the expression, "Just do it!" Let me spell this out.

Give up the search for a canonical representation. Since Leibniz's Characteristica Universalis, there have been numerous attempts to find the perfect language (Yaguello, 1984; Eco, 1995). If a consistent, canonical representation of concepts could be found, it would be ideal for representing concepts in a computer: The meanings of every word and phrase would be represented and sentences could then be understood and generated by composing the representations. Machine translation programs would convert the source language into the canonical representation, and then convert the canonical representation into the target language. The task of reasoning automatically would be simplified—instead of having several inference rules for dealing with alternative representations of a concept, there would only be one. A number of researchers in linguistics and AI (starting with, for example, Lakoff, 1971; Jackendoff 1972; Schank, 1975) have therefore proposed various deep structures, semantic primitives, logical forms, or interlinguas for representing language-independent meaning.

There is some initial mileage to a canonical representation. But researchers who take this to the limit eventually find that it breaks down. Ludwig Wittgenstein, having studied with Bertrand Russell, took a logic-based approach at first, defining the world as a set of complex statements (*Tatsache*) composed of atomic statements (*Sachverhalte*) (Wittgenstein, 1921/1961). Eventually he flip-flopped, considering meaning—in particular, language—not as logic but as a game people play or a kind of labyrinth (Wittgenstein, 1953). It is very difficult to find the single, correct representation for a concept. Programs built exclusively using canonical representations suffer from brittleness, since canonical representations are unable to capture the elusiveness and open-endedness of human concepts. Anyhow, sentences are open to an infinite number of interpretations (Eco, 1990/1992).

Instead of getting lost trying to find the ultimate, elegant representational scheme, a more practical approach is to use any and all representational schemes that will enable the program to accomplish its tasks. The ThoughtTreasure database of concepts is therefore not a canonical representation of reality, but simply the basis for more detailed processing in C. For example, the database contains a list of linguistic expressions referring to a relative day and part of the day:

	day	start	stop
the night before last	-2	2100	2400
last night	-1	2100	2400
this morning	0	0600	1200
tonight	0	2100	2400
...			

In parsing one of the above expressions, ThoughtTreasure's *time text agent* accesses the list in order to convert the expression into a timestamp range, which is later used to modify a concept. The relations used to represent the relative day and starting and stopping times are specialized—they are of use only to the time text agent (or to any future agents which might desire this information). Does *night* really extend from 2100 to 2400 hours? This question leads one into the canonical representation trap.

Avoid building tools. Many attempts have been made in AI and computer science to find the right tool—a general architecture for cognition, a powerful declarative representation language, or an elegant programming language. If only we had the right tool, the argument goes, it would be easy to solve the problem at hand. But tools built too early in the game restrict future developments. They increase total programming time when much effort is put into the development of tools that turn out to be the wrong tool.

One AI tool that seemed promising—and though much work went into it did not end up helping much—was the *production rule* (Newell and Simon, 1972). The idea was that each rule would be a modular chunk operating independently of other rules, and that this would make it easy to build systems that learned by adding or deleting rules or conditions. But in practice production rules had to be used in conjunction with one another to accomplish a task. As production systems were built, rules would sometimes fire in the wrong order. To enforce the proper ordering, conditions had to be added to the rules. In essence, in order to accomplish A B C D, one was forced to write the rules:

```
if true then A
if A then B
if B then C
if C then D
```

when it would have been easier and more transparent simply to code:

```
A;B;C;D;
```

in a traditional programming language.

Ad hoc code is allowed, even encouraged. Related to the tools issue is generality of code: Much of ThoughtTreasure's code is ad hoc—there are many messy segments of code designed to cope with particular situations, rather than one elegant general mechanism (see Schank's *scruffy-neat* distinction [Abelson, 1981]). For example, first- and second-person pronouns are treated separately from third-person pronouns, where perhaps a generalization could be made. The trouble with a generalization is that it becomes very tempting to subsume more and more —perhaps everything—under it. You are then left with a set of residual cases that do not fit into that generalization, and reluctant to create a new one to handle them. Better to create lots of small overlapping islands of generalization that cover the cases, than to create one generalization that does not. A program containing multiple generalizations will be less confined to a single paradigm and less brittle as a result.

In ThoughtTreasure, there is a set of constructs for grouping related but distinguishable concepts: enums (such as liquid/solid/gas/plasma), value range names (such as days of the week), weighted attributes and relations (such as excellent/good/adequate/bad), and contrast objects (such as menswear/womenswear/uniwear). With enums and value range names, the distinction is expressed in the predicate position of the assertion. With weighted attributes and relations, the distinction is expressed in the last position of the assertion. With classificational contrasts, the distinction is expressed by location in the hierarchy. Some of these constructs probably could and should be merged into others, but they each arose in the context of a particular processing task and they perform their function. A generalization might not buy much in terms of operational behavior, and might cause further problems.

Chapter 2: The representation agency

The representation agency of ThoughtTreasure consists of a database and basic procedures and data structures for representing concepts, space, time, actors, and contexts. This agency is best understood through an example of how it is used and extended in building a particular application for movie review understanding.

Representation and the movie review application

The purpose of the movie review application is to extract as much information as possible from natural language text containing a movie review. This information includes: the name of the movie; the writer, director, and stars of the movie; the reviewer; the reviewer's overall rating of the movie; descriptive information regarding the movie and the performances of the actors; and so on. Once this information is extracted, it is stored in the database. Information may later be retrieved from the database by asking questions in natural language or by forming queries in the ThoughtTreasure representation language. For example, one could query the system for all movies recommended by a particular reviewer and released within the last 2 weeks.

Collecting data from a corpus

We begin by forming a corpus of 50 movie reviews from the Usenet newsgroup `rec.arts.movies.reviews` which contains postings of formal reviews written by people on the net. We use a news reader to access articles and then append them into a file. (Using the Unix news reader called `rn`, we would go to the newsgroup by typing `grec.arts.movies.reviews` and then issue the command `1-$scorpus` in order to append all available articles of the newsgroup into the file `corpus`.)

To extend the representation agency to handle movie reviews, we must extend the ThoughtTreasure *ontology* or model of what concepts exist in the world and how they are related. We go through the corpus and collect an informal list of concepts we would like to add (if not already present):

```
date of review
reviewer
reference to web page with more reviews by reviewer
```

```
name of movie
star of movie
writer of movie
distributor of movie
production studio of movie
director of movie
producer of movie
cinematographer of movie
composer of movie's music
language(s) of movie
whether movie has subtitles
movie that movie is a remake of
book that movie is based on
Motion Picture Association of America (MPAA) rating of
movie (G, PG, PG-13, R, NC-17, NR)
running time of movie
date movie opens
reviewer's rating of movie
genre of movie: action movie, comedy, murder mystery,
  thriller, B movie, sports movie, horror movie, noirish
various descriptions of movie
various descriptions of actors in movie
```

Adding media objects to the ontology

We then figure out where these concepts should fall in the existing ontology and begin entering them. The top-level ThoughtTreasure ontology is organized as follows:

```
=concept//
==object//
===abstract-object//
===being//
===matter//
====particle//
====chemical//
====physical-object//
==situation//
===state//
====relation//
====attribute//
====enum//
===action//
```

Hierarchy is expressed in ThoughtTreasure database file format via indentation level, with equal signs used for indentation. Thus concepts are broken down into (1) objects or entities or things, and (2) situations. Situations are broken down into (1) states of affairs or static situations, and (2) actions or dynamic situations or activities or processes or events (see Lyons, 1977, p. 483). States are broken down into (1) relations or relationships or connections between concepts, such as `weight-of`, (2) attributes or properties or characteristics of concepts, such as `heavy`, and (3) enumerated attributes or enums or collections of mutually exclusive (or simply related) attributes such as `male` and `female`.

A film is an `abstract-object`, in particular a `media-object`, so we enter the concept for film into the database file `mediaobj.txt` under the existing `media-object`:

```
=media-object/information/
==advertisement//
==art//
==computer-program//
==dance//
==datafeed//
==film//
==genetic-code//
==opera//
==play//
==text//
===book//
===magazine//
```

Newly entered items for the movie review application are shown here in **boldface** (and surrounded by the `MRBEGIN` and `MREND` keywords in the ThoughtTreasure distribution). We can enter the concepts in alphabetical order for convenience. Some of the items shown here are simplified for clarity; see the actual database files in the distribution for more details.

Although indentation is usually used to indicate parent-child relationships in the hierarchy, we may also specify additional parents using the notation:

```
=media-object/information/
```

which is equivalent to:

```
=information//
==media-object//
```

Next we expand the `film` ontology by adding various subclasses:

```
==datafeed//
==film//
==-film-length-contrast//
====feature-film//
====short-film//
==-film-budget-contrast//
====blockbuster//
====B-movie//
==-film-genre//
====action-film//
====adventure-film//
====animated-film//
====cinema-verite//
====comedy-film//
====documentary-film//
====drama-film//
====fantasy-film//
====horror-film//
====musical-film//
====mystery-film//
=====murder-mystery-film//
====science-fiction-film//
====sports-film//
====thriller-film//
==genetic-code//
```

The film genres noted in the corpus are expanded with additional genres collected from newspapers, magazines, the web, and the local video store. (The definition of lexical entries and synonyms such as *horror film* and *horror movie* will be discussed in the next chapter.)

The children of `film-length-contrast`, `film-budget-contrast`, and `film-genre` provide alternative schemes for classifying films. A given film might be classified as a `feature-film`, `B-movie`, and `thriller-film`. The top concept of each scheme is flagged as being a *contrast concept* by replacing the last equal sign with a dash.

We choose concept names that are descriptive and not already taken in the system. For example, `musical` might apply to a film or play, so we create concepts `musical-film` and `musical-play`. To find out whether a concept name is taken, we can use the `obj` command of the ThoughtTreasure shell:

```
* obj
Welcome to the Obj query tool.
Enter object name: musical
musical
ancestors: musical personality-trait 2:../db/attr.txt
   2:attribute 3:state 4:situation film-genre
   2:film 3:media-object 4:../db/mediaobj.txt
   4:information
descendants: musical
musicien.Ay/
musical.Az /
assertions involving:
Enter object name: musical-film
Obj not found
Enter object name:
```

Thus we see that the name musical is already used for a personality trait, but the name musical-film is not yet taken. (A search command such as fgrep under Unix may also be used to search the database files.) If a name is accidentally reused, ThoughtTreasure will print a warning message when the database file is loaded:

```
19960831144756 <musical>: name <musical> reused
```

Adding relations and attributes to the ontology

Next we add relations on films to the ontology. There is already a concept media-object-relation in the database file relation.txt that specifies relations on media objects, so we insert the new relations under that concept:

```
=media-object-relation/relation/
==author-of//
==composer-of//
==newscaster-of//
==viewer-of//
==actor-of//
==cinematographer-of//
==director-of//
==language-of//
==MPAA-rating-of//
==producer-of//
==writer-of//
...
```

Now we enter a sample film into the ontology, to illustrate how the above relations are used:

```
====documentary-film//
====drama-film//
=====RDP/feature-film/|
[director-of RDP MALE:"Eric Rohmer"]|
[actor-of RDP FEMALE:"Clara Bellar"]|
[actor-of RDP MALE:"Antoine Basler"]|
[actor-of RDP MALE:"Mathias Megard"]|
[actor-of RDP FEMALE:"Aurore Rauscher"]|
|@1992|[media-object-release na RDP]|
...
```

We assert information about the film Rendez-Vous de Paris (RDP) into the database: that Eric Rohmer is the director of the film, that Clara Bellar and others are actors of the film, and that the film was released by some unknown studio in 1992. (The concept na indicates information which is not available or unknown. media-object-release is an action which was already present in the ontology.)

After defining new concepts, ThoughtTreasure can be started in order to find any entry errors. For example, if we enter:

```
====drama-film/
=====RDP/feature-film/
```

instead of:

```
====drama-film//
=====RDP/feature-film/
```

(omitting a slash), the message is printed:

```
19960831172256: reading ../db/mediaobj.txt
19960831172257 <drama-film>: = present in <=====RDP>
thought to be isa
```

We can now query the ThoughtTreasure database to find out who directed *Rendez-Vous de Paris* using the db command of the ThoughtTreasure shell:

```
* db
Welcome to the Db query tool.
Enter timestamp (?=wildcard): ?
Next element: director-of
Next element: RDP
Next element: ?
Next element:
query pattern: @na|[director-of RDP ?]
results:
@-inf:inf|[director-of RDP Eric-Rohmer]
Enter timestamp (?=wildcard): pop
*
```

(We are not quite ready to query ThoughtTreasure in natural language, since lexical entries for the film domain have not yet been added. This is addressed in the next chapter.)

To represent the studio that produced the movie, we specify the studio as the actor (first argument) of the `media-object-release` action:

```
====animated-film//
=====Hunchback-of-Notre-Dame/feature-film/
|@1996|media-object-release¤Disney|
```

The notations:

```
media-object-release¤Disney
media-object-release=Disney
```

are shorthand for:

```
[media-object-release Disney Hunchback-of-Notre-Dame]
[media-object-release Hunchback-of-Notre-Dame Disney]
```

respectively, inside the definition of the concept `Hunchback-of-Notre-Dame`. Additional studios may be entered in the database file `company.txt` under `entertainment-industry`.

To enable use of the relation `MPAA-rating-of`, we first define its possible values. A short list of values is usually represented in ThoughtTreasure either as an enum or as an abstract object. In this case, there is already a `rating` concept in the database file `absobj.txt`, so we add the MPAA ratings there:

```
=rating/abstract-object/
==Q-rating//
==popularity-rating//
==television-audience-rating//
===Nielsen-rating//
===Audimat-rating//
==MPAA-rating//
===MPAA-G//
===MPAA-NC-17//
===MPAA-PG//
===MPAA-PG-13//
===MPAA-R//
===MPAA-NR//
```

We may then specify:

```
=====Hunchback-of-Notre-Dame/feature-film/
|@1996|MPAA-rating-of=MPAA-G|
```

Now we turn to representing judgments of the reviewer. We attempt to use existing concepts wherever this is acceptable for the application. The ThoughtTreasure attribute ontology contains a variety of attributes such as:

```
====attribute//
=====personality-trait//
======arrogant//
======courageous//
======easygoing//
======litigious//
======preppy//
======sane//
=====object-trait//
======condition//
======sick//
=======earache//
======fashionable//
======good//
======interesting//
======profound//
```

If a reviewer Jim Denby thinks somewhat highly of *Rendez-Vous de Paris*, yet feels it is shallow, according to a review dated August 31, 1996, this is represented as:

```
@19960831:na|[believe Jim-Denby [good RDP 0.5u]]
@19960831:na|[believe Jim-Denby [profound RDP -0.9u]]
```

That is, all the various star rating systems will be converted into a value from -1.0 to 1.0 of the good attribute, where -1.0 means extremely bad and 1.0 means extremely good. (If we wanted to, we could retain the rating peculiar to the reviewer such as "3 on the Renshaw scale of 0 to 10 beast intentions," in a fashion similar to that used to store the MPAA rating.) Other ThoughtTreasure attributes are used to describe the film in more detail, and new attributes are added when they are not already present. We will add more attributes in the next chapter, where we continue the example of the movie review application and show how to add lexical entries to ThoughtTreasure so it can parse natural language movie reviews.

A brief tour of the ontology

The complete ontology is defined in the database files of the ThoughtTreasure distribution and consists of over 20,000 concepts. Just to give an idea of its contents, we quickly run through some excerpts. (The previous section presented abbreviated versions of the top-level and attribute ontologies.)

Humans

Humans are located in the ontology as follows:

```
=concept//
==object//
===being//
===matter//
====physical-object//
=====animate-object//
=====living-thing//
======animal/being,animate-object/
=======chordate//
========vertebrate//
=========mammal//
==========homo//
===========Homo-sapiens//
============human//
=============group//
```

22

Particular humans are located under human, while parts of humans (such as hand, finger, fingernail, lunula) are located under living-thing.

Relations

Here are some excerpts from the relation ontology, defining relations on humans:

```
====relation//
=====human-relation//
======age-of//
======name-of//
======residence-of//
======occupation-of//
======attitude//
=======admire//
=======like//
======goal//
=======active-goal//
=======failed-goal//
=======succeeded-goal//
=====ipr//
======familial-relationship//
======signed-ipr//
======pos-ipr//
========acquaintance-of//
========friend-of//
========lover-of//
=======spouse-of//
======neg-ipr//
========enemy-of//
=====object-relation//
======similar//
======part-of//
======cpart-of//
======owner-of//
```

Enums

Here are some excerpts from the enum ontology, defining enums on humans:

```
====enum//
=====phase-of-life//
======alive//
======not-alive//
=======not-yet-conceived//
=======unborn//
```

```
=======dead//
=====body-position//
======standing//
======sitting//
======lying//
```

Actions

Here are some excerpts from the action ontology, defining actions performed by humans or parts of humans (such as hand or mouth):

```
===action//
====primitive-action//
=====grasp//
=====ingest//
======eat//
======drink//
=====atrans//
=====mtrans//
======speech-act//
=======insult//
=======perlocutionary-act//
========indicate//
=====ptrans//
======leave//
======arrive//
=====create//
====script//
=====call//
=====transaction//
======buy//
=====holiday//
=====teach//
=====meal//
======brunch//
=====leisure-activity//
======read-book//
=====personal-script//
======cognitive-process//
=======remember//
======dress//
======sleep//
=====interpersonal-script//
======maintain-friend-of//
======appointment-script//
======conversation//
```

Physical objects

Here are some excerpts from the physical object ontology:

```
===matter//
====physical-object//
=====topographic-feature//
======landmass//
=======island//
=====building//
======house//
======shopping-center//
=======mall//
========mini-mall//
======skyscraper//
=====exterior-area//
======grass//
======roadway//
=====boundary//
======wall//
=====interior-area//
======subway-platform//
======room//
=======attic//
=====furniture//
======chair//
=====musical-instrument//
======woodwind//
=======piccolo//
=====personal-article//
======credit-card//
======umbrella//
=====material//
======fabric//
=======corduroy//
=====electronic-device//
======electronic-appliance//
=======computer-equipment//
========CPU//
=========microprocessor//
========computer//
=========workstation//
```

Related work

Previous hierarchical ontologies include:

- The U.S. Library of Congress subject headings (Library of Congress, 1987), begun in 1898 and consisting of 145,000 records in 1987. The database includes relations between headings such as USE/UF (synonym), BT/NT (hierarchical), and other associative links such as RT (related term) and SA (see also).
- The Cyc ontology (Lenat and Guha, 1990; Lenat, 1995), begun in 1983 and consisting of 100,000 atomic concepts in 1995. The concepts are connected by thousands of types of relations.
- WordNet (Miller, 1995b), a lexical database consisting of 90,000 concepts. Word forms are connected by the following relations: synonymy, antonymy, hyponymy (hierarchical), meronymy (part-whole), troponymy (manner), and entailment.
- Oracle ConText, a hierarchy of 250,000 concepts and 10 million cross-references (Steinberg, 1996).

Lehmann (1995) provides a more detailed list of ontologies.

Objects

We now discuss ThoughtTreasure objects, which are intended to represent concepts, in more detail. Objects fall into several categories: atomic objects, lists, and constants.

Atomic objects

An *atomic object* (also known as a *symbol*) has a *name*, which is a character string built from the characters 0-9, a-z, A-Z, and "-" (dash). It has hierarchical links: zero or more *parents* and zero or more *child* objects. Atomic objects are also linked to lexical entries. Example atomic objects in ThoughtTreasure are:

object	parents	children
Rutgers-Law-School	university	
bean	seed-vegetable	butter-bean kidney-bean ...
Jim	human	
color	light attribute ...	red orange yellow green ...
sister-of	familial-relationship	
ingest	primitive-action	eat drink ...

There are three types of atomic object: *abstract*, *contrast*, and *concrete*. An abstract atomic object represents a *class* of objects in the world, while a concrete atomic object represents a particular *instance* of an object in the world. (This type-token distinction is not always obvious-for example, is the University of California a type whose instances are UC Irvine and UC Davis or is it a token having the parts UCI and UCD?) Thus human is abstract while Jim is concrete-Jim here refers to a particular Jim, not to all possible Jims. Concrete atomic objects are indicated in database file format by replacing the last indentation equal sign with an asterisk:

```
=human/Homo-sapiens/
=*Jim//
```

A contrast atomic object represents a class of objects in the world whose children are abstract atomic objects used to classify other objects:

```
=phone/electronic-appliance/
=-single-multi-line-contrast//
===single-line-phone//
===multiline-phone//
=-phone-type-contrast//
===butt-set//
===desk-phone//
===pay-phone//
===videophone//
===wall-phone//
===wireless-phone//
=-phone-signaling-contrast//
===manual-phone//
===dial-phone//
====WE-500/single-line-phone,desk-phone/
===DTMF-phone//
```

According to this portion of database file format code, a telephone can be classified according to three contrasts: whether the phone is single-line or multi-line, whether it is a desk or wall phone, and whether it is a dial or DTMF phone. A WE-500 is a single-line, desk, dial phone.

Lists and assertions

A *list object* consists of a sequence of objects. For example:

```
[eat Jim kidney-bean]    = Jim eats the kidney bean.
```

```
[active-goal Jim [eat Jim kidney-bean]]
                        = Jim wants to eat the kidney bean.

[red kidney-bean]       = The kidney bean is red.

[sister-of Jim Karen]   = Karen is Jim's sister.
```

(Each element of a list object also contains an optional pointer to the parse node it derives from, not usually displayed.)

Lists may be asserted into the database for later retrieval. They are then referred to as *assertions*. The first element of an assertion is called its *predicate*. The remaining elements are called the *arguments* of the predicate.

A relation assertion of the form:

```
[X-of A B]
```

generally maps to English as "a/the X of A is B" or "B is a/the X of A." Attribute assertions are of the form:

```
[ATTRIBUTE A WEIGHT]
[ATTRIBUTE A]
```

A *weight* is a value from -1.0 to +1.0. If a weight is not provided, it is assumed to be 0.55. Weights are used to represent gradable adjectives (Lyons, 1977, p. 271) such as *hot*:

object	English
[hot A]	A is hot.
[hot A 1.0]	A is extremely hot.
[hot A 0.55]	A is hot.
[hot A 0.2]	A is slightly hot.
[hot A 0.0]	A is not at all hot.
[hot A -0.55]	A is cold.
[hot A -0.7]	A is very cold.

Weights may also be provided for relation assertions:

```
[like-human A B 0.9]
```

Lists contain a *timestamp range*:

```
@19940309083437:19940309083440|[eat Jim kidney-bean]
```

which specifies the start and stop timestamps of the represented action or state. If the second timestamp is not specified, it is assumed to be equal to the first timestamp plus one second.

As we saw above, assertions are begun, separated, and ended with a vertical bar ("|"):

```
=human/Homo-sapiens/
=*Jim//|[sister-of Jim Karen]|
@19940309083437:19940309083440|[eat Jim kidney-bean]|
```

Shorthand notations are available. An attribute may be defined for an atomic object using:

```
==kidney-bean//|red|
```

which is equivalent to:

```
==kidney-bean//|[red kidney-bean]|
```

Predicates taking two arguments, where one of the arguments is the current object, may be defined using:

```
=*Jim//|sister-of=Karen|employee-of¤France-Telecom|
```

which is equivalent to:

```
=*Jim//|[sister-of Jim Karen]|
[employee-of France-Telecom Jim]|
```

Several values of a predicate may be specified by separating them with commas:

```
===plant-bulb//|part-of¤bud,scale-leaf,
fleshy-leave,underground-stem,stem,root,bulbil|
```

which is equivalent to:

```
===plant-bulb//|[part-of bud plant-bulb]|
[part-of scale-leaf plant-bulb]|[part-of fleshy-leave
```

```
plant-bulb]|[part-of underground-stem plant-bulb]|
[part-of stem plant-bulb]|[part-of root plant-bulb]|
[part-of bulbil plant-bulb]|
```

A timestamp range applies to all of the assertions following it in the atomic object definition until another timestamp range is specified. Thus:

```
=*Jim//|@1992:1994|[friend-of Jim Donald-Blair]|
[friend-of Jim Donald-Kreisel]|@1993:1995|
[friend-of Jim Donald-Livingston]|
```

is equivalent to:

```
=*Jim//|@1992:1994|[friend-of Jim Donald-Blair]|
@1992:1994|[friend-of Jim Donald-Kreisel]|@1993:na|
[friend-of Jim Donald-Livingston]|
```

Several timestamp ranges may be specified separated by commas, in which case the lists that follow are asserted for all of those ranges. For example:

```
=*Jim//|@1992:1994,1995:na|
[friend-of Jim Donald-Blair]|
```

is equivalent to:

```
=*Jim//|@1992:1994|[friend-of Jim Donald-Blair]|
@1995:na|[friend-of Jim Donald-Blair]|
```

Another convenience syntax is the "Ð" character which is used after a timestamp range in order to retract previous assertions with the same predicate as of the start timestamp of the current assertion. For example:

```
=====Paris//|@1817:na|population-of=714000u|
@1900:naÐ|population-of=2714000u|
@1962:naÐ|population-of=2790000u|
@1990:naÐ|population-of=2152423u|
```

is equivalent to:

```
=====Paris//|@1817:1900|population-of=714000u|
@1900:1962|population-of=2714000u|
@1962:1990|population-of=2790000u|
@1990:na|population-of=2152423u|
```

Assertions also contain a list of justification assertions—reasons why the assertion is believed to be true. These cannot be specified in database file format files, but rather are added by the program in various situations.

Atomic objects of various types may be quickly defined inside lists via the following formats:

```
HUMAN:lexentry
MALE:lexentry
FEMALE:lexentry
GROUP:lexentry
BUILDING:lexentry:street-number:street-name:
  postal-code:city:state:country
FLOOR:lexentry:level:street-number:street-name:
  postal-code:city:state:country
APARTMENT:lexentry:apt:level:street-number:street-name:
  postal-code:city:state:country
ROOM:lexentry:room:apt:level:street-number:street-name:
  postal-code:city:state:country
PLAY:lexentry:playwright:composer
OPERA:lexentry:composer:librettist
DANCE:lexentry:choreographer:composer
MUSIC:lexentry:composer
```

These formats are used to define an atomic object and a standard set of assertions about the object. They are used when no further assertions are expected to be made. For example, instead of defining a human in the human ontology as follows:

```
=*Joan Rivers.Fº//|female|
```

and then defining a TV show in the broadcasting ontology:

```
====Joan-Rivers-Show//|host-of=Joan-Rivers|
```

one may simply define the human on the fly in the broadcasting ontology:

```
====Joan-Rivers-Show//|host-of=FEMALE:Joan Rivers|
```

Here are some more examples of the quick forms:

```
GROUP:Opéra de Chambre de Varsovie
BUILDING::15:Columbus Circle:10023:New York City:
  New York:United States
```

```
FLOOR::18:1230:Avenue of the Americas:10020:
  New York City:New York:United States
PLAY:Ce qui arrive et ce que on attend:
  Jean-Marie Besset:
DANCE:Casse-Noisette::
```

Constants

ThoughtTreasure enables arbitrary character strings and double-precision floating-point numbers to be stored as objects with parent classes (abstract atomic objects). Here are some examples in database file format:

```
123u                        = the unitless number 123
NUMBER:u:123                = the unitless number 123
1m                          = 1 meter
1mi                         = 1609.3 meters
8khz                        = 8000 Hertz
1g                          = 1 gram
1Kbyte                      = 1024 bytes
1.50$                       = US$1.50
NUMBER:USD:1.50             = US$1.50
STRING:cc:"33"              = the country code "33"
STRING:email-address:"someone at somewhere.com"
                            = the email address
                              "someone at somewhere.com"
"this is a string"          = the string "this is a string"
```

Constants representing measures such as length and mass are stored in canonical units such as meters and grams. Input measures are converted into canonical units, and canonical units are converted into other units for output.

In all cases, ranges of the form:

```
number¯number
```

can be entered instead of a single number.

The following entities, to be described in the sections to follow, may also be stored as ThoughtTreasure objects: timestamp ranges, grids, grid subspaces, trip legs, and human names.

Object routines

The representation agency contains routines for creating and destroying objects, generating unique object names, retrieving objects by name (using a hash table), converting various C data structures (such as strings and grid subspaces) into objects, converting objects into various C data structures, copying list objects (top-level and deep), making a copy of a list object in which one object has been substituted with another, processing various standard types of list objects used in parsing and understanding (intensions, weights), and reading and pretty printing objects.

Hierarchical routines are provided for adding parents and children to an object, retrieving an object's parents, children, ancestors, and descendants, and finding the common ancestors of two objects. The ISA function determines whether an object O is *an instance of* another object C, by following hierarchical links. (We use the phrase "an instance of" for both the IS-A and A-KIND-OF relationships discussed by other authors such as Winston, 1977).

Access and modification routines are provided for getting and setting the *i*th element of a list object, getting and setting the *i*th parse node of a list object, getting an object's name and lexical entries, and getting and setting an object's justifications. Comparison routines are provided for determining whether two nonlist objects are equal, determining whether two list objects are similar (have the same contents), evaluating numerically how similar two objects are, and determining whether an object is contained inside another object (top-level or deep).

The representation of time

Time is represented in ThoughtTreasure as points or instants of time called *timestamps*, and intervals of time (see Allen, 1983) called *timestamp ranges*.

Timestamps

Timestamps are represented in database file format as any of the following:

```
YYYYMMDDHHMMSS   = year month day hour minute second
YYYYMMDDHHMM     = year month day hour minute
YYYYMMDDHH       = year month day hour
YYYYMMDD         = year month day
YYYYMM           = year month
YYYY             = year
```

```
na                  = not available
-Inf                = negative infinity
+Inf                = positive infinity
Inf                 = positive infinity
```

An indication of the time zone may be appended to the above:

```
pt   Pacific Time
et   Eastern Time
gt   Coordinated Universal Time (= Greenwich Mean Time)
ts   Central European Time (default)
```

Thus the assertion:

```
@199302031503ts|
[publish Dictionnaires-Le-Robert Nouveau-Petit-Robert]
```

states that Dictionnaires Le Robert published the *Nouveau Petit Robert* on February 3, 1993 at 3:03:00 pm, Central European Time.

The assertion:

```
[issue-date-of 912794L44 19940331et]
```

states that the issue date of the T-bill 912794L44 was March 31, 1994 (at midnight Eastern Time).

ThoughtTreasure timestamps are implemented using the timestamps of the host operating system. (Under Unix, timestamps are 32-bit integers representing the number of seconds since 00:00:00 Coordinated Universal Time, January 1, 1970.)

Timestamp ranges

The assertion:

```
@19890120et:19930120et|
[President-of United-States George-Bush]
```
states that George Bush was the President of the United States between January 20, 1989 and January 20, 1993, while:

```
@19930120et:na|
[President-of United-States Bill-Clinton]
```

states that Bill Clinton is the President of the United States between January 20, 1993 and some unknown date. General truths are represented using timestamps of negative and positive infinity, as in:

```
@-inf:inf|[atomic-number-of ytterbium NUMBER:u:70]
```

which states that 70 is the atomic number of ytterbium over all time.

Time of day

The *time of day* is specified in a database file via the formats:

```
HHMMSS   = hour minute second
HHMM     = hour minute
HH       = hour
na       = not available
```

The assertion:

```
[min-value-of morning NUMBER:tod:0600]
```

states that `morning` starts at 6 am.

Time of day is represented as the number of seconds since midnight in a given time zone.

Duration

A *duration* is specified in a database file via the following formats:

```
Nsec           seconds
Nmin           minutes
Nhrs           hours
Nday           days
Nyrs           years
HHMMhhmm       hours minutes
HHMMSShhmmss   hours minutes seconds
```

For example, the assertions:

```
[min-value-of a-moment-ago -60sec]
[min-value-of a-moment-ago -1min]
```

both state that the minimum value of `a-moment-ago` is negative 60 seconds. Durations are represented as 32-bit integers measuring seconds.

Extended timestamp ranges

Extended timestamp ranges are used in ThoughtTreasure to represent repeating or regularly scheduled events such as TV shows and airplane flights. They consist of the following:

```
start timestamp
stop timestamp
days of week
start time of day
duration
```

Days of week are specified in database files in one of the following formats:

```
day+day+...+day (list of days)
day day          (range of days, inclusive)

where day = mon|tue|wed|thu|fri|sat|sun|
            lun|mar|mer|jeu|ven|sam|dim
```

The assertion:

```
@19931003et:na:thu:2100et:30min|
[video-channel-of Seinfeld NBC-East-Coast-feed]
```

states that starting on October 3, 1993 until some unknown date, *Seinfeld* is carried over the NBC East Coast feed every Thursday from 8 pm Eastern Time until 8:30 pm Eastern Time. The assertion:

```
@19930401:na:mon sun:130000:0755hhmm|
[destination-of flight1 JFK-gate-26]
```

states that starting on April 1, 1993, a flight to JFK takes place every day of the week at 1 pm Central European Time for 7 hours and 55 minutes.

Time routines

ThoughtTreasure contains a number of routines for comparing timestamps (equal, greater than/less than), incrementing a timestamp by a duration, counting the number of days between two timestamps, parsing and dumping timestamps, and so on.

ThoughtTreasure defines the following relations (and others) on timestamp ranges (see Davis, 1990, pp. 148-154):

equal	overlaps	contained	greater-than

- A timestamp range TSR1 is *equal* to a timestamp range TSR2 when TSR1.START = TSR2.START and TSR1.STOP = TSR2.STOP.
- A timestamp range TSR1 *overlaps* a timestamp range TSR when (TSR1.START >= TSR2.START and TSR1.START < TSR2.STOP) or (TSR1.STOP > TSR2.START and TSR1.STOP <= TSR2.STOP) or (TSR2.START >= TSR1.START and TSR2.START < TSR1.STOP) or (TSR2.STOP > TSR1.START and TSR2.STOP <= TSR1.STOP).
- A timestamp range TSR1 is *contained* in a timestamp range TSR2 when TSR1.START >= TSR2.START and TSR1.STOP <= TSR2.STOP.
- A timestamp range TSR1 is *properly contained* in a timestamp range TSR2 when TSR1.START > TSR2.START and TSR1.STOP < TSR2.STOP.
- A timestamp range TSR1 is *greater than* a timestamp range TSR2 when TSR1.START > TSR2.STOP.

(TSR.STOP is assumed to be greater than TSR.START.)

The following relations are defined on a timestamp and a timestamp range:

1. A timestamp TS is *contained* in a timestamp range TSR when TS >= TSR.START and TS <= TSR.STOP.
2. A timestamp TS is *properly contained* in a timestamp range TSR when TS > TSR.START and TS < TSR.STOP.

The representation of space

Space is represented in ThoughtTreasure as *grids* connected by *wormholes*.

Grids

A *grid* is a ThoughtTreasure object consisting of a 2-dimensional array of cells used to represent a rectangular space containing physical objects. Each physical object occupies a *grid subspace* or collection of grid cells. The physical objects in a grid and their locations may vary over time (both program time and simulated time). Thus a simulated human inside a grid might pick up an object, walk to another location, and set it down again. By convention, objects in a grid are represented in plan view as in Flatland (Abbott, 1884/1991) rather than in section as in the Planiverse (Dewdney, 1984).

A 2-dimensional representation of space was chosen over a more realistic 3-dimensional representation in order to reduce the computational expense and to simplify the task of representing the world. Humans are represented, for example, as single grid cells. The parts of a human—and parts of parts such as head, face, eyes, and pupils—are represented using assertions rather than as cells in the grid. Similarly, mental and physical states of humans and states of other objects (such as what channel a TV is tuned to or whether a water faucet is open or closed) are represented not in the grid, but as database assertions. Some physical objects (such as walls, tables, streets) consist of several cells. Despite the coarse granularity of the grid representation, many useful inferences can be drawn such as the distance between objects, the relative position of objects (left, right, front, back), whether it is possible to get from one location to another, whether two humans can see or hear each other, and so on.

For example, here is a simple Italian restaurant grid and snapshot of its state on February 1, 1994, as defined in ThoughtTreasure database file format:

```
==Italian-restaurant1/floor/|col-distance-of=.185m|
row-distance-of=.275m|level-of=0u|orientation-of=north|
polity-of=9arr|has-ceiling|@19940201:naÐ|GS=
   wwwwwwwwwwwwwwwwwwwwwwwwwwwwwwwwwwwwwwwwwwwwwwwwwwww
   w                                                 w
   w    ttt      ttt     ctttc                       w
   w   ctttc    ctttc     ttt        w               w
  2q                                 w               w
   q                                 w               w
   w    ttt      ttt     ctttc       w               w
   w   ctttc    ctttc     ttt        w               w
   w1                                w               w
   wwwwwwwwwwwwwwwwwwwwwwwwwwwwwwwwwwwwwwwwwwwwwwwwwwww
   .
c:side-chair
q:door-with-lock
```

```
t:table
w:wall
1.wq:Italian-restaurant
2:&Italian-restaurant1-Entrance
 .
 |
```

When the above definition is read into ThoughtTreasure, a new grid object `Italian-restaurant1` is created and assertions are made regarding the length and width of its cells in meters, what polity it is located in, its compass orientation, and whether it has a ceiling:

```
[col-distance-of Italian-restaurant1 NUMBER:metre:0.185]
[row-distance-of Italian-restaurant1 NUMBER:metre:0.275]
[level-of Italian-restaurant1 NUMBER:u:0]
[orientation-of Italian-restaurant1 north]
[polity-of Italian-restaurant1 9arr]
[has-ceiling Italian-restaurant1]
```

(`9arr` refers to the ninth arrondissement of Paris.)

When reading a database format file, the `GS` predicate is treated specially. It indicates that a definition of the contents of the grid follows. The bottom of the definition is a key which specifies what characters stand for what objects. "c" defines instances of the class `side-chair`. Wherever a "c" is present, a new instance of a side chair is created and asserted to be at that grid location:

```
@19940201000000:na|[at-grid side-chair693 Italian-
restaurant1 <gridsubspace 7 19>]
@19940201000000:na|[at-grid side-chair694 Italian-
restaurant1 <gridsubspace 7 15>]
...
```

The grid reader attempts to group contiguous characters into single objects: Thus 6 table objects are created even though there are 36 "t" characters:

```
@19940201000000:na|[at-grid table706 Italian-
restaurant1 <gridsubspace length 6: 6 25>]
@19940201000000:na|[at-grid table707 Italian-
restaurant1 <gridsubspace length 6: 6 16>]
@19940201000000:na|[at-grid table708 Italian-
restaurant1 <gridsubspace length 6: 6 7>]
@19940201000000:na|[at-grid table709 Italian-
restaurant1 <gridsubspace length 6: 2 25>]
```

```
@19940201000000:na|[at-grid table710 Italian-
restaurant1 <gridsubspace length 6: 2 16>]
@19940201000000:na|[at-grid table711 Italian-
restaurant1 <gridsubspace length 6: 2 7>]
```

The grid subspace occupied by one of the tables is shown in the following as asterisks:

```
&&&&&&&&&&&&&&&&&&&&&&&&&&&&&&&&&&&&&&&&&&&&&&&&&&&&&&
&                                                  &
&                                                  &
&         ttt       ttt      sttts                 &
&        sttts     sttts      ttt                  &
&   d                                              &
&   d                                              &
&         ttt       ***      sttts                 &
&        sttts     s***s      ttt                  &
&                                                  &
&                                                  &
&&&&&&&&&&&&&&&&&&&&&&&&&&&&&&&&&&&&&&&&&&&&&&&&&&&&&&
```

The above is a grid snapshot generated by ThoughtTreasure from assertions about the locations of objects at a given timestamp. The letter shown at a grid location is the first character of the name of the ThoughtTreasure object at that location. There may be several objects at a given grid location; only one letter is displayed. (In order to fit lots of clothes in a closet or groceries in a store, they are often placed in the same grid cell.)

The definition:

```
1.wq:Italian-restaurant
```

specifies that the location of Italian-restaurant is obtained by filling a region containing "1" whose boundary is given by "w" and "q":

```
@19940201000000:na|[at-grid Italian-restaurant715
Italian-restaurant1 <gridsubspace length 394: 8 3>]
```

The restaurant thus occupies the subspace shown as asterisks:

```
&&&&&&&&&&&&&&&&&&&&&&&&&&&&&&&&&&&&&&&&&&&&&&&&&&&&&&&&&&
&   wwwwwwwwwwwwwwwwwwwwwwwwwwwwwwwwwwwwwwwwwwwwwwwwwwwww&
&   w**************************************************w&
&   w**************************************************w&
&   w****************************w***********************w&
&   d****************************w***********************w&
&   d****************************w***********************w&
&   w****************************w***********************w&
&   w****************************w***********************w&
&   w****************************w***********************w&
&   wwwwwwwwwwwwwwwwwwwwwwwwwwwwwwwwwwwwwwwwwwwwwwwwwwwww&
&&&&&&&&&&&&&&&&&&&&&&&&&&&&&&&&&&&&&&&&&&&&&&&&&&&&&&&&&&
```

If an ampersand ("&") precedes the ThoughtTreasure object name, as in:

```
2:&Italian-restaurant1-Entrance
```

the specified object instance is used instead of creating a new instance of the specified class:

```
@19940201000000:na|[at-grid Italian-restaurant1-Entrance
Italian-restaurant1 <gridsubspace 4 1>]
```

The following other grids are defined in ThoughtTreasure:

```
Apartment of single person
Apartment of small family
(2) Apartment building common areas
Country house
Italian restaurant
Bar
Corner grocer
Theater (including lobby, theater hall, balcony)
Television studio (including reception area, control room)
Hotel ground floor
Hotel floor and room
Subway entrance area
(2) Subway platforms
Stretch of subway track
(4) City street areas
Country street area
(3) Stretches of highway
(2) Airport terminal and runway
Stretch of airspace
```

Wormholes

A *wormhole* is a connection between a cell in one grid and a cell in another grid through which physical objects can travel. Wormholes enable grids to be defined in manageable chunks: Building interiors are defined, exterior areas such as streets are defined, and then they are connected by wormholes. For example, the object `Italian-restaurant1-Entrance` in the above example is a wormhole located just outside the entrance to the restaurant. This same wormhole is also located in front of a building in another grid, `Richelieu-Drouot-area`, which defines an exterior area in Paris consisting of a number of streets and buildings.

Wormholes can be used to model buildings with several floors: A grid representing one floor has an up stairway which is connected by a wormhole to the down stairway in the grid representing the floor above it. Travel through elevators is also represented using wormholes.

Wormholes can be used to connect grids which represent space at varying levels of detail: A grid representing Paris streets and buildings in detail is connected by wormholes to another grid which represents highways in Paris which is connected to another grid which represents highways in France. The Paris highway grid is also connected to the Roissy airport grid whose runway is connected to the earth grid which is connected to the JFK airport grid. Similarly, a subway platform grid is connected to an underground network of tracks, which are in turn connected to other subway platforms.

Since ThoughtTreasure wormholes do not correspond to anything in the real world, mention of them is avoided when generating natural language output.

Finding paths within grids

In order for a physical object to go from one location to another inside a grid, a path must be found. The path must avoid obstacles, defined as objects in the grid which do not have an attribute which depends on the class of physical object:

```
human          walkable
motor-vehicle  drivable
train          rollable
airplane       flyable
```

Here are some examples of classes that are walkable:

```
store
apartment
driveway
grass
sidewalk
```

Here are some examples of classes that are not walkable:

```
table
wall
window
```

A path through a grid G at a particular time TS is found as follows: First, a 2-dimensional bitmap O is constructed from the asserted locations of physical objects in G at TS. Bits are set for those cells occupied by obstacle physical objects. Then, a path from cell A to cell B is found using the following recursive algorithm:

1. If a straight-line path not hitting any obstacles exists from A to B, return it.
2. Otherwise, find the midpoint along the path M from A to B and return the concatenation of the path from A to M and the path from M to B as found through recursive calls to this algorithm.

The *midpoint along the path* M from A to B is found as follows: Create two blank bitmaps F and T which are the same size as the obstacle bitmap O. Set cell A of F and cell B of T. Until a given cell M is set in both F and T, run one cycle of the fill algorithm on F and T with boundaries defined by O. Then return M.

One cycle of the *fill algorithm* on a bitmap F with boundary bitmap O consists of setting a cell in F which is (1) not already set in F, (2) adjacent to a cell already set in F, and (3) not set in bitmap O.

Here are two sample paths found through the Italian restaurant:

```
&&&&&&&&&&&&&&&&&&&&&&&&&&&&&&&&&&&&&&&&&&&&&&&&&&&&&&&
&    wwwwwwwwwwwwwwwwwwwwwwwwwwwwwwwwwwwwwwwwwwwwwwwww&
&    w                                              w&
&    w    ttt        ttt       ctttc                w&
&    w   ctttc      ctttc       ttt        w        w&
&  2q**                                    w        w&
&   q    ******                            w        w&
&    w    ttt *** ttt       ctttc          w        w&
&    w   ctttc  *ctttc       ttt           w        w&
&    w1         ****                       w        w&
&    wwwwwwwwwwwwwwwwwwwwwwwwwwwwwwwwwwwwwwwwwwwwwwwww&
&&&&&&&&&&&&&&&&&&&&&&&&&&&&&&&&&&&&&&&&&&&&&&&&&&&&&&&
```

```
&&&&&&&&&&&&&&&&&&&&&&&&&&&&&&&&&&&&&&&&&&&&&&&&&&&&&&&
&    wwwwwwwwwwwwwwwwwwwwwwwwwwwwwwwwwwwwwwwwwwwwwwwww&
&    w                                              w&
&    w    ttt        ttt       ctttc    *******     w&
&    w   ctttc      ctttc       ttt    * w    **    w&
&  2q                                 *  w      *   w&
&   q                                *   w       *  w&
&    w    ttt        ttt       ctttc *   w      **   w&
&    w   ctttc      ctttc       ttt**    w        *  w&
&    w1          *****************       w          w&
&    wwwwwwwwwwwwwwwwwwwwwwwwwwwwwwwwwwwwwwwwwwwwwwwww&
&&&&&&&&&&&&&&&&&&&&&&&&&&&&&&&&&&&&&&&&&&&&&&&&&&&&&&&
```

Finding paths between grids through wormholes

An *intergrid path* from grid-1 to grid-n is of the form:

```
grid-1      wormhole-1-2
grid-2      wormhole-2-3
...
grid-n-1    wormhole-n-1-n
grid-n
```

Such a path is found by doing a breadth-first search through the grid-wormhole space.

Objects in space

In this section we present algorithms for figuring out where an object is, calculating the distance between two objects, finding objects which enclose other objects, and deciding whether two objects are near one another.

Locating objects

To simplify this discussion, we will assume that an object has only one grid location at a time. In the future, it may be useful to allow an object to be present in more than one grid—for example, in order to represent the object's location at different levels of granularity. The source code has been designed with this possibility in mind.

The location of an object O at a given time TS is determined as follows: If an at-grid assertion is retrieved for O at TS, it is returned—it specifies O's current grid and location (subspace) within that grid. Otherwise, this algorithm is recursively invoked for each object of which O is a part, and for each human who is wearing O. (The location of a worn object is not explicitly asserted—it is inferred from the location of the human wearing that object. The locations of objects held by graspers and objects contained inside other objects are explicitly asserted.)

If the location of a human is not asserted for a given time TS, but the residence of the human is asserted, then the human is located at an arbitrary location inside the human's residence.

Calculating the distance between objects

The distance between two ThoughtTreasure objects O1 and O2 at a given time TS is determined as follows: The locations of O1 and O2 are determined at TS. If O1 and O2 are in the same grid, their distance is calculated based on their coordinates in the grid and the length and width of the grid's cells. (The coordinates of an object which occupies more than one cell are those of any cell having an empty adjacent cell—an accessible border of the object.) Otherwise if O1 and O2 are not in the same grid, their distance is the distance between the polities containing the grids.

Finding enclosing objects

In order to find objects which enclose an object O at time TS (as used by question answering agents): The location of O at TS is determined—a grid G and subspace S. Then enclosing objects of the following polity classes are sought:

```
universe
galaxy
solar-system
planet
continent
country
city
city-subdivision
city-subsubdivision
```

Polities of the specified classes are found which contain G. Then enclosing objects of the following physical object classes are sought:

```
roadway
building
apartment
room
```

Enclosing objects of the specified class C are found by retrieving the locations of all objects in G of the class C and returning any objects whose grid subspace contains S.

Nearness

The following notions of nearness of A to B are defined:

near-reachable
A is near enough to reach B: A is in the same grid cell as B, or A is in adjacent grid cell to B.
near-audible
A is near enough to hear B: A is less than 20 meters away from B, or A has a telephone connection to B.

near-graspable
A is near enough to grasp B: A is holding B, or A is `near-reachable` B and a grasper (hand) of A has moved to B.

Routines are provided for finding objects:

- within a certain radius of another object,
- nearest another object,
- of a given class,
- in a given polity,
- in a given grid, and/or
- owned by a given actor.

Polities

Polity is the generic term in ThoughtTreasure for governmental organizations such as countries, states, and cities.

The geography ontology

The geography ontology is coded in a special database file format in which equal signs are used to represent part-whole rather than inheritance relationships. Each indentation level corresponds to a different type of polity:

```
=continent
==country
===U.S. state, France region, territories
====U.S. county, France département
=====city
======U.S. borough, France arrondissement
=======city-subsubdivision (neighborhood)
========city-subsubsubdivision
=========city-subsubsubsubdivision
==========city-subsubsubsubsubdivision
```

A polity P1 is indicated as being a capital of a polity P2 by switching an equal sign of P1 to an asterisk ("*") below the last indentation character of P2:

```
==United-States//
===District-of-Columbia//
=*==Washington-DC//
===Alabama//
```

```
==*==Montgomery//
```
...

Thus Washington, D.C. is here defined to be the capital of the United States as
well as the District of Columbia.

The dash character ("-") is used to indicate that a polity is of several classes. The
dash is placed where a polity of the given type is normally defined. Thus:

```
===New-York//
==*==Albany//
=====-New-York-City/urban/
======Staten-Island//
```

defines New York City as both a city and county.

To summarize, polity database file format allows the definition of class, part-whole
relationships, and capital relationships:

```
New-York ancestors: polity-state

Albany ancestors: city
[cpart-of Albany New-York]
[capital-of New-York Albany]

New-York-City ancestors: city county urban
[cpart-of New-York-City New-York]

Staten-Island ancestors: borough
[cpart-of Staten-Island New-York-City]
```

Calculating the distance between two polities

Spherical coordinates for polities on Earth are specified in ThoughtTreasure using
the notation:

```
latitude ["N"|"S"] longitude ["E"|"W"] "coor"
```

For example, an entry in the geography database file is:

```
=====Llanfairpwllgwyngyll.z//Llanfairpwllgwyngyll.y/
|coordinates-of=53.13N4.12Wcoor|
```

The distance between two polities is the distance along the arc from one polity to the other. If coordinates are not specified for a polity P, the coordinates for the polity of which P is a part are used.

Polity routines

Other polity routines are available for:

- Finding a superpolity of a given class which contains a given polity. For example, given `New-York-City` and `country` this routine returns `United States`.
- Determining whether one polity contains another. For example, given `New-York-City` and `Paris` this routine returns false.
- Finding the polity of a given class which contains a grid.
- Determining whether a grid is contained in a given polity.
- Determining whether an object is contained in a given polity.

Database assertion and retrieval

The ThoughtTreasure *database* contains atomic objects organized into a hierarchy, and assertions on those objects. In addition to abstract objects such as `country` or `building`, the database contains concrete objects such as `France` and `GE-building`.

In this section, we first discuss the basic mechanisms used to assert list objects into the database and later retrieve them. We then present the higher-level retrieval methods of theorem proving and intension resolution.

Assertion

Database assertions are indexed by 5 hash tables:

```
1) hashed on slots 0 and 1
2) hashed on slots 0 and 2
3) hashed on slot 0
4) hashed on slot 1
5) hashed on slot 2
```

Parts of the names of objects in the specified slots are used as hash table keys.

For example, the assertion `[ptrans Jim na store87]` is hashed in hash table 1 using the key `ptrJim`.

These hash tables ensure that retrieval is efficient when variables are present in various slots:

```
[ptrans Jim ?location store87]    use hash table 1 key ptrJim
[ptrans ?human na store87]        use hash table 2 key ptrna
[ptrans ?human ?location store87] use hash table 3 key ptrans
[?action Jim ?location store87]   use hash table 4 key Jim
[?action ?human na store87]       use hash table 5 key na
```

Asserting an object O into the database consists of adding it to the above hash tables.

Retrieval

In order to retrieve a pattern P from the database with respect to a given timestamp TS or timestamp range TSR, the following steps are performed:

1. Retrieve candidate objects from the appropriate hash table, depending on the locations of variables in P.
2. Create an empty list of objects R.
3. For each candidate object O, if TS or TSR matches the timestamp range of O, and P unifies with O, add O to R.
4. Return R.

A timestamp TS matches a timestamp range TSR when TS is na or TS is contained in TSR:

```
TS:           .              .
TSR:        _____       _____

match?    yes          no
```

A timestamp range TSR1 matches a timestamp range TSR2 when TSR1 overlaps TSR2:

```
TSR1:    _____         _____
TSR2:       _____          _____

match?    yes              no
```

Assertions may also be retrieved for which the *i*th element of the assertion is a descendant of the *i*th element of the pattern.

For example, given a pattern:

```
[action ?human]
```

and $i = 0$, the following assertions would be eligible for retrieval:

```
[smile Jim]
[frown Jim]
[blink Jim]
```

This is implemented by substituting the *i*th element of the pattern with each of its descendants (up to some maximum depth) and attempting to retrieve the resulting patterns.

Similarly, assertions may be retrieved for which the *i*th element of the assertion is an ancestor of the *i*th element of the pattern. This is commonly used to implement *inheritance* of attributes or relations. For example, given the pattern:

```
[product-of ?company 1969-Fiat-124-Spider]
```

and $i = 2$, the following assertion would be eligible for retrieval:

```
[product-of Fiat Fiat-Spider]
```

```
where Fiat-Spider is an ancestor of 1969-Fiat-124-
Spider
```

Assertions may also be retrieved for which the *i*th element of the assertion is an ancestor of the *i*th element of the pattern, and the *j*th element of the assertion is a descendant of the *j*th element of the pattern. Given:

```
[product-of automobile-industry 1969-Fiat-124-Spider]
```

$i = 2$ and $j = 1$, the following assertion would be eligible for retrieval:

```
[product-of Fiat Fiat-Spider]
```

```
where Fiat-Spider is an ancestor of 1969-Fiat-124-
Spider and Fiat is a descendant of automobile-industry
```

Various database retrieval helping functions are provided for retrieving attributes or enum values of an object, retrieving relation values, traversing `part-of` and `cpart-of` relations to find parts/wholes of objects of a given class (such as the eyebrow of a human), and retrieving all assertions involving a given object in the first three positions.

Retraction

Removal of assertions from the database is not yet implemented. However, assertions matching a pattern can be *retracted* with respect to a stop timestamp by retrieving them and setting their stop timestamps. For example, given the pattern:

```
[smile Jim]
```

and the retraction timestamp:

```
19930809102508
```

the matching database assertion:

```
@19930809102345:inf|[smile Jim]
```

would be updated to:

```
@19930809102345:19930809102508|[smile Jim]
```

Unification

Unification (Charniak, Riesbeck, and McDermott, 1980) is a pattern-matching operation performed on two list objects. The objects may contain a special kind of object called a *variable*. Two objects unify if values for variables can be found such that substituting the values for those variables in the objects would produce similar structures. For example, if unification is invoked on:

```
[ptrans ?human na ?location]
```

and

```
[ptrans Jim na store87]
```

the result is the following list of variable *bindings*:

```
?human = Jim
?location = store87
```

Unification takes two objects and an initial list of bindings, normally empty, and returns an augmented list of bindings if the two objects unify. Two cases involving variables in unification must be considered: First, an unbound variable unifies with a list object if the object is an instance of the *class* of the variable, given by the name following the question mark:

variable	class
?human	human
?location	location

When an unbound variable successfully unifies with an object, that object becomes that variable's value in the list of bindings. Second, a bound variable unifies with an object if the value of that variable unifies with the object.

Instantiation

Instantiation (Charniak, Riesbeck, and McDermott, 1980) takes a list object and binding list, and returns a copy of the object in which any variables have been replaced by their values in the binding list. For example, if the object:

```
[ptrans ?human na ?location]
```

is instantiated with the binding list:

```
?human = Jim
?location = store87
```

the resulting object is:

```
[ptrans Jim na store87]
```

Any unbound variables remain as variables in the copy. The list object may contain other list objects—the complete structure with the given object as root is copied.

Theorem proving

The *prover* is a simple theorem prover (Charniak, Riesbeck, and McDermott, 1980) which retrieves information from the database by backward chaining from a goal containing zero or more variables.

For example, if the following assertions are in the database:

```
[male Larry]
[natural-parent-of Jim Joyce]
[natural-parent-of Joyce Larry]
[ifthen [and [male ?z] [natural-parent-of ?x ?y]
[natural-parent-of ?y ?z]]
        [grandfather-of ?x ?z]]
```

and the prover is asked to prove the assertion:

```
[grandfather-of Jim ?somebody]
```

it will return that the assertion is true with the bindings:

```
?somebody = Larry
```

It also returns the proof (or proofs):

```
found proofs of [grandfather-of Jim ?somebody]
```

```
[grandfather-of Jim ?somebody] because
  [ifthen [and [male ?z]
               [natural-parent-of ?x ?y]
               [natural-parent-of ?y ?z]]
          [grandfather-of ?x ?z]]
?y:Joyce ?somebody:Larry
----
>[and [male ?somebody] [natural-parent-of Jim ?y]
      [natural-parent-of ?y ?somebody]] because and
>?y:Joyce
>?somebody:Larry
>----
>>[male Larry] because true
>>?somebody:Larry
>>----
>>[natural-parent-of Jim Joyce] because true
>>?y:Joyce
```

```
>>----
>>[natural-parent-of Joyce Larry] because true
>>----
[grandfather-of Jim ?somebody]
```

A goal G is proved in the following cases:

- G is proved if it can be retrieved from the database.
- G is proved if an `ifthen` rules exists whose right-hand side (second argument) unifies with G and whose left-hand side (first argument) instantiated with the bindings from the unification is proved.
- G's predicate may be `and`, `or`, and `not`. An `and` is proved if all of its arguments are proved. An `or` is proved if any of its arguments are proved. A `not` is proved if its argument is not proved.
- Finally, the prover has several hardcoded rules to deal with spatial goals: `location-of` and `near`, for example, are proved by invoking space routines.

The intension resolver

An *intension* is an abstract description of a set of objects such as "all X such that X is a physical object and X is green", while an *extension* is an enumeration of the objects in a set such as "grass34, pool-table82, book43" (Lyons, 1977, pp. 146-147, pp. 158-161). In ThoughtTreasure, the *intension resolver* is employed to resolve intensions into extensions. It finds all atomic objects O in the database satisfying a set of restrictions stored in an *intension data structure*, which consists of the following fields:

class
The object O must be an instance of this class.
propositions
The object O must satisfy all these propositions, expressed in terms of the class. For example, given:

```
class:        human
propositions: [brother-of human Karen]
```

and the database assertion:

```
[brother-of Jim Karen]
```

Jim is an O satisfying the restrictions.

isas

This is a list of class lists. O must be an instance of at least one of the classes in each list. Thus the structure of this list is:

```
{and {or CLASS CLASS ...} {or CLASS CLASS ...} ...}
```

attributes

This is a list of attribute lists. O must possess at least one of the attributes in each list.

created timestamp

The object O must have created at the specified timestamp. (This is used for retrieving cars of a given year.)

context

A context in which to search for actors and physical objects near those actors.

context only flag

If true, O must be an actor in the context or physical object near an actor in the context. This is used by the anaphoric parser—the flag is set to true in order to resolve definite articles.

timestamp

This is used for database retrievals above.

timestamp range

This is used for database retrievals above.

Propositions of the form:

```
[of NONGEN GEN]
```

resulting from genitive constructions such as:

```
Jim's apartment
[of apartment Jim]
```

are satisfied if any of the following are satisfied:

1. *A part-of relation holds:* [cpart-of O GEN] where O is an instance of a NONGEN:

```
Jim's foot =>
  [of foot Jim] =>
  [cpart-of Jim-left-foot Jim]
  [cpart-of Jim-right-foot Jim]
```

```
The CRT of the TV. =>
  [of CRT TV-set48] =>
  [cpart-of TV48-CRT TV-set48]
```

2. *An ownership relation holds:* [owner-of O GEN] where O is an instance of a NONGEN:

```
Jim's apartment =>
  [of apartment Jim] =>
  [owner-of condominium32 Jim]
```

```
the market research firm of Dunn and Bradstreet =>
  [of market-research-firm Dunn-and-Bradstreet] =>
  [owner-of ACNielsen Dunn-and-Bradstreet]
  [owner-of Nielsen-Media-Research  Dunn-and-Bradstreet]
```

3. *A pseudoownership relation holds:* [REL GEN O] where O is an instance of a NONGEN and REL is a relation such as the following:

```
residence-of
headquarters-of
```

```
Jim's country =>
  [of country Jim] =>
  [residence-of Jim United-States]
```

```
NYNEX's building =>
  [of building NYNEX] =>
  [headquarters-of NYNEX building823]
```

or [REL O GEN] where O is an instance of a NONGEN and REL is a relation such as:

```
unique-author-of
```

```
Jim's article =>
  [of media-object-article Jim] =>
  [unique-author-of time-magazine-article263 Jim]
```

Propositions such as:

```
[NAME-of human NAME:"Jim"]
```

are satisfied if a human with the given first, middle, and/or family names can be found in the database (or in the context if the context only flag is set).

Contexts

A *context* (Rulifson, Derksen, and Waldinger, 1972) represents a possible world. As ThoughtTreasure processes a natural language text, it uses contexts to keep the alternative interpretations separate. For example:

```
Jim is friends with Donald Blair and Donald Kreisel.
=>
  Context #1:
  [friend-of Jim Donald-Blair]
  [friend-of Jim Donald-Kreisel]

Jim spoke to Donald.  =>
  Context #11:
  [friend-of Jim Donald-Blair]
  [friend-of Jim Donald-Kreisel]
  [conversation Jim Donald-Blair]

  Context #12:
  [friend-of Jim Donald-Blair]
  [friend-of Jim Donald-Kreisel]
  [conversation Jim Donald-Kreisel]
```

Any and all state changes made by understanding agents are made in a context. A context consists of the following state information: *story time*, the actors of the text, the mental state of the actors (including subgoals, emotions, interpersonal relationships), and arbitrary assertions. (In principle, all state could be stored as assertions. Specialized data structures are part of contexts as a convenience to understanding agents.)

Story time is the time of the events described in the input text—called "the 'then' of the narrative reference" by Greenbaum and Quirk (1990, p. 441). Story time, which is associated with each ThoughtTreasure context, is to be contrasted with the "'now' of both the narrator and the hearer or reader" (p. 441), which is part of each entry on ThoughtTreasure's *deictic stack*. (The constructs of story time and now are insufficient for handling more complicated cases such as narratives within narratives, but merely adjusting story time and now is already a difficult problem.)

When natural language input, parsed in a context P, has two interpretations, two new contexts C1 and C2 are *sprouted* from P. The states of C1 and C2 are then modified appropriately for the two interpretations. A context C sprouted from P is simply a copy of P: all the assertions and other state contained in P are copied and stored in C.

Contexts and database assertion/retrieval

All database assertions and retrievals are performed with respect to a particular context. Every timestamp and timestamp range contains a pointer to a context. An assertion is only retrieved from the database when the context of the retrieval timestamp or timestamp range matches the context of the assertion. A retrieval context P matches an assertion context C when P = C or C is the *root context*. The root context contains all the assertions read in from database files upon startup of the program.

Each context contains a list of assertions that hold in that context, other than those in the root context. When a context C is sprouted from P, each of the assertions of P is copied and asserted into C.

For example, the following assertion is placed in the root context upon program initialization:

```
@-inf:inf|[first-name-of Jim aamgn-Jim]
```

Then a sentence is parsed and the following assertions are made in context 1:

```
@-inf:inf#1|[friend-of Jim Donald-Blair]
@-inf:inf#1|[friend-of Jim Donald-Kreisel]
```

Then another sentence is parsed which has two interpretations. Therefore two contexts 11 and 12 are sprouted, which involves asserting the following:

```
@-inf:inf#11|[friend-of Jim Donald-Blair]
@-inf:inf#11|[friend-of Jim Donald-Kreisel]

@-inf:inf#12|[friend-of Jim Donald-Blair]
@-inf:inf#12|[friend-of Jim Donald-Kreisel]
```

The interpretations are then asserted into the two contexts:

```
@19950607102308:19950607103143#11|
[conversation Jim Donald-Blair]
@19950607102308:19950607103143#12|
[conversation Jim Donald-Kreisel]
```

At this point, the database retrieval pattern:

```
@na:na#12|[? Jim ?]
```

would retrieve the assertions:

```
@-inf:inf|[first-name-of Jim aamgn-Jim]
@-inf:inf#12|[friend-of Jim Donald-Blair]
@-inf:inf#12|[friend-of Jim Donald-Kreisel]
@19950607102308:19950607103143#12|
[conversation Jim Donald-Kreisel]
```

Actors inside contexts

An *actor* data structure is maintained for each actor in a context. It consists of the actor object, the actor's subgoals (planning agents), antecedents, and caches of assertions regarding emotions, interpersonal relationships, appointments, and rest and energy levels.

Natural language references to physical objects are resolved using two methods: (1) If the physical object was previously referred to, either by the user or in ThoughtTreasure output, then it will be present in the context as an actor—albeit one without subgoals, emotions, and so on. (2) Otherwise, physical objects of the appropriate class are identified by looping through all actors and locating physical objects spatially near those actors.

Discourse

ThoughtTreasure is designed to participate in several discourses at the same time. The *discourse* data structure holds all the state information for a particular discourse. It consists of the following information:

A list of communication channels. Each *channel* consists of a flag indicating whether the channel is for input or for output, an input or output stream, a language (English, French), a dialect (American, British, Canadian, old, other dialect, none), and a style (formal, informal, slang, none). Input channels contain an input text buffer and the parse node forest created by the text agency and syntactic component.

Input comes from a single input channel. Input is echoed to all output channels with the same language, dialect, and style. Remaining channels receive an interlingual translation of the input. Output from ThoughtTreasure is generated on all output channels in the appropriate language, dialect, and style. In the output, echoed input is preceded by a greater than sign (">") and translated (paraphrased) input is preceded by a right parenthesis (")").

A list of contexts. One context is designated as the *best context* or ThoughtTreasure's current best understanding of the discourse.

Mode flags. The following flags may each be true or false:

Turing mode
ThoughtTreasure should pretend to be a human. This causes code to be selected which gives shorter and less computer-like answers. Output is generated by a *typing simulator* which imitates human typing. A time delay occurs after each character is output, and typographical errors are generated and then corrected. After a typographical error, the simulator continues typing a few correct characters before backspacing to correct the error. Sometimes the errors are not corrected. Typographical errors are generated via the following transformations, each performed with some probability:

- A character is modified to a nearby character.
- A nearby character is inserted.
- Two characters are transposed.

Nearby characters are found by consulting the keyboard layout: A qwerty layout is used when the channel is for English or Canadian French; an azerty layout is used when the channel is for Parisian French.

Programmer mode
The user is a programmer. This causes more implementation information to be produced on output, such as feature characters and ThoughtTreasure object names.

Conversational mode
ThoughtTreasure may ask questions of the user in order to narrow down alternatives or request missing information.

Thought stream mode

ThoughtTreasure should generate its internal stream of thought or all the assertions it makes as it runs. This can be used to obtain a natural language trace of the sequence of events in a simulation (or daydream). The thought stream text is preceded by an ampersand ("&").

The most recent answer data structures. Each such structure contains information regarding the last answer to a user's question, including the answer, a rephrased version of the answer, and a further explanation of the answer. These can then be produced if the user asks "What?" or "Why?".

The deictic stack. This contains information about the speakers, listeners, and time of the discourse.

Exercises

1. Pick another domain, such as the stock market or recipes, and add the necessary concepts, lexical entries, and agents, paralleling the work done on the movie review understanding application throughout this book.

2. Extend the movie review application beyond what is described in this book, by filling in additional appropriate concepts, lexical entries, text agents, and understanding agents.

3. Reimplement timestamps to enable the representation of events prior to 1970 such as Aristotle's birth or the big bang.

4. Implement partially specified timestamps: Currently, if a month is not supplied it is assumed to be January; if a day is not supplied it is assumed to be the first of the month; and so on. Unknown "parts of a timestamp" should be represented as such.

5. Implement time zones and daylight savings time properly. Support all time zones.

6. Implement the following durations:

```
Nns          nanoseconds
Nms          milliseconds
```

7. Modify the program to store ranges properly such as:

```
number‾number
```

Currently only a single number, the average, is stored.

8. Implement a graphical interface for grids and wormholes. When the user clicks on a location, information about the objects at that location should be produced. Clicking on a wormhole should take the user through the wormhole to another grid. The interface should produce animations of a simulation in progress.

9. Instead of keeping complete copies, store only the differences between contexts, as in Barrow and Tipler's (1986, pp. 472-489) incremental implementation of the many-worlds interpretation of quantum mechanics.

Chapter 3: The lexical component

The lexical component is concerned with *lexical entries*—words and phrases such as:

lexical entry	part of speech, type
green	adjective, word
yellow-green	adjective, phrase
essentially	adverb, word
practically speaking	adverb, phrase
microwave	noun, word
vinyl disc	noun, phrase
until	preposition, word
up to	preposition, phrase
nobody	pronoun, word
no one	pronoun, phrase
leave	verb, word
go out	verb, phrase

The lexical component is best understood by continuing with our example application, showing how lexical entries are added to ThoughtTreasure to enable it to parse movie reviews.

The lexicon and the movie review application

We start by incorporating lexical information into the items added to the ontology in the previous chapter. For example, we enter two English lexical entries for film and one French lexical entry:

==film.z//movie.Àz/film.My/

The characters after the periods are *features*. Their meanings are:

```
z = English
À = American English
M = masculine gender
y = French
```

(A complete list of ThoughtTreasure feature characters is provided in Appendix C.)

If a part of speech feature is not specified after the period, the lexical entry is assumed to be a noun. Other parts of speech are specified by adding a part-of-speech feature character:

```
A = adjective
B = adverb
D = determiner
H = pronoun
K = conjunction
N = noun
R = preposition
V = verb
U = interjection
x = sentential lexical entry
0 = expletive
9 = element
« = prefix
» = suffix
```

For example:

```
==film.z//movie.Àz/filmic.Az/film.My/
```

Thus words of various parts of speech can be specified for a single concept. In this case we have defined a noun *film* and a corresponding adjective *filmic*.
We then enter lexical entries for the other subclasses of `film`:

```
==-film-length-contrast//
====feature# film*.z//feature#A-length# film*.z/
full#A-length# film*.z/feature.Tz/long*A métrage*.My/
====medium#A-length# film*.z//moyen*A métrage*.My/
====short#A film*.z//short.Tz/court*A métrage*.My/
...
==-film-genre//
====animated#A film*.z//animated#A movie*.Àz/
=====Hunchback* of#R Notre#Dj Dame#Nj.kz/feature-film/
====drama-film//drama.z/
=====RDP/feature-film/Rendezvous# in#R Paris#.Éz/
Rendez#VP-Vous#HP de#R Paris#S.MPïy/
...
```

```
T = informal
k = noun preceded by definite article
É = noun preceded by empty article
j = foreign word
P = plural
ï = preferred inflection
```

Note that we specify the parts of speech of all the words that make up a phrase:

```
====medium#A-length# film*.z//
```

The phrase *medium-length film* is thus defined to be a noun built from an adjective and two nouns. (The part of speech of a word in a phrase defaults to the part of speech of the phrase, which itself defaults to noun.)

Then we define lexical entries for the relations added in the previous chapter. Rating relations are specified in the corpus using expressions such as:

```
It is rated PG.
The film is rated NC-17.
It's "PG".
It is not rated, but would get a G today.
It would get a PG-13 rating.
```

The verbs *be rated*, *be*, and *get* are thus used to specify movie ratings in English. These are captured in ThoughtTreasure as follows:

**==MPAA-rating-of//be* rated#A.Véz/be,get.Véz/|r1=film|
r2=MPAA-rating|**

```
V = verb
é = verb takes a direct object
z = English
```

The *selectional restrictions* (Chomsky, 1965, p. 95) r1=film and r2=MPAA-rating prevent the concept *MPAA-rating-of* from being returned by the parser whenever *be* or *get* are used in a sentence. With these selectional restrictions, this concept is only returned when the first argument (in this case, the subject) is a film and the second argument (in this case, the direct object) is an MPAA rating, as defined in the rating ontology:

**==MPAA# rating*.z//Motion# Picture# Association# of#R
America# rating*.z/**

```
===MPAA-G//G.¹Éz/G# rating*.z/
===MPAA-NC-17//NC#-17*.¹Éz/NC#-17# rating*.z/
===MPAA-PG//PG.¹Éz/PG# rating*.z/
===MPAA-PG-13//PG#-13*.¹Éz/PG#-13# rating*.z/
===MPAA-R//R.¹Éz/R# rating*.z/
```

```
R = preposition
¹ = frequent
É = noun preceded by empty article
```

Another meaning of *get* is abstract transfer of possession:

```
=atrans//get.Véz/|r1=human|r2=physical-object|
```

The assertions preceded by an asterisk do not satisfy the selectional restrictions:

```
*[atrans Mary MPAA-PG]
*[atrans Mary film54]
 [atrans Mary video-cassette12]
*[atrans film54 MPAA-PG]
```

Using the above selectional restrictions, the system is able to disambiguate *get* in the following sentences:

```
The movie got a PG rating. [MPAA-rating-of film54 MPAA-PG]
Mary got a video cassette. [atrans Mary video-cassette12]
```

(In general, a selectional restriction is an assertion of the following form:

```
[r1/r2/r3/... predicate restriction-specification]
```

A restriction-specification may be:

```
class
[and restriction-specification restriction-specification ...]
[or restriction-specification restriction-specification ...]
[not restriction-specification]
```

Selectional restrictions are inherited by descendant predicates unless overridden.)

We also define a noun for the relation:

```
==MPAA-rating-of//rating,MPAA# rating*.z/
```

which enables ThoughtTreasure to parse the sentences (not found in the corpus):

```
The MPAA rating of the film is PG.
PG is the MPAA rating of the film.
The film's MPAA rating is PG.
The rating of the film is PG.
PG is the rating of the film.
The film's rating is PG.
```

The `actor-of` relation is specified in the corpus using expressions such as:

```
KANSAS CITY stars Jennifer Jason Leigh [as Blondie]
Michael J. Fox plays (character) [in (film)]
Robin Williams is (character) [in (film)]
Eric Roberts stars as a fencing instructor [in (film)]
```

We see that `actor-of` is a relation with three arguments-a *ternary relation*. The first argument is the film, the second argument is the actor, and the third argument is the character played in the film:

```
0         1              2                       3
[actor-of film-Kansas-City Jennifer-Jason-Leigh character-Blondie]
```

The lexical entries for this relation will thus be:

```
==actor-of//actor,star.z/
star* as_.Véz/; FILM stars HUMAN as CHARACTER
play* in_.Vúëz/; HUMAN plays CHARACTER in FILM
be* in_.Vúëz/; HUMAN is CHARACTER in FILM
star* in_ as_.Vúz/; HUMAN stars as CHARACTER in FILM
```

By default, the subject of the sentence goes into slot 1 and the direct object goes into slot 2 of the result concept. This behavior is overridden using the features:

```
ú = subject placed in slot 2
é = direct object placed in slot 2
ë = direct object placed in slot 3
```

Indirect objects indicated by prepositions such as *as* and *in* are placed in available slots starting with slot 1.

Similarly, we define:

```
==director-of//director.z/
direct.Vúèz/; HUMAN directs FILM
```

è = direct object placed in slot 1

We continue by identifying descriptive words and expressions used in the corpus of 50 Usenet movie reviews:

```
description of movie
  good:   amazing, exciting, well crafted, imaginative,
          hilarious, extremely funny, a surefire success,
          takes risks, will do well, has things going for it,
          laugh one's head off
  mixed: mixed bag
  bad:    awful, derivative, sloppy, unoriginal, cliched,
          cliche-ridden, stupid, shallow, predictable,
          formula-ridden, crap, cheesy, ridiculous,
          unbearable, a strike-out, a letdown,
          will not do well
  language: mild language, mildly offensive language,
            offensive language
  other: outlandish, bittersweet, political, dubbed, topless,
         nudity, violence

description of performances of actors in movie
  good:   solid, fun, flawless, intense, imploding
  bad:    atrocious

description of actors in movie
  good:   perfectly cast, the star of the show,
          steals the screen
  bad:    miscast
```

We then enter these into the ontology and lexicon when they are not already present. For example, we extend the entry for the good attribute as follows:

```
=object-trait/attribute/
==good.Az//
[.8⁻Inf]/fantastic.Az/fabulous.TAz/awesome.aAz/
amazing.TAz/
[.5⁻.8]/good.Az/have* things#NP going#V for#R it#H.Vz/
[.1⁻.5]/acceptable.Az/OK.TAz/
[-.1⁻.1]/inoffensive.Az/mixed#A bag*.z/
```

```
[-Inf⁻-.1]/bad.Az/barfy.aAz/atrocious,awful.Az/
```

The parser and generator will make use of this information, enabling the correspondences:

```
[good A 1.0]           A is amazing.
[good A 0.55]          A has things going for it.
[good A 0.2]           A is acceptable.
[good A 0.0]           A is a mixed bag.
[good A -0.55]         A is awful.
```

No changes are needed for the *extremely funny* noted in the corpus, since the existing adverb *extremely* can be used to modify the existing adjective *funny*:

```
[humorous A 1.0]       A is extremely funny/humorous.
[humorous A 0.55]      A is funny/humorous.
[humorous A 0.2]       A is slightly funny/humorous.
[humorous A -0.55]     A is not funny/humorous.
```

We similarly extend other attributes:

```
=personality-trait/attribute/
==courageous.Az//take* risks#NP.Vz/
==unexpected#A star*.z//steal* the#D screen#N.Vz/steal*
the#D show#N.Vz/
star* of#R the#D show#.z/
==well#B cast#.Az//perfectly#B cast#.Az/
[-Inf⁻-.1]/miscast.Az/
=object-trait/attribute/
==bearable.Az//
[-Inf⁻-.1]/unbearable.Az/
==excellent.Az//flawless.Az/
[-Inf⁻-.1]/mediocre.Az/cheesy.Az/
==exciting.Az//thrilling.Az/
==humorous.Az//funny.Az/hilarious.Az/
==normal.Az//
[-Inf⁻-.1]/strange.Az/outlandish.Az/
==novel.Az//original.Az/
[-Inf⁻-.1]/unoriginal.Az/derivative,cliched,cliche#N-
ridden#.Az/
==nude.Az//nudity.z/
===topless.Az//
==predictable.Az//formula#N-ridden#.Az/
==violent.Az//violence.z/
==well#B crafted#.Az//
```

```
====bittersweet.Az/positive-emotion,negative-emotion/
====disappointment.mz/prospect-based-emotion/
letdown.Tz/

==-goal-status//
====failed-goal//not do* well#B.Vz/strike#V out#R ½.Tz/
====succeeded-goal//do* well#B.Vz/
```

success is already in the lexicon under the concept *succeeded-goal*, though how *a surefire success* will be parsed is unclear.

Some reorganization of the existing ontology is often necessary in order to add new items in a clean and consistent fashion. No matter how much is added to the ontology, there is always more to add. Human knowledge is infinitely divisible and distributed among humans, subcultures, and cultures: We have the concept of a phone, which can be broken down into desk phone and wall phone. Desk phone can further be broken down into Western Electric 500 set and France Telecom S63. Western Electric 500 set can be broken down into 500CD and 500DM. 500CD can be broken down by whether it has a 7A or 7D dial or the number of windings in hybrid coil A/2. An expert in the art of coil winding will break down hybrid coil A/2 according to type of winding. A physicist will break down the phone's color, weight, and date of manufacture into particles and fields. A social psychologist will describe the use of the phone in terms of interpersonal relationships. We can go on and on: phones relate to human communication, language, speech acts, history, evolution, interior decorating. There seems to be no limit.

Thus when entering information into ThoughtTreasure, it is easy to become overwhelmed with possibilities. At this point, we step back and ask: What does the application *do*? What type of information must the application represent in order to do this? And we add only the necessary information. (Then again, entering items into ThoughtTreasure can be an amusing pastime.)

At this point we can start ThoughtTreasure with the updated database files and ask it questions in English:

```
> Who directed Rendezvous in Paris?
Eric Rohmer directed Rendezvous in Paris.
> Who starred in the film?
Clara Bellar starred in Rendezvous in Paris. Antoine
Basler starred in Rendezvous in Paris. Mathias Megard
starred in Rendezvous in Paris. Aurore Rauscher starred
```

```
in Rendezvous in Paris.
> Is the Hunchback of Notre Dame rated PG?
No, the Hunchback of Notre Dame is not rated PG.
> The animated movie got a G rating?
Yes, the Hunchback of Notre Dame was in fact rated g.
```

In the chapter on semantic parsing, we will see how the above questions are parsed and how the answers are generated. But first, in the next chapter, we show how text agents are added to enable ThoughtTreasure to parse ratings such as "4 stars".

Coding lexical entries

We now review how to code lexical entries in more detail, including the specification of their features and argument structure. A lexical entry consists of:

- A character string giving the *citation form* (see Lyons, 1977, p. 19) of the lexical entry, such as the infinitive form of a verb or the singular form of a noun.
- A list of *features*, including the part of speech and language of the lexical entry.
- A list of *inflections*, each of which consists of a character string and list of features (such as singular or plural).
- Separator characters, such as apostrophes and dashes, which are part of the phrase but not stored in the inflection strings.
- Links to the atomic object *meanings* of the lexical entry. Each link itself contains *argument structure* and feature information which apply to the lexical entry when used with the given meaning.

Lexical entries for atomic objects or concepts are defined in ThoughtTreasure database files along with definitions of concepts and assertions about those concepts. A simple definition is:

```
=window/physical-object/window.z/fenêtre.Fy/
```

This defines a concept `window` which is a kind of `physical-object` and two words for `window-`*window* in English and *fenêtre* of feminine gender in French. This may be abbreviated to:

```
=window.z/physical-object/fenêtre.Fy/
```

That is, if a lexical entry specification—recognized because it contains a period—occurs in the initial position, it is used both as the concept name and as a lexical entry for the concept.

As we have seen, the second element of a definition specifies the parent of a concept and hierarchical relationships among concepts are also specified by level of indentation:

```
=boundary.z/physical-object/
==window.z//fenêtre.Fy/
===bay# window*.z//fenêtre* en#R baie#.Fy/
==door.z//doorway.z/
===folding# door*.z//porte* pliante*A.Fy/
===hinged#A door*.z//porte* à#R charnière#.Fy/
```

Here a `bay-window` is a kind of `window`, which is a kind of `boundary`, which in turn is a kind of `physical-object`. A `door` is a kind of `boundary`, and so on.

Coding words

When specifying a word, as in:

```
=window.z//
```

if the word is not already contained in the inflections file, ThoughtTreasure automatically generates inflections for it. Nouns are inflected in the singular and plural:

```
SING window
PL   windows
```

(The inflections for a word may be viewed with the dictionary tool.)

Some words are *invariant*—they do not inflect. Any word marked with the feature "ß" is invariant. In addition, invariance is determined by a set of rules: In English, any word that is neither a noun nor verb is invariant. In French, any word that is neither a noun, verb, nor adjective is invariant. In addition, in French, trademarks (marked with "®"), acronyms, and non-`polity` proper nouns are invariant. See Grevisse (1986, sections 510-513) for more details.

Coding phrases

The lexical entry

```
bay# window*.z/
```
is phrasal—it consists of two words. Upon reading the definition of a phrase, ThoughtTreasure must generate its inflections if they are not already specified in the inflections file. The inflection of a phrase is produced by inflecting its component words appropriately. The character "*" indicates that the preceding word should be inflected, while the character "#" indicates that the preceding word should not be inflected.

Since this lexical entry is a noun, it needs to be inflected for singular and plural. To generate the singular inflection, ThoughtTreasure constructs the string "bay " followed by the singular inflection for the word *window*, which is "window". Then to generate the plural inflection, ThoughtTreasure constructs the string "bay " followed by the plural inflection for *window*, which is "windows". The inflections of *bay window* are therefore:

```
SING bay window
PL   bay windows
```

Inflections are generated for phrasal verbs in all the appropriate tenses, numbers, and persons. In French, adjective inflections are generated for masculine and feminine, singular and plural.

To facilitate later retrieval, any white space characters in the phrasal inflection (such as apostrophes or commas) are mapped to spaces. For example, "Macy's" is stored as:

```
Macy s
```

These separator characters are saved in another data structure so they can be reconstituted by the generator.

Above we saw some additional characters in the phrase definitions:

```
===hinged#A door*.z//
```

The character "A" indicates that the preceding word is an adjective. This is used for two reasons: If there is not already a word in the lexicon having an inflection of "hinged", this enables a new word to be created with the correct part of speech.

And if "hinged" is a known inflection, then the "A" helps disambiguate which inflection and word is intended—for example, one "hinged" might be an adverb and the other an adjective. In addition to the "A", other features might have been used for disambiguation. For example:

```
lots#NP of#R.Az/
```

This defines a phrasal adjective *lots of* consisting of the plural of the noun *lot* followed by the preposition *of*.

There are a number of cases where a given string is ambiguous, even restricted as to part of speech. For example, *pops* could be the plural of *pop* (a sound), or the singular of *pops* (informal for *father*). *Evans* could be the plural of the first name *Evan*, or the singular of the last name *Evans*.

Here are some other examples of phrasal inflection:

```
luminance* and#K saturation*.z/
SING    luminance and saturation
PL      luminances and saturations

brain#N dead#.Az/
        brain dead

super#B-bon*.Ay/
M SING super bon
M PL    super bons
F SING super bonne
F PL    super bonnes

couleur#NF pêche#NF.Ay/
M SING couleur pêche
M PL    couleur pêche
F SING couleur pêche
F PL    couleur pêche
```

Several lexical entries that have the same features after the period may be defined by separating them with commas:

```
==turnpike.z//parkway,pike,thruway,toll# highway*,
toll# road*.z/
```

This notation is not permitted in the initial position; the following does not work:

```
==turnpike,parkway.z//
```

The name of a concept is derived from a lexical entry in initial position by removing "#", "*", and features, and by mapping all nonalphanumeric characters to "-". Some examples:

```
=purplish#A red*.z//                    purplish-red
=adverb* of#R common#A knowledge#.z// adverb-of-common-
knowledge
```

Coding verb argument structure

Verb argument structure is represented in a ThoughtTreasure database file using a compact feature-based notation designed to speed entry of lexical entries. In this section, we provide examples of how to code the various verb classes and types of sentences, such as those discussed by Greenbaum and Quirk (1990), Alexander (1988), and Lyons (1977).

Intransitive verbs

An intransitive verb is coded as:

```
===smile.Vz//
```

which is expanded to the following argument structure:

```
<smile>.<Vz> <> <smile>
  1:    subj
```

(Argument structure expansions of items in ThoughtTreasure's lexicon such as the above can be obtained by typing lexentry into the ThoughtTreasure shell. This command starts the lexical entry tool which will prompt for words or phrases.) The verb *smile* has one argument, the subject NP (noun phrase), which maps to slot 1 of the smile concept. subj is a *case-frame role* filled by the semantic parser when it parses the subject NP of a sentence; in order for *smile* to parse, a subj must be present in the case frame.

The sentence:

```
Pete smiles.
```

is thus parsed as:

```
[smile Pete]
```

Transitive verbs

A transitive verb is coded as:

```
===eat.Véz//|r1=animal|r2=food|
```

which expands to:

```
<eat>.<Vz₃> <¹> <eat>
   1:      subj                    animal
   2:      obj                     food
```

The verb *eat* takes a subject NP and an object NP, which map to slots 1 and 2 of the `eat` concept. The `obj` case-frame role is filled by the semantic parser when it parses an NP verb argument within a verb phrase. Both the `subj` and `obj` case-frame roles must be present in the case frame in order for *eat* to parse. (The verb is parsed after all its arguments have been parsed.) A selectional restriction of `animal` is specified for `subj` and `food` for `obj`. Except in relaxed parsing, if the concepts do not obey the selectional restrictions, the given meaning of the verb will not parse.

The sentence:

```
Pete eats bread.
```

is parsed as:

```
[eat Pete bread]
```

(The semantic parses shown here are simplified—for example, tense and intensions are ignored.)

A verb which can be both intransitive and transitive (with similar enough meanings) is coded as:

```
===eat.Vé_z//|r1=animal|r2=food|
```

An underscore ("_") is used after any object feature to indicate that the object is optional. The above expands to:

```
<eat>.<Vz˳> <¹> <eat>
   1:    subj                    animal
( 2:     obj                     food)
```

Now sentences involving *eat* are parsed as follows:

```
Pete eats bread.  [eat Pete bread]
Pete eats.        [eat Pete food]
```

Note that for optional arguments which are not supplied, ThoughtTreasure uses the selectional restriction (in this case food) to fill the slot.

Verbs with prepositional phrase arguments

A verb with a single indirect object prepositional phrase is coded as:

```
====attend-look//look* at+.¹Vz/
```

We saw above that NP arguments are encoded using features (after the period). In contrast, PP (prepositional phrase) arguments are encoded using words (before the period) which are followed by a plus sign ("+") or underscore ("_"). A plus sign indicates a required PP argument, while an underscore indicates an optional PP argument. The above expands to:

```
<look>.<Vz> <¹> <attend-look>
  1:    subj
  2:    iobj          at. Rz˳
```

The iobj case-frame role is filled in by the semantic parser when it parses a prepositional phrase argument to a verb.

A verb with an optional prepositional phrase argument is coded as:

```
===wink//wink* at_.Vz/
```

which expands to:

```
<wink>.<Vz> <> <wink>
   1:    subj
( 2:    iobj              at. Rz    )
```

The specified preposition (in this case *at*) must agree with the head preposition of the PP argument in order for the parse to succeed. Thus

```
The cat winks at Pete.
```

parses as:

```
[wink cat Pete]
```

while

```
The cat winks in Pete.
```

parses as:

```
[prep-inside [wink cat na] Pete]
```

That is, *in Pete* is interpreted as an *adjunct* rather than an argument.

A verb with several PP arguments is coded as:

```
==ptrans//go* from_ to_.¹Vz/|r1=animal|
```

which expands to:

```
<go>.<Vz,> <¹> <ptrans>
   1:    subj                       animal
( 2:    iobj      from.   Rz              )
( 3:    iobj        to.   Rz,             )
```

Sentences involving this use of *go* are parsed as follows:

```
Pete goes.                [go Pete na na]
Pete goes from A.         [go Pete A na]
Pete goes to B.           [go Pete na B]
Pete goes from A to B.    [go Pete A B]
Pete goes to B from A.    [go Pete A B]
```

Note that arguments following the verb parse in any order.

Verbs with noun phrase and prepositional phrase arguments

A verb having both object NP and indirect object PP arguments is coded as follows:

```
==connect//connect* to+.Véz/
```

which expands to:
```
<connect>.<Vz> <> <connect>
    1:      subj
    2:       obj
    3:      iobj           to. Rz¸
```

Thus

```
John connects the antenna to the TV set.
```

parses as:

```
[connect John antenna TV-set]
```

Slot numbers

What if we would like to alter which slots arguments are assigned to? For subject NPs, one of the following feature characters is added:

```
ú = subject assigned to slot 2
ü = subject assigned to slot 3
otherwise subject assigned to slot 1
```

Indirect object PPs are assigned to available slots starting at 1. Thus:

```
====emotion-miss//miss.¹Véz/manquer* à+.¹Vúy/
```

expands to:

```
<miss>.<Vz> <¹> <emotion-miss>
    1:     subj
    2:      obj
```

```
<manquer>.<Vy¸> <¹> <emotion-miss>
```

```
1:     iobj              à. Ry
2:     subj
```

Both of the sentences:

```
John misses Mary.
Mary manque à John.
```

parse to:

```
[emotion-miss John Mary]
```

For object NPs, a different feature character is used:

```
è = object assigned to slot 1
é = object assigned to slot 2 (the most frequent case)
ë = object assigned to slot 3
otherwise no object
```

For example:

```
====chair-of//run.Vúèz/|r1=company|r2=human|
```

expands to:

```
<run>.<Vz > <> <chair-of>
  1:     obj                     company
  2:     subj                    human
```

Multiple object NPs are coded by using several object features as in:

```
===owe//owe.Véëz/|r1=human|r2=human|
r3=financial-instrument|
```

which expands to:

```
<owe>.<Vz> <> <owe>
  1:     subj                    human
  2:     obj                     human
  3:     obj                     financial-instrument
```

Then the sentence:

```
John owes Peter 2 dollars.
```

parses to:

```
[owe John Peter $2]
```

The assignment of indirect object PPs to slots may also be specified using the following feature characters:

```
ö = indirect objects assigned after slot 3 inclusive
ō = indirect objects assigned after slot 4 inclusive
otherwise indirect objects assigned after slot 1 inclusive
```

Prepositions followed by "+" or "_" are assigned from left to right to slot numbers, starting from the first available slot after and including slot 1, 3, or 4 as specified. For example:

```
===ptrans-sink//sink* into_.Vöz/|r1=animal|
```

expands to:

```
<sink>.<Vz> <> <ptrans-sink>
   1:    subj                      animal
 ( 2:      na                      )
 ( 3:    iobj        into. Rz,     )
```

Here a placeholder is entered for slot 2—nothing in the input syntax fills this argument but na is nonetheless inserted into slot 2 of a successful parse. So

```
John sinks into the swamp.
```

parses as:

```
[sink John na swamp]
```

Verbs with clause arguments

Subordinate clause verb arguments are specified using the following *subcategorization restrictions* regarding the tense and mood of the clause:

```
÷ = indicative          "(that) he goes"
O = subjunctive         "(that) he go"
ï = infinitive          "(for him) to go"
± = present participle  "(him) going"
```

These can be applied to both NP and PP arguments. For an NP argument, the feature is placed after the object feature ("è", "é", or "ë"). For a PP argument, the feature is placed after the "_" or "+".

For example:

```
=====say-to//say* to_.¹Vë÷z/tell.Véë÷z/
```

expands to

```
<say>.<Vz¸> <¹> <say-to>
   1:    subj                          human
( 2:    iobj            to. Rz¸        human)
   3:    obj                    ÷      list

<tell>.<Vz> <> <say-to>
   1:    subj                          human
   2:    obj                           human
   3:    obj                    ÷      list
```

That is, these uses of *say* and *tell* both take a sentence as argument whose main verb is in the indicative ("÷"), which is assigned to slot 3. Here are how some sample sentences are parsed:

```
Peter said he ate.              [say-to Peter na [eat Peter]]
Peter said that he ate.         [say-to Peter na [eat Peter]]
Peter said to John that he ate. [say-to Peter John [eat Peter]]
Peter said that he ate to John. [say-to Peter John [eat Peter]]
Peter told John that he ate.    [say-to Peter John [eat Peter]]
```

Similarly,

```
====active-goal//want.¹Véïz/|r1=human|r2=list|
```

expands to:

```
<want>.<Vz> <¹> <active-goal>
   1:    subj                          human
   2:    obj                    ï      list
```

The sentence

```
Peter wants John to eat.
```

parses to:

```
[active-goal Peter [eat John]]
```

A subordinate clause PP argument is coded as follows:

```
=====intimidate//intimidate* into_ɫ.¹Véz/|r1=human|
r2=human|r3=list|
```
which expands to:

```
<intimidate>.<Vz> <¹> <intimidate>
   1:    subj                        human
   2:    obj                         human
 ( 3:    iobj      into. Rz‸ ɫ       list)
```

A number of different subordinate clause verb arguments are defined in the speech act ontology. The following concepts can be used as a test suite to test the coding and generation of speech act lexical entries:

```
[SPEECH-ACT Lucie Martine-Dad
            [hand-to Lucie Martine-Dad saltshaker]]
[SPEECH-ACT Lucie na
            [hand-to Lucie Martine-Dad saltshaker]]
[SPEECH-ACT Lucie Martine-Dad na]
[SPEECH-ACT Lucie na na]
[SPEECH-ACT Lucie Martine-Dad
            [hand-to Martine-Dad Lucie saltshaker]]
[SPEECH-ACT Lucie na
            [hand-to Martine-Dad Lucie saltshaker]]
```

By typing the following commands in the ThoughtTreasure shell:

```
testsa -lang z -dialect À -dcout outsae.txt
testsa -lang y -dialect ? -dcout outsae.txt
```

English and French output files will be produced containing generated sentences for each of the above concepts for a list of speech acts. For example:

```
intimidate//intimidate* into_ɫ.Véz/
faire* pression#NF sur_ pour_O.Vy/
  Lucie Paret intimidates François Guérin.
  She intimidates someone.
  She intimidates François Guérin into handing a saltshaker
  to her.
```

Lucie Paret fait pression sur François Guérin pour que
Lucie Paret passe une salière à François Guérin.
Elle fait pression pour qu'elle lui passe une salière.
Elle fait pression sur lui.
Elle fait pression.
Lucie Paret fait pression sur François Guérin pour que
François Guérin passe une salière à Lucie Paret.
Elle fait pression pour qu'il lui passe une salière.

=====say-to//say* to_.Vë÷z/
    She says that she hands a saltshaker to him.
    She says something to François Guérin.
    She says something.
    Lucie Paret says to him that he hands a saltshaker to Lucie
    Paret.
    She says that he hands a saltshaker to her.

======deny//deny* to_.Vë±z/
    Lucie Paret denies handing a saltshaker to him.
    She denies something to him.
    She denies something.
    She denies to François Guérin handing a saltshaker to her.
    Lucie Paret denies him handing a saltshaker to Lucie Paret.

======urge//urge.VëOz/
    She urges that she hand a saltshaker to François Guérin.
    She urges something.
    She urges something.
    Lucie Paret urges that François Guérin hand a saltshaker to
    Lucie Paret.
    She urges that François Guérin hand a saltshaker to her.

=======plead//plead* with+.Vëïz/
    She pleads to hand a saltshaker to him.
    She pleads something with him.
    She pleads something.
    She pleads with him to hand a saltshaker to her.
    She pleads for him to hand a saltshaker to her.

Phrasal verbs

Phrasal verbs contain *expletive elements* that do not contribute concepts to any slot
of the result concept. For example:

==died//kick* the#D bucket#N.TVz/|r1=animal|

expands to:

```
<kick>.<Vz> <T> <died>
   1:    subj                           animal
    :    expl the bucket.  0z    V_O
```

There is no slot number associated with "the bucket", since "the bucket" is not part of the result concept. "the bucket" must however be provided in order for the parse to succeed. "V_O" indicates the position of the expletive element: after the main verb. "0" (the digit zero, not the letter "O") is the part of speech used for unanalyzed expletives. "T" means informal. Thus

```
Peter kicked the bucket.
```

parses to:

```
[died Peter]
```

Phrasal verbs may include NP and PP arguments as described above for nonphrasal verbs:

```
===exaggerate//get* carried#V away#B with_.Vz/

<get>.<Vz¸> <> <exaggerate>
   1:    subj
( 2:    iobj          with. Rz¸          )
    :    expl carried away.  0z    V_O

Peter got carried away with the story.

[exaggerate Peter story]

====appointment//
have* an#D appointment#N with_ at_ to_ï on_.@¹ôVz/
|r1=human|r2=human|r3=location|r4=list|r5=time-range|

<have>.<Vz¸> <¹ô> <appointment>
   1:    subj                           human
( 2:    iobj          with. Rz¸          human)
( 3:    iobj            at. Rz¸          location)
( 4:    iobj            to. Rz¸ ï        list)
( 5:    iobj            on.·Rz¸          time-range)
    :    expl an appointment.  0z    V_O
```

```
Peter has an appointment with Mary.
```

```
[appointment Peter Mary na na na]
```

Expletive elements prefer certain locations over others:

```
John put it away in the refrigerator.
*John put away it in the refrigerator.
John put the mustard away in the refrigerator.
?John put away the mustard in the refrigerator.
```

In ThoughtTreasure, the character "ø" is used to indicate the location of an object NP within a phrase:

```
===put-away//put* ø away#B in_.Véz/
```

The above expands to:

```
<put>.<Vz¸> <> <put-away>
   1:     subj
   2:     obj
 ( 3:     iobj          in.·Rz¸          )
   :      expl          away.  0z    VO_
```

"VO_" indicates that "away" follows the object NP. (This information is used only in generation—parses which disobey this restriction are accepted.)

Note the distinction between an expletive preposition (also known as a particle or adverb), and a preposition used to mark a PP argument:

```
John put on the shirt.
John put the shirt on.
John put it on.
*John put on it.
```

which contrasts with:

```
John sat on the chair.
*John sat the chair on.
*John sat it on.
John sat on it.
```

These two cases are coded differently:

```
===put-on//put* ø on#R.¹Véz/

<put>.<Vz,> <¹> <put-on>
    1:      subj
    2:       obj
     :      expl                on.   0z   VO_

==sit//sit* on+.¹Vz/

<sit>.<Vz> <¹> <sit>
    1:      subj
    2:      iobj                on.·Rz,
```

Pronominal and negative phrasal verbs

Pronominal phrasal verbs contain expletive pronouns, or pronouns which do not contribute additional concepts to any slot of the result concept (but which are often necessary to identify the verb as an instance of the given concept). For example, in:

```
Peter treated himself to a schnaps.
```

there are three syntactic arguments to the verb:

```
subject NP:         Peter
object NP:          himself
indirect object PP: to a schnaps
```

But *himself* is redundant with *Peter* and we would like the result to be simply:

```
[treat Peter schnaps]
```

Such an example is handled in ThoughtTreasure by coding it as:

```
===treat//himself treat* to+.¹Vz/

<treat>.<Vz> <¹> <treat>
    1:      subj
    2:      iobj              to. Rz,
     :      expl      himself. Hz,      _V
```

This type of verb is very common in French:

```
===rise.Vz//s'élever*.Vy/

<élever>.<Vy> <> <rise>
  1:    subj
   :    expl           se.·Hy˛      _V


===hobby-of//se brancher* sur+.TVêy/

<brancher>.<Vy˛> <T> <hobby-of>
  1:    subj
  2:    iobj           sur. Ry˛
   :    expl           se.·Hy˛      _V

===leave//s'en aller*.Vy/

<aller>.<Vy˛> <> <leave>
  1:    subj
   :    expl           se.·Hy˛      _V
   :    expl           en.·Hy˛      _V
```

"_V" indicates that the expletive element precedes the verb.

Note that there is nothing preventing us from defining uses of pronouns such as *himself* that do fill slots:

```
==atrans//give.Véëz/

<give>.<Vz˛> <> <atrans>
  1:    subj
  2:    obj
  3:    obj
```

```
Peter gave himself a car.
```

```
[atrans Peter Peter car]
```

Negative phrasal verbs contain a negative element which does not appear in the result concept:

```
===like//not can* resist#.Véz/
```

```
<can>.<Vzˏ> <> <like>
   1:    subj
   2:      obj
    :    expl           not.·Bzˏ      _V
    :    expl        resist.  0z    V_O
```

Peter can't resist pizza.

[like Peter pizza]

===different//ne rien avoir* à#R voir#V avec+.TVy/

```
<avoir>.<Vyˏ> <T> <different>
   1:    subj
   2:    iobj        avec. Ryˏ
    :    expl        rien.·Byˏ      _V
    :    expl      à voir.  0y    V_O
```

John n'a rien à voir avec Peter.

[different John Peter]

To speed coding, a hardcoded set of expletive elements are permitted before the verb, without having to specify their inflection with "#" or "*". For English lexical entries:

```
not
himself
```

For French lexical entries:

```
ne pas
ne point
ne plus
ne rien
jamais
se
s'
en
s'en
s'y
```

Coding lexical entries for gradable concepts

The *range specification*:

```
[LOWERBOUND~UPPERBOUND]/
```

applies to all lexical entries that follow, until superseded by another range specification. At the beginning of each concept definition, the range specification is reset to the default, which is `[.1~1.0]`.

For example:

```
===like-human//
[.8~Inf]/love.vÔéz/
[.5~.8]/like.vÔéz/
[-Inf~-.1]/hate.véz/

[like-human A B 1.0]   A loves B.
[like-human A B 1.0]   A totally likes B.
```

Coding relations and roles

ThoughtTreasure relations are most often expressed as nouns. For example, a relation `President-of` is defined with a noun lexical entry *President* as follows:

```
==President-of//President.áz/
```

The object:

```
[President-of United-States Bill-Clinton]
```

is expressed in natural language (parsed or generated) as:

```
The President of the United States is Bill Clinton.
```

or:

```
Bill Clinton is the President of the United States.
```

Whether the definite article *the* or indefinite article *a* is used depends on the type of mapping:

```
[relation A B]
```

```
many-to-one:
```

```
    a0 ---+
    a1 ---+--> b0
    a2 ---+

    a3 ------> b1
```

```
one-to-many:
```

```
          +--> b0
    a0 ---+--> b1
          +--> b2

    a1 ------> b3
```

```
one-to-one:
```

```
    a0 ------> b0
    a1 ------> b1
    a2 ------> b2
    a3 ------> b3
```

```
many-to-many:
```

```
    none of the above
```

Many-to-one and one-to-one relations are expressed using a definite article:

```
==mother-of//mother.áz/|many-to-one|
[mother-of Jim Joyce]
The mother of Jim is Joyce.
Joyce is the mother of Jim.
```

```
==nationality-of//nationality.áz/|many-to-one|
[nationality-of Bill-Clinton United-States]
The nationality of Bill Clinton is the United States.
The United States is the nationality of Bill Clinton.
```

```
==spouse-of//spouse.áz/|one-to-one|
[spouse-of Jim Juliet]
The spouse of Jim is Juliet.
Juliet is the spouse of Jim.
```

while one-to-many and many-to-many relations are expressed using an indefinite article:

```
==friend-of//friend.áz/|many-to-many|
[friend-of Jim Tom]
A friend of Jim is Tom.
Tom is a friend of Jim.
```

The nouns defined above using the feature "á" apply to the second *role* of the relation: The word *nationality* describes the filler of the second argument of the `nationality-of` relation. Nouns which apply to the first role of the relation are defined using the feature "à":

```
==nationality-of//citizen.àz/nationality.áz/
|many-to-one|
[nationality-of Bill-Clinton United-States]
A citizen of the United States is Bill Clinton.
Bill Clinton is a citizen of the United States.
```

Note that an indefinite article is used here. The choice of articles is determined by the type of mapping and the role:

```
role feature                           á                    à
role slot                              1                    2
             +---------------------------------------------
many-to-one  |   definite-article  indefinite-article
one-to-many  | indefinite-article    definite-article
one-to-one   |   definite-article    definite-article
many-to-many | indefinite-article  indefinite-article
```

Role features may be coded for concepts other than relations, such as actions:

```
==publish//publish.Véz/publisher.àz/
[publish Garamond Les-Templiers]
Garamond publishes Les Templiers.
The publisher of Les Templiers is Garamond.
Garamond is the publisher of Les Templiers.
```

```
==stay//stay* with_.Vz/guest.àz/host.áz/
[stay Jim Karen]
Jim stays with Karen.
The guest of Karen is Jim.
Jim is the guest of Karen.
The host of Jim is Karen.
Karen is the host of Jim.
```

Nouns which describe the filler of the third slot are defined using the feature "ä":

```
==advise//advise.Vëëïz/advisor.àz/advisee.áz/advice.äz/
[advise Jim Karen [happy Karen]]
Jim advises Karen to be happy.
The advisor of Karen is Jim.
Jim is the advisor of Karen.
The advisee of Jim is Karen.
Karen is the advisee of Jim.
The advice of Jim is for Karen to be happy.
For Karen to be happy is the advice of Jim.
```

Relations may also be expressed by other parts of speech such as verbs:

```
==residence-of//residence.áz/reside* in+.Vz/
[residence-of Bill-Clinton White-House]
The residence of Bill Clinton is the White House.
Bill Clinton resides in the White House.
```

and adjectives:

```
==addiction-of//addiction.áz/addicted* to+.Az/
[addiction-of Jim chocolate]
An addiction of Jim is chocolate.
Jim is addicted to chocolate.
```

Attribute-relation connections

A canonical representation might represent the meaning of each pair of these sentences similarly:

```
Jim is artistic.              / Jim is an artist.
Jim is tall.                  / Jim is 6 foot 2.
A is more expensive than B.   / A costs $2 and B costs $1.
```

But instead of searching for such a canonical representation, we represent the left-hand sentences using attributes and the right-hand sentences using relations. Then attributes and relations are connected via a set of specialized inference rules, which are accessed from the appropriate C code such as the question answering agents.

The `attr-rel-value` relation equates a particular value (weight) of an attribute with a particular value of a relation. For example, the assertions:

```
[attr-rel-value artistic occupation-of 0.9u artist]
[attr-rel-value artistic occupation-of 0.8u musician]
```

represent the equivalences:

```
[artistic ?person 0.9u] <=> [occupation-of ?person artist]
[artistic ?person 0.8u] <=> [occupation-of ?person musician]
```

The `attr-rel-range` relation equates a particular range of weights of an attribute with a particular range of values of a relation, so that:

```
[attr-rel-range tall height-of +0.2u +0.7u 1.8m 2.0m]
```

represents:

```
[tall ?person 0.2u]  <=> [height-of ?person 1.8m]
...
[tall ?person 0.45u] <=> [height-of ?person 1.9m]
...
[tall ?person 0.7u]  <=> [height-of ?person 2.0m]
```

Several such relations may be asserted on a given attribute-relation pair:

```
[attr-rel-range tall height-of +0.7u +Inf  2.0m +Inf]
[attr-rel-range tall height-of +0.2u +0.7u 1.8m 2.0m]
[attr-rel-range tall height-of -0.2u +0.2u 1.6m 1.8m]
[attr-rel-range tall height-of -Inf -0.2u 0.0m 1.6m]
```

The `attr-rel-proportion` relation states that the weights of an attribute are proportional to the values of a relation:

```
[attr-rel-proportional heavy weight-of]
[attr-rel-proportional big circumference-of]
[attr-rel-proportional expensive ap]
```

(`ap` means asking price.) Code can then infer, for example, that one object is *heavier* than another when it has a greater weight.

The `attr-rel-inv-proportion` relation states that the weights of an attribute are inversely proportional to the values of a relation.

Coding attachments

A set of lexical entries, which we will call *attachments*, refer to a relation and a filler of the relation simultaneously. For example, *American* in *Jim is an American* refers to the relation `nationality-of`, and the value of that relation `United-States`. Similarly, *French* refers to `nationality-of` and `France`.

Attachments, which may be nouns or adjectives, are defined using the "þ" feature. The following types of attachments are common:

```
relation                filler class      example
────────────────────    ────────────      ────────────────────────────────
residence-of            polity            New#A York*.z/New#A Yorker*.þz/
nationality-of          country           Spain.z/Spaniard.þz/
political-affiliation-of political-system Democratic#A Party*.z/Democrat.þz/
occupation-of           occupation        psychology.z/psychologist.þz/

religion-of             religion          Taoism.z/Taoist.þz/
```

Attachment lexical entries allow an economical representation of classes such as occupations and religions. Instead of defining a hierarchy of religions, then a hierarchy of persons holding certain religious beliefs, and linking the two, we define a single hierarchy containing both.

Attachments provide a *lexical parallel universe* of lexical entries for objects. Lexical entries coded as attachments are not interchangeable with lexical entries not coded as attachments:

```
Jim is an American.
*Jim is a United States.
Jim lives in the United States.
*Jim lives in the American.
```

A word that is both a noun and an adjective may be coded using both the "N" (noun) and "A" (adjective) features:

```
==Paris.z//Parisian.þNAz/
==west.NAz//
```

Coding isms

Another type of lexical parallel universe is provided by *isms*. These are nouns defined with the feature "Î" which refer to the quality, condition, act, practice, result, doctrine, or school of a given concept. For example:

```
==good.Az//good#A thing*.þz/goodness.Îz/
==male#A chauvinist*.Az//male#A chauvinist*.þz/
male#A chauvinism*.Îz/
==yogic.Az//yogi.þz/yoga.Îz/
==Plato.Mz//Platonic.Az/Platonist.þNz/Platonism.Îz/
==United#A States#.kPïz//American.þz/americanism.Îz/
```

Parsing- and generation-only predicates

Certain predicates are only used in parsing and generation. They are indicated with a `parsegen` assertion, as in:

```
==ingest.Véz//|r1=animal|
===eat.Véz//|r2=food|parsegen|
===drink.Véz//|r2=beverage|parsegen|
```

On parsing, eat and `drink` are converted to `ingest`:

```
[eat Jim]               => [ingest Jim food]
[eat Jim green-pepper] => [ingest Jim green-pepper]
[drink Jim]             => [ingest Jim beverage]
[drink Jim Perrier]     => [ingest Jim Perrier]
```

If an argument is not supplied, it is filled in with the selectional restriction class when available.

On generation, `ingest` is converted to `eat` or `drink` depending on what is being ingested:

```
[ingest Jim green-pepper] => [eat Jim green-pepper]
[ingest Jim Perrier]      => [drink Jim Perrier]
```

Here are some other examples where selectional restrictions can be used to select an appropriate concept (and associated lexical entries) in generation:

```
[gold hair]   => [blond hair]
[stupid film] => [sappy film]
```

```
[tall Jim]    => [human-tall Jim]      ("grand" in French)
[tall desk]   => [nonhuman-tall desk]  ("haut" in French)
```

Wholes for parts: Metonymy coercion

In natural language, one type of *metonymy* (Hobbs, Stickel, Appelt, and Martin, 1993, pp. 79-81, 104-107; Moeschler and Reboul, 1994, pp. 399-422) is that in which a whole stands for a part, as in:

```
The dog bit Jim.
   dog => dog's teeth
Jim opened the jar.
   Jim => Jim's hands
```

A coercion from a whole to a part may be specified for each argument of a predicate, as in:

```
==bite.Véz//|r1=tooth|r2=physical-object|whole1=animal|
==open.Véz//|r1=grasper|r2=physical-object|
whole1=animal|
```

In semantic parsing, if a given argument W (such as dog or Jim) does not satisfy its selectional restriction SRP (such as tooth or grasper), but does satisfy its whole coercion restriction SRW (such as animal), then the parser attempts to find a part of W which satisfies SRP. If such a part P is found, W is replaced with P:

```
[bite dog23 Jim]  => [bite dog23-tooth Jim]
[open Jim jar98]  => [open Jim-left-hand jar98]
```

The reverse procedure is employed in generation: If a given argument P satisfies its selectional restriction SRP but does not satisfy its whole coercion restriction SRW, then the generator attempts to find a whole of P which satisfies SRW. If such a whole W is found, P is replaced with W.

Coding human names

A shorthand notation is used for coding human names:

```
Henri Bidault.Mº/
Florence Bidault.Fº/
```

The name text agent is invoked in order to parse the name into first, middle, last name, and other components, and make the necessary database assertions. "M" indicates male, "F" indicates female.

Lexical tools

ThoughtTreasure incorporates several tools useful in doing lexicographic research, coding lexical entries, and understanding the contents of the ThoughtTreasure lexicon.

Lexical entry scanner

The lexical entry scanner is obtained by typing *lexentryscan* into the ThoughtTreasure shell. This finds and prints all lexical entries having all of the specified list of features, and all the lexical-entry-to-object links having all of the specified list of usage features.

For example, we could get a printout of all lexical-entry-to-object links marked as being from an unspecified dialect:

```
* lexentryscan
[Lexical entry scanner]
Enter features: î
==admire//ain respect.î.Nz/
==version//generic.î.Nz/
==women-s-G-string//T back.Pîï.Nz/
==blouse//caraco.î.MNy/
==palourde//clovisse.î.FNy/
==cat//gib cat.gîq.Nz/
==cat//coon cat.î.Nz/
==displeasure//oy.î.Uz/
==good//pisser.aî.Nz/
==good//bonny.Tgî.Az/
==good//twitchin.aî.Az/
==good//wicked pisser.aî.Az/
==good//gnarly.aî.Az/
...
```
Or we could get a list of all the element lexical entries in the system:
```
Enter features: 9
s.9z¸/
s.·9yj¸/
t.9y¸/
```

Inflection scanner

The inflection scanner is obtained by typing *inflscan* into the ThoughtTreasure shell. This finds and prints all inflections having all of the specified list of features.

For example, this could be used to print out all the past tense modal auxiliaries in the system:

```
* inflscan
[Inflection scanner]
Enter features: μi
needed.μiVz /durst.oμiVz /dared.μiVz /should.μi·Vz /
shouldn.Áμi·Vz /should.gμi1P·Vz /d.Ígμi1P·Vz /
would.gμi1P·Vz /should.gμi1S·Vz /d.Ígμi1S·Vz /
would.gμi1S·Vz /d.Íμi·Vz /would.μi·Vz /wouldn.Áμi·Vz /
might.μiVz /mightn.Áμi·Vz /could.μiVz /couldn.Áμi·Vz /
```

Another example would be a list of all the informal inflections in the system:

```
Enter features: T
anyways.TÀBz /yeahs.TP·Nz /yeah.TS·Nz /yeah.T·Uz
yeah.T·Bz /okays.TP·Nz /okay.TS·Nz /okay.T6·Uz /
okay.T6·Bz /okay.T6·Az /&.TKz /em.TÍ3P·Hz /
er.TÍ3SF·Hz /im.TÍ3SM·Hz /em.TÍ3S·Hz /
you all,y all,y uns,youse.Tî2PHz /
ça.THy /t.ÁT2SHy /
```

Note the distinction between inflections marked as informal, and lexical-entry-to-object links marked as informal. Informal inflections such as the above are fairly rare-they can potentially be substituted for any meaning of a lexical entry. Normally, the informal feature is attached to a particular meaning of a lexical entry, as in the word *pond*, which is entered as informal British English for the *Atlantic Ocean*, but also as the standard word for a pond.

Polysemous lexical entry dumper

Typing *polysem* into the ThoughtTreasure shell will dump to the log a list and count of the polysemous words in the system:

```
<translator.Nz> unique-translator-of translator-of
<edited.Az> unique-editor-of author-editor-of
<head.Vz> president-of ceo-of chair-of
<care.Vz> like-human consider-important
```

```
<fond.Az> like-human like
<passion.Nz> love hobby-of
<ex.Nz> ex-wife-of ex-husband-of ex-lover-of
<parent.Nz> ako natural-parent-of
<U47.Nz> Neumann-U47-microphone
Telefunken-U47-microphone
<4 track.Nz> 4-track-reel-to-reel-tape-recorder
4-track-portastudio
<Stingray.Nz> SPARCserver-390 SPARCstation-370 4-360
SPARCstation-330
<cassette.Nz> cassette-recorder audio-cassette
<DAT.Nz> DAT-recorder DAT-tape
<concern.Nz> goal company
<Star Trek.Nz> TOS Star-Trek
<Channel 13.Nz> KCOP-TV WNET-TV
<folk music.Nz> traditional-folk-music modern-folk-
music
...
1971 polysemous out of 50151 words
```

Ambiguous part-of-speech inflection dumper

Typing *posambig* into the ThoughtTreasure shell will dump to the log file a list and count of all inflections in the system which are ambiguous as to part of speech:

```
...
<mean.VNA>
  mean f·Vz, meaning-of
  mean f·Vz, like-human
  mean p1S·Vz, meaning-of
  mean p1S·Vz, like-human
  mean pP·Vz, meaning-of
  mean pP·Vz, like-human
  mean Az, good
  mean Az, kind
...
<work.NV>
  work SNz, music-form-of-piece
  work SNz, media-object-book
  work SNz, occupation
  work fVz, condition-electronic-component
  work p1SVz, condition-electronic-component
  work pPVz, condition-electronic-component
...
2629 ambiguous out of 52475 words
```

Coverage checker

A set of commands check how many words in the text file In are found in ThoughtTreasure's lexicon:

covcheckeng
Check English coverage. Print count.
covcheckfr
Check French coverage. Print count.
covcheckengm
Check English coverage. Print missing words and count.
covcheckfrm
Check French coverage. Print missing words and count.

For example, the coverage for *Of Human Bondage* downloaded from Project Gutenberg is:

```
228984 of 266109 words found (86 percent)
```

Using the French lexicon, the coverage is:

```
73194 of 266109 words found (27 percent)
```

The French percentage is as high as it is because many English function words (such as *of*, *to*, *and*) are in the French lexicon as borrowings, and function words are frequent. A number of the other matches are proper nouns, numbers, and Latinate words.

Concordance generator

ThoughtTreasure includes a tool for generating concordances from a corpus, useful in lexicographic research. A corpus is first loaded from a file or directory via the ThoughtTreasure shell commands:

```
For English:
  corpusload -lang z -dir dirname
  corpusload -lang z -file filename

For French:
  corpusload -lang y -dir dirname
  corpusload -lang y -file filename
```

Then a concordance for a word may be generated with the commands:

```
For English: cfe -w word
For French:  cff -w word
```

For example, here is a portion of a concordance:

```
* cfe -w become
os2.misc e many niche >markets that will become the next industry giant.  I hop
dMeaning , the alterations at each level become the objects for the next. The m
croscope rge as the lengths of two paths become the same; to measure those leng
os2.misc buy os/2 apps from them, I have become tired of asking them to carry p
ognitive he control structures that have become traditional in the literatures
.solaris            useful functions to become unavailable. However,
.telecom that the good examples of these become universal.  Here are some answe
unix.aix ptys' may   cause the 'pty' to become unusable.     This program was
avel.air hat's going on", and therefore >become useless. Even if something goes
ketplace fications are.  So what if he's become very competent >at providing hi
st-class the internal file structure may become very inefficient. The best solu
aq/emily e publicity for the net, you'll become very well known.  People on the
st-class black & white light colors will become white (vanish) while darker
/maclang s that up-to-date GCC stuff may become widely available soon.  COBOL:
.powerpc users are >: going to see Win95 become Win NT after the fork out more
ai.alife ndergo many revisions before we become word perfect. It is a commonpla

q/usenet hin the past four months,  will become:     ....Discussion of Star Trek
```

Corpus-based adverbial finder

A tool for finding potential adverbials is provided with the `adverbial`
ThoughtTreasure shell command:

```
adverbial -dir dirname
adverbial -file filename
```

This command reports all sentences which begin with 6 or less words followed by
a comma. The output is appended to the file `outadv.txt`. After running this
through Unix `sort` and `uniq`, output such as the following is produced:

```
At Gravier's where they ate,
At King's School,
At last he came,
At last it was finished,
At last Lawson,
At last Philip saw Mildred,
At last she came,
At last,
At night the porter,
At that moment two men passed,
At the beginning of May,
```

```
At the bottom of his heart,
Athelny did not speak,
Athelny entered into his humour,
```

Corpus-based lexicon verifier

Features encoded in ThoughtTreasure's lexicon can be checked for agreement with a corpus by typing *corpusvalagainst* into the ThoughtTreasure shell. French genders are checked by looking for determiners before a given word.

For example, type:

```
* corpusload -lang y -dir dirname
* corpusvalagainst
```

Exercises

1. Enter more attributes on physical objects, such as their typical color, size, and weight.

2. Enter more geographical entities such as the counties for New York state.

3. Merge into the ThoughtTreasure database detailed databases maintained by each discipline such as the USDA Nutrient Data Base, the USGS Geographic Names Database, and the Library of Congress Z39.50 BOOKS file.

4. Make the above databases available to ThoughtTreasure on a demand basis via the net.

5. Implement selectional restrictions associated with lexical entries instead of with predicates. (As a side effect the `parsegen` feature can be eliminated.)

6. Handle the word *cannot*, a modal auxiliary and negative adverb all rolled up into one.

7. Add pointers from words to the phrases they are in, for use by the dictionary tool.

8. Investigate the use and meaning of isms, and extend ThoughtTreasure appropriately. (Isms are currently treated the same as regular nouns by the program.)

9. Fix the program to handle subordinate clauses properly. Currently, the subject is always carried down into the subordinate clause, so that the following results are produced:

```
want.Véïz/
Peter wants to eat.          [active-goal Peter [eat Peter]]
Peter wants John to eat.     [active-goal Peter [eat John]]

promise.Vé_ëïz/
Peter promises to eat.       [promise Peter na [eat Peter]]
```

The above results are correct, but there are other cases in which the simple rule fails:

```
Peter promises John to eat.  [promise Peter John [eat Peter]]
                            *[promise Peter na [eat John]]
```

That is, when John is the object NP of promise in the syntactic parse tree:

```
[Z
 [X [NAME Peter]]
 [W
  [W
   [W [V promises]]
   [X [NAME John]]]
  [X
   [Z
    [W
     [R to]
     [W [V eat]]]]]]]]
```

the correct semantic parse is obtained. But when there is no NP object of *promise* and John is instead the subject NP of the infinitival subordinate clause:

```
[Z
 [X [NAME Peter]]
 [W
  [W [V promises]]
  [X
   [Z
    [X [NAME John]]
    [W
     [R to]
     [W [V eat]]]]]]]]
```

an incorrect semantic parse is obtained. In other cases, the correct semantic parse is never even obtained:

```
ask.Véëïz/
Peter asks John to eat.      *[ask Peter John [eat Peter]]
```

In this case, the object, not the subject, must be carried down as the subject of the subordinate clause. A feature should be added because some verbs require the subject to be carried down (*promise*), while others require the object to be carried down (*ask*, *require*).

10. Fix the program to handle the following distinction:

```
John is eager to please. (= John is eager to please someone.)
John is easy to please.  (= John is easy for someone to please.)
```

Neither sentence parses in ThoughtTreasure because a required object of *please* is missing. See Alexander (1988, pp. 305-312) for a discussion of the above cases and more.

11. Fix the program to fan out single verb arguments to multiple slots. For example, in the case of:

```
Mary made friends with Peter.
[initiate-friend-of Mary Peter]
```

two arguments result in two slots. But in:

```
Mary and Peter made friends.
[initiate-friend-of Mary Peter]
```

a single argument, the subject, is fanned out to two slots. ThoughtTreasure currently parses this incorrectly as:

```
[initiate-friend-of [and Mary Peter]]
```

Other similar examples:

```
Mary talked with Peter.      [conversation Mary Peter]
They talked.                 [conversation Mary Peter]

Mary married Peter.          [marry Mary Peter]
They married.                [marry Mary Peter]
```

```
Mary is a friend of Peter.     [friend-of Peter Mary]
Mary and Peter are friends.    [friend-of Peter Mary]

Mary added up the numbers.
```

The ThoughtTreasure feature "ù" has already been provided to indicate that the subject is to be fanned out to slots 1 and 2, but this is not yet exploited in the parser or generator:

```
===initiate-friend-of//make* friends#NP.Vùz/
===conversation//talk.Vùz/
===marry//marry.Vùz/
```

12. Fix the following case not properly handled by the phrase inflector:

```
==ecstasy//
think* he*H has* died#V and#K gone#V to#R heaven.Vz/
```

This should be inflected for every person, gender, and tense:

```
(I) think I have died and gone to heaven.
(He) thinks he has died and gone to heaven.
(She) thinks she has died and gone to heaven.
...
(I) thought I had died and gone to heaven.
...
```

13. Fix the following case not properly handled by the phrase inflector:

```
==leave//be* on#R his*D way#N.z/
```

This should be inflected as:

```
(I) am on my way.
(You) are on your way.
(He) is on his way.
(She) is on her way.
...
```

14. Fix the program to inflect adjectives inside French phrasal verbs properly, as in:

```
==name-of//être* appelé*A.Véy/
```

Again this should be inflected for masculine and feminine gender:

```
(Il) est appelé
(Elle) est appelée
```

A possible solution would be to code it as an adjective:

```
==name-of//appelé.Aéy/
```

But direct objects to adjectives are not yet fully implemented.

15. Implement direct objects to adjectives.

16. Fix the program to treat properly phrases which include elements which can be contracted (such as *is/'s* and *que/qu'*). Currently the contracted versions are not always recognized.

17. Provide a better way to refer to phrasal prepositions when coding indirect object prepositional phrases such as:

```
except for
in spite of
on the other side of
on to
out of
prior to
```

One might code:

```
===send-memo//send* a#D memo#N in#R regard#N to+.Vz/
```

but what is really intended is something like:

```
===send-memo//send* a#D memo#N in_regard_to+.Vz/
```

18. Extend the program to handle prepositions which take arguments sandwiched in the middle. In English one can say:

```
at ___ish
```

which means basically the same thing as:

```
at around ___
```

In French there is:

```
à ___ près
```

which is similar in meaning to

```
sauf ___
```

Handle the following French determiners: `ce ___-ci`
```
cet ___-ci
cette ___-ci
ces ___-ci
ce ___-là
...
```

19. Handle postpositions. (But is this necessary, considering they cannot be used in a general fashion in English or French? They are usually employed in frozen expressions such as *the world over* which can be defined as a synonym for *worldwide*.)

20. Modify the program to generate expletive pronouns in the proper location in the following French sentences:

```
Je m'en vais.
Je vais m'en aller.
Je m'en suis allé.
Va-t'en!
```

Chapter 4: The text agency

The *text agency* consists of a collection of *text agents* (TAs) which recognize different types of textual entities, such as words, phrases, human names, and phone numbers. We start by considering how the text agency is extended in order to improve the parsing ability of the movie review application.

The text agency and the movie review application

Let's extend the existing set of text agents with a new agent for parsing star-based movie ratings. We start by searching for all instances of "*" (asterisk) in the corpus of 50 Usenet movie reviews and sort the results in order to obtain a subcorpus of star-based ratings. Under Unix, we issue the following pipeline:

```
fgrep \* reviews | sort | uniq
```

After editing out some spurious and duplicate results by hand, we obtain:

```
(1983) **1/2 - C:Charles Bronson, Andrew Stevens, Wilford Brimley.
(1991) ** - C:Eric Roberts, F. Murray Abraham, Mia Sara.
(1993) *** - C:Tommy Lee Jones, Hiep Thi Le, Joan Chen, Haing S.
Ngor,
(1995) *** (out of four)
(1995) *1/2 (out of four)
(1996) ** (out of four)
(1996) **** - C:Robert De Niro, Wesley Snipes, Ellen Barkin, John
(1996) *1/2 - C:Tom Arnold, David Paymer, Rod Steiger, Rhea Perlman.
*1/2 (out of ****)
Alternative Scale: ** out of ****
Alternative Scale: **** out of ****
Alternative Scale: *1/2 out of ****
give it my strongest recommendation and my top rating of ****.
I award it ***.
I recommend the movie to you and give it ***.
I give the original just barely one *.
RATING (0 TO ****):   *
RATING (0 TO ****):   ** 1/2
RATING (0 TO ****):   ***
RATING (0 TO ****):   ****
RATING (0 TO ****):   1/2
RATING:   ***
the wonderful soundtrack make this film worth ** out of ****.
TIN CUP (1996) ** 1/2  Directed by Ron Shelton. Written by John
Norville
```

Now we code a text agent in C to recognize star ratings. Some text agents are invoked only at the beginning of each line for efficiency. In this case, a star rating can occur anywhere in the line, so the new text agent must be invoked on every character.

The text agent will sense the potential presence of a star rating when it sees one of the strings:

```
*
1/2
Alternative Scale:
RATING (0 TO ****):
```

Then it will calculate the numerator by counting each star as 1.0 and a final "1/2" as 0.5. It then parses an optional specification of the denominator (which defaults to 4.0). If the calculated numerator is less than or equal to the denominator, the text agent returns a communicon parse node containing the concept:

```
[good na RATING]
```

where RATING ranges from -1.0 to 1.0.

(The task of determining who thinks what is good will be assigned to the understanding agency, discussed in a later chapter.)

The code for the new text agent is:

```
Bool TA_StarRating(char *in, Discourse *dc,
                   /* RESULTS */ Channel *ch, char **nextp)
{
  Float numer, denom;
  char *orig_in;
  Obj  *con;
  numer = 0.0;
  denom = 4.0; /* Assume 4.0 as default. */

  orig_in = in;
  /* Sense presence of rating. */
  if (StringHeadEqualAdvance("RATING (0 TO ****):", in, &in)) {
    denom = 4.0;
    in = StringSkipWhitespace(in);
  } else if (StringHeadEqualAdvance("RATING:", in, &in)) {
    in = StringSkipWhitespace(in);
  } else if (StringHeadEqualAdvance("Alternative Scale:", in, &in)) {
    in = StringSkipWhitespace(in);
  } else if (StringHeadEqualAdvance("1/2", in, &in)) {
    numer = 0.5;
```

```
      goto post;
    } else if (*in != '*') {
      /* Rating not present. */
      return(0);
    }

    /* Parse rating numerator. */
    if (*in == '0') {
      numer = 0.0;
      in++;
    } else if (*in == '*' || *in == '1') {
      while (*in == '*' || *in == '1') {
        if (*in == '*') {
          numer += 1.0;
        } else {
          in++;
          if (!StringHeadEqualAdvance("/2", in, &in)) return(0);
          numer += 0.5;
          break;
        }
        in++;
        if (*in == ' ' && *(in+1) == '1') {
        /* "* 1/2" */
          in++;
        }
      }
    } else {
      return(0);
    }

post:
    /* Parse optional rating denominator. */
    in = StringSkipWhitespace(in);
    if (StringHeadEqualAdvance("(out of four)", in, &in)) {
      denom = 4.0;
    } else if (StringHeadEqualAdvance("(out of ****)", in, &in)) {
      denom = 4.0;
    } else if (StringHeadEqualAdvance("out of ****", in, &in)) {
      denom = 4.0;
    }
    /* todo: Parse other denominators. */

    if (numer > denom) return(0);
    con = L(N("good"), ObjNA, D(Weight01toNeg1Pos1(numer/denom)), E);
    ChannelAddPNode(ch, PNTYPE_COMMUNICON, 1.0,
                    ObjListCreate(con, NULL),
                    NULL, orig_in, in);
    *nextp = in;
    return(1);
}
```

The text agent is incorporated into the program by calling it from the function
TA_ScanAnywhere:

```
void TA_ScanAnywhere(Channel *ch, Discourse *dc)
{
  char        *p, *rest;
  ...
  for (p = (char *)ch->buf; *p; ) {
    if (TA_StarRating(p, dc, ch, &rest)) p = rest;
    else p++;
  }
}
```

We then use the parse shell command on the subcorpus of star-based ratings in
order to test the new text agent. By looking for communicon parse nodes in the
output log file, we can verify that all star ratings were correctly parsed:

```
[COMMUNICON [good na NUMBER:u:0.25] 7-12:<**1/2 >]
[COMMUNICON [good na NUMBER:u:0] 74-76:<** >]
[COMMUNICON [good na NUMBER:u:0.5] 131-134:<*** >]
[COMMUNICON [good na NUMBER:u:0.5] 202-218:<*** (out of four)>]
[COMMUNICON [good na NUMBER:u:-0.25] 227-244:<*1/2 (out of four)>]
[COMMUNICON [good na NUMBER:u:0] 253-268:<** (out of four)>]
[COMMUNICON [good na NUMBER:u:1] 277-281:<**** >]
[COMMUNICON [good na NUMBER:u:-0.25] 343-347:<*1/2 >]
[COMMUNICON [good na NUMBER:u:-0.25] 405-422:<*1/2 (out of ****)>]
[COMMUNICON [good na NUMBER:u:0] 424-456:]
[COMMUNICON [good na NUMBER:u:1] 458-492:]
[COMMUNICON [good na NUMBER:u:-0.25] 494-528:]
[COMMUNICON [good na NUMBER:u:1] 587-590:<****>]
[COMMUNICON [good na NUMBER:u:0.5] 604-606:<***>]
[COMMUNICON [good na NUMBER:u:0.5] 650-652:<***>]
[COMMUNICON [good na NUMBER:u:-0.5] 691-691:<*>]
[COMMUNICON [good na NUMBER:u:-0.5] 694-716:]
[COMMUNICON [good na NUMBER:u:0.25] 717-744:]
[COMMUNICON [good na NUMBER:u:0.5] 745-769:]
[COMMUNICON [good na NUMBER:u:1] 770-795:]
[COMMUNICON [good na NUMBER:u:-0.75] 796-820:]
[COMMUNICON [good na NUMBER:u:0.5] 821-833:]
[COMMUNICON [good na NUMBER:u:0] 880-893:<** out of ****>]
[COMMUNICON [good na NUMBER:u:0.25] 911-918:<** 1/2 >]
```

Discussion of the movie review application resumes in the chapter on the semantic
component, where we give a detailed trace of syntactic and semantic parsing of the
sentence *Who directed Rendezvous in Paris?*.

A tour of the text agency

The text agency is invoked as the first step in parsing an input text in order to create parse nodes for use by the syntactic parser. Some text agents—such as the product and table text agents—extract information directly, and no further parsing is required. Text agents such as the product and media object agents are able to learn new products and media objects. In this section, we consider an example, which enables us to run through the capabilities of the text agency.

We feed the text agency the following input text:

```
From jim Mon Mar 11 09:35 EST 1996
Return-Path: <jim@trollope.com>
Received: by trollope.com (SMI-8.6/SMI-SVR4)
        id JAA00384; Mon, 11 Mar 1996 09:35:17 -0500
Date: Mon, 11 Mar 1996 09:35:17 -0500
From: jim@trollope.com (Jim Garnier)
Message-Id: <199603111435.JAA00384@trollope.com>
To: karen@netabulous
Subject: Re: What's up?
Content-Type: text
Content-Length: 16
Status: RO

On Mar 8, 11:53am, Karen Garnier wrote:
>What's up?

Not much. I saw the film "Horizons lointains" in Saumur
(Maine-et-Loire).

BTW, my new phone number is 212-555-3845.

Jim

P.S. I sold my 1977 Fiat Spider for $600. 8-)
```

The lexical entry text agent recognizes the following words:

```
[[On ]][[Mar ]]8, 11:53am, Karen Garnier [[wrote:
>]][[What']][[s ]][[up?

]][[Not ]][[much. ]][[I ]][[saw ]][[the ]][[film
"]]Horizons lointains"
  [[in ]][[Saumur
```

```
(]]Maine-et-Loire).
```

```
[[BTW, ]][[my ]][[new ]][[phone ]][[number ]][[is ]]
[[212-]]555-3845.
```

```
Jim
```

```
P.S. [[I ]][[sold ]][[my ]]1977 [[Fiat ]][[Spider ]]
[[for ]]$600. 8-)
```

The agent adds a parse node for each word:

```
[0 <On.0z:on> 377-379:<On >]
[R <On.·Rz˛:on> 377-379:<On >]
[A <On.·Az˛:on> 377-379:<On >]
[N <Mar.qSNz˛:March> 380-383:<Mar >]
[V <wrote.iVz˛:write><:\n>> 410-417:<wrote:\n>>]
[U <What.·Uz˛:what><'> 418-422:<What'>]
[H <What.·Hz˛:what><'> 418-422:<What'>]
[D <What.·Dz˛:what><'> 418-422:<What'>]
...
```

The lexical entry text agent recognizes the following phrases:

```
On Mar 8, 11:53am, Karen Garnier wrote:
>[[What's up?
```

```
]][[Not much. ]]I saw the film "[[Horizons
lointains" ]]in Saumur
([[Maine-et-Loire)]].
```

```
BTW, my new [[phone number ]]is 212-555-3845.
...
[x <What s up.xzQ:what s up><?\n>
316-326:<What's up?\n>]
[A <Not much.Az:not much> 430-439:<Not much. >]
[N <Horizons lointains.Nz><" >
456-475:<Horizons lointains" >]
[N <Maine et Loire.SNz><)> 487-501:<Maine-et-Loire)>]
[N <phone number.SNz> 517-529:<phone number >
```

The name text agent recognizes:

```
On Mar 8, 11:53am, [[Karen Garnier ]]wrote:
```

>What's up?

Not much. I saw the film "Horizons lointains" in Saumur
(Maine-et-Loire).

BTW, my new phone number is 212-555-3845.

[[Jim

]]P.S. I sold my 1977 Fiat Spider for $600. 8-)
...
[NAME:N <Karen Garnier>:<>G<Karen:> <:><:>S<Garnier:>
<:>P<> 396-409:<Karen Garnier >]
[NAME:N <Jim>:<>G<Jim:> <:><:>S<:> <:>P<>
548-552:<Jim\n\n>]

The French polity text agent recognizes:

Not much. I saw the film "Horizons lointains" in
[[Saumur (Maine-et-Loire)]].
...
[POLITY:N Saumur 479-501:<Saumur\n(Maine-et-Loire)>]

The time text agent recognizes:

P.S. I sold my [[1977]]Fiat Spider for $600. 8-)
...
[TSRANGE:B @19770101000000:19770101000000
568-572:<1977 >]

The telephone number text agent recognizes:

BTW, my new phone number is [[212-555-3845]].
...
[TELNO:N string-pstn2341 533-544:<212-555-3845>]

The media object text agent recognizes:

Not much. I saw the film "[[Horizons lointains"]] in
Saumur
...
[MEDIA_OBJ:N Horizons-lointains
456-474:<Horizons lointains">]

The product text agent recognizes:

```
P.S. I sold my[[ 1977 Fiat Spider ]]for $600. 8-)
...
[PRODUCT:N 1977-Fiat-1800-Spider
567-584:< 1977 Fiat Spider >]
```

The price text agent recognizes:

```
P.S. I sold my 1977 Fiat Spider for [[$600.]] 8-)
...
[NUMBER:N NUMBER:USD:600 589-593:<$600.>]
```

The end of sentence text agent recognizes:

```
On Mar 8, 11:]]53am, Karen Garnier wrote:]]
>What's up[[?

]]Not much[[. ]]I saw the film "Horizons lointains" in
Saumur (Maine-et-Loire)[[.

]]BTW, my new phone number is 212-555-3845[[.

]]Jim

P.S[[. ]]I sold my 1977 Fiat Spider for $600. 8-)
```

The communicon text agent recognizes:

```
P.S. I sold my 1977 Fiat Spider for $600. [[8-)]]
...
[COMMUNICON [smile Jim] 595-597:<8-)>]
```

The email header text agent recognizes:

```
[[From jim Mon Mar 11 09:35 EST 1996
Return-Path: <jim@trollope.com>
Received: by trollope.com (SMI-8.6/SMI-SVR4)
        id JAA00384; Mon, 11 Mar 1996 09:35:17 -0500
Date: Mon, 11 Mar 1996 09:35:17 -0500
From: jim@trollope.com (Jim Garnier)
Message-Id: <199603111435.JAA00384@trollope.com>
To: karen@netabulous
```

```
Subject: Re: What's up?
Content-Type: text
Content-Length: 16
Status: RO
]]
...
[EMAILHEADER <standard-email-header><string-message-ID>
<19960311093500>FROM<Jim><jim@trollope.com>
TO<human2342>SUBJ<What's up?>
0-375:<From jim Mon Mar 11 09:35 EST >]
```

The attribution text agent recognizes:

```
[[On Mar 8, 11:53am, Karen Garnier wrote:
]]>What's up?
...
[ATTRIBUTION <19940308115300>SPEAKER<Karen>
  377-416:<On Mar 8, 11:53am, Karen Garni>]
```

Some text agents are invoked at the beginning of each line, others are invoked at the beginning of each word, and yet others are invoked for every character.

Once all text agents have run, lower priority parse nodes are deleted whose source text is contained inside that of a higher priority parse node marked with an asterisk ("*"):

```
LOWEST PRIORITY
 lexical entry
 name
 organization name
 polity
*timestamp range
*media object
*product
 number
 communicon
*attribution
*email header
*table
HIGHEST PRIORITY
```

For example, this results in the deletion of many parse nodes for words, phrases, dates, names, and so on, inside an email header. Only the email header parse node remains.

Parse nodes for phrases are deleted if their source text is contained inside another phrase consisting of 3 or more words. (This strategy is intended to reduce alternative parses; unfortunately, it sometimes eliminates valid ones.) Once the above has been completed, syntactic parsing is ready to begin. The parse node forest created by the text agency must be segmented into sentences (and other units such as email headers called *blocks*). This is done in a loop which scans to the next end of sentence parse node whose character position is after that of the end of the last sentence. For each sentence, the syntactic parser is invoked with the parse node forest and the start and stop character positions of the sentence.

Lexical entry text agent

The *lexical entry text agent* examines input text and identifies known words and phrases. It creates a parse node for every known inflection consisting of a given character string. For example the word *first* results in the following parse nodes:

```
[1.00000:N <first.S·Nz > 111–116:<first >]
[1.00000:B <first.6·Bz > 111–116:<first >]
[1.00000:A <first.6·Az > 111–116:<first >]
```

("1.00000" is the score of the parse node and "111-116" refers to the location of the string "first " in the input text.)

Scanning lexical entries

The lexical entry agent scans the input text from left to right, looking for the beginning of a word or phrase, defined as a non white space character preceded by a white space character. White space characters are:

```
  space
- dash
" single quote
' double quote
, comma
; semicolon
: colon
/ slash
« left guillemets
» right guillemets
( left parenthesis
) right parenthesis
```

Non white space characters are:

```
alphabetic characters
numeric characters
$ dollar sign
% percent sign
@ at sign
```

A period (".") functions as white space when it is an end of sentence character or as non white space when it is part of an abbreviation.

At the beginning of a word or phrase, the agent attempts to find phrases in the lexicon: first it looks for phrases consisting of 1 word (that is, words), then it looks for phrases consisting of 2 words, then 3 words, and so on, up to the maximum phrase length in the lexicon. It converts the input text into a canonical form by eliminating redundant white space. For example, given:

```
True;  if, you've "realized" ...
```

The agent attempts to look up the following phrases:

```
True
True if
True if you
True if you ve
True if you ve realized
...
```

This implies that phrases having embedded elements or modifiers will not be recognized (such as *from the particular point of view of*, where *particular* is inserted into the phrase *from the point of view of*). However, phrasal verb (and also adjective and nominalization) parsing makes use of expletives which do enable embedded elements such as adverbs, and certain ordering changes.

All inflections and their corresponding lexical entries are indexed in a hash table. (There are separate hash tables for English and French.) Given, for example, the string "are", the following is retrieved from the hash table:

```
features lexical entry
-------- -------------
pPVz     be.Vz/
SNz      are.Nz/
```

These are the plural present form of the verb *be* and the singular form of the noun *are* (a unit of measure). A parse node is created for each inflection. Some other examples:

```
"am":
p1SVz       be.Vz/
Bz          am.Bz/      (as in "10 am")

"drink":
fVz         drink.Vz/
p1SVz       drink.Vz/
pPVz        drink.Vz/
SNz         drink.Nz/

"s":
Íp3SVz      be.Vz/      (as in "he's here")
Íp3SVz      do.Vz/      (as in "what's it matter?")
Íp3SVz      have.Vz/    (as in "he's arrived")
Í9z         s.9z/       (as in "Peter's sister")
19960213122
```

("Í" indicates a contraction: the word must be preceded by an apostrophe in order to be added as a parse node.)

If nothing is found in the hash table, and the phrase length is 1, word formation is invoked, which attempts to derive the unknown word from existing words by adding affixes.

If the phrase length is 2 or higher, or if word formation fails, spell correction is invoked at progressively higher levels of relaxation until a match is found. The levels of relaxation are:

```
1 insensitive to case
2 above + insensitive to accents (mostly applicable to
French)
3 above + insensitive to nonalphanumeric characters
4 above + insensitive to duplicate characters
5 above + insensitive to consonant voicing ("t"="d",
"f"="v"="ph", ...)
6 above + insensitive to vowels
```

Spell correction is implemented by reducing all inflections in the database to level 6 and using the result to index the inflections and their corresponding lexical entries in a spell hash table. For example, the hypothetical inflection *Parallélogramm.* is reduced as follows:

```
1 parallélogramm.
2 parallelogramm.
3 parallelogramm
4 paralelogram
5 paralelokram
6 perelelekrem
```

When an unknown phrase is encountered, it is reduced to level 6 and used to look up potentially relevant inflections in the spell hash table. Then starting with level 1, the program looks for inflections which level-1 reduce to the same string that the unknown phrase level-1 reduces to. If any are found, they are returned. Otherwise, this process continues at a higher level. If nothing is found after level 6, words are searched for in the other language via the same procedure. (It is important to search the other language, because proper nouns such as place or brand names might only be coded in one language.)

Part-of-speech tagging

Quite a few parse nodes are often generated for a word and these may lead to an explosion of syntactic parses. Research in corpus-based part of speech tagging has produced taggers whose accuracy is around 97 percent. As good as this sounds, 97 percent accuracy for each word implies a 73.7 percent accuracy for a 10-word sentence. Still, the accuracy of these taggers continues to improve, and something is still needed to prevent ThoughtTreasure's parser from blowing up on long sentences.

ThoughtTreasure therefore (optionally) calls a statistical part-of-speech tagger after generating lexical entry parse nodes, before calling the syntactic parser. Any Penn Treebank compatible part-of-speech tagger (Marcus, Santorini, and Marcinkiewicz, 1993) may be used. Taggers which generate a single guess may be used, as well as taggers which generate several guesses, called *n-best taggers*. ThoughtTreasure creates a file of input text in Penn Treebank format, uses the *system* library function to invoke the tagger on it as a separate program:

```
./tagger InputFilename OutputFilename
```

and then uses the output of the program to prune the lexical entry parse nodes.

Pruning works as follows: Given several tags assigned to a word by the tagger, those parse nodes compatible with the first tag are accepted, those parse nodes compatible with the remaining possible (nonbest) tags are accepted with a reduced score, and the remaining parse nodes are rejected. However, if all of the parse nodes for a word would be rejected, none are rejected. (Pruning applies only to words, not to phrases and other entities such as the names and telephone numbers recognized by specialized text agents.)

A Penn Treebank tag is compatible with a ThoughtTreasure lexical entry's features if their parts of speech, number, and tense match. (There are slight differences in the Penn Treebank and ThoughtTreasure feature sets. In cases where they are difficult to compare, the features are deemed compatible.)

Thus, given parse nodes for the word *first*, and based on the context, the part-of-speech tagger might eliminate the B (adverb) and N (noun) parse nodes but not the A (adjective):

```
[1.00000:N <first.S·Nz˛> 111-116:<first >]
[1.00000:B <first.6·Bz˛> 111-116:<first >]
[1.00000:A <first.6·Az˛> 111-116:<first >]
```

Experiments were run using Eric Brill's (1994) freely available rule-based part-of-speech tagger. The fact test suite, which consists of 43 short sentences for a total of 183 words, was run without tagging, with Brill best tagging, and with Brill n-best tagging. (The training sets used were as provided with the downloaded tagger: the Brown and Wall Street Journal lexicon, the Brown lexical rules, and the Brown contextual rules.)

The results were as follows:

	syn (#)	sem (#)	time (sec)
no pruning	168	140	204
1-tag pruning	104	102	189 (including 17 seconds for tagging)
n-best tag pruning	121	112	212 (including 31 seconds for tagging)

Use of the single-tag Brill tagger reduced the total time spent processing the test suite, even given that the tagging process itself took 9% of the total time. (Timings were performed on a PC with two 100 MHz Pentium processors running Solaris

2.4.) The number of syntactic and semantic parses was considerably reduced. Three sentences failed to parse properly due to tagging errors:

```
there/RB should be there/EX:
  How/WRB many/JJ breads/NNS are/VBP there/RB ?/.
  How/WRB many/JJ foods/NNS are/VBP there/RB ?/.
```

```
least/JJS should be least/RBS:
  What/WP is/VBZ the/DT least/JJS dense/JJ atom/NN ?/.
```

Use of the n-best Brill tagger increased the total time spent, and only repaired one of the above tagging errors:

```
What/WP is/VBZ_NNS the/DT_NNP least/JJS_RBS dense/JJ
atom/NN ?/.
```

Name text agent

The *name text agent* is able to recognize and parse human names in the following formats:

```
Jim
Garnier
Karen(-)Anne
Rey-Debove
J. Garnier
Jim Garnier
Garnier, J.
Garnier, Jim
K. Rey-Debove
Karen Rey-Debove
Rey-Debove, K.
Rey-Debove, Karen
J. A. Garnier
Jim A. Garnier
J. Alfred Garnier
Jim(-)Alfred Garnier
Karen Rey Debove
Garnier, J. A.
Garnier, Jim A.
Garnier, J. Alfred
Garnier, Jim(-)Alfred
J. Alfred B. Garnier
Garnier, J. Alfred B.
```

```
K. A. Rey-Debove
Karen A. Rey-Debove
Karen(-)Anne Rey-Debove
Rey-Debove, K. A.
Rey-Debove, Karen A.
Rey-Debove, Karen(-)Anne
K. A. M. Rey
Karen A. M. Rey
Karen Anne Marie Rey
Rey, K. A. M.
Rey, Karen A. M.
Rey, Karen Anne Marie
K. A. M. Rey-Debove
Karen A. M. Rey-Debove
Karen Anne Marie Rey-Debove
Rey-Debove, K. A. M.
Rey-Debove, Karen A. M.
Rey-Debove, Karen Anne Marie
```

Each of the above may optionally be preceded and followed by titles, as in:

```
Karen Rey Debove, PhD
Mr Jim Garnier
```

The name text agent makes use of the name ontology, which contains common personal and family names, as well as many pre and post titles. Spell correction is employed when parsing components of a name.

Representing names

Names are represented in ThoughtTreasure using the following relations:

pre-title-of
A title which precedes the name, such as *Dr*.
first-name-of
The given or Christian name.
second-name-of
The second name. This may be further broken down into:

- **second-given-name-of** (for U.S. *Lee* in *Mary Lee*, or French *François* in *Jean-François*),
- **middle-name-of** (for English middle names), and
- **middle-surname-of** (for *Fitzgerald* in *John Fitzgerald Kennedy*).

third-name-of
A third name or second middle name.
first-surname-of
The family name or first family name of a hyphenated or compound last name.
second-surname-of
The second family name of a hyphenated or compound last name.
post-title-of
A title which follows the name, such as *Esq*.
used-name-of
The personal name used by the person. This is usually the first name, but it is sometimes the second name.
nickname-of
A nickname.
maiden-surname-of
The maiden name.
first-initial-of
The first initial.
middle-initial-of
The middle initial. In the U.S., some have a middle initial but no middle name.
first-last-initial-of
The first last initial.
second-last-initial-of
The second last initial.
full-name-of
The full name consisting of all known components.

Human objects in the database are linked to name objects via the above relations. This representation enables resolution of name references to a person in any of the above formats. Name assertions in the database can be associated with different time intervals, which enables the modeling of name changes (in marriage or other cases).

Learning new names

If the name text agent encounters an unknown word in a context where it is likely to be a name, such as after a first name, if it has a prefix or suffix commonly used in names, it learns the new name. The number of occurrences of name prefixes and suffixes of length 3 to 5 is stored and counted. In relaxed matching, words are recognized as being names if they match a stored prefix or suffix having a count of more than 8.

Here are some of the name affixes and counts found during training:

```
First name prefixes
    78 Mar 31 Car 28 Sha 25 Ste 24 Fran 24 Fra 23 Chr 22 Chri
    21 Ale 21 Geo 20 Ber 20 Cha 20 Chris 18 Kat 18 Mari 17 Marg
First name suffixes
    54 ine 36 lle 34 nne 30 nda 28 ard 26 ina 26 sha 26 elle
    22 yne 20 nna 20 ell 20 nie 20 ick 20 nny 20 lla 20 ana
Last name prefixes
    32 Sch 28 Cha 27 Per 27 Car 27 Bar 22 Sha 22 Wal 21 Mar
    20 Gar 20 Bra 19 Bur 19 Wei 18 McC 18 She 17 Man 17 Wil
Last name suffixes
    98 son 82 man 58 ler 54 ton 48 ley 38 ner 37 sky 36 ell
    34 berg 34 erg 30 ard 28 ter 26 ing 24 ier 22 ick 22 ers
```

Time text agent

The *time text agent* is actually several agents that recognize various time and date formats and language expressions.

Date expressions such as the following are recognized:

```
Monday March 11, 1996
March 11, 1996
March 1996
March '96
lundi le 11 mars 1996
le 11 mars 1996
11 mars 1996
mars 1996
1996
'96
this morning
cette nuit-là
```

Lexical entries for days of the week and months of the year are contained in the value name ontology. Parts of the day (such as *afternoon*) are contained in the value range name ontology.

Computer date and time formats such as the following are recognized:

```
16:34
16:34:02
9:34:23
10:09a
10:09p
09-29-93
09-29-93   10:09p
Mar 8, 11:53am
Fri Jan 21 22:52:33 1994
Thu Jan 20 16:57:47 MET 1994
Tue 01 Feb 1994  0:49 EST
Fri, 21 Jan 1994 10:38:10 +0000
Fri, 21 Jan 94 11:58:29 +0100
Fri, 21 Jan 94 11:07:36 GMT
Fri, 21 Jan 1994 16:52:07 -0500 (EST)
6 Jul 89 13:42:43 GMT
16 Feb 95 16:00:40 -0700
Jeudi 16 Février 1995 23:00:40
Mercredi 4 Janvier 1995 1:19:00
```

Once all the basic text agents have run, an additional set of text agents called *parse node pattern text agents* are run, which take parse nodes as input and produce other parse nodes as output. Typically, the agent recognizes a pattern of several adjacent input parse nodes, creates a new parse node that contains all the information in those input parse nodes, and deletes the input parse nodes. The parse node pattern text agents are run in several phases, since some of them produce parse nodes that are later used by other agents.

In the first phase, parse nodes representing time expressions such as the following are recognized and replaced with new parse nodes:

```
quarter to six
quarter to six o'clock
quarter to six pm
quarter past six
midnight
six seconds
a moment ago
six heures et demie
six heures moins quart
six heures
```

(The agent recognizes various lexical entries stored in the temporal adverb, value name, and number ontologies.)

In the second phase, parse nodes of the form:

```
NUMBER-TRAIT-LEXICAL-ITEM-PARSE-NODE  TIME-PARSE-NODE
```

such as:

```
around six pm
```

are recognized and replaced.

In the third phase, date and time of day parse nodes are combined, as in:

```
 _____     _____
March 11, 1996 at around six pm
 _____     _____
```

In the final phase, various time combinations are built up into larger structures:

```
on TIME
in TIME
in DURATION
il y a DURATION
DURATION from now
DURATION ago
at TIME-OF-DAY / à TIME-OF-DAY
since TIME / depuis TIME
until TIME / jusqu'à TIME
between TIME and TIME / entre TIME et TIME
from TIME to TIME / de TIME jusqu'à TIME
```

as in the example:

```
between January 8, 1988 at about 8 o'clock and January
12, 1988 at 9 o'clock
```

The generator uses similar strategies as the above—except in reverse—in order to generate time expressions. These are called into play when timestamp range generation advice is set by question answering agents.

Timestamp generation can be tested by typing `testts` into the ThoughtTreasure shell. Various timestamps relative to now will be generated with various generation advice combinations:

```
19940710090000
the day before yesterday at nine am
two days ago
earlier
Sunday July 10, 1994
nine am
the day before yesterday
avant hier à neuf heures
il y a deux jours
précédemment
dimanche le 10 juillet 1994

19940711140000
yesterday afternoon at two pm
one day ago
Monday July 11, 1994
hier après midi à quatorze heures
il y a 1 jour
lundi le 11 juillet 1994

19940711234552
last night
la nuit dernière

19940712084416
this morning
one hour ago
ce matin
il y a 1 heure

19940712094316
sixty seconds ago
il y a soixante seconds

19940712094417
instantly
sur le champ
```

19940712094418
in two seconds
dans deux seconds

19940712094547
in two minutes
shortly
dans deux minutes
avant peu

19940712114416
in two hours
in a while
dans deux heures
tout à l'heure

19940712135916
this afternoon at two pm
before long
cette après midi à quatorze heures
avant longtemps

19940712234416
tonight
ce soir

19940713092916
tomorrow morning
demain matin

19940714090016
the day after tomorrow at nine am
in two days
après demain à neuf heures
dans deux jours

19940715091516
on Friday morning
in three days
vendredi matin
dans trois jours

Telephone number text agent

The *telephone number text agent* recognizes phone numbers in the U.S. and France in the following formats:

```
(NXX) NXX=XXXX
(NXX)NXX=XXXX
NXX=NXX=XXXX
1=NXX=NXX=XXXX
+1=NXX=NXX=XXXX
19=1=NXX=NXX=XXXX
16 (1) XX=XX=XX=XX
16=1=XX=XX=XX=XX
16=XX=XX=XX=XX
(1) XX=XX=XX=XX
1=XX=XX=XX=XX
XX=XX=XX=XX
```

```
where
X in "0123456789"
N in "23456789"
= in " -+."
other characters are literal
```

Insignificant characters such as delimiters are removed from the parsed number, it is converted into a worldwide unique phone number, and a parse node containing the number is created.

Media object text agent

The *media object text agent* recognizes the names of media objects such as newspapers, books, films, songs, and so on:

```
{L'Aurore}
{La passion de Maximilien Kolbe}
_Cyc Programmer's Manual_
L'émission "Hot Country Night"
une chanson, "I will always love you"
l'album "Dangerous"
the "Dangerous" album
```

It is triggered by the following opening characters:

{
«
"
'

—

A string is then read up to the corresponding closing character:

}
»
"
'

—

Certain heuristics are then used to eliminate possibilities, because the above strategy produces many matches in text. Then media objects having the string as a lexical entry are looked up. If any are found, then a parse node containing them is created. Otherwise, the agent scans for a media object class word (such as *book* or *film*) before the opening character or after the closing character. If one is found, a new media object is learned of the specified class.

Product text agent

The *product text agent* recognizes product names such as:

```
Adobe Type Library
chrome Nikon FM2
red 67 Alfa Romeo GTV
Apple Macintosh Centris 650
```

The agent is triggered by a company name and will only recognize products that are an instance of the class of product manufactured by the company. (All brand names and the corresponding product classes must be entered into the company ontology.)

The agent then scans backward and forward from the company name to find other *product elements*:

- Attributes such as color.
- Year of manufacture/issue.
- A lexical entry such as *brand*, *model*, *series*, which is ignored.

- An arbitrary class that is an instance of the class of product manufactured by the company. Included here are generic descriptive classes such as *multiline* and *convertible*, and trademarks such as *Trimline* and *Spyder*.
- When scanning forward, an unrecognized word of length 5 or less consisting of uppercase letters and digits, probably a model number not in the database.

Scanning backward or forward stops when a product element is not recognized, or when certain punctuation characters are reached.

Once product elements have been collected, the intension resolver is invoked in order to find objects which (1) are a product of the company, (2) have the specified attributes, (3) were issued on the specified year, and (4) are instances of the specified classes. If such objects are found, a new product parse node is created containing those objects.

If no matching objects are found, a new product is learned as follows: The collected product elements are concatenated in an appropriate order to generate a lexical entry for the new product. The new lexical entry and a corresponding object are created in memory and dumped to the learning file. The new product's attributes, year of issue, and additional product element classes are then learned in memory and dumped. A product parse node is then created containing the new product.

Adding products to the database

So that the product text agent will recognize products properly, products should be added to the database according to the following procedure:

1. Define the brand name as a company and insert it into an appropriate industry group in the company ontology:

```
=====WE.®z//|manufacturer-of¤phone|
```

2. Define the basic product class:

```
===phone.z//
```

3. Define generic product contrasts:

```
===phone.z//
===-single-multi-line-contrast//
=====single#A-line# phone*.z//single#-line#N.Az/
```

```
=====multiline# phone*.z//multiline.Az/
===-phone-signaling-contrast//
=====dial# phone*.z//dial.Az/
=====DTMF# phone*.z//DTMF.Az/
```

4. Define model names or trademarks:

```
===phone.z//
===-single-multi-line-contrast//
=====single#A-line# phone*.z//single#-line#N.Az/
======WE# Trimline*.®z//Trimline.¹®z/|product-of¤WE|
```

The lexical entry "WE Trimline" is for generation and the lexical entry "Trimline" is for parsing by the product text agent.

5. Define specific models:

```
===phone.z//
===-single-multi-line-contrast//
=====single#A-line# phone*.z//single#-line#N.Az/
======WE# Trimline*.®z//Trimline.¹®z/|product-of¤WE|
=======WE# dial#A Trimline*.®z/dial-phone/
========red#A WE# dial#A Trimline*.®z//|red|
=========red#A 1967# WE# dial#A Trimline*.®z//|@1967|
create¤WE|
```

The lexical entry "red 1967 WE dial Trimline" is for generation only. Product parsing is done based on the asserted attributes and relations of the product, so that, for example, "red 1967 Western Electric Trimline dial phone" will be recognized as an instance of the same product.

Every product should appear below some contrast rather than directly under the main class (in our example, phone).

Price text agent

The *price text agent* recognizes prices in U.S. dollars, triggered by a dollar sign, such as:

```
$6000
$ 2.00
$51,900
```

It creates a number parse node whose class is USD.

End of sentence text agent

The *end of sentence text agent* adds an end of sentence parse node in the following situations:

- Any semicolon: One sentence; another sentence.
- Any colon: One sentence: another sentence.
- A period followed by white space followed by an uppercase letter or left parenthesis: One sentence. Another sentence. (Yet A.N.O.T.H.E.R. sentence.)
- An exclamation point or question mark, optionally followed by white space, followed by an uppercase letter or left parenthesis: A question? A question!
- A period, exclamation point, or question mark which is last in the input stream (except for white space).
- A blank line.
  One sentence

  Another sentence.

After all text agents have run, end of sentence parse nodes are eliminated which fall inside portions of input text determined to be names by the name text agent. This prevents the periods from being considered the end of sentence in:

Ms. K. Garnier

Communicon text agent

The *communicon text agent* recognizes some common communicons and converts them into parse nodes containing assertions about the speaker or listener:

```
:)          [smile SPEAKER]
:]          [smile SPEAKER]
:-)         [smile SPEAKER]
8-)         [smile SPEAKER]
;-)         [smile SPEAKER]
<g>         [smile SPEAKER]
:(          [frown SPEAKER]
;)          [wink SPEAKER]
:-(         [sadness SPEAKER .5u]
```

```
:-<         [sadness SPEAKER .5u]
:-|         [emotionless SPEAKER]
:-o         [surprise SPEAKER .9u]
:-O         [shock SPEAKER .9u]
:-0         [shock SPEAKER .9u]
:*)         [drunkenness SPEAKER]
(@@)        [sane listener -.9u]
:->         sarcastic
;>          mischievous
-o-         over
-oo-        over-and-out
```

Email header text agent

The *email header text agent* recognizes and parses email headers. The agent triggers on a line of one of the following forms:

```
Article NUMBER of NEWSGROUP
From USER TIME
Path: STRING-CONTAINING-AN-EXCLAMATION-POINT
ASCII-US ASCII-FORMFEED
0, unseen,,
*** EOOH ***
--- Internet Message Header Follows ---
```

Then it parses the header lines which follow. The following fields are parsed:

```
Article
Cc
Date
From
Message-Id/Message-ID
Mime-Version
Newsgroups
Received
Reply-To
Resent-Cc
Resent-Date
Resent-From
Return-Path
Resent-To
Subject
To
```

The following fields are recognized but ignored:

```
Approved
Content-Length/Content-length
Content-Transfer-Encoding
Content-Type
Distribution
In-Reply-To/In-reply-to
Keywords
Lines
NNTP-Posting-Host/Nntp-Posting-Host
Path
Organization
References
Resent-Message-Id
Sender
Status
Summary
X-Administrivia-To
X-Authenticated
X-Client-Port
X-Ident-Sender
X-Mailer
X-Newsreader
X-Nntp-Posting-Host
X-Nntp-Posting-User
X-Posted-From
X-Sender
X-Submissions-To
X-Url/X-URL
X-UserAgent
Xref
```

A parse node is added containing the parsed header field values, including timestamps, email addresses, actors, newsgroups, article number, message ID, and subject text.

The agent parses email addresses contained in header lines into full name, username, and domain. Examples handled include:

input text	full name	username	domain
kcol@cs.com (Ken Col)	Ken Col	kcol	cs.com
KCOL@cs.com (Ken Col)	Ken Col	kcol	cs.com

```
Ken_Col@cs.com            Ken Col    Ken_Col   cs.com
Ken.Col@cs.com            Ken Col    Ken.Col   cs.com
Ken Col <kcol@cs.com>     Ken Col    kcol      cs.com
"Ken Col" <kcol@cs.com>   Ken Col    kcol      cs.com
"Ken Col" <kcol>          Ken Col    kcol      localhost
<kcol@cs.com>                        kcol      cs.com
kcol@cs.com                          kcol      cs.com
```

Then the agent resolves the above information into a ThoughtTreasure actor, such as the object representing the human Ken Col, as follows:

1. Actors A1 are looked up in the database which have the email address (obtained by concatenating the username, an at sign ("@"), and the domain). If no actors are found, a new email address string object is created.
2. The name text agent is invoked in order to parse the full name (if available), and actors A2 in the database matching the name are retrieved.
3. If A1 and A2 are nonempty, one of the elements in the intersection of A1 and A2 is deemed to be the actor referred to by the email address.
4. Otherwise, if A1 is empty and A2 is nonempty, then the actor is deemed to be one of the elements of A2, and the email address is learned for the actor.
5. Otherwise, if A2 is empty and A1 is nonempty, then the actor is deemed to be one of the elements of A1, and the full name (if available) is learned for the actor.
6. Otherwise, if both A1 and A2 are empty, then a new human is learned with the specified full name (if available) and email address.

New Usenet newsgroups are also learned.

Attribution text agent

The *attribution text agent* deals with nested attributions as in:

```
In article <880227113646.2480a904@cs.com> kcol (Ken Col)
writes:
>On Fri, 11 Dec 97 09:38:16 +0100, jim (Jim Garnier) said:
>>On Dec 10, 09:34am, Ken Col wrote:
>>> I wonder if anyone could post a summary of all the
>>> major telephone companies in the US besides the RBOCs.
>> So do I.
>>-- End of excerpt from Jim Garnier
> Now now.
```

Has anyone else noticed how this newsgroup has deteriorated
in the last few months?

It parses attribution lines into parse nodes, recognizes redundant indications of an
end of an excerpt, and counts greater than (">") signs.

When an email header is processed by the semantic parser, the deictic stack is
cleared and a new entry is pushed onto the stack:

```
speakers = From actors in email header
listeners = To actors in email header
now = Date in email header
```

When an attribution is processed by the semantic parser, a new entry is pushed
onto the deictic stack:

```
speakers = speaker in attribution
listeners = previous speakers from top of deictic stack
now = Date in attribution
```

The attribution text agent is invoked at the beginning of each line in the input text.
It counts the number of greater than (">") signs, and sets the level of the deictic
stack accordingly. (Note that the deictic stack can be unpopped—popped items
remain until overwritten by new items.)

French polity text agent

The *French polity text agent* recognizes polities in the French format such as:

```
New Haven (Connecticut)
Colombier-Châtelot (Doubs)
Saumur (Maine-et-Loire)
```

Exercises

1. Enhance the star rating text agent to handle other rating schemes in the movie
review corpus such as:

```
Grade: C
Rate it a +1 on the -4 to +4 scale.
On the Renshaw scale of 0 to 10 bombs in Gilead:  4.
```

2. Improve the heuristics for deciding whether a period (".") is white space or non white space.

3. Enhance the name text agent to handle hyphenated or compound maiden names.

4. Enhance the name text agent to distinguish second name, middle name, and middle surname.

5. Extend the system to be able to parse parenthetical elements.

Chapter 5: The syntactic component

The text agency of ThoughtTreasure scans input text and produces leaf parse nodes for words, phrases, and other entities in the text. The *syntactic component* of ThoughtTreasure is responsible for constructing parse trees out of those leaf parse nodes.

For example, the text agency scans the text:

```
The cat sat on the mat.
```

and produces the following leaf parse nodes:

```
[D The]
[N cat]
[V sat]
[R on]
[D the]
[A mat]
[N mat]
```

The *syntactic parser* takes these parse nodes and constructs the following parse tree:

```
[Z
 [X
  [D The]
  [X [N cat]]]
 [W
  [W [V sat]]
  [Y
   [R on]
   [X
    [D the]
    [X [N mat]]]]]]
```

The ThoughtTreasure syntactic parser is a simple bottom-up parser which repeatedly applies base or phrase structure rules (Chomsky, 1957) subject to constraints or filters (Chomsky, 1982) to parse nodes until all possible sentence parses are found.

The base component

Base rules in ThoughtTreasure consist of a left-hand side whose length is one and a right-hand side whose length is one or two. The base rules currently employed in ThoughtTreasure, for both French and English, are the following:

```
E -> A
E -> B E
E -> D E
E -> E B
E -> E E
E -> E Y
E -> K E
W -> B W
W -> H W
W -> R W
W -> V
W -> W 0
W -> W B
W -> W E
W -> W H
W -> W V
W -> W X
W -> W Y
X -> D X
X -> E X
X -> H
X -> K X
X -> N
X -> X 9
X -> X E
X -> X W
X -> X X
X -> X Y
X -> X Z
X -> Z
Y -> B Y
Y -> K Y
Y -> R B
Y -> R X
Y -> Y Y
```

```
Z -> B Z
Z -> E W
Z -> E Z
Z -> H X
Z -> K Z
Z -> U
Z -> W
Z -> x
Z -> X E
Z -> X W
Z -> X Z
Z -> Y Z
Z -> Z B
Z -> Z Z
```

The characters employed here are ThoughtTreasure feature codes. The following feature codes are defined for parts of speech:

```
A = adjective
B = adverb
D = determiner
H = pronoun
K = conjunction
N = noun
R = preposition
V = verb
U = interjection
x = sentential lexical entry
0 = expletive
9 = element
« = prefix
» = suffix
```

The following feature codes are defined for *constituents* or nodes of the parse tree that are not leaf nodes:

```
E = adjective phrase (ADJP)
L = adverb phrase (ADVP)
W = verb phrase (VP)
X = noun phrase (NP)
Y = prepositional phrase (PP)
Z = sentence (S)
```

Filters

ThoughtTreasure *filters* restrict the application of base rules. For example, the filter
on case (Chomsky, 1982/1987, pp. 35-36) states that X must be in the nominative
case in the rule:

```
Z -> X W
```

Filters are written in C and consist of various constraints from X-bar (Chomsky,
1970) and government-binding theories (Chomsky, 1982), constraints from
grammatical reference works such as those of Grevisse (1986), Alexander (1988),
Greenbaum and Quirk (1990), and Battye and Hintze (1992), and constraints
found through trial and error during the development of the program.

Filters make use of *filter features* associated with lexical entries. A filter feature on
a lexical entry blocks or enables the application of certain rules whose right-hand
side contains that lexical entry. Filter features are associated with a particular
meaning (ThoughtTreasure object) of a lexical entry, since a lexical entry with one
meaning may be acceptable in a context where it would be unacceptable with
another meaning. For example, the type of *marble* used in a sculpture is a mass
noun, while a *marble* used in the game marbles is a count noun (and the game
marbles is a mass noun).

In syntactic parsing, a rule is blocked when all of the meanings of the lexical entry
have a filter feature which blocks that rule. That is, if any meaning of the lexical
entry is not blocked for the rule, the rule applies. A rule is enabled when any of the
meanings of the lexical entry contains a filter feature that enables that rule.

Semantic parsing considers all the meanings of a lexical entry in a parse tree
passed to it from the syntactic parser. If a given meaning is blocked (enabled) in a
given syntactic environment, it is rejected (accepted). The filter features are also
used by the generator, in order to select appropriate base rules, lexical entries, and
inflections.

Just as lexical entries are filtered based on features associated with their links to
objects, lexical entries can be filtered based on their linked objects (meanings).
Grammatical lexical entries such as pronouns have meanings defined in the
linguistics ontology which are used by filters to help decide whether to apply base
rules whose right-hand side contains those lexical entries. A filter is satisfied if any
of the linked objects is an instance of a particular class. If there are 10 meanings,
but only one of the meanings passes, the syntactic parse tree must be generated so

it can be passed to the semantic parser to consider that one meaning. The semantic parser usually reinvokes the same filter as the syntactic parser in order to weed out the 9 syntactically invalid meanings.

Some filters are *soft constraints* in that they return neither 0 nor 1, but a *score* between 0 and 1 indicating how probable a parse node is.

X-bar filters

In an X-bar grammar (Jackendoff, 1977), a *maximal projection* corresponds to each constituent category:

```
E    E-MAX
W    W-MAX
X    X-MAX
Y    Y-MAX
Z    Z-MAX
```

A maximal projection parse node is the top-level parse node of a given category that has a *head* and takes *arguments*. Maximal projections also serve as arguments to other maximal projections.

For example, in:

```
[Z-MAX
 [X-MAX
  [D The]
  [X [N cat]]]
 [W-MAX
  [W [V sat]]
  [Y-MAX
   [R on]
   [X-MAX
    [D the]
    [X [N mat]]]]]]
```

```
The cat sat on the mat.
```

the W-MAX is a top-level verb phrase whose head is the verb *sat* and whose arguments are the X-MAX *The cat* and the Y-MAX *on the mat*. The head of the Y-MAX is the preposition *on* and its single argument is the X-MAX *the mat*. The head of the X-MAX *the mat* is the the noun *mat*; this X-MAX has no arguments.

The following X-MAX has two arguments:

```
[X-MAX
 [X
  [X
   [D the]
   [X [N sitting]]]
  [Y-MAX
   [R of]
   [X-MAX
    [D the]
    [X [N cat]]]]]
 [Y-MAX
  [R on]
  [X-MAX
   [D the]
   [X [N mat]]]]]
```

```
the sitting of the cat on the mat
```

The following E-MAX has one argument:

```
[E-MAX
 [E [A angry]]
 [Y-MAX
  [R at]
  [X-MAX
   [D the]
   [X [N cat]]]]]
```

```
angry at the cat
```

Maximal projections are not represented using features in ThoughtTreasure, but according to the rule:

```
A PN of category X is a maximal projection parse node
when the parent parse node of PN is not of category X
(or PN is the top-level parse node).
```

Note however that during bottom-up parsing this rule cannot always be applied since the parent of a given parse node might not yet be known. A filter has to be defined on a higher-level parse node to get around this problem. Furthermore, alternative parses in ThoughtTreasure share parse nodes, so that a given parse node may have several parents. The parent referred to in the above rule is the parent "looking down" from a particular parse node.

Filters are used to constrain the number of arguments to a maximal projection according to the following matrix:

```
                   arguments
          E-MAX  W-MAX  X-MAX  Y-MAX
head-MAX  _____  _____  _____  _____
E-MAX       0      0      0     0-2
W-MAX      0-1     0     0-3    0-3
X-MAX      0-1     0      0     0-4
Y-MAX       0      0      1      0
```

Thus a W-MAX takes from 0 to 3 X-MAX arguments, as in the following sentences:

X-MAXes

```
_____
     0 Eat!
     1 Jim ate.
     2 Jim ate dinner.
     3 Jim made Karen dinner.
```

An E-MAX takes from 0 to 2 Y-MAX arguments:

Y-MAXes

```
_____
     0 angry
     1 angry at the cat
     2 angry with the cat about the glass
```

All arguments to a maximal projection must be maximal projections.

A soft constraint is that X-MAX arguments precede Y-MAX arguments:

```
Jim set the glass on the table.
?Jim set on the table the glass.
Jim set on the table the most amazing glass.
```

The case filter constrains the case of arguments to Z-MAXes, W-MAXes, and Y-MAXes:

```
rule        case filter
_____    _____
Z -> X W    X nominative for finite W
            X accusative for nonfinite W
W -> W X    X accusative
Y -> R X    X dative
```

Finite verbs are those with person, number, and tense. Infinitives and participles are nonfinite. For example, the case filter rejects the following sentences:

```
*Him laughed.            Z -> X W, laughed finite,
                         X not nominative
*She heard he laughing.  Z -> X W, laughing nonfinite,
                         X not accusative
*She heard he.           W -> W X, X not accusative
*She gave it to he.      Y -> R X, X not dative
```

It accepts the following:

```
He laughed.
She heard him laughing.
She heard him.
She gave it to him.
```

The following recursive algorithm is employed to verify that a given parse node PN is consistent with a case C0:

1. If PN is a *barrier* (Chomsky, 1986, pp. 10-16), return false. In ThoughtTreasure, any maximal projection is considered a barrier. This condition prevents the following sentence from being rejected:

```
[Z-MAX
 [X-MAX <- (1)
  [Z-MAX <- (2)
   [W-MAX <- (3)
    [W [V Understanding]]
    [X-MAX [H her]]]]]] <- (4)
 [W-MAX <- (5)
  [W [V was]]
  [E-MAX [A easy]]]]
```

```
Understanding her was easy.
```

Although the accusative *her* (4) is contained in (1), the subject argument to (5), whose verb is finite, (4) is separated by the barriers (2) and (3) from (1).

2. Otherwise, if PN is a leaf node: If the case C1 of PN is known, return whether C0 equals C1; otherwise, return true. The case is only known in English and French for personal pronouns (and for genitives in English). (The cases of personal pronouns are defined using the `case-of` relation in the personal pronoun ontology.)

3. Otherwise, if PN consists of two noun phrases joined by a coordinating conjunction:

```
[X
 [X ...]
 [X
  [K ...]
  [X ...]]]
```

then return true (see Pinker, 1994, pp. 390-392).

4. Otherwise, the children of PN must all be consistent with case C0.

Adjective filters

The following features enable or block the application of rules involving adjectives:

	W -> W E	X -> E X	X -> X E	description
b English		blocked	enabled	postposed adjective
b French		enabled	blocked	preposed adjective
ó	blocked			epithetic adjective
ú		blocked	blocked	predicative
adjective				

(We use the word *epithetic* to describe an attributive adjective to avoid confusion with the French expression for a predicative adjective, *adjectif attribut*.)

For example, here are some adjectives and the features used to encode them:

```
to die for
_____
b It's a chocolate sundae to die for.     (postposed epithetic)
  *It's a to die for chocolate sundae.    (preposed epithetic)
  This chocolate sundae is to die for.    (predicative)
```

```
galore
_____
b There are chocolate sundaes galore.     (postposed epithetic)
  *There are galore chocolate sundaes.    (preposed epithetic)
ó *The chocolate sundaes are galore.      (predicative)
```

```
well
____
ú *The well patient ate a sundae.         (epithetic)
  The patient is well.                    (predicative)
```

```
cheerful
_____
  *The patient cheerful ate a sundae.     (postposed epithetic)
  The cheerful patient ate a sundae.      (preposed epithetic)
  The patient is cheerful.                (predicative)
```

Adverb filters

The following filter features apply to adverbs:

```
feature   blocked
_____   _____
     °    Z -> B Z
     ¿    Z -> Z B
     Þ    W -> B W
     ð    W -> W B
     Æ    E -> B E
```

For example, here are some adverbs, examples of their use in each of the above contexts, acceptability judgments, and the features used to encode those judgments:

```
very
____
° *Very he wanted to finish the painting.
Þ *He very wanted to finish the painting.
ð *He wanted very to finish the painting.
```

¿ *He wanted to finish the painting very.
   That is a very funny thing.

very much

_____
° *Very much he disappeared.
   He very much wanted to finish the painting.
   He wanted very much to finish the painting.
   He wanted to finish the painting very much.
Æ *He is very much funny.

somewhat

_____
° *Somewhat he wanted to finish the painting.
   He somewhat wanted to finish the painting.
   He wanted somewhat to finish the painting.
   He wanted to finish the painting somewhat.
   He is somewhat funny.

it's like

_____
   It's like he ran upstairs.
Þ *He it's like wanted to finish the painting.
ð *He wanted it's like to finish the painting.
¿ *He wanted to finish the painting it's like.
Æ *He is it's like funny.

and all

_____
° *And all he ran upstairs.
Þ *He and all ran upstairs.
ð *He ran and all upstairs.
   He wanted to finish the painting and all.
Æ *He is and all funny.

carefully

_____
   Carefully he ran upstairs.
   He carefully ran upstairs.
   He ran carefully upstairs.
   He ran upstairs carefully.
   He is carefully funny.

By typing `filtfeat` into the ThoughtTreasure shell and then an adverb (or conjunction), a list of example sentences will be generated similar to the above, enabling the user to decide which filter features to use. One has to try to make only syntactic and not semantic acceptability judgments.

Conjunction filters

Conjunctions are introduced via the following base rules:

```
E -> E E
E -> K E
X -> X X
X -> K X
Y -> Y Y
Y -> K Y
Z -> Z Z
Z -> K Z
```

For example, the noun phrase *the cat and the dog* is represented as:

```
[X
 [X [D The] [X [N cat]]]
 [X
  [K and]
  [X [D the] [X [N dog]]]]]
```

The sentence *the cat sat and the dog ate* is represented as:

```
[Z
 [Z
  [X [D The] [X [N cat]]]
  [W [W [V sat]]]]
 [Z
  [K and]
  [Z
   [X [D the] [X [N dog]]]
   [W [W [V ate]]]]]]
```

Coordination of maximal projections other than sentences is enabled by the following feature associated with a conjunction:

```
feature  enabled
_____  _____
    ©  X  ->  K  X
       E  ->  K  E
       Y  ->  K  Y
```

The rule:

```
X  ->  K  X
```

applies provided that (1) K is enabled for coordination with "©" and (2) the right-hand side X is not itself of the form `[X [K ...] [X ...]]`. The second condition is to prevent the rule from recursing and producing the structure:

```
[X
 [K ...]
 [X [K ...] [X ...]]]]
```

The conditions for adjective and prepositional phrases are similar.
The following features associated with conjunctions enable or block the rule $Z \rightarrow Z\ Z$:

```
feature  behavior
_____  _____
    O  ENABLE  Z  ->  Z1  Z2  where  Z1  or  Z2  is  of  form
                      [Z  [K  ...]  [Z  ...subjunctive  verb...]]
    ÷  ENABLE  same  as  above,  except  indicative
    ï  ENABLE  same  as  above,  except  infinitive
    ±  ENABLE  same  as  above,  except  present  participle
    w  BLOCK   Z  ->  Z1  Z2  where  Z1  of  form  [Z  [K  ...]  [Z  ...]]
```

For example, here are some conjunctions and the features used to encode them:

```
and
____
    *He  is  working  hard  and  to  finish  the  painting.
 ÷  He  is  tired  and  he  is  happy.
 w  *And  he  is  tired,  he  is  happy.
    He  is  happy,  and  he  is  tired.
 ©  Carrie  and  Karen  work  hard.
```

although
_____

÷ He works hard although he never finishes a painting.
  Although he works hard, he never finishes a painting.
  *Carrie although Karen work hard.

before
_____

± He is working hard before finishing the painting.
  *He is working hard before to finish the painting.
÷ He is tired before he is happy.
  *Carrie before Karen work hard.

Noun filters

The following features are soft constraints (for parsing) or hard constraints (for generation) on the base rule `X -> D X`:

k = Noun is preceded by definite article.
É = Noun is preceded by empty article.
m = Mass noun. If not specified, count noun is assumed.

For example:

France
_____

É *I flew to the France.
  I flew to France.

the Who
_____

  I listened to the Who's album Live at Leeds.
k *I listened to Who's album Live at Leeds.

Internet
_____

  ?I connected to Internet.
  I connected to the Internet.

chair
_____

  He bought a chair.
  *He bought chair.
  *He bought some chair.

```
music
```
_____

```
m   *He listened to a music.
     He listened to music.
     He listened to some music.
```

The feature "ï" indicates that the lexical entry is usually employed in the given meaning with a certain inflection. This is used for nouns which are typically used in the plural:

```
==game-marbles//marbles.Pïz/
==toy-marble//marble.z/
```

Noun groups are difficult to analyze because of the many groupings of a sequence of nouns:

```
[[desk lamp] [counter holder]]
[desk [[lamp counter] holder]]
[desk [lamp [counter holder]]]
[[[desk lamp] counter] holder]
[[desk [lamp counter]] holder]
```

ThoughtTreasure deals with noun groups using the following strategies: First, many noun groups are defined as phrasal entries in the lexicon and recognized by the lexical entry text agent. Second, text agents deal with specialized noun group subgrammars, such as those for media objects:

```
the film "Horizons lointains"
```

for product names:

```
Apple Macintosh Centris 650
```

and human names. Finally, the remaining noun groups are syntactically parsed by the base rule X -> X X.

The base rule X -> X X is used for (1) conjunctions as described above, (2) English genitive constructions such as *Jim's stereo*, and (3) appositives such as *her friend Jim*.

English genitives are handled by the base rules X -> X1 X2 and X -> X 9. The first rule applies when X1 is of the form [X [X ...] [9 ...]]. The second rule applies when 9 is the genitive element 's.

Various filter strategies are employed for appositives handled with the base rule X -> X X:

1. The right hand side may not contain a Z (sentence).

2. Longer appositives get a lower score:

appositive	length
my friend Jim	2
Jim, a doctor,	2
?Jim, a doctor, a jogger,	3
my friend Jim, a doctor	3
?my friend Jim, a doctor, a jogger	4

3. Appositives consisting of two proper nouns receive a low score:

```
*Jim, James
*Wiesen Alley, Mrs. Püchl
```

4. Unbalanced appositive trees receive lower scores.

Relative pronoun filters

Relative pronouns are divided into two types: *representative* and *nominal* (Grevisse, 1986, section 678; Greenbaum and Quirk, 1990, sections 15.7, 17.1-17). Representative relative pronouns refer back to antecedents and are used in the following cases:

1. When a noun phrase functions as subject in the following relative clause:

```
[X [X the friends] [W [H who] [W like theater]]]
[X [X the train] [W [H that] [W goes downtown]]]
```

In order for the rule W -> H W to apply, the H must be a subject representative relative pronoun, as defined in the representative relative pronoun ontology. This restriction is also checked in X -> X W: in order for this rule to apply, the W must be of the form [W [H ...] [W ...]] where the H is a subject representative relative pronoun.

2. When a noun phrase functions as object (or indirect object in French) in a following relative clause:

```
[X [X the friends] [Z [X [H whom]] [Z she took to the
theater]]]
[X [X the train] [Z [X [H that]] [Z she took
downtown]]]
```

In order for the rule Z -> X Z to apply, the X must consist of an object representative relative pronoun or, in French, an indirect object representative relative pronoun with the preposition built in such as *dont*. This restriction is also checked in the rule X -> X Z.

3. When a noun phrase functions as indirect object in a following relative clause:

```
[X [X the friends] [Z [Y [R with] [X [H whom]]] [Z she
went to the play]]]
[X [X the train] [Z [Y [R of] [X [H which]]] [Z she
spoke]]]
```

In order for the rule Z -> Y Z to apply, the Y must be of the form [Y [R ...] [X [H ...]]] where the H is an indirect object representative relative pronoun. This restriction is also checked in the rule X -> X Z.

Nominal relative pronouns are relative pronouns in which a wh-element is merged with its antecedent.

For example, the sentence employing the nominal relative pronoun *what*:

```
I took what they offered me.
     ‾‾‾‾‾
```

has a similar meaning to the sentence employing the representative relative pronoun *that*:

```
I took the thing that they offered me.
     ‾‾‾‾‾‾‾‾‾‾‾‾‾‾‾‾‾‾
```

Nominal relative pronouns are used in the following cases:

1. When the pronoun functions as subject in the following relative clause:

```
[X [X [H what]] [W brought them to the city]]
```

In order for the rule X -> X W to apply, the X must consist of a subject nominal relative pronoun, as defined in the nominal relative pronoun ontology.

2. When the pronoun functions as object or indirect object (in French) in the following relative clause:

```
[X [X [H what]] [Z they saw]]
[X [X [H ce dont]] [Z je me souviens]]
[X [X [H de quoi]] [Z rire]]
```

In order for the rule X -> X Z to apply, the X must consist of an object or indirect object nominal relative pronoun.

Verb filters

The rule Z -> X W only applies if the person and number of the subject agree with the person and number of the auxiliary verb of W:

	subject	verb
*He are drunk.	3S	P
*I is drunk.	1S	3S
*You am drunk.	2P	1S
He is drunk.	3S	3S

The base rule W -> W H is used for subject-auxiliary verb inversion in English and French, and for pronouns that occur inside a verb phrase in French such as direct and indirect object pronouns, reflexive pronouns, *en*, and *y*. Subject-auxiliary verb inversion requires that (1) H be a subject pronoun, (2) W be a simple (not compound) verb, and in English, (3) W be one of a short list of helping verbs, namely, *be*, *do*, and the modal auxiliaries. For example:

sentence	disobeys
Will he go to school?	
Is he going to school?	
*Is him going to school?	(1)
*Is going he to school?	(2)
*Goes he to school?	(3)

```
Does he like school?
*Likes he school?                    (3)
```

In order for the rule W -> W E to apply, the main verb of W must be a copula such as *be, seem, remain, become*, and so on. The subcategorization restrictions for verbs are discussed in the chapter on the lexical component. Here we simply mention the following filter features:

```
1 = French verb taking être as an auxiliary verb.
Ô = English verb which does not occur in the
progressive.
ô = Verb whose arguments may not be reordered (by heavy
NP shift).
```

Other filters

Punctuation is taken into account by filters. For the rule Z -> Z1 Z2, the presence of punctuation (such as commas or dashes) between Z1 and Z2 increases confidence in the rule application. Punctuation is also used to increase or decrease the score of various parses of appositives and relative clauses.

Various filters are concerned with collapsing redundant alternative trees. For example, the parse tree:

```
[X
 [X [D the] [X [N grocer]]]
 [Y [R of] [X [N Wiesen Alley]]]]
```

is allowed, whereas the parse tree:

```
[X
 [D the]
 [X [X [N grocer]] [Y [R of] [X [N Wiesen Alley]]]]]
```

is disallowed.

Several filters are used to restrict the use of lexical entries for various tasks:

feature	¾	a	q	else
semantic parser	no	no	yes	yes
generator	no	yes	no	yes
translation parse	no	no	yes	yes
translation gen	yes	yes	no	yes

The feature "¾" indicates that a lexical entry should only be used when a concept is being generated in transfer-based translation. This enables a translation to be produced when there is no word for a given concept in the target language. For example, the following ensures that a translation will be produced if, for some reason, the concept `prep-time-before-hour-french` needs to be translated into English:

```
prep-time-before-hour-french//less.¾Rz/moins.¹Ry/
```

But given the English word *less*, we do not wish to parse it into `prep-time-before-hour-french`. The strategies employed by the standard generator when a word does not exist for a concept are: (1) ascend the hierarchy, or (2) print the word in a foreign language enclosed in quotes. For example, given the following:

```
==cocktail.z//
===kir.My//
```

`kir` would be generated as one of the following in English:

```
"kir"
cocktail
```

The feature "ᵃ" indicates that a lexical entry should only be used in generation. It may be used to prevent the lexical entry from being semantically parsed, as in:

```
===location-interrogative-pronoun//where.Hz/où.Hy/
====location-interrogative-pronoun1//where.ᵃHz/
où# ça#.Hy/
```

In French, the location interrogative pronoun is *où* when used in a larger sentence, and *où ça* when used alone. In English, *where* is used in both situations:

```
Where did you go?
Where?
```

Use of the feature "ᵃ" prevents both `location-interrogative-pronoun` and `location-interrogative-pronoun1` from being generated when parsing *where*.

The feature "q" has five uses:

1.   The lexical entry is monosemous—it is always used with this meaning—
     but it is infrequent. (The meaning of a concept is best described by the
     lexical entry marked with the frequent feature "¹".)
2.   The lexical entry is polysemous and its use with this meaning is
     infrequent.
3.   The lexical entry is not used with this exact meaning, but it was entered
     here as an expedient. Instances of this case should be moved into separate
     concepts.
4.   The lexical entry should not be generated.
5.   The lexical entry is a common spelling error.

The bottom-up syntactic parser

A forest of parse nodes is passed to the syntactic parser from the text agency along
with the start and stop character positions of the sentence to be parsed. For
efficiency reasons, those parse nodes that are part of the sentence are collected into
a new forest area to be used by the syntactic parser.

The *syntactic parsing* algorithm is:

```
. Set CHANGED = TRUE.
. While CHANGED:
  . Set CHANGED = FALSE
  . For each parse node PN1 in forest:
    . If singleton rules have not been applied to PN1:
      . If applying singleton rules to PN1 returns TRUE:
        . Set CHANGED = TRUE.
    . If applying rules to PN1 returns TRUE:
      . Set CHANGED = TRUE.
```

The algorithm for *applying singleton rules* to PN1 whose part of speech or
constituent feature is F1 is:

```
. Set CHANGED = FALSE.
. For each base rule R of the form ?F0 -> F1
  . If, according to filters, R can be applied to PN1
    with score S > 0.0:
    . Add to the forest a new parse node
        whose score is S combined with the score of PN1,
        whose constituent feature is ?F0,
        whose first child is PN1,
        whose start position is that of PN1, and
```

```
        whose stop position is that of PN1.
  . Set CHANGED = TRUE.
. Return CHANGED.
```

The algorithm for *applying rules* to PN1 whose part of speech or constituent feature is F1 is:

```
. Set CHANGED = FALSE.
. For each parse node PN2 in forest:
  . If PN1 == PN2, continue (with the next iteration of
    this loop).
  . If the start character position of PN2 is equal to the
    stop character position of PN1 plus 1:
    . If the combination of PN1 with PN2 was already
      considered, continue.
    . For each base rule R of the form ?F0 -> F1 F2,
      where F2 is the feature of PN2:
      . If, according to filters, R can be applied to PN1
        and PN2 with score S > 0.0:
        . Add to the forest a new parse node whose
            score is S combined with the scores of PN1 and
            PN2, whose constituent feature is ?F0,
            whose first child is PN1 and second child is PN2,
            whose start character position is that of PN1,
            and whose stop character position is that of PN2.
        . Set CHANGED = TRUE.
  . If the stop character position of PN2 is equal to the
    start character position of PN1 minus 1:
    . (Analogous to the above with PN1 and PN2 switched.)
. Return CHANGED.
```

The filters referred to in the above algorithms are those described in the previous section. Associated with each parse node PN is a list of other parse nodes PN has been considered against, which is maintained and consulted in the above loop. Scores are combined by multiplying them (see Allen, 1995, p. 215).

When a parse node is added to the forest, in integrated parsing the parse node may immediately be passed to the semantic parser. Otherwise, the semantic parser is not invoked until a sentence parse node is added. A sentence parse node is one whose feature is Z (sentence) and whose start and stop positions equal those of the sentence.

If after all possibilities are exhausted, a sentence parse was not found, then the semantic parser is invoked on sentence *fragments* as follows:

```
. Set POSITION = start character position of sentence.
. While POSITION < stop character position of sentence:
   . Find the longest parse nodes in the forest which
start at POSITION-those with the greatest stop
character position.
   . Semantically parse those parse nodes.
   . Set POSITION = the stop position of the parse
nodes.
```

(The algorithm ensures that all input text is spanned. This is essential in transfer-based translation where some translation must be produced for all source language text even when that text cannot be fully parsed.)

Transformations

Transformational rules (Chomsky, 1965) are used in ThoughtTreasure by the generator and for post-editing of output from the transfer-based translator. They are not used in parsing, since the syntactic and semantic parsers deal directly with structures such as subject-auxiliary verb inversion and French clitic pronouns.

In this section we present transformations which apply to both English and French parse trees, followed by English-only transformations, and French-only transformations.

English and French transformations

A construction in which a pronoun is the argument of *of* is transformed into a construction involving a possessive determiner:

```
[X [X [D a] [X [N friend]]] [Y [R of] [X [H you]]]]
=> [X [D your] [X [N friend]]]

   a friend of you => your friend
```

In English and French, the inflection of some words depends on whether the following word begins with a vowel sound:

```
a house        ce chat
an umbrella    cet arbre
```

Sometimes an apostrophe is also added:

```
is not          le chat
isn't           l'arbre
```

Therefore, inflections which (1) occur before vowel-initial words and (2) occur with an apostrophe before vowel-initial words in French (or occur with an apostrophe in other situations in English) are marked as such in the inflections file:

```
feature English examples French examples

Ä (1)    an thine           mon cet nouvel
Á (2)    isn' 'n' o'         l' d' s' n' qu'
```

An inflection I1 marked with one of the above features, which is of the same gender, number, and person as inflection I0, is called an *alteration* of I0. For example, *qu'* is an alteration of *que*.

When a vowel-initial word is preceded by a word with an alteration, a transformation replaces the word with its alteration (and possibly inserts an apostrophe):

```
?1 ?2 where ?2 is a vowel-initial word
=> ?3(')?2 where ?3 is the alteration of ?1

  a umbrella => an umbrella
```

A vowel-initial word, for the purposes of the above transformation, is not necessarily pronounced starting with a vowel sound, just as a non-vowel-initial word is not necessarily pronounced starting with a nonvowel: In French, the h at the beginning of a word is not pronounced (except in some regional dialects and for occasional emphasis in words such as *hop !*). However, some words, called *h-aspiré* words, are pronounced starting with a vowel sound, but act as if they were not pronounced with a vowel sound for the purposes of the above transformation. Similarly in English, words such as *historic* are occasionally preceded by *an* even when the h is pronounced.

Since ThoughtTreasure is currently not a speech recognition or generation system, the program merely needs to know whether a word is vowel-initial or not for the purposes of the above transformation. By default, a word is considered vowel-initial if it begins with certain characters that depend on the language:

```
English    French
```
_____ _____
```
aeiouAEIOU aàâäeéèêhiîïoòôöuüÀAÉEHIOÒUÜ
```

Override features are then added in the inflections file to lexical entries which are exceptions to the default rule:

```
feature                English examples French examples
```
_____ _____ _____
```
È (non-vowel-initial) Europe union U   onze haut H
Ì (vowel-initial)     honest hour L    y
```

Some inflections are also marked as contractions in the lexicon with the feature "Í":

```
've    have
'm     am
't     not
```

This feature is used in generation in order to generate an apostrophe before the inflection, and in parsing to require an apostrophe before the inflection.

English transformations

A genitive construction involving a pronoun is transformed into a possessive determiner:

```
[X [X [X [H you]] [9 s]] [X [N sister]]]
=> [X [D your] [X [N sister]]]

  you's sister => your sister
```

The word *that* introducing a subordinate finite clause is deleted:

```
[X [Z [K that] [Z ?1]]] => [X [Z ?1]]

  She said that she liked ice cream.
  => She said she liked ice cream.
```

The subject of a subordinate nonfinite clause is deleted by a transformation if it is identical to the subject or object of the main clause:

```
She wanted for her to have ice cream.
```

(where she and her refer to the same person)
=> She wanted to have ice cream.

She persuaded him for him to go to the store.
=> She persuaded him to go to the store.

A prepositional phrase involving a pronoun of location is transformed into a noun phrase consisting only of the pronoun:

```
[Y [R ?1] [N [H ?2]]] where ?1 is in/at/to and
   ?2 is there/where
=> [N [H ?2]]

   at there => there
   to where => where
```

French transformations

A number of transformations are employed to convert pronouns initially placed in direct or indirect object position by the generator into clitic pronouns connected to the verb:

```
[Y [R de] [H ?1]] where ?1 not interrogative
=> [H en] connected to verb
   Il parle de le. => Il en parle.

[Y [R à] [H là-bas]] => [H y] connected to verb
   Il va à là-bas. => Il y va.

[X [H ?1]] where ?1 is a direct object pronoun
=> [H ?1] connected to verb
   Il aime la. => Il la aime.
   (later transformed to Il l'aime.)

[Y [R ?] [H ?1]] where ?1 is a reflexive pronoun
=> [H ?1] connected to verb
   Il parle à se. => Il se parle.

[Y [R à] [H ?1]]
=> [H ?2] connected to verb
     where ?2 is an indirect object pronoun of
     the same gender, number, and person as ?1
   Il téléphone à elle. => Il lui téléphone.
```

A number of transformations are responsible for combining articles:

```
[Y [R à] le ?1] => [Y [R au] ?1]

[Y [R de] le ?1] => [Y [R du] ?1]

[Y [R de] les ?1] => [Y [R des] ?1]

[Y [R en] la ?1] where ?1 refers to a polity
=> [Y [R en] ?1]

[Y [R en] les ?1] where ?1 refers to a polity
=> [Y [R aux] ?1]

[Y [R en] le ?1] where ?1 is a vowel-initial
word referring to a polity
=> [Y [R en] ?1]

[Y [R en] le ?1] where ?1 is a non-vowel-initial
word referring to a polity
=> [Y [R au] ?1]
```

Exercises

1. Tune the values of the soft constraints of filters (see Hindle and Rooth, 1993).

2. Improve the set of adverb filters to correspond more closely to the grammatical environment.

3. Extend the base rules, filters, and semantic parser, to handle all conjoined parts of speech. For example, verbs cannot currently be conjoined.

4. Extend ThoughtTreasure to handle English deferred or stranded prepositions such as in the following:

```
the friends she went to the play with
the train she talked about
```

Chapter 6: The semantic component

With all of the things that need to be done in understanding a sentence—syntactic parsing, semantic parsing, anaphoric parsing, and deep understanding—what order should ThoughtTreasure do them in? Dyer (1983) argued for *integrated parsing* in which all parsing processes work in close cooperation. Integrated parsing is valid from a cognitive standpoint: humans are able to understand in real time as words are read or heard; there is no need to wait until the end of a sentence in order to understand it.

The main benefit of integrated parsing is efficiency: The longer one waits to reduce alternatives, the more those alternatives explode. With integrated parsing, incorrect possibilities can be eliminated sooner rather than later. (On the other hand, there may be a penalty to integrated parsing when chunks are processed that would have been later ruled out. For example, a syntactic subtree might undergo expensive semantic or deep-understanding-level processing that would never have made it into the final sentence parse anyway due to inexpensive syntactic filters.)

The approach opposite to integrated parsing, *modular parsing*, has the advantage that each component (such as syntax and semantics) can be coded separately, and it is presumably easier to understand each component in isolation. But the complication here is that more information has to be constructed and passed between modules. For example, intensions have to be constructed that would otherwise have been resolved immediately into extensions. In any case, if integrated parsing is broken down into the appropriate chunks, it can perhaps be modular as well.

Unfortunately, a number of Catch-22s arise when trying to implement an integrated parser. Integration is difficult to achieve since the right information is not always available at the right time. One problem relates to the integration of anaphoric parsing into semantic parsing: In order to perform anaphoric parsing, the antecedents must be available. But only those antecedents from prior sentences are available inside semantic parsing; antecedents (or postcedents in the case of cataphora) within the current sentence might not yet be available, since those are the very concepts that semantic parsing is in the process of constructing. (What concepts are available inside semantic parsing depends on where one is in the tree and the order of traversal of branches.)

Another problem relates to the integration of semantic parsing into syntactic parsing: A syntactic subtree may not contain all the information needed to parse it. For example, a verb phrase cannot be semantically parsed in isolation, since selectional restrictions on the unavailable subject cannot be used to disambiguate the verb sense. A partial solution is to invoke semantic parsing only on maximal projections (Chomsky, 1982) where the head lexical entry's arguments are all available. This effectively limits early semantic parsing to noun phrases and embedded clauses (sentences). But many subordinate clauses cannot be parsed in isolation either since they inherit arguments from their superordinate clauses.

Some type of parallel algorithm is clearly needed in which a society of agents (Minsky, 1986) play give and take until the system converges on a result. But it is far from clear how to implement such a system.

ThoughtTreasure's parsing control structure

ThoughtTreasure is basically a modular parser with the following hooks to enable integrated parsing:

- The semantic parser may be invoked whenever the syntactic parser adds a parse node. By default, it is invoked only when the parse node is a sentence node spanning the input sentence text. But it can also be invoked on smaller trees. (An attempt to do this can be enabled in the source code via `#define INTEGSYNSEM`.) Though this strategy usually works, it does not reduce processing by much since there are many restrictions on when it can be applied.
- The anaphoric parser may be invoked after the semantic parser is invoked in syntactic processing. (The `#ifdef INTEGSYNSEMANA` in the source code disables an unsuccessful attempt to do this.) Due to Catch-22s, the parsing fails on many cases of intrasentential anaphora.
- The outermost loop loops through contexts, so that all processes from the syntactic parser onward can make use of the context.

The algorithm used by ThoughtTreasure to process an input sentence is as follows:

```
. Run text agents on input to produce parse nodes.
. For each context:
  . For each base rule application creating a new parse node:
    . If new parse node satisfies certain conditions:
      . Semantically parse the parse node.
  . For each semantic parse collected above:
    . Perform anaphoric parsing on the parse.
    . For each anaphoric parse collected above:
      . Run understanding agents on the parse, sprouting
        a new context for each interpretation.
. Prune contexts sprouted above and select best context.
. Generate output from best context.
```

The following diagram illustrates the basic flow of control and what types of data are processed at each stage of parsing and generation:

```
Parsing:

    TEXT -----------text agency----------->
    PARSE NODES ----syntactic parser------>
    PARSE NODES ----semantic parser------->
    LIST OBJECTS ---anaphoric parser------>
    LIST OBJECTS ---understanding agency-->
    LIST OBJECTS, C DATA STRUCTURES

Generation:

    LIST OBJECTS ---generator------------->
    PARSE NODES  ---trivial mapping------->
    TEXT
```

Parsing and the movie review application

We return to our movie review application, presenting a detailed trace of how a question about a movie is syntactically and semantically parsed. We then present an example of how ThoughtTreasure parses and answers questions about a simple movie review.

Parsing and answering a question

The question *Who directed Rendezvous in Paris?* is typed into the file inex.txt and the following commands are typed into the ThoughtTreasure shell:

```
dbg -flags synsem -level detail
parse -dcin inex.txt -outsyn 1 -outsem 1 -outana 1
    -outund 1 -dcout outex.txt
```

The first command turns on detailed debugging of syntactic and semantic parsing. The second command initiates parsing of the file inex.txt with output of the syntactic, semantic, anaphoric, and understanding-level parses to the file outex.txt.

The debugging output is always placed into the log file. This file starts as follows:

```
19960901160211: created Context 1
Deictic stack level 0 <computer-file> 19960901160211
speakers: Jim
listeners: TT
```

A speaker of Jim and a listener of ThoughtTreasure are pushed onto the deictic stack—this is hardcoded for now.

The text agents are then run. The lexical entry text agent and the end of sentence text agent add the following parse nodes:

```
[H <Who.Hz:who> 0-3:<Who >] [N <Who.SNz> 0-3:<Who >]
[V <directed.iVz:direct> 4-12:<directed >]
[V <directed.dVz:direct> 4-12:<directed >]
[A <directed.Az> 4-12:<directed >]
[N <Rendezvous in Paris.Nz><?\n>
13-33:<Rendezvous in Paris?\n>]
[0 <in.0z> 24-26:<in >]
[N <in.·Nz‚> 24-26:<in >]
[R <in.·Rz‚> 24-26:<in >]
[A <in.·Az‚> 24-26:<in >]
[N <Paris.SNz‚><?\n> 27-33:<Paris?\n>]
```

Several different inflections of each word are added:

- pronoun and singular noun instances of *Who* found in the input text from characters 0 to 3 (including trailing white space),
- preterit verb, past participle verb, and adjective instances of *directed*,
- the phrasal singular noun *Rendezvous in Paris*,
- expletive (as in phrasal verbs), noun (as in *inch*), preposition, and adjective (as in *fashionable*) instances of *in*, and
- the singular noun *Paris*.

The locations of items found by the text agents above are then shown:

```
LEXITEM words:
[[Who ]][[directed ]]Rendezvous in Paris?
```

```
LEXITEM phrases:
Who directed [[Rendezvous in Paris?
]]
```

```
END_OF_SENT:
Who directed Rendezvous in Paris[[?
]]
```

Next, syntactic parsing begins:

```
19960901160211: **** PROCESS SENTENCE BEGIN ****
19960901160211: **** PROCESS SENTENCE IN CONTEXT #1
****
19960901160211: **** SYNTACTIC PARSE BEGIN ****
Who directed Rendezvous in Paris?\n
SYN X <- [N <Rendezvous in Paris.Nz>]
SYN E <- [A <directed.Az>]
SYN W <- [V <directed.dVz:direct>]
SYN W <- [V <directed.iVz:direct>]
SYN X <- [N <Who.SNz>]
SYN X <- [H <Who.Hz:who>]
```

Singleton base rules N -> X, H -> X, A -> E, and V -> W are applied to the lexical entries: noun phrases are built from nouns and pronouns, adjective phrases are built from adjectives, and verb phrases are built from verbs.

A nonsingleton base rule H W -> W is applied, creating a verb phrase out of the pronoun *Who* and the verb phrase containing the verb *directed*:

```
SYN W <- [H <Who.Hz:who>] +
[W [V <directed.iVz:direct>]]
```

It so happens that this parse node will not end up in any final sentence parse, but the syntactic parser nonetheless carries out all possible base rule applications subject to the set of filters (constraints).

Another verb phrase and a sentence node are then added:

```
SYN W <- [H <Who.Hz:who>] +
         [W [V <directed.dVz:direct>]]
SYN Z <- [X [H <Who.Hz:who>]] +
         [W [V <directed.iVz:direct>]]
```

Although a sentence node has been added, it is not semantically parsed since it does not span the entire input sentence.

A number of other base rules are applied, adding yet more nodes to the parse node forest:

```
SYN Z <- [X [H <Who.Hz:who>]] +
         [W [V <directed.dVz:direct>]]
SYN X <- [X [H <Who.Hz:who>]] + [E [A <directed.Az>]]
SYN Z <- [X [H <Who.Hz:who>]] + [E [A <directed.Az>]]
SYN Z <- [X [N <Who.SNz>]] +
         [W [V <directed.iVz:direct>]]
SYN Z <- [X [N <Who.SNz>]] +
         [W [V <directed.dVz:direct>]]
SYN X <- [X [N <Who.SNz>]] + [E [A <directed.Az>]]
SYN Z <- [X [N <Who.SNz>]] + [E [A <directed.Az>]]
SYN Z <- [W [V <directed.iVz:direct>]]
SYN W <- [W [V <directed.iVz:direct>]] +
         [X [N <Rendezvous in Paris.Nz>]]
SYN Z <- [W [V <directed.dVz:direct>]]
SYN W <- [W [V <directed.dVz:direct>]] +
         [X [N <Rendezvous in Paris.Nz>]]
SYN X <- [E [A <directed.Az>]] +
         [X [N <Rendezvous in Paris.Nz>]]
SYN X <- [X [X [N <Who.SNz>]][E [A <directed.Az>]]] +
         [X [N <Rendezvous in Paris.Nz>]]
SYN W <- [H <Who.Hz:who>] +
         [W [W [V <directed.dVz:direct>]]
            [X [N <Rendezvous in Paris.Nz>]]]
SYN W <- [H <Who.Hz:who>] +
         [W [W [V <directed.iVz:direct>]]
            [X [N <Rendezvous in Paris.Nz>]]]
SYN X <- [X [N <Who.SNz>]] +
         [X [E [A <directed.Az>]]
            [X [N <Rendezvous in Paris.Nz>]]]
SYN Z <- [W [W [V <directed.dVz:direct>]]
            [X [N <Rendezvous in Paris.Nz>]]]
```

Finally a sentence node is added that spans the input sentence, and the semantic parser is invoked:

```
SYN Z <- [X [H <Who.Hz:who>]] +
         [W [W [V <directed.dVz:direct>]]
            [X [N <Rendezvous in Paris.Nz>]]]
19960901160212: **** SEMANTIC PARSE TOP SENTENCE ****
19960901160212: **** SEMANTIC PARSE BEGIN ****
[Z
 [X [H <Who.Hz:who>]]
 [W
  [W [V <directed.dVz:direct>]]
  [X [N <Rendezvous in Paris.Nz>]]]]
SC [Z [X [H <Who.Hz:who>]]
      [W [W [V <directed.dVz:direct>]]
         [X [N <Rendezvous in Paris.Nz>]]]]
>SC [X [H <Who.Hz:who>]]
>>SC [H <Who.Hz:who>]
>>SR human-interrogative-pronoun [H <Who.Hz:who>]
>SR human-interrogative-pronoun [H <Who.Hz:who>]
```

SC indicates a recursive call to the semantic parser and SR indicates a return. Greater than signs (">") indicate recursion level. The semantic parser is invoked on the entire tree, a sentence, which then invokes itself on the noun phrase ("X"). To parse the noun phrase, it invokes itself on the pronoun ("H"). The pronoun lexical entry is linked to one meaning in the database, human-interrogative-pronoun, which it returns along with a pointer to the parse node from which it derives.

The semantic parser is next invoked on the verb phrase ("W"), with a *case frame* containing the subject obtained above:

```
>SC [W [W [V <directed.dVz:direct>]]
       [X [N <Rendezvous in Paris.Nz>]]]
>{subj: human-interrogative-pronoun
  [X [H <Who.Hz:who>]]}
```

In order to parse a verb phrase, verb arguments must first be parsed. This parse contains one direct object argument—*Rendezvous in Paris*. The semantic parser is invoked on this argument:

```
>>SC [X [N <Rendezvous in Paris.Nz>]]
>>>SC [N <Rendezvous in Paris.Nz>]
```

```
>>>SR 0.900:RDP [N <Rendezvous in Paris.Nz>]
>>SR 0.900:RDP [N <Rendezvous in Paris.Nz>]
```

The one meaning linked to *Rendezvous in Paris* is returned.

The embedded verb phrase is then called with a case frame containing one subject and one object:

```
>>SC [W [V <directed.dVz:direct>]]
>>{obj: RDP [X [N <Rendezvous in Paris.Nz>]]}
>>{subj: human-interrogative-pronoun
[X [H <Who.Hz:who>]]}
>>>SC [V <directed.dVz:direct>]
>>>{obj: RDP [X [N <Rendezvous in Paris.Nz>]]}
>>>{subj: human-interrogative-pronoun
[X [H <Who.Hz:who>]]}
```

A new concept is constructed and semantic parsing returns with one concept as the result:

```
>>>SR 0.810:[director-of RDP
human-interrogative-pronoun] [V <directed.dVz:direct>]
>>SR 0.810:[director-of RDP
human-interrogative-pronoun] [V <directed.dVz:direct>]
>SR 0.810:[director-of RDP
human-interrogative-pronoun] [V <directed.dVz:direct>]
SR 0.810:[director-of RDP
human-interrogative-pronoun] [V <directed.dVz:direct>]
19960901160212: **** SEMANTIC PARSE END ****
```

The syntactic parser then continues its process of applying base rules. Another sentence is found and semantic parsing is again invoked:

```
SYN Z <- [X [N <Who.SNz>]] +
         [W [W [V <directed.dVz:direct>]]
            [X [N <Rendezvous in Paris.Nz>]]]
19960901160212: **** SEMANTIC PARSE TOP SENTENCE ****
19960901160212: **** SEMANTIC PARSE BEGIN ****
[Z
 [X [N <Who.SNz>]]
 [W
  [W [V <directed.dVz:direct>]]
  [X [N <Rendezvous in Paris.Nz>]]]]
```

```
SC [Z [X [N <Who.SNz>]]][W [W [V <directed.dVz:direct>]]
[X [N <Rendezvous in Paris.Nz>]]]]]
>SC [X [N <Who.SNz>]]
>>SC [N <Who.SNz>]
>>SR 0.630:rock-group-the-Who [N <Who.SNz>]
>SR 0.630:rock-group-the-Who [N <Who.SNz>]
```

This parse involves the noun *Who*, whose only known meaning is the rock group
the Who. But since this meaning of the word is marked in the lexicon as preferring
a definite article (a filter feature of "k"), it is assigned a score of 0.630.
Parsing then continues:

```
>SC [W [W [V <directed.dVz:direct>]]
       [X [N <Rendezvous in Paris.Nz>]]]
>{subj: rock-group-the-Who [X [N <Who.SNz>]]}
>>SC [X [N <Rendezvous in Paris.Nz>]]
>>>SC [N <Rendezvous in Paris.Nz>]
>>>SR 0.900:RDP [N <Rendezvous in Paris.Nz>]
>>SR 0.900:RDP [N <Rendezvous in Paris.Nz>]
>>SC [W [V <directed.dVz:direct>]]
>>{obj: RDP [X [N <Rendezvous in Paris.Nz>]]}
>>{subj: rock-group-the-Who [X [N <Who.SNz>]]}
>>>SC [V <directed.dVz:direct>]
>>>{obj: RDP [X [N <Rendezvous in Paris.Nz>]]}
>>>{subj: rock-group-the-Who [X [N <Who.SNz>]]}
>>>SR 0.510:[director-of RDP rock-group-the-Who]
[V <directed.dVz:direct>]
>>SR 0.510:[director-of RDP rock-group-the-Who]
[V <directed.dVz:direct>]
>SR 0.510:[director-of RDP rock-group-the-Who]
[V <directed.dVz:direct>]
SR 0.510:[past-participle
[director-of RDP rock-group-the-Who]]
[V <directed.dVz:direct>]
19960901160212: **** SEMANTIC PARSE END ****
```

The resulting concept may be paraphrased as *Did the Who direct Rendezvous in
Paris?*

Further syntactic parses are considered, which lead to further semantic parses:

```
...
[Z
[X [H <Who.Hz:who>]]
```

```
[W
 [W [V <directed.iVz:direct>]]
 [X [N <Rendezvous in Paris.Nz>]]]]
...
SR 0.810:[preterit-indicative
[director-of RDP human-interrogative-pronoun]]
[V <directed.iVz:direct>]
...
[Z
 [X [N <Who.SNz>]]
 [W
  [W [V <directed.iVz:direct>]]
  [X [N <Rendezvous in Paris.Nz>]]]]
...
SR 0.510:[preterit-indicative
[director-of RDP rock-group-the-Who]]
[V <directed.iVz:direct>]
```

Finally, all possible syntactic parses have been considered and the following semantic parses are returned:

```
19960901160212: **** SYNTACTIC PARSE END ****
19960901160212: **** RESULTS OF SEMANTIC PARSE ****
0.810:[preterit-indicative
 [director-of *RDP *human-interrogative-pronoun]]
0.810:[past-participle
 [director-of *RDP *human-interrogative-pronoun]]
0.510:[preterit-indicative
 [director-of *RDP *rock-group-the-Who]]
0.510:[past-participle
 [director-of *RDP *rock-group-the-Who]]
19960901160212: 4 semantic parse(s) [session total 4]
of <Who direct>
```

Next, each semantic parse is considered by the anaphoric parser and understanding agency. In this example, there is no anaphora to be resolved, so the anaphoric parser just returns back its input:

```
19960901160212: **** ANAPHORIC PARSE BEGIN ****
AC [preterit-indicative
[director-of *RDP *human-interrogative-pronoun]]
>AC preterit-indicative
>AR preterit-indicative
>AC [director-of *RDP *human-interrogative-pronoun]
```

```
>>AC director-of
>>AR director-of
>>AC RDP
>>AR RDP
>>AC human-interrogative-pronoun
>>AR human-interrogative-pronoun
>AR [director-of RDP human-interrogative-pronoun]
AR [preterit-indicative
[director-of RDP human-interrogative-pronoun]]
Accepted [preterit-indicative
[director-of *RDP *human-interrogative-pronoun]]
  with anaphors:
anaphor <RDP> <RDP> 1 [X [N <Rendezvous in Paris.Nz>]]
anaphor <human-interrogative-pronoun>
<human-interrogative-pronoun>
  1 [X [H <Who.Hz:who>]]
19960901160212: **** ANAPHORIC PARSE END ****
```

The understanding agency is then run on the output of the anaphoric parser:

```
19960901160212: **** UNDERSTANDING AGENCY BEGIN ****
19960901160212: sprouted Context 12
UNROLLED QUESTION CONCEPT
[director-of *RDP *human-interrogative-pronoun]
UnderstandUtterance3 returns 1.000000
19960901160212: **** UNDERSTANDING AGENCY END ****
```

It sprouts a new context for an interpretation of the input question. The question makes complete sense (1.000000) because a question answering agent finds an answer to the question in the database, which we will see below.

The above is repeated for each semantic parse. To see the results, we skip to the point in the trace where the sprouted contexts are printed out:

```
...
19960901160212: freed Context 1
19960901160212: **** UNPRUNED UNDERSTANDING CONTEXTS
****
```

```
Context 14 sense 0.104985 MODE_STOPPED
@19960901160211:19960901160211#14
  tensestep 0
last concept [preterit-indicative
  [director-of RDP rock-group-the-Who]]
```

```
last pn:
[Z
 [X [N <Who.SNz>]]
 [W
  [W [V <directed.iVz:direct>]]
  [X [N <Rendezvous in Paris.Nz>]]]]
Answer <UA_QuestionYesNo2> <Yes-No-question> sense 0.1
Q: [director-of RDP rock-group-the-Who]
A: [sentence-adverb-of-negation
     [not @na:na#14|
      [director-of RDP rock-group-the-Who]]]
```

The Yes-No question answering agent interprets the input as *Did (the rock group) the Who direct Rendezvous in Paris?*, and generates the answer *No, the Who did not direct Rendezvous in Paris.* This interpretation does not make very much sense (0.104985).

The next interpretation is assigned a sense of 0 because the top-level tense is a past participle:

```
Context 13 sense 0 MODE_STOPPED
@19960901160211:19960901160211#13 tensestep 0
last concept [past-participle
[director-of RDP rock-group-the-Who]]
last pn:
[Z
 [X [N <Who.SNz>]]
 [W
  [W [V <directed.dVz:direct>]]
  [X [N <Rendezvous in Paris.Nz>]]]]
```

A context is then displayed in which the pronoun question answering agent found an answer to an interpretation of the question:

```
Context 12 sense 1.0009 MODE_STOPPED
@19960901160211:19960901160211#12 tensestep 0
last concept [preterit-indicative
[director-of RDP human-interrogative-pronoun]]
last pn:
[Z
 [X [H <Who.Hz:who>]]
 [W
  [W [V <directed.iVz:direct>]]
```

```
[X [N <Rendezvous in Paris.Nz>]]]]
Answer <UA_QuestionPronoun> <question-word-question>
sense 1
Q: [director-of RDP human-interrogative-pronoun]
A: @19920101000000:19920101000001|
[director-of RDP Eric-Rohmer]
```

This interpretation is of high sense (1.0009).

The last interpretation is assigned a sense of 0:

```
Context 11 sense 0 MODE_STOPPED
@19960901160211:19960901160211#11 tensestep 0
last concept [past-participle
[director-of RDP human-interrogative-pronoun]]
last pn:
[Z
 [X [H <Who.Hz:who>]]
 [W
  [W [V <directed.dVz:direct>]]
  [X [N <Rendezvous in Paris.Nz>]]]]
```

Then contexts are pruned. Currently only the context with the highest sense rating
is retained:

```
19960901160212: freed Context 14
19960901160212: freed Context 13
19960901160212: freed Context 11
19960901160212: **** PRUNED UNDERSTANDING CONTEXTS ****
```

```
Context 12 sense 1.0009 MODE_STOPPED
@19960901160211:19960901160211#12
   tensestep 0
```

The answer is then generated and processing completes:

```
19960901160212: QUESTION <UA_QuestionPronoun>
<question-word-question>
@na:na#12|[director-of *RDP
*human-interrogative-pronoun]
19960901160212: INPUT TEXT
<Who directed Rendezvous in Paris?>
19960901160212: ANSWER sense 1
```

```
@19920101000000:19920101000001|
[director-of RDP Eric-Rohmer]
ASPECT focus @19920101000000:19920101000001 obj
  @19920101000000:19920101000001
  [director-of RDP Eric-Rohmer] nonsituational:
<aspect-unknown>
ASPECT <aspect-unknown> tensestep -4 literary 0 =>
  TENSE <preterit-indicative>
19960901160212: **** PROCESS SENTENCE END ****
Deictic stack empty
Time spent on command = 1 seconds
```

The requested output is placed into the outex.txt file:

```
> Who directed Rendezvous in Paris?
SEMANTIC PARSE CONCEPTS:
0.810:[past-participle
 [director-of RDP human-interrogative-pronoun]]
0.810:[preterit-indicative
 [director-of RDP human-interrogative-pronoun]]
0.510:[past-participle
 [director-of RDP rock-group-the-Who]]
0.510:[preterit-indicative
 [director-of RDP rock-group-the-Who]]
ANAPHORIC PARSE CONCEPT:
[past-participle
 [director-of RDP human-interrogative-pronoun]]
ANAPHORIC PARSE CONCEPT:
[preterit-indicative
 [director-of RDP human-interrogative-pronoun]]
ANAPHORIC PARSE CONCEPT:
[past-participle
 [director-of RDP rock-group-the-Who]]
ANAPHORIC PARSE CONCEPT:
[preterit-indicative
 [director-of RDP rock-group-the-Who]]
UNDERSTANDING TREE:
[Z
 [X [H ]]
 [W
  [W [V ]]
  [X [N ]]]]
UNDERSTANDING CONCEPT:
@na:na#12|[preterit-indicative
```

```
[director-of RDP human-interrogative-pronoun]]
Eric Rohmer directed Rendezvous in Paris.
```

Parsing a movie review

All the modifications to ThoughtTreasure are now in place enabling it to parse, understand, and answer questions about simple movie reviews. For example, we invoke the parser on the following review:

```
Article 5464 of rec.arts.movies.reviews:
From: jim@trollope.com (Jim Garnier)
Newsgroups: rec.arts.movies.reviews
Subject: Review of film "Emma"
Date: 01 Sep 1996 15:01:02 GMT

Douglas McGrath directed "Emma". The film is
passionate. It's rated PG.

Emma stars Gwyneth Paltrow as Emma Woodhouse. She's
lovely.

I give it a **** (out of four).
```

ThoughtTreasure extracts the following from the review:

```
[email-address-of Jim
STRING:email-address:"jim@trollope.com"]
[part-of
STRING:Usenet-newsgroup:"rec.arts.movies.reviews"
Usenet]
=*Emma.z/film/
[director-of Emma Douglas-McGrath]
[strong-feeling Emma]
[MPAA-rating-of Emma MPAA-PG]
[actor-of Emma Gwyneth-Paltrow Emma-Woodhouse-]
[beautiful Gwyneth-Paltrow]
[COMMUNICON [good na NUMBER:u:1]
323-340:<**** (out of four)>]
```

We may then ask ThoughtTreasure questions which can be answered based on the extracted information:

```
> Who directed Emma?
Douglas McGrath directs Emma.
> Emma is rated what?
```

```
Emma is rated PG.
> Who stars in the film?
Gwyneth Paltrow stars in Emma.
```

The semantic parser

We now discuss the *semantic parser* in detail. This is invoked by the syntactic parser in order to convert a syntactic parse tree into one or more semantic parse list objects. This parser operates in a recursive fashion, taking a parse node, case frame, and discourse structure as arguments, and producing a list of list objects.

The top semantic parsing function invokes an appropriate subfunction depending on the type of parse node, which may be one of the following:

```
constituent (having one or two child parse nodes)
lexical entry
name
timestamp range
telephone number
media object
product
number
communicon
attribution
email header
table
```

Case frames

Case frames are data structures used to hold intermediate results from semantic parsing to be used in further semantic parsing. For example, given the following syntactic parse tree:

```
[Z
 [X Jim Garnier]
 [W [W [W [V connected]]
       [X the aerial]]
    [Y to the television set]]]
```

Jim Garnier connected the aerial to the television set.
the semantic parser first parses the subject noun phrase, indirect object prepositional phrase, and object noun phrase, entering the meanings of these phrases into a case frame:

```
case    concept prep
        _____  ____
{subj:      Jim    }
{obj:   antenna    }
{iobj:  TV-set to }
```

The verb *connected* is then parsed by consulting this case frame in order to create
the list object [connect Jim antenna TV-set].

Case frames consist of a sequence of *entries*. Each entry consists of a case,
concept, parse node (the argument prepositional phrase or noun phrase), and other
information.

ThoughtTreasure case frames are temporary data structures used in semantic
parsing and not to be confused with the case frames of Fillmore (1968) or
Jackendoff (1972) used to represent the meanings of all sentences in terms of a
small number of roles such as agent, patient, source, goal, instrument, and so on.
The ThoughtTreasure equivalent to this level of representation is the list object,
where thematic roles are represented economically by their position in the list:

```
thematic role position
_____ _____
Predicate           0
Actor               1
Source              2
Destination       2,3
Location            3
Goal              2,4
Time                5
...
```

(The above are typical; the assignment of thematic roles to list positions depends
on the particular predicate.) Thus the list object:

```
[go Jim grocery-story deli-store]
(Jim went from the grocery to the deli.)
```

is a shorthand notation for:

```
[Predicate:    go
 Actor:        Jim
 Source:       grocery-store
 Destination: deli-store]
```

However, the ThoughtTreasure list object is not considered to be a canonical "semantic representation" of the "deep structure" of a sentence, but merely the starting point for further understanding by the understanding agency in terms of various other representations such as grids, timestamp ranges, planning agent states, emotional data structures, and so on. The meaning of a sentence depends on what task is being performed, and different tasks may call for different representations. Therefore, there is no requirement in ThoughtTreasure that sentences such as:

```
Jim broke the TV with the ray gun.
The ray gun broke the TV.
The TV broke.
```

be represented in a unified fashion.

Semantic Cartesian product

A constituent consisting of two children PN1 and PN2 is generally parsed by taking the *semantic Cartesian product* of the two children, which consists of recursively parsing the meaning of PN1, and then recursively parsing the meaning of PN2 for each of the parsed meanings of PN1. When PN2 is parsed, the meaning of PN1 is available in the case frame. The algorithm in more detail is:

```
SemCartesianProduct(PN1, PN2, CF1, CASE):

. Set OBJS1 = SemParse(PN1, CF1).
. Set R = empty list.
. For each OBJ1 in OBJS1:
  . CF2 = CF1 augmented with {CASE: OBJ1}.
  . OBJS2 = SemParse(PN2, CF2).
  . Append OBJS2 to R.
. Return R.
```

For example, in order to parse the sentence:

```
[Z [X Jim] [W ate]]
```

the semantic parser is first recursively invoked on:

```
[X Jim]
```

resulting in two possible meanings:

```
Jim1
Jim2
```

The semantic parser is then recursively invoked on:

```
[W ate]
```

with the case frame:

```
{subj: Jim1}
```

which produces the list of objects:

```
[eat1 Jim1]
[eat2 Jim1]
```

Then the semantic parser is invoked on `[W ate]` with the case frame:

```
{subj: Jim2}
```

which produces the list of objects:

```
[eat1 Jim2]
[eat2 Jim2]
```

The final result of the parse is:

```
[eat1 Jim1]
[eat2 Jim1]
[eat1 Jim2]
[eat2 Jim2]
```

Parsing maximal projections

Maximal projections whose heads are adjectives, nouns, prepositions, and verbs, are parsed using a procedure called *theta marking* (Chomsky, 1982).

Adding arguments to the case frame

Consider how the sentence:

```
[Z [X [NAME Jim]] [W [W [V spoke]]
   [Y [R to] [X [NAME John]]]]]
```

is parsed. The semantic parser is first invoked on the sentence, which consists of a noun phrase and a verb phrase, and an empty case frame CF. The sentence is parsed by taking the semantic Cartesian product of the following arguments:

```
PN1:   [X [NAME Jim]]
PN2:   [W [W [V spoke]] [Y [R to] [X [NAME John]]]]
CF1:   CF
CASE:  subj
```

This results in a recursive call to the semantic parser on PN1 which returns Jim, and then the semantic parser is recursively invoked on:

```
PN:   [W [W [V spoke]] [Y [R to] [X [NAME John]]]]
CF:   case    concept
      _____ _____
      {subj:     Jim}
```

(For simplicity, the handling of names as intensions is ignored here.) This verb phrase is then parsed by again taking the semantic Cartesian product of its components:

```
PN1:   [Y [R to] [X [NAME John]]]
PN2:   [W [V spoke]]
CF1:   case    concept
       _____ _____
       {subj:     Jim}
CASE:  iobj
```

The semantic parser is invoked on PN1, returning $John$ and the parser is then invoked on:

```
PN:   [W [V spoke]]
CF:   case    concept prep
      _____ _____ ____
      {subj:     Jim     }
      {iobj:     John  to}
```

All parse nodes having only one child such as PN are parsed by recursing on that child:

```
PN:    [V spoke]
CF:    case    concept prep
       _____ _____ ____
       {subj:     Jim     }
       {iobj:     John  to}
```

Theta marking is then performed, as descibed in the next section, producing the result list object:

```
[speak Jim John]
```

Above we discussed how arguments are collected by taking appropriate semantic Cartesian products in the following situations:

```
structure    PN1 PN2 case
_____   ___ ___ ____
[Z ?X ?W]     ?X  ?W subj
[W ?W ?Y]     ?Y  ?W iobj
```

Arguments to the maximal projections of verb, adjective, noun, and preposition are similarly collected in the following situations:

```
structure    PN1 PN2 case
_____   ___ ___ ____
VERB:
[W ?W ?X]     ?X  ?W obj

ADJECTIVE:
[E ?E ?X]     ?X  ?E obj
[E ?E ?Y]     ?Y  ?E iobj
[X ?X ?E]     ?X  ?E aobj-postposed
[X ?E ?X]     ?X  ?E aobj-preposed

NOUN:
[X ?X1* ?X2] ?X1 ?X2 iobj prep=of
[X ?X ?Y]     ?Y  ?X iobj
[X ?D ?X]     ?D  ?X dobj

PREPOSITION:
[Y ?R ?X]     ?X  ?R pobj
* must be the genitive construction [X [X ...] [9 s]]
```

Preposition parse nodes are parsed simply by returning the `pobj` contained in the case frame:

```
PN:        [R to]
CF:        case      concept
           _____  _____
           {pobj:    John}
```

RESULT: John

Prepositions contribute to meaning elsewhere: (1) in theta marking where they serve to flag particular `iobj` arguments, and (2) in adjunct parsing.

Some movement phenomena are handled as follows:

```
structure                 PN1 PN2 case               example
_____  ___ ___ _____   _____
[W [W [W ?] ?X] ?E]*  ?X  ?E  aobj-predicative       Is she cheerful?
[W [W [W ?] ?H] ?E]*  ?H  ?E  aobj-predicative       Is Karen cheerful?
[W ?W ?X]*                ?X  ?W  subj               Aimé-je ?
[Z ?Y ?Z]                ?Y  ?Z  iobj               To the house she went.
[Z ?E ?W]                ?E  ?W  obj                How big is the house?
[Z ?X ?E]                ?X  ?E  aobj-predicative   The house, big.
```

`* must pass tests for inversion`

Recursion on only one of the child parse nodes is performed in the following situations:

```
structure   recurse on   comments
_____  _____   _____
[?1 ?2]           ?2     singleton node
[E ?D ?E]         ?E     determiner ignored
[W ?W ?E]         ?E     copula ignored
[Y ?B ?Y]         ?Y     adverb ignored for now
[Y ?R ?TSR]     ?TSR     timestamp range, ignore preposition
[W ?W ?0]         ?W     expletive, ?0 is added to case frame
```

Theta marking

Theta marking for a meaning object O linked to a lexical entry LE of parse node PN with argument structure AS, and a case frame CF, is as follows:

1. If O is a copula, invoke copula parsing with O, AS, and CF.
2. Otherwise, invoke noncopula theta marking on O, AS, and CF.

For example, theta marking is invoked with:

```
O:   connect
LE:  connect* to+.Véz/
PN:  [V connected]

AS:  <connect>.<Vz> <> <connect>
       1:      subj
       2:      obj
       3:      iobj              to. Rz
```

```
CF: case     concept prep
    _____  _____ ____
    {subj:       Jim     }
    {obj:     antenna    }
    {iobj:    TV-set to }
```

The argument structure specifies the mapping between positions of the result object [connect Jim antenna TV-set] and cases of the case frame.

Noncopula theta marking

Theta marking for an object O, argument structure AS, and case frame CF proceeds as follows:

1.   Clear the *theta marked flag* in each entry of CF. This flag indicates whether an entry has been theta marked in this procedure.
2.   If O is a predicate (AS is non-empty), set O1 to the object returned by applying predicate theta marking to O, AS, and CF. Otherwise, set O1 to O.
3.   Set R to the result of invoking adjunct parsing on O1 and CF.
4.   Apply the theta criterion: If any entry for the cases obj, iobj, or expl is not theta marked, return an empty result. Otherwise, return R.

Parsing predicates

Predicate theta marking for an object O, argument structure AS, and case frame CF proceeds as follows:

1.   Create a result object O1. Set its predicate to O.

2. For each entry of AS consisting of a result object position I, case C, lexical entry LE, subcategorization restriction SR, and optionality flag OPT:
    1. If C is `expl` (expletive): Retrieve the entry E of CF whose case is `expl` and whose parse node contains LE. If no such entry is found, return an empty result; otherwise, set the theta marked flag of E and continue with the next iteration of the loop (nothing is added to O1 because this is an expletive element). Otherwise:
    2. Retrieve the entry E from CF whose theta marked flag is false, whose case is C, whose lexical entry is LE, and whose parse node satisfies the subcategorization restriction SR.
    3. If such an entry E is not found: If OPT is false, return an empty result; otherwise, set position I of O1 to `na` and continue with the next iteration of the loop. Otherwise, if an entry E is found:
    4. Set the theta marked flag of E.
    5. Set position I of O1 to the concept of E.
3. If O1 disobeys selectional restrictions, return an empty result. Otherwise, return O1.

A parse node PN satisfies a subcategorization restriction SR when PN is of the appropriate structure and the auxiliary verb of PN is of the appropriate tense and mood:

SR	description	PN example
none	NP or PP	[X him] or [Y to him]
÷	indicative	[Z (that) he goes]
o	subjunctive	[Z (that) he go]
ï	infinitive	[Z (for him) to go]
±	present participle	[Z (him) going]

Parsing adjuncts

Adjunct parsing for an object O1 and case frame CF is as follows:

1. Set R to a list of objects containing the single element O1.
2. For each entry E of CF whose theta marked flag is false:
    1. If the case of E is `iobj`: Set R1 to the empty list. For each meaning object PO linked to the preposition of the prepositional phrase parse node of E, and for each element O1' of R1, if O1' satisfies the selectional restriction on the first argument of PO

and the concept O2 of E satisfies the selectional restriction on the second argument of PO, add the list object [PO O1' O2] to R1. If R1 is nonempty, set the theta marked flag of E and set R to R1. Otherwise:

2.   If the case of E is `tsrobj`, update the timestamp range of each element of R to the timestamp range concept of E and set the theta marked flag of E.

3.   Return R.

For example, when parsing the adjective *happy* in the sentence:

```
François is happy for Jacques.
```

the case frame contains:

case	concept	prep
{aobj-predicative:	Francois	}
{iobj:	Jacques	for}

Two meanings were defined for the lexical entry *happy*:

```
==happy-for//happy* for+.Az/
==happiness//happy.Az/
```

All the case frame entries are theta marked in the first case, resulting in:

```
[happy-for Francois Jacques]
```

In the second case, only the `aobj-predicative` case is theta marked, leaving the `iobj` case still unmarked. The following meaning was defined for the preposition *for*:

```
=====prep-because-of//for.Rz/
```

Adjunct parsing retrieves this meaning, theta marks the `iobj`, and returns the concept:

```
 [prep-because-of
  [happiness Francois]
  Jacques]
```

Parsing copulas

Copula parsing for an object O, argument structure AS, and case frame CF is as follows:

1. Retrieve the entry ES of CF whose case is `subj`, the entry EO of CF whose case is `obj`, and the entry EIO of CF whose case is `iobj`. (The exact algorithm depends on the argument structure AS.)
2. If ES, EO, and EIO are found (and there are no other entries in CF), invoke equative role parsing.
3. Otherwise, if ES and EO are found (and there are no other entries in CF), CS is the concept of ES, CO is the concept of EO, and CS is an interrogative pronoun, return the list object `[O CS CO]`. For example: `[standard-copula human-interrogative-pronoun Jim]` (Who is Jim?)
4. Otherwise, if ES and EO are found (and there are no other entries in CF), invoke ascriptive attachment parsing.
5. Otherwise, copula parsing was unsuccessful, so invoke noncopula theta marking.

Parsing equative roles

Equative role parsing for case frame entries ES, EO, and EIO is as follows:

1. Let CS be the concept of ES, CO the concept of EO, CIO the concept of EIO, and LE the lexical entry in the parse node of EO. For example:

CS	CO	CIO	LE
Bill-Clinton	President-of	United-States	President.áz/
Bill-Clinton	nationality-of	United-States	citizen.àz/

2. Set O1 to the list object `[CO CIO CS]` or `[CO CS CIO]` depending on whether the role feature in LE is "á" or "à":
```
[President-of United-States Bill-Clinton]
[nationality-of Bill-Clinton United-States]
```
(The role feature is associated with the particular meaning CO of LE.)
3. If O1 disobeys selectional restrictions, return an empty result. Otherwise, return O1.

Parsing ascriptive attachments

Ascriptive attachment parsing for case frame entries ES and EO is as follows:

1. Let CS be the concept of ES, CO the concept of EO, and LE the lexical entry in the parse node of EO.
2. If LE is not marked with "þ", return an empty result. Otherwise:
3. Retrieve attachments of CO from the database. For example:

```
CS: Bill-Clinton
CO: United-States
LE: American.þz/
attachments: [attachment-rel-of country nationality-of]
             [attachment-rel-of polity residence-of]
```

The United States is both a polity and country, so there are two possible attachment meanings: Bill Clinton lives in the United States, or Bill Clinton is a citizen of the United States.

4. Set R to the empty list.
5. For each attachment consisting of filler F and relation REL: Set O1 to the list object [REL CS F]. If O1 obeys selectional restrictions, add O1 to R.
6. Return R:

```
[nationality-of Bill-Clinton United-States]
[residence-of Bill-Clinton United-States]
```

Parsing compound tenses

Compound tenses are defined in the tense ontology via phrase structure rules such as the following, enabling the production of arbitrarily complex structures:

```
future-perfect -> aux-have:future + past-participle    will have been
   future -> aux-will:present-indicative + infinitive   will have
      infinitive -> inflection feature "f"              have
   past-participle -> inflection feature "d"            been

present-progressive ->
      aux-be:present-indicative + present-participle    am being
   present-indicative -> inflection features "pG"        am
   present-participle -> inflection feature "e"          being
```

Compound tenses are parsed as follows: A nonleaf verb phrase node PN is parsed by recursively parsing the children PN1 and PN2 of PN into tenses T1 and T2, finding a rule whose right-hand side matches PN1 and T1 and PN2 and T2, and returning the left-hand side of that rule. A leaf verb parse node L is parsed by finding a rule whose right-hand side matches the inflection features of L and returning the left-hand side of the rule.

For example:

```
->[W [W [W [V will.pG]]][V have.f]] [V been.d]]
--->[W [W [V will.pG]]][V have.f]]
----->[W [V will.pG]]]
------->[V will.pG]
<-------present-indicative
<-----present-indicative
----->[V have.f]
<-----infinitive
<---future
--->[V been.d]
<---past-participle
<-future-perfect
```

Compound tenses may also contain adverbs, pronouns (for French), and prepositions (for English infinitives with *to*).

Compound tenses are generated in the reverse fashion. Adverbs including negatives (such as *not* in English and *ne*, *pas*, *rien* in French) are generated in the appropriate position.

The following English compound tenses are defined (shown in second person plural, where applicable):

```
infinitive: [W [V be]]
infinitive-with-to: [W [R to][W [V be]]]
past-infinitive: [W [W [V have]][V been]]
past-infinitive-with-to: [W [W [R to][W [V have]]][V been]]
present-participle: [W [V being]]
past-participle: [W [V been]]
past-present-participle: [W [W [V having]][V been]]
progressive-past-participle: [W [W [V been]][V being]]
pluperfect-indicative: [W [W [V had]][V been]]
conditional-perfect: [W [W [W [V would]][V have]][V been]]
past-past-recent: [W [W [W [V had]][B just]][V been]]
preterit-indicative: [W [V were]]
preterit-subjunctive: [W [V were]]
do-past: [W [W [V did]][V be]]
past-progressive: [W [W [V were]][V being]]
perfect-indicative: [W [W [V have]][V been]]
perfect-subjunctive: [W [W [V have]][V been]]
past-future-near: [W [W [W [V were]][V going]][W [R to][W [V be]]]]
conditional: [W [W [V would]][V be]]
```

```
conditional-progressive: [W [W [W [V would]][V be]][V being]]
past-recent: [W [W [V were]][B just]]
present-indicative: [W [V are]]
do-present: [W [W [V do]][V be]]
present-progressive: [W [W [V are]][V being]]
present-process-progressive: [W [W [V are in the process of]][V
being]]
present-subjunctive: [W [V be]]
imperative: [W [V be]]
future-near: [W [W [W [V are]][V going]][W [R to][W [V be]]]]
future-perfect: [W [W [W [V will]][V have]][V been]]
future-perfect-progressive:
  [W [W [W [V will]][V have]][W [W [V been]][V being]]]
future: [W [W [V will]][V be]]
future-progressive: [W [W [W [V will]][V be]][V being]]
should-simple: [W [W [V should]][V be]]
should-progressive: [W [W [W [V should]][V be]][V being]]
should-perfect-simple: [W [W [W [V should]][V have]][V been]]
should-perfect-progressive:
  [W [W [W [W [V should]][V have]][V been]][V being]]
```

The following French compound tenses are defined (shown in second person
plural, where applicable):

```
infinitive: [W [V attendre]]
infinitive-with-to: past-infinitive: [W [W [V avoir]][V attendu]]
past-infinitive-with-to: present-participle: [W [V attendant]]
past-participle: [W [V attendu]]
past-present-participle: [W [W [V ayant]][V attendu]]
pluperfect-indicative: [W [W [V aviez]][V attendu]]
pluperfect-subjunctive: [W [W [V eussiez]][V attendu]]
preterit-anterior: [W [W [V eûtes]][V attendu]]
conditional-perfect: [W [W [V auriez]][V attendu]]
past-past-recent: [W [W [V veniez]][W [R de][W [V attendre]]]]
imperfect-indicative: [W [V attendiez]]
imperfect-subjunctive: [W [V attendissiez]]
past-progressive: simple-past: [W [V attendîtes]]
perfect-indicative: [W [W [V avez]][V attendu]]
perfect-subjunctive: [W [W [V ayez]][V attendu]]
past-future-near: [W [W [V alliez]][V attendre]]
conditional: [W [V attendriez]]
past-recent: [W [W [V venez]][W [R de][W [V attendre]]]]
present-indicative: [W [V attendez]]
present-process-progressive: [W [W [V êtes en train de]][V attendre]]
present-subjunctive: [W [V attendiez]]
imperative: [W [V attendez]]
future-near: [W [W [V allez]][V attendre]]
future-perfect: [W [W [V aurez]][V attendu]]
future: [W [V attendrez]]
double-compound-perfect-indicative:
  [W [W [W [V avez]][V eu]][V attendu]]
double-compound-pluperfect-indicative:
```

```
[W [W [W [V aviez]][V eu]][V attendu]]
double-compound-future-perfect:
  [W [W [W [V aurez]][V eu]][V attendu]]
double-compound-preterit-anterior:
  [W [W [W [V eûtes]][V eu]][V attendu]]
double-compound-conditional-perfect:
  [W [W [W [V auriez]][V eu]][V attendu]]
double-compound-perfect-subjunctive:
  [W [W [W [V ayez]][V eu]][V attendu]]
double-compound-pluperfect-subjunctive:
  [W [W [W [V eussiez]][V eu]][V attendu]]
double-compound-past-participle:
  [W [W [W [V ayant]][V eu]][V attendu]]
double-compound-past-infinitive:
  [W [W [W [V avoir]][V eu]][V attendu]]
```

Tense generation and parsing may be tested by typing `testcomptense` in the ThoughtTreasure shell.

Associated with each tense in the tense ontology is a *tensestep* used to order tenses.

Here are a few representative examples:

compound tense	tensestep	example
pluperfect-indicative	-7	I had gone
past-past-recent	-5	I had just gone
preterit-indicative	-4	I went
past-future-near	-3	I was going to go
past-recent	-1	I just went
present-indicative	0	I go
future-near	1	I am going to go
future	3	I will go

Also stored are the subjunctive and progressive versions of each tense for French, American English, and British English, and normal and literary style:

```
present-indicative
```

```
  eng-progressive-of=present-progressive
  US-eng-subjunctive-of=present-subjunctive
  UK-eng-subjunctive-of=should-simple
  fr-subjunctive-of=present-subjunctive
```

```
imperfect-indicative
```

```
  fr-subjunctive-of=present-subjunctive
  fr-literary-subjunctive-of=imperfect-subjunctive
```

. . .

In generation, these are employed to convert a tense into an appropriate tense as specified by subcategorization restrictions. In parsing, they are employed to simplify various tenses to the nonprogressive indicative.

Parsing verbs

The compound tense parsing algorithm returns the compound tense T, and pointers to the auxiliary verb parse node PNA and main verb parse node PNM. Given this information and a case frame CF, a verb is parsed as follows:

1. Set R to the empty list.
2. For each meaning O linked to the lexical entry LE of PNM:
    1. If O is an auxiliary verb object, continue (with the next iteration of this loop). Otherwise:
    2. If T is a progressive tense and LE is marked with the no progressive filter feature "Ô", continue. Otherwise:
    3. Add to R the result of invoking theta marking on O, PNM, and CF.
3. Return R.

Parsing nouns

A noun parse node PN is parsed as follows, given a case frame CF:

1. Set R to the empty list.
2. For each meaning O linked to the lexical entry LE of PN with argument structure AS:
    1. Retrieve the determiner concept DET from the dobj case of CF. If it is not present in CF, set DET to an empty object.
    2. If O is a predicate (AS is non-empty, as in a nominalization such *Jim's connection of the antenna to the TV*), then set R1 to the result of invoking theta marking on O, PN, and CF. Otherwise, set R1 to the result of invoking noun adjunct parsing on O and CF.

3. Expand any attachments in R1: Set R2 to the empty list. For each O1 in R1, if LE is marked with "þ", retrieve attachments of O1 from the database:

```
O1: United-States
LE: American.þz/
attachments: [attachment-rel-of country nationality-of]
             [attachment-rel-of polity residence-of]
```

```
O1: grocer
LE: grocer.þz/
attachment: [attachment-rel-of grocer occupation-of]
```

For each relation REL in an attachment, add to R2 the list object [such-that human [REL human O1]]:

```
[such-that human [nationality-of human United-States]]
[such-that human [residence-of human United-States]]
(an American)
```

```
[such-that human [occupation-of human grocer]]
(a grocer)
```

Otherwise, if LE is not marked with "þ", add O1 to R2. Set R1 to R2.

4. Wrap R1 in determiners and modify the score of R1 based on the filter features "k" (takes definite article) and "É" (takes an empty article): Set R2 to the empty list. For each O1 in R1, add to R2 a non-empty O2 as follows:

LE feat	DET	score	O2
	interrogative-determiner	1.0	[question-element O1 DET]
	determiner	1.0	[DET O1]
k	definite-article	1.0	O1
k	empty	0.7	O1
k	indefinite-article	0.5	O1
k	possessive-determiner	0.0	empty
k	anything else	0.2	O1
É	empty	1.0	O1
É	possessive-determiner	0.0	empty
É	anything else	0.5	O1
	anything else	1.0	O1

Set R1 to R2.

5. Append R1 to R.

3. Return R.

A noun adjunct O is parsed given case frame CF as follows:

1. If the concept IO is retrieved from the iobj case of CF whose preposition is *of*, as in:

```
O:   apartment
CF:  case    concept prep
     _____  _____ ____
     {iobj:  Jim     of }
IO:  Jim
```

```
the apartment of Jim
```
invoke genitive parsing with a genitive object of IO and a nongenitive object of O.

2. Otherwise, invoke adjunct parsing on O and CF.

Parsing adjectives

Adjectives arise in three syntactic environments in ThoughtTreasure:

Predicative
The semantic parser has been (recursively) invoked with a verb phrase consisting of a verb phrase and an adjective phrase, and a case frame CF1:

```
[W ?1 ?2] where ?1 = [W ...] and ?2 = [E ...]
```

```
Example: Karen [W [W [V is]] [E [A cheerful]]].
```

A new case frame CF2 is created by augmenting CF1 with a copy of the subj entry of CF1 whose case is aobj-predicative:

```
CF1:
{subj: Karen}
```

```
CF2:
{subj: Karen}
{aobj-predicative: Karen}
```

The semantic parser is then recursively invoked on the adjective phrase ?2 and CF2.

Preposed epithetic
The semantic parser has been invoked with a noun phrase consisting of an adjective phrase and a noun phrase, and a case frame CF1:

```
[X ?1 ?2] where ?1 = [E ...] and ?2 = [X ...]
```

```
Example: [X [E [A cheerful]] [X [NAME Karen]]]
```

This is parsed by taking the semantic Cartesian product with PN1 = ?2, PN2 = ?1, CF1, and CASE = `aobj-preposed`.

Postposed epithetic

The semantic parser has been invoked with a noun phrase consisting of a noun phrase and an adjective phrase, and a case frame CF1:

```
[X ?1 ?2] where ?1 = [X ...] and ?2 = [E ...]
```

This is parsed by taking the semantic Cartesian product with PN1 = ?1, PN2 = ?2, CF1, and CASE = `aobj-postposed`.

When the semantic parser is invoked with an adjective parse node PN and case frame CF, it examines CF to determine what kind of `aobj` is present. Then for each meaning O linked to the lexical entry of PN with filter features F, if F is compatible with the type of `aobj` (preposed epithetic, postposed epithetic, predicative), theta marking is invoked on O, PN, and CF.

Inside noncopula theta marking, a different result is generated for predicative and epithetic adjectives:

```
Predicative:
[cheerful [such-that human [NAME-of human
NAME:"Karen"]]]
(cheerful Karen)

Epithetic:
[such-that human [cheerful human] [NAME-of human
NAME:"Karen"]]
(Karen is cheerful)
```

Parsing adverbs

Arguments to adverbs are contained in the `bobj` entry of the case frame. They are collected in the following situations, via a semantic Cartesian product:

structure	PN1	PN2	case
[E ?B ?E]	?E	?B	bobj
[E ?E ?B]	?E	?B	bobj
[Z ?B ?Z]	?Z	?B	bobj
[Z ?Z ?B]	?Z	?B	bobj

An adverb node PN is parsed as follows given a case frame containing the `bobj` entry with concept BC:

1. Create an empty list of objects R.
2. For each meaning O linked to the lexical entry of PN:
    1. If O is an interrogative adverb (such as *where*, *when*, and others stored in the adverb ontology), add the list object `[O  BC]` to R. Otherwise:
    2. If O is an adverb of absolute negation (*not* in English and *pas* in French), add the list object `[O  BC]` to R. Otherwise:
    3. If O is a first adverb of absolute negation (*ne* in French), add BC to R. Otherwise:
    4. If O is an adverb of absolute degree, use O to modify the weight of BC according to the value of O specified in the ontology:

```
o                                       example      value-of
```

o	example	value-of
adverb-of-highest-degree	totally	1.0
adverb-of-extremely-high-degree	extremely	0.9
adverb-of-high-degree	very	0.7
adverb-of-average-degree	somewhat	0.5
adverb-almost	nearly	0.35
adverb-of-low-degree	slightly	0.2
adverb-of-near-negation	barely	0.05
adverb-of-negation	not at all	0.0

text	input BC	modified BC
slightly unfriendly	[friendly Jim -1.0]	[friendly Jim -0.2]
extremely friendly	[friendly Jim 1.0]	[friendly Jim 0.9]

        Add the modified BC to R. Otherwise:

    5. Otherwise, add the list object `[O  BC]` to R.
3. Return R.

Parsing conjunctions

Arguments to conjuctions are collected by semantic Cartesian product in the following situations:

structure	PN1	PN2	case
[E ?E1 ?E2*]	?E1	?E2	mkobj2
[E ?K ?E]	?E	?K	mkobj1
[X ?X1 ?X2*]	?X1	?X2	mkobj2
[X ?K ?X]	?X	?K	mkobj1
[Y ?Y1 ?Y2*]	?Y1	?Y2	mkobj2

```
[Y ?K ?Y]        ?Y   ?K   mkobj1
[Z ?Z1** ?Z2]    ?Z2  ?Z1  kobj2
[Z ?Z1 ?Z2**]    ?Z1  ?Z2  kobj2
[Z ?K ?Z]        ?Z   ?K   kobj1
```

```
*  must begin with a coordinating conjunction
** must begin with a conjunction
```

A conjunction node PN with case frame CF is parsed as follows:

1. Retrieve the concept A1 from the `mkobj1` or `kobj1` case of CF, and A2 from the `mkobj2` or `kobj2` case.
2. Create an empty list of objects R.
3. For each meaning O linked to the lexical entry of PN, add the list object `[O A1 A2]` to R.
4. Return R.

Parsing genitives

The genitive constructions:

```
(1) [X
       [X [D the] [X [N President]]]
       [Y [R of] [X [N France]]]]
    the President of France
```

```
(2) [X [X [X [N France]] [9 s]] [X [N President]]]
    France's President
```

are parsed by first parsing the component genitive and nongenitive noun phrases (*France* and *President*). A *genitive parsing* algorithm is then invoked on each pair <GEN, NONGEN> of result objects, which operates as follows: If NONGEN is a relation, its selectional restrictions are retrieved:

```
[r1 President-of country]   SR1 = country
[r2 President-of human]     SR2 = human
```

If GEN is an instance of SR1, an intension is created and returned of the form:

```
[such-that SR2 [NONGEN GEN SR2]]
```

which in this case is:

```
[such-that human [President-of France human]]
```

If NONGEN is not a relation, as in:

```
(1) [X
      [X [D the] [X [N apartment]]]
      [Y [R of] [X [NAME Jim]]]]
    the apartment of Jim
```

```
(2) [X [X [X [NAME Jim]] [9 s]] [X [N apartment]]]
    Jim's apartment
```

then an intension of the form [such-that NONGEN [of NONGEN GEN]] is returned:

```
[such-that apartment [of apartment Jim]]
```

The anaphoric parser later passes this to the intension resolver in order to resolve it into a concrete object.

In order to parse the construction:

```
[X [D his] [X [N sister]]]
```

the semantic parser passes the concept:

```
[possessive-determiner sister-of]
```

to the anaphoric parser which resolves the determiner into a GEN object and invokes genitive parsing on GEN and the NONGEN object (sister-of).

Parsing appositives

In order to parse an appositive structure of the form:

```
[X ?X1 ?X2]
```

the parse node ?X1 is parsed resulting in a list of objects OBJS1, and ?X2 is parsed resulting in a list of objects OBJS2. Then all pairs of objects in OBJS1 and OBJS2 are considered. O1 and O2 will be generally be intensions which need to be merged:

```
text: the grocer Mrs. Püchl
O1:   [such-that human [occupation-of human grocer]]
O2:   [such-that human [NAME-of human NAME:"Mrs. Püchl"]]
MERGED RESULT:
[such-that human
  [NAME-of human NAME:"Mrs. Püchl"]
  [occupation-of human grocer]]
```

The result of parsing the appositive is the list of all such merged results.

Parsing relative clauses

Relative clauses are subordinate clauses containing a verb which is missing one of its arguments such as the subject, object, or indirect object. The missing argument is passed in from the main clause.

Parsing nominal relative clauses

In order to parse a nominal relative clause, the semantic parser is recursively invoked on the subordinate clause with a case frame containing an entry for the missing argument (subject, object, or indirect object). The case and concept of the entry depend on the type of nominal relative pronoun:

pronoun class	case	concept
nominal-rel-pronoun-subj	subj	
nominal-rel-pronoun-obj	obj	
nominal-rel-pronoun-iobj	iobj	
nominal-rel-pronoun-human		human
nominal-rel-pronoun-nonhuman		nonhuman

Each nominal meaning of a pronoun is defined in the linguistic ontology as an instance of one of the top classes and one of the bottom classes shown above. For example:

lexical entry	class	class
who	nominal-rel-pronoun-subj	nominal-rel-pronoun-human
who	nominal-rel-pronoun-obj	nominal-rel-pronoun-human
what	nominal-rel-pronoun-subj	nominal-rel-pronoun-nonhuman
what	nominal-rel-pronoun-obj	nominal-rel-pronoun-nonhuman
that which	nominal-rel-pronoun-subj	nominal-rel-pronoun-nonhuman
that which	nominal-rel-pronoun-obj	nominal-rel-pronoun-nonhuman
...		

For indirect objects in French, the preposition built into the pronoun is added to the case frame entry for later use in recognizing (theta marking) the prepositional phrase verb argument:

pronoun class	built in preposition	examples
nominal-rel-pronoun-iobj-of	prep-of (de)	de quoi, ce dont
nominal-rel-pronoun-iobj-to	prep-to (à)	ce à quoi

Each list object OBJ resulting from the semantic parse of the subordinate clause is then wrapped in an intension as follows:

```
[such-that CONCEPT OBJ]
```

where CONCEPT is the human or nonhuman concept added to the case frame above. The resulting intensions are then returned as the semantic parse of the nominal relative clause.

For example, in order to parse the relative clause:

```
[X [X [H what]] [Z Jim likes]]
```

the subordinate clause:

```
[Z Jim likes]
```

is recursively parsed with a case frame of:

```
{obj: nonhuman}
```

The recursive call to the parser returns:

```
[like Jim nonhuman]
```

and the caller then returns:

```
[such-that nonhuman [like Jim nonhuman]]
```

Parsing nonnominal relative clauses

A nonnominal relative clause is parsed via a semantic Cartesian product: Given a relative clause consisting of a noun phrase and subordinate clause, such as:

```
noun phrase:            [X a friend]
subordinate clause:    [W who likes theater]
```

the noun phrase is first parsed. Then for each returned meaning OBJ1 of the noun phrase, the subordinate clause is parsed with a case frame containing an entry whose concept is OBJ1 and whose case and preposition depend on the structure of the subordinate clause and the type of relative pronoun:

subordinate clause	case	preposition
`[W ?3]` (who likes theater)	subj	none
`[Z [X [H ?2]] [Z ?3]]` (whom she took to the theater)	obj	none
`[Z [X [H ?2]] [Z ?3]]` (dont elle parle)	iobj	that built into ?2
`[Z [Y [R ?1] [X [H ?2]]] [Z ?3]]` (of which she spoke)	iobj	?1

Each result OBJ2 of the subordinate clause parse is wrapped in an intension:

```
[such-that OBJ1 OBJ2]
```

and added to a list which is eventually returned as the parses of the relative clause.

For example, in order to parse:

```
[X [X a movie]
   [Z [X [H which]] [Z Jim likes]]]
```

the noun phrase:

```
[X the movie]
```

is parsed into the concept:

```
film
```

Then the subordinate clause:

```
[Z Jim likes]
```

is parsed with a case frame of:

```
{obj: film}
```

which returns:

```
[like Jim film]
```

The caller then returns:

```
[such-that film [like Jim film]]
```

Parsing other parse nodes

The following types of nodes are parsed simply by returning the list of meanings
linked to the lexical entry of the node:

```
[D ...]   determiner
[H ...]   pronoun
[U ...]   interjection
[x ...]   canned sentence
```

Name parse nodes are parsed by wrapping them in an intension as follows:

```
[NAME "Karen Garnier"] =>
[such-that human [NAME-of human "Karen Garnier"]]
```

What is shown as a quoted character string above is actually a name data structure
broken down into first name, middle name, last name, and so on.
In order to parse the nodes created by text agents such as the time, telephone
number, media object, product, price, communicon, and French polity text agents,
the object or objects contained in those nodes are simply returned—the parsing
work has already been done by the text agent. The processing by the semantic
parser of email headers and attributions was described in the text agent chapter.

The anaphoric parser

The *anaphoric parser* takes an object from the semantic parser and resolves the
following types of *anaphoric entities* contained within the object: pronouns,
indefinite and definite articles, possessive determiners, and arbitrary intensions
resulting from language constructions involving adjectives, relative clauses,
genitives, names, and so on.

The semantic parser takes a syntactic parse tree PN and produces a number of parse objects. The anaphoric parser is then invoked for each parse object O, returning one or more result objects for each O. In particular, given an object O and parse node PN, the anaphoric parser performs the following steps:

1. If O is an anaphoric entity, resolve O and PN into one or more result objects using methods to be described below, and return those objects. Otherwise:

2. Invoke the anaphoric parser recursively on each object and parse node element of O. Elements of O are linked to the parse node from which they derive:

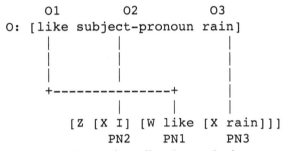

```
        O1            O2           O3
O: [like subject-pronoun rain]
        |             |            |
        |             |            |
        |             |            |
     +---------------+            |
        |       |     |
    [Z [X I] [W like [X rain]]]
        PN2     PN1      PN3
```

Each recursive call to the anaphoric parser returns a list of objects:

```
anaphoric-parser(O1, PN1) -> O1.1
anaphoric-parser(O2, PN2) -> O2.1 O2.2 O2.3
anaphoric-parser(O3, PN3) -> O3.1 O3.2
```

3. Return the Cartesian product of all the returned results:

```
[O1.1 O2.1 O3.1]
[O1.1 O2.1 O3.2]
[O1.1 O2.2 O3.1]
[O1.1 O2.2 O3.2]
[O1.1 O2.3 O3.1]
[O1.1 O2.3 O3.2]
```

Antecedents

Associated with each actor in a context is a list of *antecedent* data structures, one per input or output channel. Each antecedent structure contains: (1) the features (gender, number, and person) of the last lexical entry used to refer to the actor on the channel, and (2) integer activation levels corresponding to references to the actor in different syntactic environments as proposed by Huls, Bos, and Claassen (1995):

major
Subject, direct object, or indirect object of a sentence.
subject
Subject of a sentence.
nested
Anything other than a top-level subject, direct object, or indirect object. For example, a direct object inside a relative clause.

The sum of the major, subject, and nested activation levels is called the *salience* of the antecedent, which can be used by the anaphoric parser to choose among alternative referents (say, of a pronoun or definite noun phrase).

At the end of an understanding cycle, anaphors are *committed* as follows: All activation levels are first *decayed*—decremented by 1. Then antecedents are *refreshed* as follows: The understanding agency produces a result concept linked with its parse tree, such as:

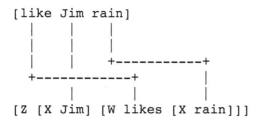

```
[like Jim rain]
   |    |    |
   |    |    |
   |    |    +-----------+
   +-----------+         |
        |        |       |
[Z [X Jim] [W likes [X rain]]]
```

For each actor contained in the result concept (such as Jim and rain), the actor's antecedent structures in the context are refreshed (or created for the first time) for all relevant channels. Relevant channels are those which are the same language and dialect as the input, including the input channel. Other channels receive a translation of the input, produced by the generator, instead of an exact copy of the input; decaying and refreshing antecedents is a responsibility of the generator. Refreshing consists of (1) incrementing the appropriate activation levels by different amounts—major by 3, subject by 2, nested by 1—and (2) setting the features to those of the lexical entry linked to the actor. If the above example is the first sentence, then the activation levels are updated to:

	gender	number	person	major	subject	nested	SALIENCE
Jim	M	S	3	3	2	0	5
rain	C	S	3	3	0	0	3

If the next sentence were:

```
Jim spoke with John.
```

then the activation levels would first be decayed:

	gender	number	person	major	subject	nested	SALIENCE
Jim	M	S	3	2	1	0	3
rain	C	S	3	2	0	0	2

and then refreshed:

	gender	number	person	major	subject	nested	SALIENCE
Jim	M	S	3	5	3	0	8
rain	C	S	3	2	0	0	2
John	M	S	3	3	0	0	3

Jim has the highest salience, so use of the pronoun *he* at this point is most likely referring to Jim, though the possibility that it is referring to John needs to be considered as well. (Note that, despite the name "actor", physical objects are actors in a context as are humans, at least for the purpose of storing antecedents.)
A separate antecedent structure must be maintained for each channel since the features and syntactic environment of a reference to an actor might be different on different channels. For example, Jim might be the indirect object on one channel and the subject on another:

```
Parisian French channel:   "La pluie plait à Jim."
American English channel:  "Jim likes rain."
```

Note also that in French, grammatical gender differs from sex, so that for example, a feminine word such as *personne* can be used to refer to a male in one sentence, and then a masculine word can be used in another sentence.

Resolving pronouns

Resolution of a pronoun O given the corresponding parse node PN proceeds as follows:

1. If O is an expletive pronoun (such as *it* in *it is raining*), return O. Otherwise:
2. Retrieve the gender G, number N, and person P of the pronoun from PN.

3. If P = 1 or 2 (*I* and *you*), invoke deictic pronoun resolution. Otherwise:
4. If English and O is *there*, invoke *class specific* pronoun resolution on O, PN, and the class `location`. Otherwise:
5. If English, G = neuter, and N = singular (*it*, *itself*, and so on), invoke class specific pronoun resolution on O, PN, and the class `nonhuman`. Otherwise:
6. If English and N = plural (*they*), invoke class specific pronoun resolution on O, PN, and the classes `human` and `nonhuman`. Otherwise:
7. If English and N = singular (*he*, *she*), invoke class specific pronoun resolution on O, PN, and the class `human`. Otherwise:
8. If French, invoke class specific pronoun resolution on O, PN, and the classes `human` and `nonhuman`.

Class specific resolution of a third-person pronoun O given gender G, number N, and class C consists of combining the results from intersentential and intrasentential pronoun resolution.

Resolving third-person pronouns

Intersentential resolution of a third-person pronoun O given gender G, number N, and class C is as follows:

1. Create an empty list of objects R.
2. For each actor A in the context, if A's antecedent for the current channel has positive salience and its features match G and N, then add A to R. Unknown features match any feature:

```
f1  f2  matches?
```

f1	f2	matches?
S	S	yes
P	S	no
?	S	yes
S	P	no
P	P	yes
?	P	yes
S	?	yes
P	?	yes
?	?	yes

3. If N = singular, return R. Otherwise:
4. Create an empty list of objects S.
5. For each actor A in the context, if A's antecedent for the current channel has positive salience, A's number is singular, and (in French) it is not the case that G is feminine and A's gender is masculine, then add A to S. (The

actual rule in French is that a plural pronoun referring to a group is masculine if one or more of its members are male.)

6. Add to R an and object consisting of the elements of S (or, if there is only one element in S, that element).
7. Return R.

For example, given the subject pronoun *they* and the antecedents:

actor	gender	number	person
John	M	S	3
Peter	M	S	3
Mary	F	S	3
jeans		P	3

the anaphoric parser returns the following two objects:

```
jeans
[and John Peter Mary]
```

The first object results from step 2 above since *they* is a plural pronoun which can refer to nonhumans, and jeans is nonhuman and plural. The second object results from step 5 above since *they* is an unknown gender pronoun which can refer to humans, and the humans John, Peter, and Mary are all singular. The pronoun *he* would result in:

```
John
Peter
```

The French masculine plural subject pronoun *ils* would produce one result object:

```
[and John Peter Mary]
```

since a pair of jeans is referred to in the singular in French. The feminine pronouns *elle* and *elles* would result in:

```
Mary
```

The masculine singular pronoun *il* would result in:

```
John
Peter
jeans
```

since *jean* is masculine in French.

The method for intrasentential pronoun resolution is similar to that for intersentential pronoun resolution, except that instead of looping through actors in the context, the method loops through all objects contained inside the top-level object from the semantic parse.

Resolving deictic pronouns

Deixis refers to the function of linguistic entities such as pronouns (*I*, *you*), adverbs (*now*, *here*, *there*), and pronouns (*this*, *that*) which relate an utterance to the location in space and time of the utterance (Lyons, 1977, pp. 636-690). ThoughtTreasure has a *deictic stack* which is stored in the discourse data structure. Each element of the stack consists of:

- a *list of speakers*,
- a *list of listeners*,
- *now*, the narration time or the timestamp of the discourse such as the current time in a realtime discourse, or the time an email message was sent or a file was modified,
- a *discourse class* such as `computer-file` or `online-chat`, and
- a *flag* indicating whether the discourse is taking place in real time.

When a discourse is first started (such as when the `parse` command is issued from the ThoughtTreasure shell), an entry is pushed onto the initially empty deictic stack. The speaker defaults to `Jim` and the listener to ThoughtTreasure, but these can be modified using the `-speaker` and `-listener` arguments of the `parse` ThoughtTreasure shell command. Entries are pushed onto the deictic stack whenever a new deictic context is introduced by an email message header or attribution of a quotation. When the message or quotation ends, the entry is popped off the deictic stack.

Resolution of a deictic pronoun O given number N and person P proceeds as follows:

1. If N is singular and P is first person, return each speaker in the top entry of the deictic stack as a possible meaning. (If there are multiple speakers, it is left to the understanding agency to decide which speaker is intended by *I*.)
2. If N is singular and P is second person, return each listener in the top entry of the deictic stack.

3.   If N is plural and P is first person (as in *we*), return a single result object consisting of the and of all the speakers in the top entry of the deictic stack (or simply the speaker if there is only one).
4.   If N is plural and P is second person, return a single result object consisting of the and of all the listeners in the top entry of the deictic stack (or simply the listener if there is only one).

Thus given:

```
O:         subject-pronoun
P:         1
N:         S
speakers:  Jim
listeners: Karen
```

this method returns:

```
Jim
```

Resolving articles and intensions

Intensions of the following forms:

```
[ARTICLE CLASS]
[such-that CLASS PROPOSITION PROPOSITION ...]
[such-that [ARTICLE CLASS] PROPOSITION PROPOSITION ...]
```

result from the following linguistic entities and constructions

```
Indefinite articles:
  a ball
  [indefinite-article ball]

Definite articles:
  the ball
  [definite-article ball]

Adjectives:
  a red ball
  [such-that [indefinite-article ball] [red ball]]
  the red ball
  [such-that [definite-article ball] [red ball]]

Relative clauses:
  a ball which is red
  [such-that [indefinite-article ball] [red ball]]
```

```
the ball which is red
[such-that [definite-article ball] [red ball]]
```

Genitives:
```
[such-that human [President-of France human]]
France's President
```

Attachments:
```
[such-that human [nationality-of human United-States]]
an American
```

Names:
```
Jim
[such-that human [NAME-of human NAME:"Jim"]]
```

The above entities and others may be combined:

```
Genitive + name:
  [such-that human
   [sister-of
    [such-that human [NAME-of human NAME:"Jim Garnier"]]
    human]]
  Jim Garnier's sister

Appositive + name:
  [such-that human
   [nationality-of human United-States]
   [NAME-of human NAME:"Karen Garnier"]]
  Karen Garnier, an American

Appositive + genitive + name:
  [such-that human
   [sister-of
    [such-that human
     [NAME-of human NAME:"Jim Garnier"]] human]
   [NAME-of human NAME:"Karen Garnier"]]
  Karen Garnier, Jim Garnier's sister

Adjective + attachment:
  [such-that human
   [cheerful human]
   [nationality-of human United-States]]
  a cheerful American
```

An intension consisting of a class C, propositions P, and optional article A is handled as follows:

1. If A is an indefinite article, invoke the *intension instantiator* on C and P. Otherwise, if A is a definite article or no article is supplied:
2. Invoke the intension resolver on C and P. If A is a definite article, instruct the intension resolver to look only for actors in the context or physical

objects near an actor in the context. Otherwise, all atomic objects in the program are considered.

3. If the intension resolver returned results in the step above, return them. Otherwise:

4. Invoke the intension instantiator on C and P.

(The return values from invocations are returned by the invoker, unless otherwise specified.)

The intension instantiator is invoked on class C and propositions P in order to create and return a new object of class C for which the propositions P are true. It operates as follows:

1. If C is human and P contains a NAME-of proposition, learn a new human O with the specified name. Otherwise, if C is human, learn a new human O with an unknown name. Otherwise, create a new instance O of C.

2. For each element P1 of P, assert P1 with O substituted for C.

3. Return O.

Learned humans are added to the database and dumped to the file outhuman.txt.

When the anaphoric parser resolves an intension into an extension, it returns the original intension in addition to the extension, since some understanding agents (especially question answering agents) require intensions.

Resolving possessive determiners

In order to resolve a possessive determiner of the form:

```
[possessive-determiner CLASS]
```

pronoun resolution is first invoked on the possessive determiner object and its parse node (which contains the gender, number, and person features of the determiner). Then genitive parsing is invoked on each result of pronoun resolution and CLASS. Any results of genitive parsing which are intensions are recursively processed by the anaphoric parser.

For example, given the object:

```
[possessive-determiner foot]
```

```
where possessive-determiner.person = 1
      possessive-determiner.number = S
(my foot)
```

pronoun resolution is invoked which returns the speaker:

```
Jim
```

Genitive parsing is then invoked with a genitive object of Jim and a nongenitive object of foot. Genitive parsing returns:

```
[such-that foot [of foot Jim]]
```

Since this is an intension it is passed to the anaphoric parser, which resolves it into two possibilities:

```
Jim-left-foot
Jim-right-foot
```

Applying coreference constraints

Coreference between noun phrases is not possible when those noun phrases are in certain syntactic environments relative to one another (Lasnik, 1976; Bresnan, 1978, p. 11). The rule for when coreference is possible makes use of the following definitions of relations between nodes in a parse tree: First, A *c-commands* B if and only if:

```
(1) A is not an ancestor of B,
(2) B is an ancestor of A, and
(3) the parent of A is an ancestor of B.
```

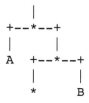

Second, A *governs* B (Chomsky, 1986, pp. 8-9) if and only if:

```
(1) A c-commands B, and
(2) there is no barrier between A's parent and B
(noninclusive).
```

Thus in the following tree, if C is a barrier, then A does not govern B; if C is not a barrier, A does govern B:

```
        |
   +--*--+
   |     |
   A   +--C--+
       |     |
       *     B
```

Barriers are defined in the section on X-bar theory in the chapter on the syntactic component.

Then, coreference between two noun phrases NP1 and NP2 is possible (Allen, 1995, p. 369) if and only if:

```
(1) NP2 is a reflexive pronoun and NP1 governs NP2,
(2) NP2 is a nonreflexive pronoun and NP1 does not
govern NP2, or
(3) NP2 is not a pronoun and NP1 does not c-command
NP2.
```

Before the anaphoric parser returns a list of result objects, it removes any objects not satisfying the coreference constraints: For every pair of anaphors associated with a result object O built during anaphoric parsing, if A1 and A2 refer to the same concept, and coreference is not possible between the noun phrases of A1 and A2, then O is removed from the list of result objects.

Generating pronouns

In the generator, pronoun concepts are selected appropriately based on case, language, and whether the noun phrase refers to the same concept as the subject-called a *same-as-subject flag*:

```
case         sas pronoun concept        examples

subj             subject-pronoun        He goes, Il va
obj          0   direct-object-pronoun He washes her, Il lave la*
             1   reflexive-pronoun     He washes himself, Il lave se*
iobj         0   disjunctive-pronoun He talks to her, Il parle à elle**
             1   reflexive-pronoun   He talks to himself, Il parle à se*
complement le    reflexive-pronoun     He is himself
                 disjunctive-pronoun   It's him, C'est lui
```

```
1e = English and same as subject
* fixed by transformations to "il la lave, il se lave, il se parle"
** fixed by a transformation to "il lui parle" (including replacement
of disjunctive-pronoun with indirect-object-pronoun)
```

In particular, given a concept O, case C, and same-as-subject flag SAS, a pronoun is selected as follows:

1. If O is contained in the list L of speakers in the top entry of the deictic stack: Select a pronoun concept P according to the above table. Return a pronoun lexical entry for P inflected in the first person and with number equal to that stored along with O in L. (If O is a human the number is singular; if O is a group the number is plural.) Otherwise:

2. If O is contained in the list L of listeners in the top entry of the deictic stack: Select a pronoun concept P according to the above table. Return a pronoun lexical entry for P inflected in the second person and with number equal to (1) singular if the speaker uses *tu* with O (in French), otherwise (2) the number stored along with O in L. Who uses *tu* with whom is defined via the `tutoyer` relation. Otherwise:

3. If C is `subj` and O is a location, set the pronoun concept P to `pronoun-there-location`. Otherwise, set P according to the above table.

4. Invoke the pronoun resolution algorithm used in parsing to find a list of objects RO along with their saliences which P (with gender, number, and person derived from the noun lexical entry passed in by the generator) could be used to refer to (on the current input/output channel in the best context). If O is the unique object with the highest salience in RO, then use of P to refer to O is probably acceptable, so return a pronoun lexical entry for P.

5. Otherwise, return an empty result. (In this case, the generator will generate the noun lexical entry rather than a pronoun.)

Generating articles

Articles are generated according to the following table:

condition	article	example
~N & ~H	empty-article	cheerfully
N & GA & P & z	empty-article	Elephants are smart.
N & GA & P & y	definite-article	Les éléphants sont intelligents.
N & GE & S	INDEFINITE-ARTICLE	An elephant is a mammal.
N & GE & P & z	empty-article	Elephants are mammals.
N & GE & P & y	definite-article	Les éléphants sont des mammifères.
É	empty-article	France
N & k	definite-article	the United States
H & k	definite-article	le même
H	empty-article	one
KNOWN	definite-article	the car
TRUE	INDEFINITE-ARTICLE	a car

Conditions are scanned starting from the top until a true condition is reached. The corresponding article is then returned. The symbols used in the conditions are:

```
~  = not
&  = and
H  = pronoun
N  = noun
S  = singular
P  = plural
y  = French
z  = English
k  = definite article filter feature
É  = empty article filter feature
m  = mass noun filter feature
GA = generality-ascriptive aspect
GE = generality-equative aspect
TRUE = true
```

KNOWN is true when the concept being generated is either a member of the list of listeners or speakers on top of the deictic stack, an actor in the context, or a physical object (spatially) near an actor in the context. INDEFINITE-ARTICLE is determined according to the table:

condition	article	example
m & z	empty-article	milk
m & y	partitive-article	du lait
TRUE	indefinite-article	a car

Particular articles may also be forced by the calling routine.

Aspect

The notion of *aspect* is more important in story understanding than tense. For example, the following sentences are in a past tense (tensestep = -4):

```
(1) Jim slept for 8 hours. (= Jim has slept for 8
hours.)
(2) Jim slept. (= Jim was sleeping.)
```

In (1), the reader understands that the event is over and the narrative is going to proceed to something else—Jim is no longer asleep in story time. But in (2), the reader understands that the event is unfolding—Jim is asleep in story time.

Aspect representation

The aspect ontology of ThoughtTreasure is based on the French/English aspect ontology of Boulle (1978, 1988, 1992), and Perrin (1995).

Aspect is classified in terms of the following contrasts:

Accomplished vs. inaccomplished
Accomplished is concerned with a result rather than the process which led to that result:

```
Peter repaired the table.
Peter has repaired the table.
```

Inaccomplished focuses on an unfolding process:

```
Peter is repairing the table.
Peter was repairing the table.
```

Aorist vs. situational
Aorist aspect is detached from what is described, as in a narrative of a succession of events:

```
Jim opened the door and walked in.
I take two eggs and beat them in this bowl.
```

Situational is involved in the described situation:

```
I am beating the eggs.
Come look, I have painted the wall.
```

In English, aorist aspect is typically expressed by simple verb forms, while situational aspect is typically expressed by verb forms with an auxiliary.

State vs. action

Whether the described concept is a state—perhaps a change of state:

```
The house belongs to my grandmother.
I became happy.
```

or an action:

```
Jim is painting the wall.
We used to go see movies.
```

Different types of aspect are then classified according to the above contrasts:

aspect	Acc/ Ina	Aor/ Sit	Sta Act	example
inaccomplished-situational	Ina	Sit	Act	He is painting the wall.
accomplished-situational	Acc	Sit	Act	He has painted the wall.
accomplished-aorist	Acc	Aor	Act	He painted the wall.
habitude			Act	He used to paint the wall.
generality		Aor		Red is a color.
performative		Aor	Act	I apologize.
demonstration		Aor	Act	I place the rabbit in the box.
stable-situation			Sta	He is happy.
changed-situation			Sta	He became happy.

Aspect is expressed in natural language using various devices. Aspect may be *grammaticalized*, as when it is expressed by verb tense:

```
He has painted the wall.
Il a été content.
```

Aspect may be *lexicalized*, as when it is expressed by means of a particular verb:

```
He became happy.
```

Or aspect may be expressed using arbitrary constructions such as adverbials:

```
All of a sudden, he was happy.
He was happy for 8 hours.
```

A set of tense-aspect relations is used in ThoughtTreasure to store mappings between compound tense and aspect. A given aspect maps to several tenses depending on tensestep:

```
     English                         French
     ─────────────────────────       ─────────────────────────
     inaccomplished-situational
-4   past-progressive                imperfect-indicative
     past-process-progressive        past-process-progressive
 0   present-progressive             present-indicative
     present-process-progressive     present-process-progressive
 3   future-progressive

     stable-situation
-4   preterit-indicative             imperfect-indicative
 0   present-indicative              present-indicative

     changed-situation
-4   preterit-indicative             perfect-indicative
 0   present-indicative              present-indicative

     accomplished-situational
-4   perfect-indicative              perfect-indicative

     accomplished-aorist
-4   preterit-indicative             perfect-indicative

     aspect-habitude
-4   conditional                     imperfect-indicative
```

Note the lack of a one-to-one mapping between French and English tenses. (Not shown above are additional mappings for the literary style, such as the *passé simple* for the accomplished aorist aspect.)

Aspect in parsing

Aspect is used in parsing and generation. Understanding agents make use of aspect in determining how to adjust the simulation and story time. For example, consider the following sentences, their tense, and the possible types of aspect corresponding to the tense:

sentence	parsed tense	possible aspect
(1) Jim has slept.	perfect-indicative	accomplished-situational
(2) Jim was sleeping.	past-progressive	inaccomplished-situational
(3) Jim slept.	preterit-indicative	accomplished-aorist
		inaccomplished-situational

Given (1), the only possibility is that the sleeping has been accomplished, so Jim's sleep agent can be set to the awake state in the simulation. Given (2), the only possibility is that the sleeping is inaccomplished and taking place in the current story time, so Jim's sleep agent is set to the asleep state in the simulation. Given (3), both choices are possible. In this case, the simulation may be split into two contexts. In one context the sleep agent is set to awake, and in the other it is set to asleep. The agent may also simply choose the more likely possibility (the inaccomplished situational use of the preterit is more common in literary style) and adjust the state later if it proves to be in error.

Aspect in generation

The generator makes use of aspect in order to select an appropriate tense for expressing a concept.

Generating adverbial clauses of time

Given two concepts:

```
@19940606080000:19940606081000|[take-shower Jim]
@19940606080500:19940606080502|[put-on Jim hat]
```

ThoughtTreasure could generate them separately as:

```
Jim took a shower.
Jim put a hat on.
```

However, since the timestamp ranges are available for the concepts, a better strategy is to generate them as a single sentence composed of two clauses connected by a conjunction expressing the temporal relation between them (see Grevisse, 1986, section 1081; Greenbaum and Quirk, 1990, section 15.14; ter Meulen, 1995, p. 14; Gagnon and Lapalme, 1996):

```
While Jim was taking a shower, he put a hat on.
Jim put a hat on while he was taking a shower.
```

In order to generate the above sentences, ThoughtTreasure (1) determines the temporal relation T between the two concepts O1 and O2, (2) determines the aspect of O1 and O2, (3) determines the tense of O1 and O2, and (4) generates O1 and O2 using the selected tenses connected by a lexical entry for the temporal relation T.

Following the convention that a temporal relation assertion of the form:

```
[?relation ?1 ?2]
```

is expressed in natural language as one of the following forms:

```
?relation ?1, ?2      (While Jim X, Jim Y.)
?2 ?relation ?1       (Jim Y while Jim X.)
?2, ?relation ?1      (Jim Y, while Jim X.)
```

the basic ThoughtTreasure temporal relation ontology is as follows:

```
relation                          English      timestamp ranges of ?1, ?2

                                               ---------time---------->
posteriority
  disjoint-posteriority           after        (---1---)    {---2---}
  adjacent-posteriority           as soon as   (---1---){---2---} & 1 short
  persistent-posteriority         since        ({---1-2---- & ---2---now
priority
  disjoint-priority               before       {---2---}    (---1---)
  adjacent-priority               until        {---2---}(---1---) & 2 long
simultaneity
  subset-simultaneity             when         {--(-1-2-)--}
  superset-simultaneity           while        (--{-1-2-}--)
  equally-long-simultaneity       while        ({---1-2---)} & long
```

In persistent posteriority, 1 and 2 start at roughly the same time and 2 extends to the present.

Given two timestamp ranges TSR1 and TSR2, and the narration time NOW, the temporal relation between TSR1 and TSR2 is determined as follows:

```
. Set SEP1_2 = TSR2.START - TSR1.STOP.
. Set DUR1 = duration of TSR1 (with minimum 1).
. Set DUR2 = duration of TSR2 (with minimum 1).
. Set TIMESCALE = DUR1 + DUR2.
. If ((absolute value of SEP1_2)/TIMESCALE) < .1 and
     DUR1 <= 60 seconds:
  . Return adjacent-posteriority.
```

```
. If TSR1.STOP < TSR2.START:
  . Return disjoint-posteriority,
. Set SEP2_1 = TSR1.START - TSR2.STOP.
. If ((absolute value of SEP2_1)/TIMESCALE) < .1 and
      DUR2 >= 60 seconds:
  . Return adjacent-priority.
. If TSR2.STOP < TSR1.START:
  . Return disjoint-priority.
. Set SEP_START = TSR1.START - TSR2.START.
. Set SEP1_NOW = NOW - TSR1.START.
. If SEP1_NOW > 86400 seconds and
      ((absolute value of SEP_START)/TIMESCALE) < .1 and
      (TSR2.STOP = NA or TSR2.STOP > NOW):
  . Return persistent-posteriority.
. If TSR2 is contained in TSR1:
  . Return superset-simultaneity.
. If TSR1 is contained in TSR2:
  . Return subset-simultaneity.
. Set SEP_STOP = TSR1.STOP - TSR2.STOP.
. If ((absolute value of SEP_START)/TIMESCALE) < .1 and
      (SEP_STOP/TIMESCALE) < .1 and
      DUR1 >= 60 seconds:
  . Return equally-long-simultaneity.
. Return and.
```

In a sentence such as:

```
While Jim was taking a shower, he put a hat on.
```

each clause sets up an environment for the other: When considering *he put a hat on*, the timestamp range which serves as the environment is that of *Jim was taking a shower*:

```
he put a hat on                    _           TSR2
Jim was taking a shower     _____    TSR1
```

From the perspective or *focus* of TSR1, the situation TSR2 is of accomplished aspect since TSR2 is contained within TSR1, and of short duration with respect to it. Conversely, with TSR2 as a focus, the situation TSR1 is of inaccomplished aspect since TSR1 is a process which has already begin and which has not yet ended when viewed from TSR2.

Therefore, the aspect of two objects O1 and O2 with timestamp ranges TSR1 and TSR2, for which [T O1 O2] where T is a temporal relation, is determined by determining (1) the aspect of O1 with respect to focus TSR2 and a false situational flag, and (2) the aspect of O2 with respect to focus TSR1 and a situational flag which is true if and only if T = persistent-posteriority. Recall that persistent posteriority is the situation in which TSR2 extends into the present. A perfect tense is usually employed to express situational aspect in this situation:

```
Ever since I started learning French, I have been
interested in linguistics.
```

The aspect of O with respect to a focus timestamp range TSRF and situational flag SIT is determined as follows:

```
. If SIT is true:
  . Return accomplished-situational.
. Set TSRO = timestamp range of O.
. Set OP = predicate of O.
. If TSRO extends from negative to positive infinity
(or is na:na):
  . If OP is an attribute:
    . Return generality-ascriptive.
  . If OP is a copula or set relation:
    . Return generality-equative.
  . Return generality.
. If OP is a state:
  . If TSRF is properly contained in TSRO:
    . Return stable-situation.
  . If TSRO.START is contained in TSRF or
          TSRO.STOP is contained in TSRF:
    . Return changed-situation.
. If OP is an action:
  . If TSRF is properly contained in TSRO:
    . Return inaccomplished-situational.
  . If TSRO is contained in TSRF or
          TSRF is greater than TSRO:
    . Return accomplished-aorist.
. Return unknown.
```

Having determined the aspect A1 of O1 with timestamp range TSR1, and the aspect A2 of O2 with timestamp range TSR2, and given the temporal relation T for which [T O1 O2] and the narration time NOW, the tenses of O1 and O2 are determined as follows:

1. Determine the *spread* S among TSR1.START, TSR1.STOP, TSR2.START, TSR2.STOP, and NOW, defined as the maximum timestamp minus the minimum timestamp, with a minimum of 60 seconds.

2. *Situate the main clause relative to now*: If T is persistent-posteriority, set TENSESTEP2 to -4; otherwise, set TENSESTEP2 to the tensestep of TSR2.START with respect to NOW and S.

3. Retrieve the tense TENSE2 for aspect A2 and TENSESTEP2 from the database. For example, the English tense for inaccomplished situational aspect and tensestep -4 is the past progressive.

4. *Situate the subordinate clause relative to the main clause*: If T is a simultaneity relation, or T is adjacent posteriority, adjacent priority, or persistent posteriority, or TSR1 is contained in TSR2, or TSR2 is contained in TSR1, set STEPDIST to 0. Otherwise, set STEPDIST to the tensestep distance of TSR1.START and TSR2.START with respect to S.

5. Retrieve the tense TENSE1 for aspect A1 and TENSESTEP2 + STEPDIST from the database.

6. The results are TENSE1 and TENSE2.

The *tensestep* of a timestamp TS1 with respect to another timestamp TS2 and a spread S is determined as follows:

```
. Set R = (TS1 - TS2)/S.
. If (absolute value of R) < .02:
  . Return 0.      (present)
. If R < 0:
  . If -R < .1:
    . Return -1. (past-recent)
  . Return -4.    (past)
. If R < .1:
  . Return 1.      (future-near)
. Return 3.        (future)
```

The *tensestep distance* of timestamp TS1 and timestamp TS2 with respect to spread S is determined as follows:

```
. Set R = (TS1 - TS2)/S.
. If (absolute value of R) < .02:
  . Return 0.
. If R < 0:
  . If -R < .1:
    . Return -1.
  . Return -2.
```

. If R < .1:
  . Return 1.
. Return 2.

For example, given the objects:

```
O1: @19940606080000:19940606081000|[take-shower Jim]
O2: @19940606080500:19940606080502|[put-on Jim hat]
```

and a narration time or "now" of the following day:

```
19940607000000
```

the temporal relation between the object is determined to be superset simultaneity: the timestamp range TSR2 of O2 is contained in the timestamp range TSR1 of O1. Next, the aspect of O1 is determined to be inaccomplished situational, since TSR2 is properly contained in TSR1. The aspect of O2 is determined to be accomplished aorist, since TSR2 is contained in TSR1. The tense of O2 is then determined to be preterit indicative, which is a tense used to express the accomplished aorist aspect for tensestep -4. The tensestep of O2 is -4 because TSR2 is in the past, relative to the 1-day spread. (A few minutes ago would be considered to be in the recent past relative to a 1-day spread.) The tense of O1 is then determined to be past progressive, which is a tense used to express the inaccomplished situational aspect for tensestep -4. The tensestep of O1 is -4 since the tensestep distance between TSR1 and TSR2 relative to a 1-day spread is 0. The following sentence is thus generated:

```
Jim Garnier put a hat on, while Jim Garnier was taking
a shower.
```

In French, the following is generated:

```
Jim Garnier a mis un chapeau, pendant que Jim Garnier
prenait une douche.
```

If now is instead set to 19940606080501 — when the hat is put on — the following sentences are produced:

```
He puts a hat on, while he is taking a shower.
Il met le chapeau, pendant que il prend une douche.
```

If now is set to the previous day 19940605000000, the following sentences are produced:

```
He will put a hat on, while he will be taking a shower.
Il mettra le chapeau, pendant que il prendra une
douche.
```

As another example, suppose that Jim puts the hat on after taking the shower:

```
@19940606080005:19940606081000|[take-shower Jim]
@19940606081010:19940606081012|[put-on Jim hat]
```

The following is determined:

```
T: disjoint-posteriority
O1 aspect-accomplished-aorist tensestep -4 =>
   preterit-indicative (English)
   perfect-indicative (French)
O2 same as O1
```

The following sentences are generated:

```
He put a hat on, after he took a shower.
Il l'a mis après qu'il a pris une douche.
```

Suppose that putting on a hat for five minutes is immediately followed by a ten-minute shower:

```
@19940606075500:19940606080000|[put-on Jim hat]
@19940606080000:19940606081000|[take-shower Jim]
```

Then the following sentences are generated:

```
He put a hat on, until he took a shower.
Il l'a mis jusqu'à ce que il ait pris une douche.
```

Determining aspect and tense of simple sentences

Given a single object O with timestamp range TSR to be generated, and the narration time NOW, its aspect A is determined according to the algorithm presented above with respect to TSR and a situational flag which is set if the predicate of O is an instance of a goal status. Then, if NOW is contained in TSR, TENSESTEP is set to 0; otherwise TENSESTEP is set to the tensestep of

TSR.START with respect to NOW and the spread among TSR.START, TSR.STOP, and NOW. Then the tense is retrieved for aspect A and TENSESTEP.

The generator

The ThoughtTreasure English and French *generator* takes as arguments a list object, a discourse data structure, a current communications channel (specifying, among other things, the language), and an optional compound tense (which, if not supplied, is determined based on aspect as described above). As output, the generator produces a syntactic parse tree (parse node). A parse tree is converted into text by printing the contents of its leaf nodes in left-to-right depth-first order. Leaf nodes include lexical entries, other types of entities produced by text agents such as names. A punctuation string is also contained in each leaf node.

The operation of the generator is similar to the operation of the semantic and anaphoric parsers, except in reverse. Given a list object:

```
[predicate argument1 argument2 ...]
```

the generator recursively invokes itself in order to convert the arguments into parse trees. It then constructs a parse tree for the predicate which incorporates the parse trees of the arguments. Given an atomic object, the generator constructs a parse tree incorporating a lexical entry linked to that object.

Choices must be made in generation, such as which lexical entry to use to express a concept linked to several lexical entries. Constraints such as language, filter features, and subcategorization restrictions and situation-specific strategies such as those described above for articles and pronouns are applied in order to prune alternatives. If several alternatives remain, one is chosen arbitrarily.

Exercises

1. Verbs in ThoughtTreasure take three types of arguments: The subject noun phrase, the object noun phrase, and the indirect object prepositional phrase. But as Picoche (1995) points out, adjective phrases (ADJPs) can also be verb arguments, as in the sentences:

```
NP be ADJP:
  He's totally ecstatic.          He's what?

NP find NP ADJP:
  They found it somewhat useful.  How useful did they find it?
```

```
He painted the wall bright purple. What color did he paint the
                              wall?
```

In ThoughtTreasure, NP be ADJP is currently handled as a separate sentence type. It would be more elegant—and allow for easier addition of sentence types such as NP find NP ADJP—for adjective phrases to be just another type of verb argument. Define a set of features analogous to "è", "é", and "ë", and modify parsing and generation appropriately.

2. Fix intrasentential pronoun resolution in the anaphoric parser, which fails when an anaphor refers to another entity which is also handled by the anaphoric parser, such as a name.

3. When generating measurements, generate units appropriate to the magnitude (for example, inches for between 1 and 12 inches), and use the correct units for the listener's country. Currently, the program generates all measurements using the standard units.

4. Modify ThoughtTreasure to use a plural verb when *there* is subject and the object of the copula is plural.

5. Modify ThoughtTreasure to understand and/or generate puns.

Binsted and Ritchie (1994) showed that punning riddles such as:

```
Q: What do you call a murderer that has fiber?
A: A cereal killer.
```

can be modeled by templates such as:

```
Q: What do you call a N1 that has N2?
A: A N3 N4.
   where N5 is a homophone of N3 AND
         N5 N4 ISA N1 AND
         N2 is a part of N3
```

In this case:

```
N1 = murderer
N2 = fiber
N3 = cereal
N4 = killer
N5 = serial
```

```
serial is a homophone of cereal
serial killer ISA murderer
fiber is a part of cereal
```

Modify ThoughtTreasure to use the above template to generate riddles—both the question and the answer. ISA and part-of are already available in ThoughtTreasure. Add more items to the database and lexicon. Homophones can be approximated using a spell correction algorithm such as the one described in Chapter 4.

Modify ThoughtTreasure to solve riddles. For example, if asked the question part of a riddle, the program responds with the answer.

Analyze more riddles and implement them by adding more templates to ThoughtTreasure. For example:

```
Q: What kind of emotion has bits?
A: A love byte.

Q: What kind of N1 has N2?
A: A N3 N4.
   where N5 is a homophone of N4 AND
         N3 ISA N1 AND
         N2 is a part of N4 AND
         N3 N5 is a phrase in the lexicon

N1 = emotion
N2 = bits
N3 = love
N4 = byte
N5 = bite
bite is a homophone of byte
love ISA emotion
bits is a part of byte
love bite is a phrase in the lexicon
```

Chapter 7: The planning agency

ThoughtTreasure's *planning agency* simulates a human universe consisting of space, time, and humans and physical objects with mental and other states inside that space and time. The initial state of the simulated universe is defined by the human, grid, and other ontologies, and assertions about the initial location and goals of the human *actors* in the simulation. As a simulation runs, the state of the system is modified—information is asserted to and retracted from the database, and other data structures are modified. The simulation optionally outputs natural language descriptions of actions and states, and ASCII pictures of the contents of grids where action is taking place.

An example simulation

Here is English output for a simulation of the human Jim, who has the goal to watch TV where the TV set is not initially plugged in:

```
Jim is in the bedroom of his rented apartment.
He wants to watch television.
He grasps the three-prong French AC plug of his
KV-X2150B.
He walks to the AC outlet from his KV-X2150B.
He connects to the AC outlet the three-prong French AC
plug of his KV-X2150B.
He lets go of the three-prong French AC plug of his KV-
X2150B.
He walks from the AC outlet to his KV-X2150B.
He grasps the female television connector of his KV-
X2150B.
He walks to the antenna from his KV-X2150B.
He connects to the antenna the female television
connector of his KV-X2150B.
He lets go of the female television connector of his
KV-X2150B.
He walks from the antenna to his KV-X2150B.
He moves to the power switch of his KV-X2150B.
He flips on his KV-X2150B.
...
```

(The simulation takes place in an apartment in Paris and KV-X2150B is the model of TV set. As detailed as this simulation may seem, it is nowhere near as detailed as the real world — we tend to take the detail of our world for granted.)

Here is the ASCII picture generated when Jim walks from the bedroom to the living room of his apartment:

```
&&&&&&&&&&&&&&&&&&&&&&&&&&&&&&&&&&&&&&&&&&&&&&&&&&&&&&&&&&&&&&&&&&&&&&&&&&&&&&&&&&&&&&&&&&
&                                                  wwwwwwwwwwwwwwwwwwwwwwwwwwwwww&
&                                  wwwwwwwwww  tttwsss    ht    Aswccccccccccw&
&                           wwwwwwwwwwwwwwwww      w  tttwmss             wccccccccccw&
&wwwwwwwwwwwwwwwwwwwwwwwwwwwwwwwwwwwwwccccccccw     w      w    smwmss          wcc        w&
&w  11111111 ss   g Ecccc  ssssssssswccccccccw     w      w    smwmss          wcv        w&
&wa 11111111 ss      s     ssssssssswccccccccw     wwww  wwwww  wwmss          wcc        w&
&wA  Ec                    sswccccccccw                        wwwww    wwwwwwwww    wwww&
&w   cc                    sswccccccccw                                             w&
&wr                        sswwwwwwwww                                              w&
&wr                w       *****************************************                w&
&wr                        ************  wwwwwwwwwwwwwwwwwwwwwwwwtttttttttttttl*      lw&
&w           ************           ssw            wtttttttttttttt*                 tw&
&w      ************                ssw            wtttttttttttttt*                  w&
&w ******                   w       ssw            wA    s       *     EEEEEEEEEw&
&w                          w       Rsw            w             *     EEEEEEEEEw&
&w          s               w       sw             wls          *     EEEEEEEEEw&
&w     tttttttttt           wwwww   wwww            w s         *     EEEEEEEEEw&
&wr    sttttttttts     ss   ssw        w            w s        *     EEEEEEEEEw&
&wr    tttttttttt      ss   ssw                     w          *     EEEEEEEEEw&
&wr        s          ss   Aw                       w          *     EEEEEEEEEw&
&w    s               ss   w                        w    E     *     EEEEEEEEEw&
&w tttt     ssssssssss ss  rrw                      w         ttttttEt EEEEEEEEEw&
&w A        ssssssssss ss  rrw      w               w    rrrrr       rrrrr  Aw&
&wwwwwwwwwwwwwwwwwwwwwwwwwwwwww       wwwwwwwwwwwwwwwwwwwwwwwwwwwwwwwwwwwwwwwwwww&

&&&&&&&&&&&&&&&&&&&&&&&&&&&&&&&&&&&&&&&&&&&&&&&&&&&&&&&&&&&&&&&&&&&&&&&&&&&&&&&&&&&&&&&&&&
```

The planning agency may be used to generate stories. In the next chapter, we show how the planning agency is used to model the world when understanding a story. In our movie review application, this capability is useful for understanding the description of the movie's plot.

Sample simulations can be run by typing `simul` into the ThoughtTreasure shell and then typing the number of the desired simulation:

```
NUMBER CHARACTER GOAL
1......Jim.......watch-TV
2......Jim.......attend-performance
3......Jim.......take-shower
4......Jim.......dress
5......Jim.......near-reachable JFK-gate-26
6......Jim.......inside penny1 jar2
7......Martine...near-reachable maison-de-Lucie-Entrance
```

Related work on simulating the human universe includes the TALE-SPIN story generator (Meehan, 1976), the Daydreamer model of human daydreaming (Mueller, 1990), the Oz interactive fiction project (Bates, Loyall, and Reilly, 1992), and bots inside MUD world models (Mauldin, 1994).

Planning agents

Planning agents (PAs) are used in ThoughtTreasure to achieve subgoals on behalf of simulated actors. A planning agent is structured as a finite automaton (Lewis and Papadimitriou, 1981), consisting of a BEGIN state, final SUCCESS and FAILURE states, and intermediate states. Various actions are performed in each nonfinal state: subgoals may be started, conditions may be awaited, and transitions to other states may be effected.

Planning agents are written in C allowing them to make use of the full power of C and ThoughtTreasure in attempting to achieve a goal. For example, the dress planning agent invokes clothing routines and consults the clothing ontology in order to determine in what order to put on clothes and to select matching items of clothing.

Here is a sample description of a planning agent for an actor A with argument P:

BEGIN
Initiate subgoal-a with arguments of A's right hand and a nearby pencil. If it succeeds, go to state 1. If it fails, go to state FAILURE.
1
Initiate subgoal-b with arguments of A's right hand and P. If it succeeds, go to state 2. If it fails, go to state 3.
2
Wait 10 seconds and then go to state 3.
3
Initiate subgoal-c with argument A. If it succeeds, go to state SUCCESS. If it fails, go to state FAILURE.

In this book, we employ a short notation for the above similar to Prolog (Clocksin and Mellish, 1981):

```
goal(A, P) :-
    subgoal-a(RH = FINDP(right-hand, A), FINDO(pencil)),
    subgoal-b(RH, P) ON FAILURE GOTO 3,
    WAIT 10 seconds,
3: subgoal-c(A).
```

The goal of the planning agent is followed by ":-" and the states of the planning agent are separated by commas. Unless otherwise indicated, it is assumed that the first state is the BEGIN state, and that the planning agent proceeds to the following state if a subgoal succeeds and to FAILURE if a subgoal fails. A SUCCESS state at the end is assumed. Static local variables such as RH can be defined and later used.

The FINDP function finds a part of an object of a specified class. The FINDW function finds a whole of an object of a specified class. The FINDO function invokes the space routines in order to find a nearby object of a specified class (and, optionally, owned by a specified actor).

A planning agent may WAIT for a specified duration or WAIT until an object matching a pattern is asserted. The pattern may contain variables. Several events may be awaited:

```
WAIT 10 seconds AND GOTO 100
  OR WAIT something(class1, VAR = class2) AND GOTO 200
```

When one of the events occurs, the state of the planning agent is changed as specified and the other event is no longer awaited. When a subgoal is waiting, it is in the WAITING state.

A special type of planning agent called the *object planning agent* simulates the behavior of physical objects such as electronic devices and household appliances. Unlike standard planning agents, object planning agents (1) are not associated with a subgoal, and (2) do not themselves have a state. Rather, the object simulated by the planning agent has state information which is stored as assertions in the context. A planning agent for a physical object is invoked whenever an assertion is made which involves that object, such as lifting the handset of a phone or pressing a digit key.

Grasper planning agents and containers

A *grasper* is a part of an actor that can be used to grasp objects, such as a hand. Several *grasper planning agents* enable graspers to perform actions such as grasping objects, moving objects, connecting objects, opening containers, placing objects inside containers, and so on.

A grasper G of an actor A can *move* to any object O to which A is *near-reachable*- that is, to any object in the same or an adjacent grid cell as A. In the following grid, a grasper of A can move to O, but a grasper of B cannot move to P:

```
wwwwwwwwwwwwwwwwwwwwwwwwwwwwwwwwwwwwwwwwwwwwwwwwww
w                                                 w
w    ttt       ttt       ttt                       w
w    tOt       tPt       ttt         w             w
     A                               w             w
q              B                     w             w
w    ttt       ttt       ttt         w             w
w    ttt       ttt       ttt         w             w
w                                    w             w
wwwwwwwwwwwwwwwwwwwwwwwwwwwwwwwwwwwwwwwwwwwwwwwwwww
```

In order for a grasper of B to move to P, B first has to become `near-reachable` P, say by walking. When a grasper G moves to an object O, G is asserted to be *near-graspable* O. Note that A `near-reachable` O is defined in terms of the locations of A and O in the grid, while G `near-graspable` O is a state that is asserted and retracted appropriately as G and A move.

Thus in order for a grasper G of A to be `near-graspable` O, A must be `near-reachable` O and G must then move to O:

```
near-graspable(G, O) :-
  near-reachable(A, O),
  move-to(G, O).
```

As a simplification, it is assumed that a grasper is `near-graspable` at most one object at a time. Thus whenever a grasper becomes `near-graspable` an object, any previous `near-graspable` of the grasper is retracted. Whenever an actor A changes grid locations (say by walking or driving), any previous `near-graspables` of any of A's graspers are retracted.

Graspers can *hold* objects. In order for a grasper G to hold an object O, G must *grasp* O:

```
holding(G, O) :-
  grasp(G, O).
```
In order for G to grasp O, G must be `near-graspable` O:
```
grasp(G, O) :-
  near-graspable(G, O).
```

When an actor changes grid locations (say by walking or driving), the grid locations are changed of all objects held by graspers of the actor. For example, suppose the following assertions are true:

```
[at-grid A grid1 locA]
[at-grid O grid1 locO]
[cpart-of G A]
[holding G O]
```

If A changes grid locations by walking:

```
[grid-walk A grid1 locA locA']
```

then the grid locations of both A and O are updated as follows:

```
[at-grid A grid1 locA']
[at-grid O grid1 locA']
```

A grasper G of A can *release* an object O, with the result that G is no longer holding O. Then if A changes grid locations, the location of O remains unchanged:

```
[grid-walk A grid1 locA' locA"] ->
[at-grid A grid1 locA"]
[at-grid O grid1 locA']
```

A grasper can *connect* two objects (such as an antenna to an antenna jack) by holding the first object, moving `near-graspable` the second object, and releasing:

```
connected-to(O1, O2) :-
  connect(G, O1, O2).
connect(G, O1, O2) :-
  holding(G, O1),
  near-graspable(G, O2),
  release(G, O1).
```

There are two types of containers in ThoughtTreasure: *small containers* such as bottles and pockets, and *large containers* such as cars and trains.

Small containers

At any given time, a small container is either *open* or *closed*. In order for a small container to be open, a grasper must open it:

```
open(C) :- action-open(G, C).
```

In order for a grasper to open a small container, the grasper must be **near-graspable** the container:

```
action-open(G, C) :- near-graspable(G, C).
```

Closing a container is analogous:

```
closed(C) :- action-close(G, C).
action-close(G, C) :- near-graspable(G, C).
```

In order for an object O to be *inside* a small container C, C must be open and a grasper G must hold O, move to C, and then release O:

```
inside(O, C) :-
  open(C),
  holding(G, O),
  move-to(G, C),
  release(G, O).
```

In order for a grasper to move to an object which is inside a closed container, the container must first be opened:

```
move-to(G, O) when inside(O, C) :-
  open(C).
```

Objects are removed from small containers as follows: when an object O inside a small container C is held by a grasper G of A and either (1) G moves or (2) A changes grid locations, then the assertion that O is inside C is retracted.

We make some assumptions to simplify the representation and planning of graspers and containers: (1) items held by a grasper cannot have graspers, (2) graspers cannot have graspers, and (3) containers do not nest: an object cannot be inside a container which is inside another container. The following situations are handled:

```
    |   |
    | x |   objects inside small container
    | x |
    +---+

    | x |   objects held by grasper
    | x |
-----+---+
```

244

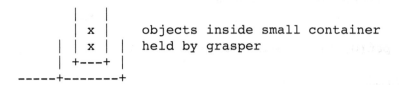

```
    |   |
    | x |        objects inside small container
    | | x | |    held by grasper
    | +---+ |
-----+-------+
```

When a container changes grid locations (say if an actor who is holding the container changes grid locations), the grid locations are changed of the container and all objects inside the container. For example, given the following assertions:

```
[at-grid A grid1 locA]
[at-grid SC grid1 locO]
[at-grid O grid1 locO]
[cpart-of G A]
[holding G SC]
[inside O SC]
```

if A changes grid locations by walking:

```
[grid-walk A grid1 locA locA']
```

then the grid locations of A, SC, and O are updated as follows:

```
[at-grid A grid1 locA']
[at-grid SC grid1 locA']
[at-grid O grid1 locA']
```

Large containers

In order for an actor A to be inside a large container LC, A must be **near-reachable** the large container:

```
inside(A, LC) :-
  near-reachable(A, LC).
```

(We ignore steps such as opening the door of a car, entering it, and sitting down.) Large containers are assumed to occupy a single grid cell.

When a large container changes grid locations, the grid location of each object A inside it is updated (and, recursively, the location of objects held by graspers of A, and the location of objects inside small containers held by graspers of A).

Whenever actor A is no longer `near-reachable` the large container (say as a result of walking), the assertion that it is inside that container is retracted.

Example: Moving a penny from one jar to another

Here is a sample run, showing Jim taking a penny out of a closed jar and putting it in another closed jar. The following states are asserted to be true at 5 am:

```
@0500:na|[at-grid Jim 20-rue-Drouot-4E <gridsubspace 20 78>]
@0500:na|[at-grid penny1 20-rue-Drouot-4E <gridsubspace 18 80>]
@0500:na|[at-grid jar1 20-rue-Drouot-4E <gridsubspace 18 80>]
@0500:na|[inside penny1 jar1]
@0500:na|[closed jar1] @0500:na|[closed jar2]
@0500:na|[at-grid jar2 20-rue-Drouot-4E <gridsubspace 16 82>]
```

(Note that Jim, jar1, and jar2 start out in different locations.) ThoughtTreasure is given the following top-level goal:

```
TOP-LEVEL GOAL [inside penny1 jar2]
```

The simulation is then started. First jar2 must be opened because it is closed:

```
SUBGOAL [open jar2]
SUBGOAL [action-open Jim-right-hand jar2]
SUBGOAL [near-graspable Jim-right-hand jar2]
SUBGOAL [near-reachable Jim jar2]
SUBGOAL [grid-walk Jim 20-rue-Drouot-4E 20 78 16 82]
SUBGOAL [standing Jim na]
SUBGOAL [stand Jim na]
@0500:0502|[stand Jim na]
@0502:inf|[standing Jim na]
@0502:0503|[grid-walk Jim 20-rue-Drouot-4E 20 78 16 82]
RETRACTED @0500:0503|[at-grid Jim 20-rue-Drouot-4E
<gridsubspace 20 78>]
@0503:inf|[at-grid Jim 20-rue-Drouot-4E <gridsubspace 16 82>]
```

(SUBGOAL refers to subgoals that are started; RETRACTED refers to assertions that are retracted; the remaining lines are assertions.) Jim stands up and walks to the location of jar2, which takes a total of 3 seconds. He then moves his right hand to the jar and opens it:

```
SUBGOAL [move-to Jim-right-hand jar2]
SUBGOAL [near-reachable Jim jar2]
@0505:0506|[move-to Jim-right-hand jar2]
@0506:inf|[near-graspable Jim-right-hand jar2]
@0506:0511|[action-open Jim-right-hand jar2]
RETRACTED @0500:0511|[closed jar2]
@0511:inf|[open jar2]
```

Next he goes to jar1 to get the penny:

```
SUBGOAL [holding Jim-right-hand penny1]
SUBGOAL [grasp Jim-right-hand penny1]
SUBGOAL [near-graspable Jim-right-hand penny1]
SUBGOAL [near-reachable Jim penny1]
SUBGOAL [grid-walk Jim 20-rue-Drouot-4E 16 82 18 80]
SUBGOAL [standing Jim na]
@0511:0512|[grid-walk Jim 20-rue-Drouot-4E 16 82 18 80]
RETRACTED @0506:0512|[near-graspable Jim-right-hand jar2]
RETRACTED @0503:0512|[at-grid Jim 20-rue-Drouot-4E
<gridsubspace 16 82>]
@0512:inf|[at-grid Jim 20-rue-Drouot-4E <gridsubspace 18 80>]
```

He opens jar1:

```
SUBGOAL [move-to Jim-right-hand penny1]
SUBGOAL [near-reachable Jim penny1]
SUBGOAL [open jar1]
SUBGOAL [action-open Jim-right-hand jar1]
SUBGOAL [near-graspable Jim-right-hand jar1]
SUBGOAL [near-reachable Jim jar1]
SUBGOAL [move-to Jim-right-hand jar1]
SUBGOAL [near-reachable Jim jar1]
@0516:0517|[move-to Jim-right-hand jar1]
@0517:inf|[near-graspable Jim-right-hand jar1]
@0517:0522|[action-open Jim-right-hand jar1]
RETRACTED @0500:0522|[closed jar1]
@0522:inf|[open jar1]
RETRACTED @0517:0522|[near-graspable Jim-right-hand jar1]
```

He then grasps the penny:

```
@0522:0523|[move-to Jim-right-hand penny1]
@0523:inf|[near-graspable Jim-right-hand penny1]
@0523:0524|[grasp Jim-right-hand penny1]
@0524:inf|[holding Jim-right-hand penny1]
```

He is now holding the penny. He then goes to jar2 in order to put the penny in it:

```
SUBGOAL [move-to Jim-right-hand jar2]
SUBGOAL [near-reachable Jim jar2]
SUBGOAL [grid-walk Jim 20-rue-Drouot-4E 18 80 16 82]
SUBGOAL [standing Jim na]
@0524:0525|[grid-walk Jim 20-rue-Drouot-4E 18 80 16 82]
RETRACTED @0523:0525|[near-graspable Jim-right-hand penny1]
RETRACTED @0500:0525|[inside penny1 jar1]
RETRACTED @0500:0525|[at-grid penny1 20-rue-Drouot-4E
<gridsubspace 18 80>]
@0525:inf|[at-grid penny1 20-rue-Drouot-4E <gridsubspace 16 82>]
```

```
RETRACTED @0512:0525|[at-grid Jim 20-rue-Drouot-4E
<gridsubspace 18 80>]
@0525:inf|[at-grid Jim 20-rue-Drouot-4E <gridsubspace 16 82>]
```

Since Jim is holding the penny, when he moves away from jar1 the penny is no longer inside jar1 and is no longer located at the coordinates of jar1. The penny and Jim are moved to the coordinates of jar2. Finally, Jim moves his hand holding the penny to jar2 and releases:

```
@0526:0527|[move-to Jim-right-hand jar2]
@0527:inf|[near-graspable Jim-right-hand jar2]
SUBGOAL [release Jim-right-hand penny1]
@0527:0528|[release Jim-right-hand penny1]
RETRACTED @0524:0528|[holding Jim-right-hand penny1]
@0528:inf|[inside penny1 jar2]
@0528:inf|[happiness Jim 0.55]
```

Jim is no longer holding the penny and the penny is inside jar2.

Trips

Trips from one location to another are arranged using various modes of transportation such as walking, driving, taking the subway, and flying. Here is a trip planned by ThoughtTreasure from Jim's apartment in Paris to JFK airport in New York, by walking to a subway stop, taking the subway to a bus stop, taking the bus to the airport, and flying across the Atlantic:

```
Trip 19940812092320 19940812205500              na
```

| | action | driver | transport | script | grid | from | to |
	wormhole path		depart	arrive	cost		
*	grid-walk		Jim		20-rue-Dro	apt4d20rd	20-rue-Dro
	yes 19940812092320		19940812092325				
	warp					20-rue-Dro	20-rue-Dro
20-rue-Dro			19940812092325	19940812092326			
	grid-walk		Jim		20-rue-Dro	20-rue-Dro	20-rue-Dro
	yes 19940812092326		19940812092339				
	warp					20-rue-Dro	Richelieu-
20-rue-Dro			19940812092339	19940812092340			
	grid-walk		Jim		Richelieu-	20-rue-Dro	metro-RD-E
	yes 19940812092340		19940812092605				
	warp					Richelieu-	metro-RD-1
metro-RD-E			19940812092605	19940812092606			
	grid-walk		Jim		metro-RD-1	metro-RD-E	metro-RD-B
	yes 19940812092606		19940812093013				
	warp					metro-RD-1	metro-RD-2

```
metro-RD-B          19940812093013 19940812093014
────────────────────────────────────────────────────────────────────────
    grid-walk                    Jim          metro-RD-2 metro-RD-B metro-RD-B
            yes 19940812093014 19940812093416
────────────────────────────────────────────────────────────────────────
* grid-condu          subway subway- metro-RD-2 metro-RD-B metro-RD-B
            yes 19940812095000 19940812095010 <numb;
────────────────────────────────────────────────────────────────────────
        warp                                metro-RD-2 Paris-unde
metro-RD-B          19940812095010 19940812095011
────────────────────────────────────────────────────────────────────────
    grid-condu          subway subway- Paris-unde metro-RD-B metro-Oper
            yes 19940812095011 19940812095054
────────────────────────────────────────────────────────────────────────
        warp                                Paris-unde Opera-area
metro-Oper          19940812095054 19940812095055
────────────────────────────────────────────────────────────────────────
    grid-condu          subway subway- Opera-area metro-Oper metro-Oper
            yes 19940812095055 19940812095500
────────────────────────────────────────────────────────────────────────
*   grid-walk                    Jim          Opera-area metro-Oper rue-Scribe
            yes 19940812095500 19940812095748
────────────────────────────────────────────────────────────────────────
* grid-drive          bus bus-tri Opera-area rue-Scribe Opera-worm
            yes 19940812101500 19940812101504 <numb;
────────────────────────────────────────────────────────────────────────
        warp                                Opera-area Paris-roug
Opera-worm          19940812101504 19940812101505
────────────────────────────────────────────────────────────────────────
    grid-drive          bus bus-tri Paris-roug Opera-worm CDG-2C-Ent
            yes 19940812101505 19940812105446
────────────────────────────────────────────────────────────────────────
        warp                                Paris-roug   CDG-2C-0
CDG-2C-Ent          19940812105446 19940812105447
────────────────────────────────────────────────────────────────────────
    grid-drive          bus bus-tri   CDG-2C-0 CDG-2C-Ent CDG-2C-bus
            yes 19940812105447 19940812110000
────────────────────────────────────────────────────────────────────────
*   grid-walk                    Jim          CDG-2C-0 CDG-2C-bus CDG-gate-6
            yes 19940812110000 19940812110322
────────────────────────────────────────────────────────────────────────
* grid-fly-p          747-400-je flight1   CDG-2C-0 CDG-gate-6 CDG-runway
            yes 19940812130000 19940812130001 <numb
────────────────────────────────────────────────────────────────────────
        warp                                CDG-2C-0      Earth-1
CDG-runway          19940812130001 19940812130002
────────────────────────────────────────────────────────────────────────
    grid-fly-p          747-400-je flight1   Earth-1 CDG-runway JFK-runway
            yes 19940812130002 19940812205328
────────────────────────────────────────────────────────────────────────
        warp                                Earth-1 JFK-intern
JFK-runway          19940812205328 19940812205329
────────────────────────────────────────────────────────────────────────
    grid-fly-p          747-400-je flight1 JFK-intern JFK-runway JFK-gate-2
            yes 19940812205329 19940812205500
────────────────────────────────────────────────────────────────────────
```

A trip consists of a series of *legs*. The following fields are shown above for each leg:

action

The type of action such as walking, driving, flying, or *warping*—going from one grid to another through a wormhole.

driver

The driver of the car. This only applies to unscheduled trips for which a driver (possibly the actor) must be arranged.

transport

The transportation device, such as a human (for walking), a car (for driving), a plane (for flying).

script

The scheduled trip object.

grid

The grid of a traversal action (such as walking or driving along a path).

from

The source physical object (for traversals) or grid (for warps).

to

The destination physical object (for traversals) or grid (for warps).

wormhole

The wormhole (for warps).

path

The grid path (for traversals).

depart

The time at which the action is begun.

arrive

The time at which the action is completed.

cost

The cost of the action.

An asterisk indicates the beginning of a *trip segment*, or sequence of grid traversals of a particular type, such as `grid-drive` or `grid-walk`.

Here is another trip planned by ThoughtTreasure from Martine's house in Paris to her aunt Lucie's house in the south of France, by having her father drive her there:

```
Trip 19940812124847 19940812173902          na
```

| | action | driver | transport | script | grid | from | to |
	wormhole path		depart		arrive	cost	
*	grid-walk		Martine		sapins-15E	Martine-ap	sapins-Ele
	yes 19940812124847 19940812124849						
	warp					sapins-15E	sapins-Rez
	sapins-Ele		19940812124849 19940812124850				
	grid-walk		Martine		sapins-Rez	sapins-Ele	sapins-Ent
	yes 19940812124850 19940812124854						
	warp					sapins-Rez	Porte-de-B
	sapins-Ent		19940812124854 19940812124855				

	grid-walk		Martine		Porte-de-B	sapins-Ent	Martine-BM
	yes 19940812124855 19940812125133						
*	grid-drive	Martine-Da	Martine-BM		Porte-de-B	Martine-BM	perif-Port
	yes 19940812125133 19940812125153						
	warp				Porte-de-B	Paris-roug	
perif-Port	19940812125153 19940812125154						
	grid-drive	Martine-Da	Martine-BM		Paris-roug	perif-Port	Paris-to-F
	yes 19940812125154 19940812131340						
	warp				Paris-roug	France-gri	
Paris-to-F	19940812131340 19940812131341						
	grid-drive	Martine-Da	Martine-BM		France-gri	Paris-to-F	Mirepoix-t
	yes 19940812131341 19940812173750						
	warp				France-gri	Lucie-area	
Mirepoix-t	19940812173750 19940812173751						
	grid-drive	Martine-Da	Martine-BM		Lucie-area	Mirepoix-t	parking-ar
	yes 19940812173751 19940812173800						
*	grid-walk		Martine		Lucie-area	parking-ar	maison-de-
	yes 19940812173800 19940812173902						

Finding trips

In order to *find trips* for an actor A from an object F to an object T, leaving F after the time TSF and arriving at T before the time TST, the following steps are performed:

1. Determine the locations of F and T at TSF—grids GF and GT and subspaces SF and ST.
2. If A and B are `near-reachable`, return a list consisting of an empty trip.
3. Initialize a list of result trips R to empty.
4. Add to R any grid-wormhole traversal trips from F to T by means of walking.
5. Add to R any driving trips from F to T.
6. Add to R any scheduled trips from F to T by means of subway.
7. Add to R any scheduled trips from F to T by means of bus.
8. Add to R any scheduled trips from F to T by means of airplane.
9. Return R.

Finding grid-wormhole traversal trips

In order to *find a grid-wormhole traversal trip* (with F, T, TSF, TST, GF, GT, SF, and ST defined as above), the following steps are performed:

1. Calculate the distance from F to T.
2. Retrieve the speed of the traversal means (walking, driving, flying) from the database.
3. If the traversal means is walking and the duration (distance times speed) is greater than an hour, return no trip.
4. If the traversal means is driving and the duration is less than two minutes, return no trip.
5. If the leave immediately flag (an argument to this algorithm) is true, set the next time to TSF. Otherwise, set the next time to TST minus the duration.
6. Find an intergrid path from GF to GT.
7. Create an empty trip R.
8. Add the following trip leg to R: a traversal action (such as walk or drive) from the initial location of F (SF in GF) to the first wormhole of the intergrid path, which is a wormhole in GF. (The traversal action is along a path found by the grid path finding algorithm.) Increment the next time appropriately.
9. For each element of the intergrid path, add the following trip legs to the end of R: (1) a warp action through the wormhole from the source grid to the destination grid, and, except in the case of the last element, (2) a traversal action from the wormhole to the next wormhole in the destination grid. Increment the next time appropriately.
10. Add the following trip leg to R: a traversal action from the last wormhole to the destination subspace ST.
11. If the time of arrival is later than TST, return no trip.
12. Return R.

Finding driving trips

In order to *find a driving trip* (with A, F, T, TSF, TST, GF, GT, SF, and ST defined as above), the following steps are performed:

1. If the distance from F to T is less than 300 meters, return no trip.
2. Find the car nearest to F owned by A.
3. Find a parking lot near T.
4. Create an empty trip R.
5. Recursively find a trip from F to the car, with the leave immediately flag set to false and the TST argument set to the TST argument of this algorithm minus the duration of the drive from the car to the parking lot near T. Add this trip to R.

6. Add to R a grid-wormhole traversal trip from the car to the parking lot near T by means of driving.
7. Recursively invoke the trip finding algorithm to find a trip from the parking lot near T to T, with the leave immediately flag set to true. Add this trip to R.
8. Return R.

Finding scheduled trips

The trip ontology contains specifications of scheduled trips. The following information is provided for means of transport which are periodic within a day, such as subways and buses:

```
start and stop time of day in service
trip frequency (how long between trips)
trip duration (how long a trip takes)
```

The following information is provided for means of transport which are not periodic within a day, such as airplane flights:

```
departure time of day
arrival time of day
```

The following information is provided for all means of transport:

```
origination location
destination location
transport vehicle
start and stop effective dates
days of week in service
checkin duration (recommended amount of time to arrive
  at origination location in advance of departure)
ticket price
```

In order to *find a scheduled trip* from F to T, the following steps are performed:

1. Find a terminal TF near F and a terminal TT near T. The type of terminal depends on the transport means:

means	action	nonobstacles	terminal
flight	grid-fly-plane	flyable	boarding-room
bus-trip	grid-drive-car	drivable	bus-stop
subway-trip	grid-conduct-train	rollable	subway-platform

2. Create an empty trip R.

3. Find a scheduled trip from TF to TT which leaves after TSF and arrives before TST.

4. Recursively invoke the trip finding algorithm to find a trip from F to TF, with the leave immediately flag set to false and the TST argument set to the departure time minus the checkin duration. Add this trip to R.

5. Add to R a grid-wormhole traversal trip from TF to TT by the indicated transport means, starting at the departure time and ending at the arrival time.

6. Recursively invoke the trip finding algorithm to find a trip from TT to T, with the leave immediately flag set to true. Add this trip to R.

7. Return R.

Ptrans planning agents

A collection of planning agents deal with goals related to physical transfer (Ptrans) (Schank, 1975) or movement through space. These planning agents make use of the trip finding algorithms described above.

The *near-reachable planning agent* enables an actor A to Ptrans to an object O:

```
near-reachable(A, O) :-
     find a trip T from A to O;
     IF T EMPTY GOTO FAILURE,
1:   IF T EMPTY GOTO SUCCESS;
     LEG = HEAD(T); I = 0;
     IF LEG.action ISA grid-walk GOTO 100
     ELSE IF LEG.wormhole GOTO 200
     ELSE IF LEG.action ISA grid-drive-car GOTO 300
     ELSE GOTO FAILURE,
100: T = TAIL(T),
101: IF I >= LENGTH(LEG.gsfrom) GOTO 1;
     grid-walk(A, LEG.grid, LEG.gsfrom[I], LEG.gsto[I])
        ON SUCCESS GOTO 101;
     I = I+1,
200: T = TAIL(T);
     warp(A, LEG.from, LEG.to, LEG.wormhole) ON SUCCESS GOTO 1,
300: drive(LEG.driver, LEG.transporter, next segment of T)
     ON SUCCESS GOTO 1; T = do enough TAILs to get to next segment
     of T.
```

(Multiple statements within a planning agent state are separated by a semicolon. Commas separate states.)

Supporting planning agents for the above are as follows:

```
grid-walk(A, G, F, T) :- standing(A).
sitting(A, O) :- sit(A, O).
standing(A) :- stand(A).
lying(A, O) :- lie(A, O).
sit(A, O) :- near-reachable(A, O).
stand(A) :-.
lie(A, O) :- near-reachable(A, O).

warp(A, F, T, W) :- .
```

The *drive planning agent* enables a driver D to drive a passenger P using a motor vehicle V according to the trip segment T:

```
drive(D, P, V, T) :-
     inside(P, V),
     inside(D, V),
     motor-vehicle-on(V),
3:   IF T EMPTY GOTO 5;
        LEG = HEAD(T); T = TAIL(T); I = 0;
        IF LEG.action ISA grid-drive-car GOTO 100
        ELSE IF LEG.wormhole GOTO 200
        ELSE GOTO FAILURE,
5:   motor-vehicle-off(V) ON SUCCESS GOTO SUCCESS,
100: IF I >= LENGTH(LEG.gsfrom) GOTO 3;
        grid-drive-car(D, V, LEG.grid, LEG.gsfrom[I], LEG.gsto[I])
          ON SUCCESS GOTO 100;
        I = I + 1,
200: warp(A, LEG.from, LEG.to, LEG.wormhole) ON SUCCESS GOTO 3.

grid-drive-car(D, V, G, F, T) :- .
```

The following planning agent enables an actor to start a motor vehicle:

```
motor-vehicle-on(V) :-
  switch(FINDP(ignition-switch, V), on),
  WAIT FOR motor-vehicle-on(V)
    OR WAIT 10 seconds AND GOTO FAILURE.
```

The Prolog-like notation for planning agents is perhaps misleading, since the `motor-vehicle-on` goal is not automatically achieved once all its subgoals are achieved. The last line above waits for the goal to be achieved. Whether the vehicle is actually on or off is determined by the *motor vehicle object planning agent* which simulates the behavior of the motor vehicle according to the following rule: A motor vehicle is on if and only if (1) it is not broken and (2) its ignition switch is on.

The following planning agent is used to turn a vehicle off:

```
motor-vehicle-off(V) :-
  switch(FINDP(ignition-switch, V), off),
  WAIT FOR motor-vehicle-off(V)
    OR WAIT 10 seconds AND GOTO FAILURE.
```

The *near-audible planning agent* enables an actor A1 to hear and speak to A2, either by calling A2 on the telephone or by being `near-reachable` A2:

```
near-audible(A1, A2) :-
   invoke space routines to determine
     distance D between A1 and A2;
     IF D < 500 meters GOTO 100;
     call(A1, A2) ON FAILURE GOTO 100
       OR WAIT FOR near-audible(A1, A2) AND GOTO
SUCCESS,
100: near-reachable(A1, A2).
```

This agent waits for the state `near-audible` to become true, instead of merely waiting for the call planning agent to succeed, since the call planning agent must stay active after A1 and A2 are `near-audible` in order to hang up the phone at the end of the conversation.

The following planning agent enables an actor A1 to take a trip and stay with A2 for a certain duration D:

```
S = stay(A1, A2, D) :-
  RETRIEVE legal-guardian-of(A1, A3 = human);
    IF A3 NOT EMPTY obtain-permission(A1, A3, S),
  obtain-permission(A1, A2, S),
  pack(A1, SC = FINDO(suitcase OWNED BY A1), S),
  near-reachable(A1, A2),
  unpack(A1, SC),
  WAIT D,
  pack(A1, SC, owner-of),
  RETRIEVE residence-of(A1, HOME = physical-object);
    near-reachable(A1, HOME),
  unpack(A1, SC).
```

The supporting planning agents for packing and unpacking are as follows:

```
pack(A, SC, S) :-
   IF S = owner-of {
      find CLOTHES owned by A within a 200 meter radius by
         invoking space routines
   } ELSE {
      select CLOTHES for S (see the section on Clothing)
   };
   IF CLOTHES EMPTY GOTO FAILURE,
1: IF CLOTHES EMPTY GOTO SUCCESS;
      inside(HEAD(CLOTHES), SC) ON SUCCESS GOTO 1;
      CLOTHES = TAIL(CLOTHES).

unpack(A, SC) :-
   holding(G = FINDP(right-hand, A), SC),
   near-reachable(A, SH = FINDO(clothing-shelf)),
   move-to(G, SH),
   release(G, SC),
3: RETRIEVE inside(O = physical-object, SC);
      IF O EMPTY GOTO SUCCESS;
      holding(G, O),
   move-to(G, SH),
   release(G, O) ON SUCCESS GOTO 3.
```

Atrans planning agents

A collection of planning agents deal with goals related to abstract transfer of possession (Atrans) (Schank, 1975).

The *purchase ticket planning agent* handles an actor A's purchase of a ticket for a performance P from an employee at a theater box office:

```
purchase-ticket(A, P) :-
   dress(A, purchase-ticket),
   RETRIEVE building-of(P, BLDG);
      near-reachable(A, BLDG),
   near-reachable(A, FINDO(box-office)),
   near-reachable(A, FINDO(customer-side-of-counter)),
2: pre-sequence(A, B = FINDO(human NEAR employee-side-of-counter)),
   WAIT FOR may-I-help-you(B, A)
      OR WAIT 10 seconds AND GOTO 2,
   interjection-of-greeting(A, B),
5: request(A, B, P),
6: WAIT FOR I-am-sorry(B) AND GOTO 13
      OR WAIT FOR describe(B, A, TKT = ticket) AND GOTO 8
      OR WAIT 20 seconds AND GOTO 5,
8: WAIT FOR propose-transaction(B, A, TKT, PRC = currency),
   IF TKT and PRC are OK accept(A, B) AND GOTO 10
   ELSE decline(A, B) AND GOTO 6,
```

```
10: pay-in-person(A, B, PRC),
    receive-from(A, B, TKT) ON FAILURE GOTO 13,
    ASSERT owner-of(TKT, A),
    post-sequence(A, B),
    SUCCESS,
13: post-sequence(A, B),
    FAILURE.
```

The *work box office planning agent* is the *other side* of the above purchase ticket planning agent. It is the script of an employee B working at a box office F:

```
work-box-office(B, F) :-
    dress(B, work-box-office),
    near-reachable(B, F),
    TKTBOX = FINDO(ticket-box);
       near-reachable(B, FINDO(employee-side-of-counter)),
/* HANDLE NEXT CUSTOMER */
100: WAIT FOR attend(A = human, B) OR
       pre-sequence(A = human, B),
    may-I-help-you(B, A),
/* HANDLE NEXT REQUEST OF CUSTOMER */
103: WAIT FOR request(A, B, R) AND GOTO 104
       OR WAIT FOR post-sequence(A, B) AND GOTO 110,
104: IF R ISA tod {
       current-time-sentence(B, A) ON COMPLETION GOTO 103
    } ELSE IF R ISA performance {
       GOTO 105
    } ELSE {
       interjection-of-noncomprehension(B, A)
       ON COMPLETION GOTO 103
    }
105: find next available ticket TKT in TKTBOX for R;
       IF none {
          I-am-sorry(B, A) ON COMPLETION GOTO 103
       } ELSE {
          describe(B, A, TKT) ON COMPLETION GOTO 106
       },
106: propose-transaction(B, A, TKT, TKT.price),
    WAIT FOR accept(A, B) AND GOTO 108
       OR WAIT FOR decline(A, B) AND GOTO 105
       OR WAIT 10 seconds AND GOTO 105,
108: collect-payment(B, A, TKT.price, FINDO(cash-register)),
109: hand-to(B, A, TKT),
110: post-sequence(B, A) ON COMPLETION GOTO 100.
```

Some supporting planning agents for the above are as follows:

```
pay-in-person(A, B, PRC) :-
  pay-cash(A, B, PRC, W = FINDO(wallet OWNED BY A))
    ON FAILURE GOTO 1;
    ON SUCCESS GOTO SUCCESS,
1: pay-by-card(A, B, PRC, W)
```

```
      ON FAILURE GOTO 2;
      ON SUCCESS GOTO SUCCESS,
2: pay-by-check(A, B, PRC, W).
pay-cash(A, B, PRC, W) :-
      = pick out PRC worth of cash from W,
2: IF CASH EMPTY {
      IF CHANGE > 0 GOTO 3 ELSE GOTO SUCCESS
   } ELSE {
      hand-to(A, B, HEAD(CASH)) ON SUCCESS GOTO 2;
      CASH = TAIL(CASH)
   },
3: collect-cash(A, B, CHANGE, W).
```

(Note that a statement which appears after a subgoal invocation is executed before that subgoal starts running—the subgoal is not actually invoked until the end of the code associated with a state has been reached.)

```
pay-by-check(A, B, PRC, W) :-
  RETRIEVE inside(CHK = check, W);
    write(A, CHK, PRC),
  write(A, CHK, signature),
  hand-to(A, B, CHK).
collect-payment(B, A, PRC, CR) :-
1: request-payment(B, A),
   WAIT FOR gesture-here(B, A, O),
   IF O ISA cash {
     collect-cash(B, A, PRC, CR)
   } ELSE IF O ISA credit-card {
     collect-card-payment(B, A, PRC, CR)
   } ELSE IF O ISA check {
     collect-check-payment(B, A, PRC, CR)
   } ELSE {
     GOTO 1
   }.
collect-cash(B, A, PRC, CR) :-
   SUM = 0,
1: receive-from(B, A, BILL = currency),
   SUM = SUM + BILL.value;
     inside(BILL, CR),
   IF SUM == PRC {
     interjection-of-thanks(B, A) ON COMPLETION GOTO SUCCESS
   } ELSE IF SUM > PRC {
     pay-cash(B, A, SUM-PRC, CR) ON COMPLETION GOTO SUCCESS
   } ELSE {
     GOTO 1
   }.
```

The following planning agents are used to give objects to another actor and to receive an object from another actor:

```
gesture-here(A1, A2, O) :-
  near-reachable(A1, A2).
hand-to(A1, A2, O) :-
  holding(G1 = FINDP(grasper, A1), O),
  gesture-here(A1, A2, O),
  WAIT FOR grasp(G2 = FINDP(grasper, A2), O),
  release(G1, O).
receive-from(A1, A2, O) :-
  gesture-here(A1, A2, O),
  WAIT a few seconds,
  grasp(G1 = FINDP(grasper, A1), O).
```

Mtrans planning agents

A collection of planning agents deal with goals related to speech acts (Searle, 1969) and transfer of mental information (Mtrans) (Schank, 1975).

The following planning agent implements a *chatterbot* which carries on an online conversation with a user in performance mode:

```
online-chat(A, B) :-
      WAIT FOR interjection-of-greeting(B, A) AND GOTO 1
        OR WAIT 20 seconds AND GOTO 20,
1:    interjection-of-greeting(A, B),
      GOTO 100,
20:   interjection-of-greeting(A, B),
      BACKTO = 20;
        WAIT FOR interjection-of-greeting(B, A) AND GOTO 100
        OR WAIT 20 seconds AND GOTO 1000,
100:  BACKTO = 100;
      how-are-you(A, B),
101:  WAIT FOR how-are-you-response-with-question(B, A)
        AND GOTO 110
        OR WAIT FOR how-are-you-response-without-question(B, A)
          AND GOTO 150
        OR WAIT 10 seconds AND GOTO 1000,
110:  how-are-you-response-without-question(A, B),
150:  request-for-news(A, B),
200:  BACKTO = 200;
        WAIT FOR mtrans(B, A) AND GOTO 200
        OR WAIT FOR leave-taking(B, A) AND GOTO 900
        OR WAIT FOR interjection-of-departure(B, A) AND GOTO 910
        OR WAIT 10 seconds AND GOTO 1000,
900:  interjection-of-departure(A, B),
901:  WAIT FOR interjection-of-departure(B, A) AND GOTO SUCCESS
        OR WAIT 5 seconds AND GOTO SUCCESS,
910:  interjection-of-departure(A, B) ON SUCCESS GOTO SUCCESS,
```

```
1000: IF BACKTO < 100 is-anybody-there(A, B)
        ELSE are-you-still-there(A, B),
      WAIT FOR I-am-here(B, A) AND GOTO BACKTO
        OR WAIT FOR mtrans(B, A) AND GOTO BACKTO
        OR WAIT 30 seconds AND GOTO 1000.
```

All inputs are run through the parser in order to answer questions or respond to requests. A number of different frozen expressions for saying hello, goodbye, and so forth are contained in the intervention ontology.

The following planning agent is used to obtain permission (say, for an appointment or stay):

```
obtain-permission(A, B, CON) :-
  propose(A, B, CON),
  WAIT FOR accept(B, A) AND GOTO SUCCESS
    OR WAIT FOR decline(B, A) AND GOTO FAILURE.
```

The following planning agent applies to all instances of the class mtrans including speech acts such as propose:

```
mtrans(A, B, CON) :-
  near-audible(A, B).
```

The following planning agent handles incoming proposals:

```
handle-proposal(A) :-
100: WAIT FOR proposal(B = human, A, CON = concept),
      evaluate CON and GOTO 300 or 400,
300: accept(A, B),
      GOTO 100,
400: decline(A, B)
      GOTO 100.
```

This handler is created for every actor in a simulation.

Telephone planning agent

The *telephone object planning agent* simulates the behavior of a telephone and network of telephones. At any moment a telephone is in one of the following states:

idle
The phone is not in use.

dialtone

A dial tone is heard in the phone's receiver.

intercept

An intercept tone or recording is heard in the phone's receiver, indicating that an unknown number has been dialed.

busy-signal

A busy signal is heard in the phone's receiver.

audible-ring

An audible ring tone is heard in the phone's receiver, indicating that the called phone is ringing.

voice-connection

A voice connection exists from this phone to another phone.

ringing

The phone's ringer is ringing.

The handset of a phone has two states: on-hook and off-hook.

The next state of a telephone T is determined by the object planning agent as follows:

```
H = FINDP(phone-handset, T)
IF condition(T, W) and W < 0 { /* T broken */
  ASSERT idle(T)
} ELSE IF idle(T) {
  IF off-hook(H) ASSERT dialtone(T)
} ELSE IF dialtone(T) {
  IF on-hook(H) ASSERT idle(T)
  ELSE IF dial(concept, FINDP(phone-dial, T), N = number) {
    phone-number-of(CLD = phone, N)
    IF CLD EMPTY ASSERT intercept(T)
    ELSE {
      CLDS = state of CLD
      IF CLDS != idle ASSERT busy-signal(T)
      ELSE {
        ASSERT ringing(CLD, T)
        ASSERT audible-ring(T, CLD)
      }
    }
  }
} ELSE IF ringing(T, CLG = phone) {
  IF off-hook(H) {
    ASSERT voice-connection(CLG, T)
    ASSERT voice-connection(T, CLG)
  }
} ELSE IF audible-ring(T, CLD = phone) {
  IF on-hook(H) {
    ASSERT idle(CLD)
    ASSERT idle(T)
  }
```

```
} ELSE IF voice-connection(T, U = phone) {
  IF on-hook(H) {
    ASSERT dialtone(U)
    ASSERT idle(T)
  }
}
```

(In each of the cases above where a new state of a phone is asserted, it is assumed that the previous state is retracted.)

Although for simplicity the above code is considered to model the behavior of a telephone, it is actually an implementation of a telephone switching system.

The following standard planning agent enables a person to call another person on the telephone, making use of the above telephone behavior:

```
call(A1, A2) :-
1:    off-hook(H = FINDP(phone-handset, T = FINDO(phone))),
      WAIT FOR dialtone(T) AND GOTO 22 OR
        WAIT 30 seconds AND GOTO 777,
22:   RETRIEVE phone-number-of(CLD = FINDO(phone NEAR A2), N =
number);
        dial(FINDP(right-hand, A1), FINDP(phone-dial, T), N),
      WAIT FOR busy-signal(T) AND GOTO 777
        OR WAIT FOR intercept(T) AND GOTO 888
        OR WAIT FOR audible-ring(T, CLD) AND GOTO 4,
        OR WAIT 10 seconds AND GOTO 777
4:    WAIT FOR voice-connection(T, CLD) AND GOTO 5
        OR WAIT 30 seconds AND GOTO 777
5:    WAIT FOR interjection-of-greeting(A3 = human, ?) AND GOTO 61
        OR WAIT 30 seconds AND GOTO 777
61:   ASSERT near-audible(A1, A3);
        IF A3 != A2 GOTO 990;
        calling-party-telephone-greeting(A1, A2),
62:   WAIT FOR mtrans(A1, A2) AND GOTO 7
        OR WAIT 5 seconds AND GOTO 990,
7:    WAIT FOR mtrans(A2, A1) AND GOTO 990
        OR WAIT 5 seconds AND GOTO 990,
777:  on-hook(H) ON SUCCESS GOTO 1,
888:  on-hook(H) ON SUCCESS GOTO FAILURE,
990:  interjection-of-departure(A1, A3),
      WAIT FOR interjection-of-departure(A3, A1)
        OR WAIT 5 seconds,
      RETRACT near-audible(A1, A3);
        on-hook(H).
```

Note that in state 62, this planning agent for actor A1 waits for an action on behalf of itself: Typically a goal of A1 leads to a subgoal for talk to an actor A2, which leads to a subgoal for A1 be near-audible A2, which leads to a subgoal for A1 to call A2. Once the near-audible is asserted by the call planning agent, the subgoal to talk generates the desired Mtrans.

The other side of the call planning agent is the *handle-call planning agent*:

```
handle-call(A2) :-
1: WAIT FOR ringing(T = phone),
   off-hook(H = FINDP(phone-handset, T)),
   telephone-greeting(A2, A1),
4: WAIT FOR M = mtrans(A1, A2) AND GOTO 5
      OR WAIT 30 seconds AND GOTO 7,
5: IF M ISA interjection-of-departure GOTO 7;
      GOTO 4,
7: interjection-of-departure(A2, A1),
   on-hook(H),
   GOTO 1.
```

Other planning agents such as the proposal handler are responsible for generating responses to A1's Mtrans.

Some supporting planning agents deal with picking up and putting down the receiver and dialing:

```
off-hook(H) :-
  pick-up(FINDP(left-hand, A), H).
on-hook(H) :-
  hang-up(FINDP(left-hand, A), H).
pick-up(G, H) :-
  grasp(G, H),
  move-to(G, FINDP(left-ear, A)).
hang-up(G, H) :-
  holding(G, H),
  move-to(G, FINDW(phone, H)),
  release(G, H).
dial(G, D, N) :-
  move-to(G, D).
```

Entertainment planning agents

The *watch TV planning agent* is as follows:

```
watch-TV(A) :-
  TV-set-on(TV = FINDO(TV-set)),
1: consult the TV show ontology to find a TVSHOW currently on;
```

```
   IF TVSHOW EMPTY GOTO 6
     ELSE knob-position(FINDP(channel-selector, TV), TVSHOW.channel),
   sitting(A, FINDO(chair)),
   WAIT UNTIL TVSHOW.end AND GOTO 1,
6: TV-set-off(TV).
```

The following planning agents are used to flip on switches or to change the position of knobs:

```
knob-position(K, P) :-
  flip-to(G, K, P).

switch(K, P) :-
  flip-to(G, K, P).

flip-to(G, K, P) :-
  near-graspable(G, K).
```

The following planning agent enables an actor to turn on a TV set:

```
TV-set-on(TV) :-
  connected-to(FINDP(AC-plug, TV), FINDO(AC-outlet)),
  connected-to(FINDP(female-television-connector, TV),
FINDO(antenna)),
  switch(FINDP(power-switch, TV), on),
  WAIT FOR TV-set-on(TV)
    OR WAIT 10 seconds AND GOTO FAILURE.
```

The *TV object planning agent* simulates the behavior of the TV set according to the following rule: A TV is on if and only if (1) it is not broken, (2) it is plugged in to an outlet, (3) neither the plug nor outlet are broken, (4) its antenna is hooked up, (5) neither the antenna connector nor antenna are broken, and (6) its switch is on.

The following planning agent is used to turn off a TV:

```
TV-set-off(TV) :-
  switch(FINDP(power-switch, TV), off),
  WAIT FOR TV-set-off(TV)
    OR WAIT 10 seconds AND GOTO FAILURE.
```

A top-level entertainment goal is achieved by watching TV:

```
s-entertainment(A) :-
  watch-TV(A).
```

The first step of attending a performance is to obtain the ticket:

```
attend-performance(A, P) :-
  purchase-ticket(A, P).
```

Clothing

The clothing ontology contains a hierarchy of items of clothing. The following parameters (enums, attributes, and relations) are defined for an item of clothing (and inherited by descendant items):

Area
The part of the body the item of clothing is to be worn on. The possible areas are:

```
clothing-top
clothing-middle
clothing-bottom
clothing-hand
clothing-forearm
clothing-wrist
clothing-thigh
clothing-calf
clothing-knee
clothing-ankle
clothing-foot
```

Layer
What the item of clothing is to be worn under and over. The possible layers are:

```
underlayerpre
underlayer
underlayerpost
shirtlayer
tielayer
vestlayer
jacketlayer
coatlayer
overlayer
overlayerpost
```

Layer and area are used in conjunction to figure out the right order for putting on or taking off clothes.

Color
The colors of the item of clothing. The percentage of the surface area taken up by the color is stored as the weight of the color attribute. Example assertions:

```
[black veston-croise-d-Ermenegildo-Zegna NUMBER:u:0.99]
[red veston-croise-d-Ermenegildo-Zegna NUMBER:u:0.01]
[dark-gray pull-De-Fursac NUMBER:u:0.55]
[orange pull-De-Fursac NUMBER:u:0.1]
[red pull-De-Fursac NUMBER:u:0.1]
[amber pull-De-Fursac NUMBER:u:0.1]
[gray pull-De-Fursac NUMBER:u:0.05]
[white pull-De-Fursac NUMBER:u:0.05]
[violet pull-De-Fursac NUMBER:u:0.05]
```

Pattern

The visual pattern of the clothing. Example assertions:

```
[triangles pull-De-Fursac]
[stripes pull-De-Fursac]
```

Material

The material of the clothing. Example assertions:

```
[cotton Russell-athletic-sweatpants NUMBER:u:0.5]
[polyester Russell-athletic-sweatpants NUMBER:u:0.49]
[rayon Russell-athletic-sweatpants NUMBER:u:0.01]
[wool veston-croise-d-Ermenegildo-Zegna]
[worsted veston-croise-d-Ermenegildo-Zegna]
[super-100-S veston-croise-d-Ermenegildo-Zegna]
```

Other

Various other relations such as the size, manufacturer, location of manufacture, model number, and price of the item of clothing. Example assertions:

```
[fr-size-of veston-croise-d-Ermenegildo-Zegna NUMBER:u:46]
[part-of veston-croise-d-Ermenegildo-Zegna
         costume-croise-en-laine-d-Ermenegildo-Zegna]
[tp cravate-en-soie-numero-21-d-Ermenegildo-Zegna NUMBER:FRF:550]
[made-in Russell-athletic-sweatpants United-States]
```

Outfits are selected based on the age and sex of the actor and what script the actor is dressing for. The following are implemented:

```
adult male business attire
adult male sport clothes
adult male casual clothing
adult male athletic sportswear
child female casual clothing
```

For example, for adult male business attire the agent selects underpants, undershirt, socks, dress shirt, pants, belt, tie, shoes, jacket, and overcoat. Matching pairs of shoes and socks are selected. Pants are selected to match the jacket, the tie to match the jacket, and the shirt to match the tie. (There is no backtracking in the event that a matching item cannot be found.)

Items of clothing are selected as follows: First a list is constructed of candidate items of the desired class (such as tie) which are near the actor and owned or currently being worn by the actor. Then a desirability rating between 0.0 and 1.0 is calculated for each candidate as:

```
forgottenness * matchness
```

Forgottenness is the number of days since the item of clothing was last worn divided by 10, with a maximum value of 1.0. Matchness is a rating of how much the item of clothing matches other items of clothing, in regard to material and color. Color matchness of A and B is the weighted sum of the matchness of each pair of colors of A and B. The item of clothing with the highest desirability rating is selected.

Color matchness of C1 and C2 is determined as follows: If C1 and C2 are certain stereotypical color combinations, hardcoded ratings assigned to those combinations are returned. Otherwise, the Euclidean distance between the hue, luminance, and saturation of C1 (stored in the color ontology) and that of C2 is calculated, normalized such that zero distance maps to 1.0 and maximal distance maps to 0.0, and returned.

Clothing planning agents

The two top-level clothing planning agents are the *strip planning agent* and the *dress planning agent*:

```
strip(A) :-
1: RETRIEVE wearing-of(A, C);
      IF C EMPTY GOTO SUCCESS;
      take-off(A, C) ON SUCCESS GOTO 1.

dress(A, SCRIPT) :-
    select CLOTHES1 for SCRIPT
/* CLOTHES1 are sorted into the right order for putting them on. */
    RETRIEVE wearing-of(A, CLOTHES0);
    CLOTHES0 = CLOTHES0 - CLOTHES1,
/* Take off clothes not in selected outfit. */
1: IF CLOTHES0 EMPTY {
    GOTO 2
    } ELSE {
```

```
      take-off(A, HEAD(CLOTHES0)) ON SUCCESS GOTO 1;
      CLOTHES0 = TAIL(CLOTHES0)
   }
/* Put on clothes in selected outfit. */
2: IF CLOTHES1 EMPTY {
      GOTO 3
   } ELSE {
      wearing-of(A, HEAD(CLOTHES1)) ON SUCCESS GOTO 2;
      CLOTHES1 = TAIL(CLOTHES1)
   }
3: RETRIEVE wearing-of(A, PANTS = pants);
      inside(FINDO(wallet OWNED BY A), FINDP(pocket, PANTS)).
```

(CLOTHES0 - CLOTHES1 indicates CLOTHES0 with the elements of CLOTHES1 removed.)

The above planning agents make use of the following support planning agents:

```
wearing-of(A, C) :-
  put-on(A, C).

put-on(A, C) :-
1: find an item of clothing C0 worn by A which is
   supposed to be worn over C;
      IF C0 EMPTY {
         GOTO 2
      } ELSE {
         take-off(A, C0) ON SUCCESS GOTO 1,
      },
2: pull-on(FINDP(right-hand, A), A, C).

take-off(A, C) :-
  pull-off(RH = FINDP(right-hand, A), C),
  near-reachable(A, FINDO(shelf)),
  release(RH, C).

pull-on(G, C) :-
  holding(G, C),
  RETRACT holding(G, C);
    RETRACT at-grid(C ...).

pull-off(G, A, C) :-
  near-graspable(G, C),
  RETRACT wearing-of(A, C);
    ASSERT holding(G, C);
    ASSERT at-grid(C ...).
```

The grid location (at-grid) of an item of clothing C is retracted when C is pulled on, since the location of the clothing can be inferred from the location of the actor wearing it. When an item of clothing is pulled off, its grid location is asserted to be the same as that of the actor who just pulled it off.

Shower planning agent

The *shower planning agent* is as follows:

```
take-shower(A) :-
  strip(A),
  shower-on(SH = FINDO(shower)),
  IF no hairwash GOTO 200,
/* HAIR WASH */
  grasp(RH = FINDP(right-hand, A), S = FINDO(shampoo)),
  action-open(LH = FINDP(left-hand, A), S),
  pour(RH, S, H = FINDP(hair, A)),
103: action-close(LH, S),
  move-to(RH, SD = FINDO(soap-dish)),
  release(RH, S),
  rub(RH, H, 30),
  move-to(H, SHD = FINDP(shower-head, SH)),
  rub(RH, H, 30),
/* WASH */
200: grasp(RH, SP=FINDO(soap)),
  move-to(F = FINDP(face,A), SHD),
  rub(RH, F),
  rub(RH, LA = FINDP(left-arm, A)),
  rub(RH, RA = FINDP(right-arm, A)),
  rub(RH, T = FINDP(trunk, A)),
  rub(RH, LL = FINDP(left-leg, A)),
  rub(RH, RL = FINDP(right-leg, A)),
  move-to(RH, SD),
  release(RH, SP),
/* RINSE */
  rub(RH, F),
  rub(RH, LA),
  rub(RH, RA),
  rub(RH, T),
  rub(RH, LL),
  rub(RH, RL),
/* DRY OFF */
  shower-off(SH),
  grasp(RH, TW = FINDO(towel)),
  rub(RH, H),
  rub(RH, F),
  rub(RH, LA),
  rub(RH, RA),
  rub(RH, T),
  rub(RH, LL),
  rub(RH, RL),
  move-to(RH, FINDO(towel-rack)),
  release(RH, TW).
```

Supporting planning agents for the shower planning agent are:

```
shower-on(S) :-
  knob-position(FINDP(cold-faucet, S), 5),
  knob-position(FINDP(warm-faucet, S), 5),
  switch(FINDP(shower-switch, S), on),
  WAIT FOR shower-on(S).

shower-off(S) :-
  knob-position(FINDP(cold-faucet, S), 0),
  knob-position(FINDP(warm-faucet, S), 0),
  switch(FINDP(shower-switch, S), off),
  WAIT FOR shower-off(S).

rub(G, O, DURATION) :-
  near-graspable(G, O).

pour(G, O1, O2) :-
  holding(G, O1),
  near-graspable(G, O2).
```

A *shower object planning agent* simulates the behavior of the shower: A shower is on if and only if its cold and hot faucets are not on position 0, its switch is on, and it is not broken.

Here are some excerpts from the English output of the simulation making use of the shower planning agent:

```
& Jim Garnier is in Jim Garnier's bedroom.
& He is dressed in a pajama top.
& He is dressed in a pajama bottom.
& His right hand is going to move to a pajama top.
& His right hand is going to be near a pajama top.
& He is going to take a pajama top off oneself.
& He will hold a pajama top.
& A pajama top will be in his bedroom.
& He will stand up.
& He will be standing.
& He will walk from his bedroom to the closet of 20 rue Drouot
apartment 4D.
& A pajama top will be in the closet of 20 rue Drouot apartment 4D.
& He will be in the closet of 20 rue Drouot apartment 4D.
& He will let go of a pajama top.
& He takes off a pajama top.
& His right hand will move to a pajama bottom.
& He will take a pajama bottom off oneself.
& He will hold a pajama bottom.
& A pajama bottom will be in the closet of 20 rue Drouot apartment
4D.
& Jim Garnier will let go of a pajama bottom.
```

& He will take off a pajama bottom.
& The bath shower is off.
& He will walk to his bathroom from the closet of 20 rue Drouot apartment 4D.
& He will be in his bathroom.
& His right hand will move to the cold faucet of the bath of the bath shower.
& He will flip to a knob position 5 the bath of the bath shower.
& The cold faucet of the bath of the bath shower will be set to 5.
& His right hand will move to the hot faucet of the bath of the bath shower.
& He will flip to a knob position 5 the bath of the bath shower.
& The hot faucet of the bath of the bath shower will be set to 5.
& His right hand will move to the shower switch of the bath shower.
& He will flip on the bath shower.
& The shower switch of the bath shower will be on.
& The bath shower will be on.
& He will walk to the Aquavital from the bath shower.
& Jim Garnier's right hand will move to the Aquavital.
& He will grasp the Aquavital.
& He will hold the Aquavital.
& Jim Garnier's left hand will move to the Aquavital.
& He will open the Aquavital.
& The Aquavital will be open.
& His right hand will move to the hair of his head.
& He will pour the Aquavital onto the hair of his head.
& He will close the Aquavital.
& The Aquavital will be closed.
& Jim Garnier will walk from the Aquavital to the bath shower.
& His right hand will move to the soap dish of the bath of the bath shower.
& He will let go of the Aquavital.
& His right hand will move to the hair of his head.
& He will rub the hair of his head.
& The hair of his head will move to the shower head of the bath shower.
& He will rub the hair of his head.
& He will walk to the soap from the bath shower.
& Jim Garnier's right hand will move to the soap.
& He will grasp the soap.
& He will hold the soap.
& He will walk from the soap to the bath shower.
& The face of his head will move to the shower head of the bath shower.
& His right hand will move to the face of his head.
& Jim Garnier will rub the face of Jim Garnier's head.
& His right hand will move to his trunk.
& Jim Garnier will rub Jim Garnier's trunk.
& His right hand will move to the soap dish of the bath of the bath shower.
& He will let go of the soap.
& His right hand will move to the face of his head.
& He will rub the face of his head.
& His right hand will move to his trunk.

& He will rub his trunk.
& Jim Garnier's right hand will move to the cold faucet of the bath
of the bath
& shower.
& He will flip to a knob position 0 the bath of the bath shower.
& The cold faucet of the bath of the bath shower will be set to 0.
& His right hand will move to the hot faucet of the bath of the bath
shower.
& He will flip to a knob position 0 the bath of the bath shower.
& The hot faucet of the bath of the bath shower will be set to 0.
& The bath shower will be off.
& Jim Garnier will walk to the towel from the bath shower.
& His right hand will move to the towel.
& He will grasp the towel.
& He will hold the towel.
& His right hand will move to the hair of his head.
& Jim Garnier will rub the hair of Jim Garnier's head.
& He will rub the face of his head.
& His right hand will move to his trunk.
& Jim Garnier will rub Jim Garnier's trunk.
& His right hand will move to the heated towel rack.
& He will let go of the towel.
& He takes a shower.
& He will be happy.

Sleep planning agent

The attributes of `energy-level` and `rest-level` are maintained for each actor (in each context). Their weights range from -1.0 (exhausted/tired) to 1.0 (energetic/well rested). The weights are *initially set* based on whether the actor is known to be asleep or awake, when the actor went to sleep or awoke, and how long the actor has been asleep or awake. For example, if the actor has been awake for more than `circadian-rhythm-of` the actor minus `ideal-sleep-of` the actor, the weight is set to -1.0. If the weights were already known and the time of day has changed since the last time the weights were calculated, then they are *incrementally adjusted*—incremented or decremented by an appropriate amount depending on whether the actor is sleeping or awake.

The *sleep planning agent* is as follows:

```
sleep(A) :-
        set initial ENERGY and REST for A,
/* AWAKE */
100: incrementally adjust ENERGY and REST for A;
        /* Go to sleep when tired: */
        IF (.2*ENERGY + .8*REST) < -0.9 GOTO 200;
        /* Go to sleep at bedtime: */
        IF current time > bedtime GOTO 200;
        WAIT 15 minutes AND GOTO 100,
```

```
/* GET READY FOR BED */
200: near-reachable(A, B = FINDO(bed)),
     strip(A),
     lie(A, B),
/* TRY TO FALL ASLEEP */
300: incrementally adjust ENERGY and REST for A;
        IF (.2*ENERGY + .8*REST) < -0.8 GOTO 400;
        WAIT 1 minute AND GOTO 300,
/* ASLEEP */
400: ASSERT asleep(A),
410: incrementally adjust ENERGY and REST for A;
        /* Wake up when rested: */
        IF (.2*ENERGY + .8*REST) > 0.9 GOTO 500;
        WAIT FOR wake(concept, A) AND GOTO 500
        OR WAIT 15 minutes AND GOTO 410,
/* AWAKEN */
500: RETRACT asleep(A);
        ASSERT awake(A);
        GOTO 100.
```

Note that this planning agent never terminates. It continues to manage an actor's sleeping and awakening as long as the actor is part of a context.

Appointment planning agent

An *appointment* has the following parameters:

- *participants* (actor and counterparty),
- *meeting place*,
- *objective*,
- *time range* (start and stop timestamps).

A separate *appointment planning agent* instance is created for each appointment with a counterparty. (A single appointment between two actors requires two appointment planning agents in ThoughtTreasure: one for each actor.)

The appointment planning agent is as follows:

```
APPT = appointment(A, B, LOC, OBJECTIVE, TSR) :-
     obtain-permission(A, B, APPT),
/* Waiting to leave for appointment */
     WAIT until time to leave (as determined by trip finder)
        AND GOTO 101,
101: (details omitted regarding missed appointments)
        near-reachable(A, LOC),
/* Waiting for counterparty */
110: IF near-reachable(A, B) GOTO 200;
        IF current time > TSR.start + A's waiting limit GOTO FAILURE;
```

```
        WAIT 60 seconds AND GOTO 110,
/* Appointment begins */
200: OBJECTIVE,
999: IF friend-of(B, A) update LAST SEEN timestamp of
        planning agent maintain-friendship(A, B).
```

When the counterparty fails to show in state 110 above, this fact is added as a cause of the appointment subgoal's failure. An anger emotion of A toward B will then be generated (inferred).

Maintain friendship planning agent

The following *maintain friendship planning agent* is initiated for each friend of an actor:

```
maintain-friendship(A, B) :-
        LAST SEEN = current time;
          SEE INTERVAL = 7 days,
100: IF current time > LAST SEEN + SEE INTERVAL
          appointment(A, B) ON FAILURE GOTO 100
             ON SUCCESS GOTO 200,
200: LAST SEEN = current time;
          GOTO 100.
```

Planning agency control structure

The possible planning modes (associated with a context) are:

Suspended
Planning agents are not currently running. They are suspended in a state.

Spinning
Certain planning agents are allowed to run freely until they reach a certain state, in order to synchronize themselves with input concepts. (Spinning will be described in more detail later.)

Daydreaming
Planning agents are allowed to run freely in order to simulate a sequence of events in an imaginary world.

Performance
Planning agents are allowed to run freely in order to perform external actions such as carrying on a conversation with the user.

The top-level planning loop is:

- Do forever:
  - If planning pass returns DONE then break.
  - If in performance mode then parse available inputs.

A *planning pass* consists of the following:

1. Determine the *lowest timestamp* among eligible subgoals. A subgoal in a final state (such as SUCCESS or FAILURE) is ineligible. In performance mode, a subgoal whose timestamp is less than the current timestamp is ineligible—you cannot change the past. When spinning, only certain subgoals specified when spinning was invoked are eligible.
2. If no lowest timestamp was found, return DONE.
3. For each actor in the context, for each eligible subgoal of the actor whose timestamp equals the lowest timestamp, run the subgoal. When spinning, if the subgoal reaches the desired destination state of the spin, return DONE.
4. If there has been no activity (subgoals running, demons firing) for more than a certain number of planning passes, return DONE. Otherwise, return NOT DONE.

Running a subgoal consists of the following:

1. If the subgoal is currently WAITing for a specified timestamp TS and the subgoal's timestamp is greater than TS, change state (as specified when the WAIT was issued) and return.
2. If the subgoal is in the WAITING state, increment its timestamp by one second and return.
3. Otherwise, run one step of the subgoal's planning agent, which may consist of various actions such as asserting concepts, invoking other subgoals, and changing to another state.

Whenever an object O is asserted into a context, for each actor in the context and for each subgoal of that actor, if the subgoal is WAITing on a pattern which unifies with O, the state of the subgoal is changed as specified when the WAIT was issued.

If an assertion is made regarding a state (attribute, enum, or relation) of an object P (such as the position of a knob on a TV set), the planning agent is invoked for the object of which P is a part (such as the TV set planning agent). This planning agent will then potentially perform other assertions (such as that the TV set is on if it is plugged in and turned on).

Exercises

1. Complete the implementation of the grocer planning agent.

2. Implement planning agents for other occupations.

3. Add attending a performance to the entertainment planning agent. The agent should decide based on various factors whether to watch TV or attend a performance.

4. Complete the attend-performance planning agent. The necessary theater grids already exist.

Chapter 8: The understanding agency

The fundamental problem of artificial intelligence is *understanding*: How can we get a computer to understand? (The definition of understanding is a hard problem, but we will assume that a computer understands if it acts appropriately—comes up with good answers to questions or carries out the desired action on behalf of the user.) Computers can understand computer programming languages, which only have mild ambiguities such as the order of evaluation of arguments to a function. In contrast, natural language is highly ambiguous: A sentence which has a single clear meaning to a human can have hundreds or thousands of possible parses for a computer.

Ambiguities arise at every level: At the level of words, "I" has at least the following uses in English:

- The subject pronoun: *I am reading a French book.*
- The letter: *I is the ninth letter of the alphabet.* (Microsoft Word suggests I change *is* to *am.*)
- The Roman numeral: *Napoleon I was born in Ajaccio.*
- The tonic in music: *That's a standard II V I progression.*
- An abbreviation for input, iodine, isospin, an integer variable, and so on.

At the level of syntax, the sequence noun-verb-noun-noun has at least the following uses:

- A subject-verb-object-object sentence: *Charlotte got Corinne dessert.*
- A subject-verb-object sentence where the object is a compound noun: *Charlotte got ice cream.*
- A vocative followed by a verb-object-object directive: *Charlotte, get Corinne dessert.*
- A vocative followed by a verb-object directive where the object is a compound noun: *Charlotte, get ice cream.*
- A subject-verb-object sentence where the object consists of two nouns in apposition: *Charlotte called coauthor Corinne.*
- A subject-verb-object sentence followed by a vocative: *Charlotte called Corinne, guys.*

For longer sentences, the number of possible syntactic parses can be quite large. By way of example, a parse by ThoughtTreasure of the sentence *Here are some country code modifications to be added* resulted in 678 potential syntactic parse trees.

At the understanding level, *Charlotte got ice cream* could mean that she purchased ice cream at a store, that she ordered ice cream at a restaurant, that she was assigned to the ice cream account at an advertising agency, that someone threw ice cream at her, and so on.

By typing `lexentryjuxt` into the ThoughtTreasure shell and then typing two words (or phrases), you can get an idea of how many meanings the words could have when combined. For example, "red" and "ball" produce at least the following possible meanings:

- A red toy ball.
- A red ball of the foot.
- A red Ball (family name).
- A red sphere.
- A red planet.
- A red Earth.
- Mars.
- A spherical communist.
- A spherical red color.
- A red baseball game.
- A red formal ball.
- The color red plays baseball.
- The color red goes to a formal ball.
- A communist plays baseball.
- A communist goes to a formal ball.

A sentence in natural language can mean many different things, just as one thing can be said using many different natural language sentences. Can we treat natural language as a very expressive computer language and write an interpreter for it? We can, but how is a computer to figure out which of the many possible interpretations of a sentence is the right one?

Understanding agents with common sense

Humans are somehow able to solve the understanding problem by picking the interpretation that *makes sense*. One way of capturing this intuitive notion is to encode knowledge of what makes sense into small, manageable, declarative chunks or rules—the approach taken in Cyc (Lenat, 1995). In contrast, the approach taken in ThoughtTreasure is to throw arbitrary C code at the problem. Why? We have tried in the past to code using rules and are convinced the problem is still too complex to be solved using a restricted notation.

Judgments of what makes sense are implemented in ThoughtTreasure at a number of levels and points in processing:

- during part-of-speech tagging,
- during syntactic parsing: syntactic filters,
- during semantic parsing: selectional restrictions, subcategorization restrictions, and anaphora heuristics, and
- *understanding agents* (UAs).

Here we focus on understanding agents.

Each understanding agent is responsible for understanding a certain set of concepts. Understanding agents can and often do interact with each other. An understanding agent takes a context and concept as input and produces as output to what degree (on a scale from 0.0 to 1.0) the concept:

- is *relevant* to the agent,
- is *novel* (previously unknown) information to the agent, and
- *makes sense* to the agent.

Understanding agents also provide *reasons* why an input concept makes sense and does not make sense.

Here is a conversation with ThoughtTreasure invoking concepts handled by the friend, emotion, and goal, understanding agents:

```
> Jacques is an enemy of François.
> He hates François.
Right, he is an enemy of François.
> He uses tu with François.
But I thought that he was an enemy of François.
> Lionel is an enemy of Jacques.
> He uses tu with Jacques.
Right, Lionel holds a "promotion Stendhal" from the
"École nationale
```

d'administration" and he holds a "promotion Vauban"
from the "École nationale d'administration".
> Jacques succeeded at being elected President of
France.
> He is happy.
Right, he succeeds at being the president of France.
> Lionel is resentful toward Jacques.
Right, he succeeds at being the president of France and
Lionel is his enemy.
> François is happy for Jacques.
True, he succeeds at being the president of France.
But I thought that he was an enemy of François.

Sentences beginning with *Right* and *True* contain make sense reasons, while sentences beginning with *But I thought that* contain not-make sense reasons. Normally ThoughtTreasure accepts an interpretation that makes sense, but if the interpretation with the highest sense contains not-make-sense reasons, it still is accepted since no better interpretation is available.

Here is a more detailed trace of the above conversation:

```
[enemy-of Francois Jacques]
  UA_Friend returns relev 1.000000 sense 0.500000
  novelty 1.000000
```

The friend understanding agent is given a concept to consider, an `ipr`, and it indicates that the concept is relevant, makes some degree of sense, and is new information.

```
[like-human Jacques Francois NUMBER:u:-0.55]
  UA_Friend returns relev 1.000000 sense 1.000000
  novelty 0.500000
  Makes sense because:
[enemy-of Francois Jacques]
```

The friend understanding agent considers the next concept, an `attitude`, which is relevant to it, is somewhat new information, and makes complete sense because of the previously learned `enemy-of` relationship.

```
[tutoyer Jacques Francois]
  UA_Friend returns relev 1.000000 sense 0.500000
  novelty 1.000000
  Does not make sense because:
  [enemy-of Francois Jacques]
```

The friend understanding agent indicates that this next concept does not make very much sense: in France, close friends use *tu* with each other, not enemies—except when being very discourteous. Still, there is no interpretation of the input text that makes more sense, so it is accepted.

```
[enemy-of Jacques Lionel]
  UA_Friend returns relev 1.000000 sense 0.500000
  novelty 1.000000
```

The friend understanding agent processes this concept without comment.

```
[tutoyer Francois Jacques]
  UA_Friend returns relev 1.000000 sense 0.500000
  novelty 1.000000
  Does not make sense because:
  [enemy-of Francois Jacques]

[tutoyer Lionel Jacques]
  UA_Friend returns relev 1.000000 sense 1.000000
  novelty 1.000000
  Makes sense because:
  [diploma-of Lionel promotion-Stendhal na ENA]
  [diploma-of Jacques promotion-Vauban na ENA]
```

The friend understanding agent considers two alternative readings of the input, since *he* is ambiguous. The first reading does not make sense, while the second one does: the friend understanding agent contains the rule that two people who have attended ENA, the prestigious graduate business school, use *tu* with each other even if they are enemies. ThoughtTreasure has in its database that Lionel and Jacques both attended ENA. Thus the program accepts the second interpretation.

```
[happiness Jacques]
  UA_Emotion returns relev 1.000000 sense 1.000000
  novelty 0.250000
  Makes sense because:
  [succeeded-goal Jacques [President-of France
  Jacques]]
```

The emotion understanding agent considers this input to make sense and not to be very new information. This is because it had already inferred the `happiness` emotion in response to the previously mentioned goal success. That emotion is linked to its cause, the goal success, which is used as the make sense reason.

```
[resentment Lionel Jacques]
  UA_Emotion returns relev 1.000000 sense 1.000000
  novelty 0.500000
  Makes sense because:
  [succeeded-goal Jacques [President-of France
  Jacques]]
  [enemy-of Jacques Lionel]
```

The emotion understanding agent considers this to make sense since one feels resentment toward an enemy for achieving a success.

```
[happy-for Francois Jacques]
  UA_Emotion returns relev 1.000000 sense 0.100000
  novelty 1.000000
  Makes sense because:
  [succeeded-goal Jacques [President-of France
  Jacques]]
  Does not make sense because:
  [enemy-of Francois Jacques]
```

The emotion understanding agent considers this to make very little sense (0.1). There is some sense to it in that one person is feeling an emotion in response to another person's achieving a goal. But it does not make sense because one does not normally feel happy for an enemy who has had a goal success.

Understanding agency control structure

Understanding agents are run on an anaphoric parse P in a context C as follows: The question asking agent is first consulted to determine whether P is an elided answer to a previous question. If so, the elided answer is expanded into a complete answer and then processed as a statement. Otherwise, P is processed as a question and then processed as a statement.

A parse P is processed as a statement in a context C as follows: A new context C' is sprouted from C. C' is initially identical to C. Tenses are stripped from P and placed in a data structure which will be passed down to all understanding agents.

For example:

```
[preterit-indicative @1400tod|[ptrans Jim na [and grocery-
store deli-store]]]
(At 2 pm, Jim went to the grocery store and deli.)
```

becomes

```
@1400tod|[go Jim na [and grocery-story deli-store]]
  dc->tense = preterit-indicative
```

Next, the parse is *unrolled* into parses which do not contain and:

```
@1400tod|[go Jim na grocery-story]
@1400tod|[go Jim na deli-store]
```

Statement understanding agents are then run on each such parse P' in context C':

1.   Run the actor-independent-pre understanding agents: the time understanding agent attempts to adjust story time based on P'. For example, assuming story time was previously set, the hour of its stop time would be updated to 2 pm:
     `cx->story_time = @19960115120000:19960115140000`
     The actor understanding agent recurses down P' in order to find new actors — any humans not already in the context C', such as Jim. Each new actor is added to the context and a standard set of planning agents is started for the actor — the sleep and handle proposals planning agents.
2.   For each actor A in C', run each of the actor-dependent understanding agents on P'. These include the occupation, emotion, goal, friend, appointment, shower, sleep, and trade understanding agents.
3.   Run the actor-independent-post understanding agents on P' in the context C': These include the relation, weather, and space understanding agents.

Thus, except in certain cases (such as the division between question and statement understanding agents), the parse concept P' is passed to all understanding agents, who have the opportunity to examine the concept and decide whether it is relevant to them. If so, they incorporate information from the concept into the context and return a make sense and novelty rating. The make sense and novelty ratings from all understanding agents for which P' was relevant are averaged and used as the make sense and novelty rating of the context C'.

A parse P is processed as a question in a context C as follows: A new context C' is sprouted from C and P is stripped of tenses and unrolled, as described above for statements. Then all the question answering agents are invoked, returning one or more answers. The maximum answer sense rating is used as the make sense rating of the context C'. (If no answers were returned, the input concept does not make sense as a question and so the make sense rating of C' is 0.)

Contexts are then pruned as follows: the contexts are sorted by make sense rating, the top *n* contexts are retained, and the remaining contexts are discarded. The *best context* is the context with the highest make sense rating. (To speed processing, set *n* = 1.)

Various actions are then taken based on the best context, which is considered to be the correct interpretation of the input:

1. If requested, output the concept and parse tree the concept derives from— the best interpretation of the input according to ThoughtTreasure.
2. Commit anaphors built during anaphoric parsing. For example, if *he* was ambiguous in an input sentence between Jim and Tim, and resolved to Jim in the best context, then the activation levels (weights) of the antecedent Jim (as stored along with each input and output channel) are refreshed. This would then increase the likelihood that a future *he* would refer to Jim.
3. If answers to questions were returned and added to this best context, output those answers: generate them in English to the English output channels and in French to the French output channels.
4. If reasons why the input concept makes sense or does not make sense were added to the best context by one or more understanding agents, generate them.
5. If questions to be asked of the user were added to the best context, generate them.

B-Brain

Minsky (1986, p. 59) proposed dividing the brain into an A-Brain and a B-Brain. The A-Brain is hooked up to the external world and the B-Brain watches and advises the A-Brain. The B-Brain recognizes various blunders of the A-Brain such as getting into a loop or concentrating too much on details.

Most of ThoughtTreasure is the A-Brain. A very simple B-Brain is used in the program to prevent certain tasks from taking too much time, such as syntactic parsing which is sometimes bogged down by too many possibilities, or operation of the understanding agency which may also be considering too many possibilities.

The B-Brain is also used to detect when the understanding agency is recursing too deep—say, more than 10 levels. The understanding agency recurses when an understanding agent makes an inference which is fed back into the understanding agency in order to see whether it makes sense.

When a task is started in ThoughtTreasure, an *A-Brain task data structure* is created, containing the timeout time, a recursion depth of 0, and the maximum recursion depth. At regular intervals in the task and at the recursion entry point, the B-Brain is called with this data structure, in order to determine whether the A-Brain task has exceeded its alloted time or recursion depth. If so, the task stops itself by breaking out of a loop or returning from a function.

Emotion understanding agent

The *emotion understanding agent* builds on previous work on the generation and comprehension of emotions by computer (Simon, 1967; Colby, 1975; Pfeifer, 1982; Dyer, 1983, pp. 103-139; Mueller, 1990, pp. 49-83). The ontology of emotions used here is based on the 22 basic emotion types identified by (Ortony, Clore, and Collins, 1988). These have been extended to 83 emotion concepts associated with 651 French and English lexical entries.

The emotion understanding agent is invoked to generate (infer) emotions and to understand emotions. Whenever a top-level goal (planning agent) is initiated or terminates, emotions are generated as follows:

- If another actor caused a goal success (failure), generate a gratitude (anger) emotion toward that actor: Assert it into the context, link it to the goal outcome via another assertion, and link it to the causes of success or failure. These causes are provided by the planning agent when it terminates.
- Generate an undirected emotion appropriate to the type of goal and link it to the goal. As in Daydreamer (Mueller, 1990), a motivation emotion is linked to active goals, and particular types of emotions are linked to particular types of goal objectives: pride to a succeeded social esteem goal, embarrassment to a failed social esteem goal, and so on.

A set of emotions is maintained for each actor in the context, and the weights of those emotions are decayed over time. If the weight of an emotion falls below a threshold, the emotion is removed.

The emotion understanding agent is invoked on an input emotion concept for an actor A. It attempts to explain that emotion as described in the following paragraphs.

If the input emotion matches one of A's existing emotions, the emotion understanding agent adds the known (asserted in the context) causes of that emotion to the reasons why the emotion makes sense, and returns with an indication that the emotion makes sense and was expected.

Otherwise, if the emotion is a fortunes-of-others emotion (O'Rorke and Ortony, 1994) in which A feels happiness or sadness toward another actor B, it is processed as follows:

1. Invoke the friend understanding agent to find out A's overall attitude toward B. (This is based on known or inferred attitudes and interpersonal relationships such as friends and enemies.) If the sign of the overall attitude is consistent with the sign of the input emotion, the emotion makes sense; otherwise, the emotion does not make sense. Consistent is defined as:

```
sign(B's goal outcome) * sign(A's attitude toward B) =
  sign(A's emotion toward B)
```

That is, the following situations make sense:

```
goal success of B, positive attitude of A toward B, A happy for B
goal success of B, negative attitude of A toward B, A resentful
toward B
goal failure of B, positive attitude of A toward B, A sorry for B
goal failure of B, negative attitude of A toward B, A gloating
toward B
```

The justifications for the overall attitude provided by the friend understanding agent are added to the reasons why the input emotion makes or does not make sense.

2. If A's attitude toward B is not known, infer it from the sign of the emotion as above. Process the inferred attitude as if it were input—that is, feed it back into the entire understanding agency.

3. Add known (asserted in the context) causes of any known emotions of B of the appropriate sign to the reasons why the input emotion makes sense. If no causes are found for the known emotion of B, add this emotion itself to the reasons why the input emotion makes sense.

4. If an emotion of B of the appropriate sign was not found above, infer it via the rule stated above. Infer a positive emotion for a goal success, and a negative emotion for a goal failure. Process the inferred emotion as if it were another input emotion—feed it back into the entire understanding agency.

Otherwise, if the emotion is not a fortunes-of-others emotion, all active top-level goals of A are considered: If the emotion is of an appropriate class for the goal, the emotion is used to infer the status of the goal—active, succeeded, or failed. For example, if a social esteem goal is active and the pride emotion is input, success of the social esteem goal is inferred. The goal understanding agent is invoked with the inferred status. If the status is the same as the goal's existing status, the input emotion makes sense and is expected. Otherwise, the goal's planning agent is spun to the inferred status—for example, if a goal success is inferred, the planning agent will run until it reaches a successful termination. (Spinning is discussed later in this chapter.) If a matching existing goal was found in this step, the emotion understanding agent returns.

Otherwise, the emotion understanding agent infers a goal based on the type of emotion. For example, if embarrassment is provided as input, a failed social esteem goal is inferred. A new planning agent is created and spun to the inferred status.

In all cases, the input emotion is asserted into the context. Recall, however, that there is a separate context for each interpretation of the input, so a particular interpretation of an emotion which does not make sense will ultimately be rejected (unless there is no better interpretation).

Goal understanding agent

The *goal understanding agent* is invoked when a goal status is explicitly provided as input, as in sentences such as:

```
He wants to be the President of France.
He succeeds at being the President of France.
He fails at being the President of France.
```

The agent considers all existing subgoals for the actor in the context. If it finds one with the same objective, it sets its status as described in the section on the emotion understanding agent. Otherwise, it creates a new top-level goal with the specified objective and instructs its planning agent to spin to the specified status.

Friend understanding agent

The *friend understanding agent* is used to understand interpersonal relationships such as friends and enemies. It also handles attitudes and tutoyer-vouvoyer relations. The friend understanding agent builds on previous models of interpersonal relationships and attitudes (Heider, 1958; Dyer, 1983, pp. 277-295; Mueller, 1990, pp. 151-162).

For each actor A and for each other actor B having an interpersonal relationship with A, the friend understanding agent maintains a data structure in the context containing the following fields:

- the *other actor* B,
- a *cache of database assertions* specifying current interpersonal relationships between A and B (such as acquaintance, friend, enemy, lover, spouse, and others in the interpersonal relationship ontology),
- the time B was *last seen*,
- the *see interval* or amount of time which is allowed to elapse before A initiates a goal to see B again, and
- a reference to the maintain friendship planning agent.

The friend understanding agent handles an input interpersonal relationship I1 between A and B as follows: For each already known relation I0 between A and B:

1. If I0 is the same class of relation as I1, the input makes complete sense and has zero novelty. Otherwise:
2. If I1 is a *next state* of I0, the input makes complete sense and is new information. I0 is added as a reason why the input makes sense. Possible next states are defined in the interpersonal relationship ontology. Examples are:

```
acquaintance-of -> friend-of -> ex-friend-of ...
             ...              -> lover-of -> ex-lover-of ...
```
Otherwise:

3. If I0 and I1 are both positive interpersonal relationships (such as friends and acquaintance), the input only makes a little bit of sense and is new information. I0 is added as a reason why the input does not make sense. Otherwise:
4. If I0 and I1 are interpersonal relationships of opposite sign (such as friends and enemies), the input only makes a little bit of sense and is new information. I0 is added as a reason why the input does not make sense.

If an already known relation I0 between A and B was not found above, then the new interpersonal relationship I1 is considered: The overall attitude of A toward B is evaluated. The make sense evaluation of the input concept I1 is calculated as:

```
0.5 * (1.0 + (sign(I1) * overall attitude))
```

For example, an enemy relation has a sign of -1.0 and a hate attitude has a value of -1.0. The above formula evaluates to 1.0 which indicates that the input concept makes complete sense. The justifications for the overall attitude are used as the reasons why the input concept does or does not make sense.

In all cases, the friend data structure is updated with the input relation I1. The old relation I0 (if any) is retracted and removed from the cache and the new relation I1 is asserted and added to the cache. Also, if an interpersonal relationship with B has changed, the appropriate maintain friendship planning agent is restarted (or a new one created) with the new relation.

The friend understanding agent *evaluates the overall attitude* of A toward B as follows:

1. *Return known attitudes*: Retrieve the attitudes of A toward B in the context and calculate their average weight. If any attitude assertions were found, return the average weight as the overall attitude and the assertions as the justifications for the overall attitude. Otherwise:

2. *Infer an overall attitude from known interpersonal relationships*: Calculate the average of the weights of known positive relations and the negative of the weights of known negative relations. Return this average along with the known interpersonal relationships as justifications. Otherwise:

3. *Infer an attitude using the rule that actors like actors who like the same things they like*: Retrieve known attitudes of A toward various objects and compare them to B's attitudes toward the same objects. Each difference between the attitude weights contributes to the returned overall attitude. When the difference is very small (agreement) or very large (disagreement), the attitudes are included as justifications for the overall attitude.

The friend understanding agent handles an input attitude of actor A toward another actor B as follows: The overall attitude of A toward B is evaluated as described above. The input concept is deemed to make sense to the extent that this overall attitude agrees with the input attitude. The returned justifications for the overall attitude are used as the reasons why the input concept does or does not make sense.

The friend understanding agent evaluates an input tutoyer-vouvoyer relation based on the sign of the average interpersonal relationship weight between A and B, and whether A and B attended the school ENA:

	ENA A	ENA B	sign(ipr(A,B))	make sense
tutoyer	yes	yes	1.0	1.0
tutoyer	yes	yes	-1.0	1.0
tutoyer	yes	no	1.0	1.0
tutoyer	yes	no	-1.0	0.5
tutoyer	no	yes	1.0	1.0
tutoyer	no	yes	-1.0	0.5
tutoyer	no	no	1.0	1.0
tutoyer	no	no	-1.0	0.5
vouvoyer	yes	yes	1.0	1.0
vouvoyer	yes	yes	-1.0	1.0
vouvoyer	yes	no	1.0	0.5
vouvoyer	yes	no	-1.0	1.0
vouvoyer	no	yes	1.0	0.5
vouvoyer	no	yes	-1.0	1.0
vouvoyer	no	no	1.0	0.5
vouvoyer	no	no	-1.0	1.0

Relation understanding agent

The *relation understanding agent* handles any input relation assertions not handled by other specialized understanding agents such as the emotion, friend, and goal, understanding agents. It checks an input assertion against existing assertions in the database, optionally updates the timestamp ranges of those existing assertions, and learns the input assertion (by asserting it into the database and dumping it to a file).

For example, if the database contains:

```
@1960:na|[chair-of Sony Morita]
```

and the following concept is provided as input:

```
@1994:na|[chair-of Sony Kimba]
(In 1994, Kimba became chair of Sony.)
```

the relation understanding agent learns the following:

```
@1960:1994|[chair-of Sony Morita]
@1994:na|[chair-of Sony Kimba]
```

The `chair-of` relation is `many-to-one`-a company only has one chair at a time. Thus when Kimba becomes chair of Sony, Morita can no longer be chair and the relation understanding agent updates the stop timestamp of the assertion involving Morita. This is the case of the *succession assertion.*

If the following concept had been provided as input:

```
@na:1994|[chair-of Sony Morita]
(Morita was chair of Sony until 1994.)
```

the relation understanding agent would have learned:

```
@1960:1994|[chair-of Sony Morita]
```

This is the case of the *identical assertion*—identical except (possibly) for timestamp range.

In the case of an identical assertion, an existing timestamp T0 is updated from a new timestamp T1 as follows: If T1 is na or T0 = T1, T0 is not updated because no new information is being provided. The new information is compatible with the old information. Otherwise, if T0 is na or T1 is a specification of T0, T0 is updated to T1. Otherwise, the new information is incompatible with the old information. For example:

T0	T1	result	
1994	na	T0 not updated	compatible
1994	1994	T0 not updated	compatible
na	1994	T0 updated to 1994	learned
1994	19940116	T0 updated to 19940116	learned
1994	1993	T0 not updated	incompatible

The relation understanding agent processes an input relation assertion A1 as follows: A1 is compared with existing assertions in the database. If A1 is identical to an existing assertion A0—that is, if A0 has the same predicate, first argument, and second argument as A1—the following is performed: If the timestamp ranges of A0 and A1 are disjoint, as in the following cases:

TSR0	TSR1
na:1965	1970:na
1960:1965	1970:na
1960:1965	1970:1994
1960:na	na:1955
. . .	

then the input concept mostly makes sense, and A0 is used as a reason why the input concept makes sense. A1 can be learned (asserted and dumped to a file). Otherwise, the start and stop timestamps of A0 are updated from the start and stop timestamps of A1, as described above. If a start or stop timestamp was incompatible, the input makes little sense, as in the cases:

TSR0	TSR1
na:1965	na:1966
1960:na	1961:na
1960:1965	1961:1966

A0 is used as a reason why the input concept does not make sense. Otherwise, if a start or stop timestamp was learned (updated), then the input makes sense, as in the cases:

TSR0	TSR1	updated TSR0
na:1965	1960:na	1960:1965
na:1965	na:19650105	na:19650105
1960:na	na:1965	1960:1965
1960:1965	19600208:19650105	19600208:19650105

A0 is used as a reason why the input concept makes sense. Otherwise, if the start and stop timestamps were both compatible, then the input concept makes sense, but no learning is done, as in the cases:

TSR0	TSR1
na:19650105	na:1965
19600208:na	1960:na
19600208:19650105	1960:1965
19600208:19650105	na:na

If A1 is instead the succession of an existing assertion A0—that is, if (1) A0 has the same many-to-one predicate and first argument, but not second argument, as A1, (2) the stop timestamp of A0 is na, (3) the start timestamp of A1 is not na, and (4) the start timestamp of A0 is na or less than the start timestamp of A1— then the input concept makes sense and the stop timestamp of A0 is learned, as in:

TSR0	TSR1	updated TSR0
1960:na	1965:na	1960:1965
na:na	1965:na	na:1965

(An A0 with the same one-to-many predicate and second argument, but not first argument, as A1 is also a succession and treated similarly.)

Question answering agents

Question answering agents, a type of understanding agent, are used to answer questions. For each active context, an input question is fed to a variety of question answering agents who add their answers to a list associated with the context.

An initial make sense rating is assigned by each question answering agent. This is modified by a structural measure of how specific the answer is—more specific answers have a higher make sense rating. Any answers are removed whose sense rating is less than 75 percent of the highest make sense rating among the answers.

At the end of the understanding cycle, the answers associated with the context with the highest sense rating (which derives from the answer sense ratings) are generated.

Each *answer* consists of the following fields:

- The *question concept.*
- The *question class*, such as question word question or Yes-No question.
- The *make sense rating* of the question, as interpreted by the question answering agent which produced this answer.
- A list of *answer concepts.*
- A list of *rephrased answer concepts*, to be generated if the user does not understand the answer concepts.
- A list of *answer texts*, one for each output channel—for example, one for the English output channel and one for the French output channel. These are used when the question answering agent desires full control over the formatting of the answer—as in the case of the dictionary agent.
- The *end of sentence character*, usually a question mark but sometimes a period (if a question mark was inadvertently omitted by the user in a question word question, or in the case of requests).
- A *sort by timestamps flag* indicating whether to sort the answer concepts by timestamp.

- A *pair generation flag* indicating whether to generate the answer concepts in pairs joined by temporal relations (such as *until*, *while*, *since*).
- A *generate timestamp range flag* indicating whether to generate the timestamp range of the answer concepts.
- *Timestamp generation advice*, used when the above timestamp range generation flag is set: whether to attempt to generate a relative timestamp (such as *in two hours*), whether to attempt to generate the day and part of the day (such as *last night*, *Friday afternoon*), whether to include the time of day, day of the week, day of the month, month, year, and duration, and whether to generate an exact or approximate time.
- The *name of the question answering agent* which produced this answer.

Yes-No question answering agent

The *Yes-No question answering agent* is invoked if the end of the sentence is a question mark. This agent attempts to prove the input assertion in the context. If a proof is found, the returned answer is *yes*, otherwise the returned answer is *no*. If the question is about an attribute, if a proof is not found, the agent also attempts to find a proof for ancestors of the attribute. For example, if an assertion of `purple` is not found, the agent attempts to find an assertion of any `color`:

```
> Are elephants purple?
No, they are not purple. Elephants are gray.
```

Since hierarchical relationships are not stored as assertions, but as pointers in the object data structure, Yes-No questions involving them are answered by a specialized ISA question answering agent. This agent answers *yes* if the queried relationship holds:

```
Mrs. Jeanne Püchl is a human?
Yes, she is in fact human.
```

Otherwise, it responds with a clarification if the queried relationship holds in reverse:

```
A human is a kind of Mrs. Jeanne Püchl?
She is human.
```

Otherwise, if the queried objects have a common ancestor, that is reported:

```
> Is Jeanne Püchl a cat?
No, but a cat and her are a type of a mammal.
```

Question word question answering agent

The *question word question answering agent* is invoked if a question word concept (such as an interrogative adverb, determiner, or pronoun) is contained within the input concept. It invokes other agents described in the following sections. The input concept is passed to all of these agents who then have the choice of responding or not responding.

Location adverb question answering agent

The *location adverb question answering agent* responds to a question containing a location interrogative adverb (such as *where*, *where on earth*), such as:

```
[location-interrogative-adverb [hang-up Jim phone26]]
(Where did Jim hang up the phone?)
```

The agent first calls the prover to get assertions matching the assertion of the question. It then looks for physical objects in those assertions (such as `Jim` and `phone26`) and calls the space understanding agent to find objects (such as Jim's living room, his apartment building, Paris, France) enclosing those physical objects, to be used as answers. Smaller enclosing objects have priority over larger ones.

Location pronoun question answering agent

The *location pronoun question answering agent* responds to a question containing an interrogative location pronoun such as:

```
[location-of Jim location-interrogative-pronoun]
(Jim is where?)
```

This is answered by finding objects (such as room or countries) enclosing the object in question.

Nearby object question answering agent

The *proximity question answering agent* responds to a question regarding nearby objects, such as:

```
[near Jim
 [question-element electronic-device
                   interrogative-identification-determiner]]
(Jim is near which electronic device?)
```

Time adverb question answering agent

The *time adverb question answering agent* responds to a question containing an absolute time interrogative adverb such as:

```
[absolute-time-interrogative-adverb [hang-up Jim phone26]]
(When did Jim hang up the phone?)
```

Proved assertions matching the assertion of the question are added as answers, with the timestamp range generation flag set and most of the timestamp range generation advice flags set.

Duration question answering agent

The *duration adverb question answering agent* responds to a question containing a duration interrogative pronoun such as:

```
[duration-interrogative-pronoun [conversation Fabienne
Lucie]]
(How long did Fabienne speak to Lucie?)
```

Proved assertions matching the assertion of the question are added as answers, with the timestamp range generation flag set and the include duration flag of the timestamp range generation advice flags set.

Temporal relation question answering agent

The *temporal relation question answering agent* responds to a question consisting of two assertions connected by a temporal relation where one of the assertions contains a question word, such as:

```
[superset-simultaneity
 [conversation Fabienne Lucie]
 [standard-copula location-interrogative-pronoun Fabienne]]
(Where was Fabienne while Fabienne spoke to Lucie?)
```

It proves the assertion not containing the question word with respect to a timestamp range implied by the temporal relation. Then it recursively invokes the entire question word question answering agent on the assertion containing the question word. For each proved assertion A and answer from the question word question answering agent B, if the specified temporal relation holds between A and B, an answer is added:

```
[superset-simultaneity
 [conversation Fabienne Lucie]
 [location-of Fabienne living-room87]]
(Fabienne was in the living room while Fabienne spoke to
Lucie.)
```

Timestamp request question answering agent

The *timestamp request question answering agent* responds with the current time of day, date, year, and so on, as requested:

```
What time is it?
What month is it?
What year is it?
What decade is it?
What century is it?
...
```

Degree adverb question answering agent

The *degree adverb question answering agent* responds to a question containing a degree interrogative adverb and attribute such as:

```
[degree-interrogative-adverb [tall Jim]]
(How tall is Jim?)
```

The agent retrieves from the database any connections between the attribute and relations, such as:

```
[attr-rel-range tall height-of -0.2u +0.2u 1.6m 1.8m]
```

It then looks up assertions in the database involving the relation and the argument of the attribute:

```
[height-of Jim 1.7m]
```

and calculates the corresponding weight of the attribute in the database which it uses for the answer:

```
[tall Jim 0.0u]
```

The weight 0.0 of the `tall` attribute is generated as *of average height*. (Positive weights are generated as *tall* and negative weights are generated as *short*.) Relation assertions retrieved from the database are used as justifications to be generated if the user later asks for an explanation. (There are other cases handled here; if an adverb such as *exactly* is used, the relation assertion is returned as the answer instead of the attribute assertion.)

Quantity question answering agent

The *quantity question answering agent* responds to questions containing an interrogative quantity determiner such as:

```
[standard-copula
 pronoun-there-expletive
 [question-element bread interrogative-quantity-determiner]]
(There are how many breads?)
```

It answers with the number of descendants of the specified class.

Pronoun question answering agent

The *pronoun question answering agent* responds to a question containing an interrogative pronoun such as:

```
[create human-interrogative-pronoun Bugs-Bunny]
(Who created Bugs Bunny?)
```

or containing an interrogative determiner such as:

```
[create
 [question-element human interrogative-identification-determiner]
 Bugs-Bunny]
```

```
(Which person created Bugs Bunny?)
```

It first builds a query pattern in which interrogative determiners and pronouns have been substituted with variables of an appropriate type:

```
object-interrogative-pronoun     => ?nonhuman
human-interrogative-pronoun      => ?human
[question-element human ...]      => ?human
action-interrogative-pronoun     => ?action
attribute-interrogative-pronoun => ?attribute
```

It then invokes the prover on the query pattern and adds the proved assertions as answers.

Top-level question element question answering agent

The *top-level question element question answering agent* responds to questions with a question element at the top level such as:

```
[question-element name object-interrogative-pronoun
  [name-of TT name]]
(What is your name?)

[question-element atom object-interrogative-pronoun
  [atomic-weight-of atom maximal]]
(What is the heaviest element?)
```

This agent invokes the intension resolver to find objects of the specified class which satisfy the specified restrictions.

Weather question answering agent

The *weather question answering agent* responds to a question regarding the weather, such as:

```
[standard-copula manner-interrogative-pronoun weather]
(How is the weather?)
```

The agent retrieves and responds with weather conditions asserted for grids in the context.

Appointment question answering agent

The *appointment question answering agent* answers questions or requests regarding appointments, such as:

```
[program-output TT [appointment Jim]]
(List my appointments.)

@199603062100:199603062400|[program-output TT
 [such-that calendar [owner-of calendar Jim]]]
(Display my calendar for tonight.)
```

It consults the list of appointments stored by the appointment planning and understanding agents, responding with those satisfying any timestamp restriction in the question.

Description question answering agent

The *description question answering agent* responds to questions asking for descriptions of humans or objects such as:

```
[standard-copula human-interrogative-pronoun Noam-Chomsky]
(Who is Noam Chomsky?)

[meaning-of object-interrogative-pronoun ball]
(What does ball mean?)
```

It invokes the dictionary agent to generate a description of the human or object.

Means adverb question answering agent

The *means adverb question answering agent* responds to a question containing a means interrogative adverb such as:

```
[means-interrogative-adverb [hang-up Jim phone26]]
(How did Jim hang up the phone?)
```

The agent first calls the prover to get assertions matching the assertion of the question. For each such assertion A, it looks for subgoals in the context having A as an objective. It uses the subgoals of those subgoals as answers.

Reason adverb question answering agent

The *reason adverb question answering agent* responds to a question containing a reason interrogative adverb such as:

```
[reason-interrogative-adverb [hang-up Jim phone26]]
(Why did Jim hang up the phone?)
```

The agent first calls the prover to get assertions matching the assertion of the question. For each such assertion A, it looks for subgoals in the context having A as an objective. It uses the supergoals of those subgoals as answers.

Explanation question answering agent

The *explanation question answering agent* does not generate explanations itself, but rather feeds back:

- *justifications* that have previously been generated and associated with database assertions,
- *justifications and rephrased answers* associated with answers previously produced by ThoughtTreasure, and
- *rephrased questions* associated with questions previously asked by ThoughtTreasure.

All agents are responsible for attaching explanations to what they produce. Given an interjection of noncomprehension such as *What?*, the agent responds with the rephrased answer to the last question as stored with the answer to the last question in the context.

If a question had been asked by ThoughtTreasure, the agent responds with the long version of the asked question as stored in the context:

```
Where?
> What?
([interjection-of-noncomprehension Jim TT])
You have an appointment with her where in one hour?
```

Given an interjection requesting an explanation such as *Why?*, or an interjection of noncomprehension, the agent responds with the justifications stored with the answer to the last question in the context. These justifications might have been generated by the question answering agent:

```
An elephant is extremely tall.
> Why?
([explanation-request Jim TT])
An elephant is extremely tall, because 3 meters is the
height of an elephant.
```

They also might have already been associated with a database assertion retrieved by a question answering agent:

```
Austria is the nationality of Mrs. Jeanne Püchl.
> Why?
([explanation-request Jim TT])
Austria is the nationality of Mrs. Jeanne Püchl,
because Austria is the nationality of Püchl.
```

One might object that since knowledge of what makes sense is not stored declaratively in ThoughtTreasure, it cannot generate deeper explanations of why an input concept makes sense. Each agent generates reasons, but those are specific to the input and might not reflect more fundamental causes.

However, once we have code that tells us whether something makes sense, we can run many examples through that code, and automatically induce generalizations satisfying to human users. Or we could generate various modifications of the inputs and look at the results, in order to produce explanations such as *Well, if Jacques had not attended ENA, then I would have been surprised that Lionel uses tu with him since they are enemies.*

Dictionary agent

The *dictionary agent* generates human readable, dictionary-like descriptions of objects and lexical entries in ThoughtTreasure's database. It is used by the description question answering agent and by the dictionary tool.

To use the dictionary tool, type dict into the ThoughtTreasure shell and then enter a word and phrase. (Separator characters such as apostrophes must be omitted: enter a single space for every sequence of one or more separator characters in the input phrase.) Definitions of all occurrences of the word or phrase as an inflection in English and French will be output to the files outdicte.txt (for English readers) and outdictf.txt (for French readers).

Dictionary definitions are structured as follows:

```
*** ENTERED INFLECTION
(A)   inflection 1 of lexical entry A
  (1) meaning 1 of lexical entry A
  (2) meaning 2 of lexical entry A
...
(A') inflection 2 of lexical entry A
...
(B)   inflection 1 of lexical entry B
...
(C)   inflection 1 lexical entry C
...
palindromes and anagrams (if any)
```

Each inflection entry is structured as follows:

```
features
lexical entry citation form if it differs from entered
  inflection
```

Each meaning entry is structured as follows:

```
ThoughtTreasure name of object
ThoughtTreasure name of parent of object
weight range for the lexical entry used with this
  meaning
features of the lexical entry used with this meaning
  (usage features)
argument structure of the lexical entry:
  selectional and subcategorization restrictions
related words:
  synonyms
  stronger forms
  weaker forms
  neutral forms
  antonyms
parents
children
siblings
(for humans, occupation and employer)
assertions involving object in textual form
assertions involving object and children of object
  in tabular form
assertion- and object-based associative thought streams
```

For example, here is (part of) the output of the dictionary tool for the inflection "winked":

```
*** WINKED
(A)   V ENG PAST wink
  (1) &wink &smile-wink-etc [SUBJECT ANIMAL] wink (IO
at+PHYSICAL OBJECT) FR
faire un clin de oeil (à); ENG wink N; FR clin de oeil
M N; ENG en clignant de l'oeil ADV, with a wink ADV;

(A') V ENG PP wink
```

This inflection is the simple past (A) and past participle (A') of the lexical entry *wink*. (The uppercase feature abbreviations such as V, ENG, and PAST used by the dictionary tool are defined in the feature report and the linguistic ontology.) The lexical entry *wink* has one meaning, the ThoughtTreasure object `wink`, whose parent is `smile-wink-etc`.

The argument structure of the lexical entry, when used with this meaning, is:

```
[SUBJECT ANIMAL] wink (IO at+PHYSICAL OBJECT)
```

Required arguments are shown with square brackets; optional arguments are shown with parentheses. In general, each argument consists of:

```
case in upper case
optional preposition in lower case
optional selectional restriction class in upper case
```

The cases include SUBJECT, DO (direct object), and IO (indirect object). Synonyms in English and French are the English noun *wink*, the French verb *faire un clin de oeil (à)*, and so on. Since the second interpretation of "wink" as a past participle of *wink* has the same meaning as the first, that meaning is not repeated. The French version of the above definition is similar, but with feature abbreviations, cases, and selectional restrictions generated in French:

```
*** WINKED
(A)   V ANGL IMP wink
  (1) &wink &smile-wink-etc [SUJET ANIMAL] wink (COI at
+OBJET PHYSIQUE) FR faire un clin de oeil (à); ANGL
wink N; FR clin de oeil M N; ANGL en clignant de
l'oeil ADV, with a wink ADV;
```

(A') V ANGL PP wink

Two types of tables are generated by the dictionary tool. The first type is an object by value table:

object	relation
child	values
child	values
...	

Frequent relations of the children of the object—those occurring for more than 25 percent of the objects—are selected for inclusion in a table. For example, the tables generated for clothing are:

wardrobe	specialty
dress	dressmaker
footwear	shoemaker shoe dealer
gloves PL	glover
hosiery	hosier
shirt	shirtmaker

wardrobe	HASA relation
pants PL	right pocket left pocket
short pants PL	right pocket left pocket

When a lexical entry is typically employed with the given meaning in the plural, this is indicated with PL.

In the French version, genders are also provided:

tenue F	spécialité F
bonneterie F	bonnetier M
chemise F	chemisier M
gants MPL	gantier M
robe F	couturière F

The second type of table is the timestamp range by value table:

```
from        to          relation
_____  _____  _____
start ts    stop ts     values
start ts    stop ts     values
...
```

For example, one table generated for `France` is:

```
                           president
_____  _____  _____
de Gaulle René Coty Vincent Auriol Léon Blum Georg
                 19740101000000  Georges Pompidou
19740101000000   19810101000000  Giscard d'Estaing M
19810101000000   19950501000000  François Mitterrand
19950501000000                   Jacques Chirac
```

(Leaders prior to about 1970 are shown without timestamps due to a bug in the implementation of ThoughtTreasure timestamps—they are implemented using the timestamps provided by the host operating system. This example was run on a Unix system whose timestamps begin in 1970. Macintosh operating system timestamps begin in 1905.)

The entered inflection does not include expletive elements, so that, for example, entering "go" causes all the phrases with *go* as the main verb to be output:

```
*** GO
(A)  V ENG INF
  (1) &like &attitude [0.5‾0.8]  [SUBJECT OBJECT] go down
well (IO with+ANIMAL)
  (2) &specialty-of &human-relation [SUBJECT HUMAN] go in [IO
for+]
  (3) &diploma-of-Bachelors-degree &diploma-of [SUBJECT
HUMAN] go to school [IO at+EDUCATIONAL INSTITUTION]
  (4) &diploma-of-Bachelors-degree &diploma-of FREQ [SUBJECT
HUMAN] go [IO to+EDUCATIONAL INSTITUTION]
  (5) &used-name-of &name-of FREQ [SUBJECT HUMAN] go by the
name [IO of+GIVEN NAME]
  (6) &lover-of &pos-ipr OLD FASH [SUBJECT HUMAN] go steady
[IO with+HUMAN]
  (7) &lover-of &pos-ipr FREQ [SUBJECT HUMAN] go out [IO with
+HUMAN]
  (8) &trance &altered-state-of-consciousness [SUBJECT] go
into a trance
```

```
    (9) &coma &altered-state-of-consciousness [SUBJECT] go into
a coma
...
    (26) &go-away &leave FREQ [SUBJECT ANIMAL] go away
    (27) &leave-building &leave FREQ [SUBJECT ANIMAL] go out
[IO of+BUILDING]
    (28) &leave &ptrans [SUBJECT ANIMAL] go out
    (29) &leave &ptrans [SUBJECT ANIMAL] go
    (30) &ptrans &primitive-action FREQ [SUBJECT ANIMAL] go (IO
from+) (IO to+)
    (31) &begin-copula &state-change-copula [SUBJECT] go [DO]
    (32) &aux-go &semi-auxiliary-verb [SUBJECT] go
(A') V ENG PRES SING 1
(A') V ENG PRES PL
```

Understanding as simulation

Given some input text, if ThoughtTreasure could construct a simulation, a detailed
mental model (Johnson-Laird, 1983; Craik, 1943) of what was happening in that
text, then it would be easy to answer questions about it. For example, given the
sentence:

```
Jim is watching TV.
```

ThoughtTreasure could construct a detailed model in which Jim is in his apartment
in a particular building in a particular city, sitting on the couch in the living room,
near a TV set which is on and tuned to a particular channel and TV show. Then
answers to questions such as the following would be read right off the simulation:

```
What room is Jim in?
  The living room.
What building is Jim in?
  His apartment building.
What city is Jim in?
  Paris.
Where is the TV set?
  On top of a TV stand near a couch.
Is Jim near a coffee table?
  Yes.
What other objects are near Jim?
  A couch, a TV set, a painting, a chair.
Is Jim standing?
  No, Jim is sitting on a couch.
How far away is Jim from a refrigerator?
  24 feet.
```

```
What channel is the TV set tuned to?
   Channel 2.
What TV show is Jim watching?
   The France 2 Evening News.
```

(This is not ThoughtTreasure output.) Some of the answers might be incorrect, but they are one plausible interpretation of the input.

Elements of the simulation need to be *defeasible*, so that if the user types:

```
No, Jim is in New York City.
```

ThoughtTreasure would revise its interpretation by transplanting the simulation to New York. That is, not all of the elements of the existing simulation need to be recreated from scratch; the location of his apartment building could perhaps simply be changed from a Paris street to a New York street. But if the user types:

```
No, Jim is in a bar in New York City.
```

the entire simulation would have to be redone, placing Jim in a completely new simulated environment. Now the answers to the questions would be different:

```
What room is Jim in?
   A bar.
What building is Jim in?
   A townhouse on 50th Street off the GE building.
What city is Jim in?
   New York.
Where is the TV set?
   Behind the counter suspended from the ceiling.
Is Jim near a coffee table?
   No.
What other objects are near Jim?
   Jim's friends, the counter, and a mug of beer.
Is Jim standing?
   No, Jim is sitting on a bar stool.
How far away is Jim from a refrigerator?
   8 feet.
What channel is the TV set tuned to?
   Channel 4.
What TV show is Jim watching?
   Monday Night Football.
```

The state of the simulated world needs to be updated as further inputs are received. Thus:

```
Jim leaves the bar.
```

causes Jim's location to be updated in the simulation:

```
Where is Jim now?
  He is in the sidewalk on 50th Street.
Is Jim wearing his coat?
  Yes.
How far away is Jim from a subway entrance?
  A subway entrance is across the street.
```

In order to implement the above, we first need to build an appropriate set of data structures for the simulation. Virtual reality (Foley et al., 1990) systems employ detailed 3-dimensional graphical models of space. In ThoughtTreasure, we have chosen a less detailed representation of space, but a more detailed representation of mental states (such as goals and emotions) of humans in that space.

Once the data structures are specified, the dynamic behavior of those data structures needs to be defined: In the above example, before Jim walks outside, he puts on his coat. Or if he drops his beer mug, the beer spills.

The human world is a very complicated one. Even given a coarse level of representation, there are many mental states, situations, human behaviors, spatial settings, objects, object states, and object behaviors which need to be engineered. The implemented planning agents of ThoughtTreasure and associated data structures such as grids and emotions, are one step toward a more complete simulation.

Building the basic simulation is not all that needs to be done. In order to do understanding, the simulation needs to be *steered* such that it mirrors the input appropriately. But steering the simulation is a difficult problem. A search must be conducted in a very large space: an input can affect any and all of the elements of the simulation, and there are many possible inputs.

When the program is told something, how much should it infer? If it infers a lot of details, then there is more steering to be done to keep those details in sync with the input (whether due to revision of previous interpretations or to new information). But if the program infers less details, there are less questions it can answer. Humans seem to create mental models at "just the right level"—not too detailed and not too vague. If a question comes up not answered by the model, then the model can be elaborated on demand. Indeed, Eco (1990/1992) shows how human interpretation of a text can be carried out indefinitely, to levels which are often far removed from what the author of the text intended. (See also R. E. Mueller, 1967, pp. 111-113).

Is simulation the right approach? Suppose we want ThoughtTreasure to understand the Solaris operating system, a version of Unix. A computer simulation of Solaris already exists: since it is already a computer program, it is its own simulation. Solaris consists of over 5,468,000 lines of code (SunSoft, 1994). If this level of simulation is the answer, then ThoughtTreasure, which so far only consists of about 135,000 lines of code (counting both the code and database files), is a long, long way from being artificially intelligent. And that's only Solaris. For it to understand how to use the phone system, we would then have to add the code for the 5ESS switch. And programs of similar complexity for simulating other aspects of the world. This program would be huge, and conducting a search through the space of possible simulations intractable.

But one does not need to understand Solaris at that level of detail in order to use Solaris. In fact, it is highly unlikely anyone — even an expert kernel hacker — is able to internalize 5,468,000 lines of code. ThoughtTreasure therefore uses simplified models, which are easier to specify and easier to steer: the modeling of telephones, for example, only consists of a few hundred lines of code.

The question remains: How do we steer the simulation?

The combination lock metaphor for understanding

In the situated action view of cognition (Ringle, 1993), intelligent behavior is more a response to the environment than a result of mental simulation. The environment provides a situation and one rapidly responds. It provides constant feedback which reduces processing requirements. For example, there is no need to remember whether a pot is currently covered or whether the water is currently boiling — all one has to do is look (or touch, taste, smell, listen). If intelligent actions — and therefore intelligence — are largely responses to the environment, then how does one understand stories? One sits on the couch reading and understanding a book, while the only overt actions are turning the pages, breathing, and so on.

Perhaps even reading a book can be viewed as situated action: As you read, you *put yourself in the situation* you are reading about. That is, whatever you do mentally when you are in a real situation, you can do when you simply read about a situation. You understand the imaginary just as quickly as you would react to the real. As seen in the documentary film *Moonblood* (Asch and Chagnon, 1976), when the shaman Dedeheiwa recounts the Yanomamo creation myth, he points to objects in the environment as if the myth were taking place then and there. Can we get a computer to understand in a direct fashion as humans do, by this sort of living an imaginary experience?

Thinking along the lines of Minsky's (1986) society of mind theory (see p. 218), suppose the mind consists of a collection of agents, each devoted to a different function such as breathing, avoiding obstacles, sleeping when you get tired, ordering when the waiter comes, and so forth. At any moment an agent is in a particular state, which we can think of as an integer. When you wake up, your sleep agent is in state 0, the rested state. When you become tired, the sleep agent enters state 1. When you go to sleep, it enters state 2, and so on—we could assign states to the various stages of sleep.

Agents can be instantiated: Instead of having a fixed number of agents, it is possible to create new agents (differing by their parameters) as necessary. Thus when you make an appointment with someone, you might instantiate a new appointment agent which keeps track of who the appointment is with, the date and time of the appointment, the meeting place, and the purpose of the appointment. When it became time to leave for the appointment, the agent would initiate a goal (another agent) to go to the meeting place.

Imagine each agent as one of the cylinders of a combination lock—a portable lock or one embedded in an attaché case:

```
   | 0| 0| 0|
   | 1| 1| 1|
->| 2| 2| 2|
   | 3| 3| 3|
   | 4| 4| 4|
```

The process of understanding consists of lining up the cylinders properly. When you read that someone is on the way to an appointment, you spin their sleep agent cylinder to 0 ("awake and rested"), their appointment agent cylinder to state 3 ("on the way to appointment"), and so on:

```
    | 8| 1| 6|
    | 9| 2| 7|
->| 0| 3| 8|
    | 1| 4| 9|
    | 2| 5| 0|
```

An entire set of agents needs to be assigned to each story character. As the story proceeds, you continue to adjust the cylinders in response to what you read. These agents or cylinders are very much like the planning agents (PAs) in ThoughtTreasure, which also have integer states. ThoughtTreasure's understanding agents (UAs) will be responsible for properly lining up the planning agents. The planning agents will be the wheels of the lock, and the understanding agents will be the thumb and forefinger which line them up.

The simulation consisting of a bunch of planning agents will therefore be steered by understanding agents, and to make this a more tractable problem, an understanding agent will be specially designed for every type of planning agent. ThoughtTreasure has the pairs:

```
UA_Appointment  PA_Appointment
UA_Grocer       PA_Grocer
UA_Shower       PA_Shower
UA_Sleep        PA_Sleep
```

The combination lock metaphor provides a way of modularizing the understanding problem—breaking it up into more manageable chunks. Instead of steering a huge simulation from afar with all of its momentum, you get in there and realign each of the little gears it is built from. But there is still a lot of complicated coding to do: A detailed script must be worked out for each area of human experience and coded as a finite automaton or planning agent. Then a multitude of possible input language constructions and concepts must be considered, and it must be determined how those inputs affect the state of the planning agent. The understanding agent consists of those procedures which modify the state of the planning agent in response to input. For example, the following input sentences affect the sleep planning agent:

```
Mary is sleeping.
Mary is lying awake in her bed.
Mary was lying asleep in her bed.
Mary was asleep and Peter did not want to wake her.
At ten in the morning, Mary was still asleep.
Mary had only slept a few hours.
. . .
```

The understanding agent will have to deal with each sentence (in the form of a ThoughtTreasure assertion provided as the output of the semantic parser). Even for a case as apparently simple as sleeping, there are many cases to deal with.

Spinning a planning agent to a state

Spinning a planning agent to a new state is not as simple as assigning its state variable. It would not work to create a new shower planning agent and simply set it to state 103 (the state in which the shampoo has just been poured on the hair), since the actor would not be in the shower, the water would not be turned on, the shampoo would not be poured on the hair, and so on. Instead, the planning agent actually has to run through all the steps leading up to state 103, to get the simulated world into the appropriate state.

In order to spin a planning agent to a particular state, that planning agent is allowed to run freely from its current state until it reaches the desired state. The spinning planning agent may invoke subgoals, which are also allowed to run freely. In contrast, other planning agents which are not subgoals of the spinning planning agent are not allowed to run, since the purpose of spinning is to line up one and only one planning agent.

What if a spinning planning agent never reaches the desired destination state? To help ensure that they do reach the desired state, planning agents may determine whether they are in spin mode and what the desired state is. This allows them to direct their activities toward that state.

Example: Sleep and shower understanding agents

Here is an example of a simple story processed by ThoughtTreasure using the sleep and shower understanding agents and planning agents:

```
> Jim Garnier was sleeping.
> He woke up.
> He poured Aquavital on his hair.
> Jim lay down on his bed when?
He lay down on his bed on Thursday January 18, 1996 at
midnight.
> Jim was asleep when?
He was asleep between Thursday January 18, 1996 at
midnight and Thursday January 18, 1996 at seven am.
> Jim stood up when?
```

```
He stood up on Thursday January 18, 1996 at seven am.
He stood up on Thursday January 18, 1996 at midnight.
> Jim was awake when?
He was awake on Thursday January 18, 1996 at seven am.
He was awake on Thursday January 18, 1996 at midnight.
> Jim was in his foyer when?
He was in his foyer on Thursday January 18, 1996 at
midnight.
> Jim was in his bedroom when?
He was in his bedroom between Thursday January 18, 1996
at midnight and Thursday January 18, 1996 at seven am.
> Jim was in his bathroom when?
He was in his bathroom on Thursday January 18, 1996 at
seven am.
```

The above conversation is processed as follows: The first sentence parses to the concept:

```
@na:na#12|[past-progressive [asleep Jim]]
(Jim Garnier was sleeping.)
```

(The above is the output of the syntactic, semantic, and anaphoric parsers.) When the time understanding agent receives the above concept, it sets the context *story time* somewhat arbitrarily to about a month in the past, since a past tense is employed.

When the actor understanding agent receives the concept, it notices that the character Jim has been mentioned for the first time. It therefore creates a new actor in the context and starts a set of planning agents which are always associated with an actor—currently, the sleep and handle proposals planning agents.

When the sleep understanding agent receives the concept, it instructs Jim's sleep planning agent to spin to state 410 (asleep). Along the way, the sleep planning agent calls the FINDO function to locate the bed nearest to Jim owned by him. As part of this process, Jim is first located. There is no assertion for Jim's location, so it is assumed that he is in his apartment (as specified by a residence-of assertion in the database). He is arbitrarily located in the apartment's foyer. Then his bed is found and returned from FINDO. (Jim's apartment—including the grid and the objects contained in the grid—has been predefined in the database files.)

The sleep planning agent then initiates the subgoal for Jim to be near the bed. A path through the grid is found, and in the simulated world Jim walks along that path from the foyer to the bed. Jim then lies down on the bed and falls asleep. The planning agent has thus reached state 410, and stops spinning.

The second sentence is then parsed into the concept:

```
@na:na#122|[preterit-indicative [awake Jim]]
(He woke up.)
```

(Actually, another concept is also produced:

```
0.675:[preterit-indicative [awake helium]]
```
since "He" is also the abbreviation for Helium, but this one makes no sense in the context.)

The sleep understanding agent then directs the sleep planning agent to spin to state 100 (awake). The sleep planning agent simulates Jim awakening after 7 hours of sleep.

The next sentence is then parsed into:

```
@na:na#1234|[preterit-indicative [pour Jim-left-hand
Aquavital Jim-head-hair]]
(> He poured Aquavital on his hair.)
```

(An interpretation that he poured the shampoo onto his body hair is rejected.) The shower understanding agent recognizes this concept as being part of the shower script, so it creates a new shower planning agent and instructs it to spin to state 103, the point when the shampoo has been poured on the hair.
The spinning shower planning agent simulates the following: Jim goes into the shower (after stripping), turns on the water, washes his face, and opens the shampoo.

The rest of the inputs are questions. The first question requests the time when Jim lay down on the bed. This assertion is found in the context and the concept and associated time are generated:

```
19960227160545: QUESTION <UA_QuestionTimeAdverb>
<question-word-question>
@na:na#12342|[absolute-time-interrogative-adverb
 [lie *Jim *Jim-bed]]
19960227160545: INPUT TEXT
<Jim lay down on his bed when?>
19960227160545: ANSWER sense 0.666667
```

```
@19960118000007:19960118000009#12342|[lie Jim Jim-bed]
```
(He lay down on his bed on Thursday January 18, 1996 at
midnight.)

Unlike the above question whose answer contained a time range of 2 seconds, the
next question involves a 7-hour time range which is big enough to generate as a
range:

```
19960227160608: QUESTION <UA_QuestionTimeAdverb>
<question-word-question>
@na:na#123421|[absolute-time-interrogative-adverb
 [asleep *Jim]]
19960227160608: INPUT TEXT <Jim was asleep when?>
19960227160608: ANSWER sense 1
@19960118000009:19960118070000#123421|[asleep Jim]
```
(He was asleep between Thursday January 18, 1996 at
midnight and Thursday
January 18, 1996 at seven am.)

The next question retrieves two times when Jim stood up. (Jim stood up at
midnight in order to walk to his bed.)

```
19960227160646: QUESTION <UA_QuestionTimeAdverb>
<question-word-question>
@na:na#1234214|[absolute-time-interrogative-adverb
 [stand *Jim na]]
19960227160646: INPUT TEXT <Jim stood up when?>
19960227160646: ANSWER sense 1
@19960118070001:19960118070003#1234214|[stand Jim na]
@19960118000001:19960118000003#1234214|[stand Jim na]
```
(He stood up on Thursday January 18, 1996 at seven am.
He stood up on Thursday January 18, 1996 at midnight.)

The rest of the questions are handled similarly, except that for location questions,
conversions must be done between the location-of used in parsing and
generation, and the more detailed at-grid used to represent locations in the
context. For example:

```
[at-grid Jim 20-rue-Drouot-4E <gridsubspace 1 83>]
```

is converted to:

```
[location-of Jim Jim-foyer]
```

for generation, since Jim is contained in a subspace of the grid that is contained in another subspace known as the foyer.

Time understanding agent

The *time understanding agent* is responsible for updating story time based on the input concept. Story time is initially set to the present time. It is then updated based either on a timestamp range provided explicitly in the input concept, or on the tense of the input concept.

If a date is specified in the input concept, the story time is updated to this date. If a time of day is specified in the input concept, the story time is adjusted (forward) to this time of day.

If no timestamp information is provided as input, the tensestep of the tense is used to adjust the story time. (Time steps are used to order tenses. For example, a past tense as in *I went* is tensestep -4 and a past future near tense as in *I was going to go* is tensestep -3.) If the tensestep of the input tense differs from the previous tensestep of the context, story time is adjusted based on the old and new tensesteps. If the tensestep change is between certain adjacent tensesteps, such as -5/-4 or -4/-3, the story time is adjusted backward or forward by a small amount. Otherwise, the story time is adjusted by a larger amount proportional to the difference between the tensesteps.

The adjustments are arbitrary. Everything in the simulation is concrete and time is no exception. Times could instead be stored on a relative basis, yet it is still necessary to know the approximate absolute time—in order to plan properly, it will be necessary to know the state of the external world such as what companies and countries exist.

Space understanding agent

The *space understanding agent* handles concepts involving stated locations or change of locations, such as:

```
[location-of Jim grocery-store]
(Jim is at the grocery store.)

[ptrans Jim na grocery-store]
```

```
(Jim goes to the grocery store.)
```

It is only invoked if the concept was not handled by other understanding agents which would be in a better position to explain the concept. The space understanding agent initiates a top-level goal for the actor to be at the input destination location.

Weather understanding agent

The *weather understanding agent* is responsible for updating the weather conditions associated with each grid. It handles input concepts such as:

```
[beautiful-day pronoun-it-expletive]   It was beautiful.
[sunny pronoun-it-expletive]           It was sunny.
[humid pronoun-it-expletive]           It was humid.
[freezing pronoun-it-expletive]        It was freezing.

[overcast-sky sky]                     The sky was overcast.
[dry air]                              The air was dry.
[cold air]                             The air was cold.
```

Ignoring exactly what is sunny, overcast, dry, and so on, this agent simply asserts the weather condition on the active grids in the context. Grids are found by locating the actors in the context.

Sleep understanding agent

Given the input concept `asleep`, the *sleep understanding agent* does the following:

If the input concept is of accomplished aspect, as in sentences such as:

```
Jim had slept.
Jim had slept for 8 hours.
Jim has slept.
Jim has slept for 8 hours.
Jim slept for 8 hours.
```

then do the following: If the sleep planning agent is in state 100 (awake), then look up last night's `asleep` assertion generated by the planning agent before entering state 100, in order to determine how long the actor is believed to have slept. Generate relevance, sense, and novelty ratings as appropriate based on to what degree the duration stated in the input concept agrees with the duration of the assertion. Otherwise, if the sleep planning agent is in state 400 or 410 (asleep), increment the current time by the duration stated in the input concept (if any) and then spin the sleep planning agent to state 100 (awake). Indicate that the concept is relevant, makes sense, and is slightly novel. Otherwise, if the sleep planning agent is in any other state, set the energy levels to 1.0 and spin the sleep planning agent to state 100 (awake). Indicate that the concept is relevant, makes sense, and is mostly novel.

If the input concept is of inaccomplished situational aspect, as in sentences like:

```
Jim was sleeping.
Jim slept.
Jim is sleeping.
```

then do the following: If the sleep planning agent is in state 410 (asleep), indicate that the input concept is relevant, makes complete sense, and is previously known information (novelty = 0.0). Otherwise, set the actor's rest and energy levels to -1.0 and spin the sleep planning agent to state 410. Indicate that the input concept is relevant, makes complete sense, and is new information.

Given the input concept `awake`, the sleep understanding agent does the following: If the sleep planning agent is in state 100 (awake), the concept is relevant, known, and makes sense. Otherwise, set the actor's rest and energy levels to 1.0 and spin the sleep planning agent to state 100.

The sleep planning agent is modified to change to the sleep or awake state based on the desired spin state (despite the current values of the energy and sleep levels), and to reset the timestamp appropriately.

Shower understanding agent

Given the input concept:

```
Jim Garnier pours some Vidal Sassoon on his hair.
```
the *shower understanding agent* does the following (in a given context):

- Find an active `take-shower` subgoal and corresponding planning agent instance for Jim Garnier.
- If there is such a planning agent, spin it to state 103—the state just after pouring some shampoo onto the hair.
- Otherwise, create a new `take-shower` top-level goal and planning agent, associate the mentioned shampoo with the planning agent, and spin

the agent to state 103.

The shower planning agent is modified to notice if it is running in spin mode and the current state is greater (later in the shower sequence) than the desired state. In this case, it goes back to the start of the cycle the desired state is in. The cycles are: beginning, hair wash, wash, and rinse.

Example: Appointment, asker, and emotion understanding agents

The following ThoughtTreasure session demonstrates a simple natural language calendar application making use of the appointment, question asking, and emotion understanding agents:

```
> I have an appointment with Ruth Norville at eleven
pm. Where?
> What?
You have an appointment with her where in one hour?
> The Four Seasons.
> Display my calendar.
You have an appointment with Ruth Norville at the Four
Seasons in one hour.
> I have an appointment with Amy Newton on March 21,
1996 at eight pm.
Where?
> List my appointments.
You have an appointment with Ruth Norville at the Four
Seasons in one hour. You have an appointment with Amy
Newton on Thursday March 21, 1996 at eight pm.
> I canceled the appointment with Amy.
> List my appointments.
You have an appointment with Ruth Norville at the Four
Seasons in one hour.
> Amy is mad at me.
Right, you cancel the appointment with her and she will
fail at having an appointment with you on Thursday
March 21, 1996 at eight pm.
```

In the first line, the appointment understanding agent is informed of an appointment with Ruth Norville which was not previously known in the context— no appointment planning agent exists with the same parameters. So the appointment understanding agent creates a new appointment planning agent.

If the program is in conversational mode (and it is), the understanding agent asks questions to fill in missing parameters of the appointment. The meeting place of the appointment is missing, so it asks *Where?*. A complete version of this question is also saved in the context.

The user then asks *What?* and the explanation question answering agent feeds back the previously saved complete question.

The user then answers the question by providing only the missing information *the Four Seasons*. (A complete sentence could also have been used.) This is recognized by the question asking agent as being an answer to the previous question, and this new information is incorporated by the appointment understanding agent into the existing appointment planning agent. No response is generated by the system.

The user then requests a list of appointments, and the appointment understanding agent complies with this request by generating the user's single active appointment planning agent and its parameters. This shows *the Four Seasons* having been incorporated into the appointment.

Another appointment with Amy Newton is then mentioned and a new list of appointments is requested and produced. Then the appointment with Amy is canceled, a list is requested, and the list no longer contains that appointment.

The user observes that Amy is mad at him, which makes sense to the emotion understanding agent, since an `anger` emotion had already been inferred in response to the failure of Amy's appointment planning agent caused by Jim's cancellation.

Appointment understanding agent

The *appointment understanding agent* creates, modifies, and destroys appointment planning agents in response to input concepts (in a given context). It recognizes new appointments, modification of the parameters of existing appointments, and cancellation of appointments. When an appointment planning agent is active, it recognizes when a participant in the appointment has gone to the meeting place and spins the planning agent to state 110.

Question asking agent

The *question asking agent* asks clarifying questions and helps interpret the answers to those questions. The questions are generated by other agents seeking information, such as the appointment, occupation, and trade understanding agents.

As understanding agents running in a context require clarification, they invoke the question asking agent which adds questions to a list associated with the context. At the end of the understanding loop, after the context which makes the most sense is selected, the question in that context with the highest importance rating is generated. A pointer is maintained to the *last question* asked in the context.

Each question stored in a context contains a number of fields. The *question class* field specifies whether the question is a question word question:

```
Where?
You have an appointment with her where today at nine
pm?
```

or a question about alternatives:

```
A 124, a 2000, or a 1800?
You want to buy a 124, a 2000, or a 1800?
```

An *importance* rating between 0.0 and 1.0 is assigned by the initiating understanding agent and used to decide which question to ask first. Only one question is asked at a time.

The *answer class* is the class of the missing information being requested. The user may answer with a complete sentence such as:

```
I want to buy a 124.
```

or with an elision such as:

```
A 124.
```

This class is used to recognize elided answers—any object which is an instance of this class is an answer to the question.

The *preface* field contains concepts to be generated before asking the question. This is used to specify how many instances of an ambiguous concept there are:

```
> I want to buy a Fiat Spyder.
There is twenty possibilities.
...
```

The *elided question* field contains a short concept to be generated first as the question, such as:

```
[or Fiat-124-Spider Fiat-2000-Spider Fiat-1800-Spider]
(A 124, a 2000, or a 1800?)
```

or

```
location-interrogative-pronoun
(Where?)
```

The *full question* field contains the complete question concept, to be generated if the user does not understand the elided question:

```
[active-goal Jim
 [buy Jim na [or Fiat-124-Spider Fiat-2000-Spider
Fiat-1800-Spider] na]]
(You want to buy a 124, a 2000, or a 1800?)
```

or

```
[appointment Jim Ruth-Norville location-interrogative-
pronoun na
 @19960226210000:19960226210000#12]
(You have an appointment with her where today at nine
pm?)
```

The *full question with variable* field contains the complete question, with the missing information replaced by a variable. Where the *full question* field contains an interrogative pronoun or list of alternatives, the *full question with variable* field contains a variable, as in:

```
[active-goal Jim [buy Jim na [itn-continuation-isa ?
answer] na]]
```

or

```
[appointment Jim Ruth-Norville ?answer na
@19960226210000:19960226210000#12]
```

The intension (itn) field contains a pending query described by timestamp ranges, classes, attributes, and arbitrary propositions.

The *asking understanding agent* field specifies which understanding agent initiated the question. This is used only for debugging.

Two examples will serve to clarify how the question asking agent operates.

First we consider the case of questions about alternatives. When the trade understanding agent receives the concept:

```
[active-goal Jim [buy Jim na Fiat-Spider na]]
(I want to buy a Fiat Spyder.)
```

it invokes the asker select routine on the object to be bought, `Fiat-Spider`, in order to retrieve concrete instances of that class from the database. Instead of `Fiat-Spider`, an arbitrary intension such as:

```
[such-that car [beautiful car]]
(a beautiful car)
```

may also be passed. 20 objects are returned to the trade understanding agent:

```
Fiat-124-Spider  1969-Fiat-124-Spider
1970-Fiat-124-Spider  1971-Fiat-124-Spider
1972-Fiat-124-Spider  1973-Fiat-124-Spider
1974-Fiat-124-Spider  1975-Fiat-124-Spider
1978-Fiat-124  Fiat-1800-Spider  1976-Fiat-1800-Spider
1977-Fiat-1800-Spider  1978-Fiat-1800-Spider
red-1978-Fiat-1800-Spider  white-1978-Fiat-1800-Spider
Fiat-2000-Spider  1979-Fiat-2000-Spider
1980-Fiat-2000-Spider  1981-Fiat-2000-Spider
1982-Fiat-2000-Spider
```

An intension data structure is returned containing the intension used to find the objects. The trade understanding agent then decides that there are too many possibilities, and invokes the narrowing down routine.

The purpose of the *narrow down* routine is to ask the user a short question which will narrow down a list of objects as much as possible. In order to narrow down the objects, the code first finds attributes and classes which can be used to distinguish the objects. Attributes of the objects are retrieved from the database:

```
red
white
A
B
```

Classes are found by looking for ancestors which are not ancestors of all the objects, and throwing out all but the most general such ancestors:

```
Fiat-124-Spider
Fiat-1800-Spider
Fiat-2000-Spider
```

The lists of attributes and classes are then partitioned into related categories—for example, those sharing the same parent or grandparent:

```
{red white} {A B}
{Fiat-124-Spider Fiat-1800-Spider Fiat-2000-Spider}
```

Then the number of objects which each attribute or class selects is tallied:

```
1 red
1 white

4 A
2 B

9 Fiat-124-Spider
5 Fiat-2000-Spider
6 Fiat-1800-Spider
```

A partition which minimizes the standard deviation of the counts and maximizes the coverage (sum of the counts) is then selected.

A question making use of that partition is then generated:

```
Question to ask  1  <Fiat-Spider>
Preface:
[standard-copula pronoun-there-expletive
 [such-that possibility [NUMBER:u:20 possibility]]]
elided question [or Fiat-124-Spider Fiat-2000-Spider
Fiat-1800-Spider]
(A 124, a 2000, or a 1800?)
full question [active-goal Jim
                [buy Jim na [or Fiat-124-Spider
                               Fiat-2000-Spider
                               Fiat-1800-Spider] na]]
```

```
(You want to buy a 124, a 2000, or a 1800?)
full question var [active-goal Jim
                  [buy Jim na [itn-continuation-isa ?answer] na]]
DbObjQuery na
```

The user then answers:

```
Fiat-124-Spider
(A 124.)
```

This is an instance of the class `Fiat-Spider`, so it is substituted into the full question:

```
19960226183325: elided answer expanded to
[active-goal Jim [buy Jim na [itn-continuation-isa
Fiat-124-Spider] na]]
```

The trade understanding agent receives this concept and invokes the asker select routine on the object to be bought:

```
[itn-continuation-isa Fiat-124-Spider]
```

The *asker select* routine sees the `itn-continuation-isa` which indicates that it is being invoked for a pending query described by the intension attached to the last question of the context. It then incorporates the user's answer into the intension, reinvokes the intension resolver, and returns the resulting objects. This time, only a few objects are returned and the trade understanding agent is satisfied. Alternatively, the agent could again invoke the narrowing down routine in order to narrow the possibilities down further.

Second we consider the case of question word questions. When the appointment understanding agent receives the concept:

```
@19960226210000#1:19960226210000#1|[appointment Jim
Ruth-Norville na na na]
(I have an appointment with Ruth Norville at nine pm.)
```

it notices the absence of information such as the meeting place, and generates a question:

```
Question to ask  0.5  <location>
elided question location-interrogative-pronoun1
(Where?)
```

```
full question [appointment Jim Ruth-Norville
                location-interrogative-pronoun
                na
                @19960226210000:19960226210000#12]
(You have an appointment with her where today at nine
pm?)
full question var [appointment Jim Ruth-Norville
                ?answer
                na
                @19960226210000:19960226210000#12]
```

The user then answers:

```
Four-Seasons.
(The Four Seasons.)
```

This is an instance of the class location, so it is substituted into the full question:

```
19960226165937: elided answer expanded to
[appointment Jim Ruth-Norville Four-Seasons na
 @19960226210000:19960226210000#-1342177268]
```

The appointment understanding agent then receives this concept (which could also have been typed in as a complete sentence), and incorporates the meeting place into the existing appointment planning agent.

Trade understanding agent

The *trade understanding agent* handles input concepts such as:

```
[present-indicative [active-goal Jim
[buy Jim na Fiat-Spider na]]]
(I want to buy a Fiat Spyder.)
```

It invokes the question asking agent in order to narrow down the product to be purchased:

```
[standard-copula pronoun-there-expletive
 [such-that possibility [NUMBER:u:20 possibility]]]
(There is twenty possibilities.)
[or Fiat-124-Spider Fiat-2000-Spider Fiat-1800-Spider]
(A 124, a 2000, or a 1800?)
```

Once the product is narrowed down to a sufficiently specific class, the agent responds with known advertisements:

```
@19950928131148:19950928131148|
   [for-sale 1978-Fiat-124
             NUMBER:USD:3000
             Todd-Spires
             na
             na
             STRING:email-address:"toddspi@quapaw.astate.edu"
             STRING:Usenet-newsgroup:"rec.autos.marketplace"
             STRING:message-ID:"toddspi.
812311772@quapaw.astate.edu"
             na]
(A 1978 Fiat 124 was for sale for 3000 dollars by Todd Spire
at "toddspi@quapaw.astate.edu" in Usenet newsgroup
"rec.autos.marketplace" in message ID
"toddspi.812311772@quapaw.astate.edu".)
```

Occupation understanding agent

The *occupation understanding agent* invokes the question asking agent in order to narrow down an input occupation. For example, if the input concept is:

```
[present-indicative [occupation-of Jim lawyer]]
(I am an attorney.)
```

the following question is generated (if the program is in conversational mode):

```
[occupation-of Jim [or specialist-lawyer trial-attorney
legal-advisor]]
(You are a specialist lawyer, a trial attorney, or a
legal advisor?)
```

Once the exact occupation is determined, a planning agent for the occupation is started on behalf of the actor, if one is not already active. The planning agent generates subgoals to go to work on a weekday morning, to perform job functions, and so on.

Analogy understanding agent

In the examples considered so far, the mentioned characters were already present in the database. In the case of Jim, an elaborate simulated environment—his apartment, the contents of his apartment, a nearby street, and so on—were already in the database. How should stories involving new characters be processed? If there are enough simulated environments already present in the database, then the program should be able to understand stories involving new characters by constructing new environments by analogy to known ones.

Planning agents invoke the FINDO routine to find an object near the actor: for example, the sleep planning agent invokes this routine to find a bed, the shower planning agent invokes it to find a shower, or the grocer planning agent invokes it to find the checkout counter. When such an object cannot be found, the *analogy understanding agent* is invoked. This agent attempts to create a new *target grid* containing the object based on a previously known *source grid*. An *analogy map* specifies how objects in the source grid map to objects in the target grid.

The type of planning agent (represented by the predicate of its subgoal, such as take-shower) and class of physical object (such as shower) are provided as input to the analogy understanding agent. A set of heuristics are hardcoded inside the analogy understanding for each type of planning agent.

If the type of planning agent is grocer, the source grid is the small city food store grid which has been manually entered into the database. The following entries are added to the analogy map:

```
small city food store          => store owned by the actor
owner of small city food store => actor
```

Otherwise, if the type of planning agent is take-shower or sleep, the source grid is either a family apartment or single person's apartment, depending on the situation of the actor. If the actor is a child, the following entries are added to the analogy map:

```
father in family apartment => the actor's father
mother in family apartment => the actor's mother
child in family apartment  => the actor
```

If the actor is a father or mother, the following entries are instead added:

```
spouse in family apartment       => the actor
other spouse in family apartment => the actor's spouse
child in family apartment        => the actor's child
```

If the actor is single, the following entry is added:

```
actor in single person's apartment => the actor
```

Once the source grid and initial analogy map have been set up, the target grid is ready to be created. The source grid is linked via assertions to objects which in turn are linked to other objects. In order to create a target grid embedded in its own network of assertions, we must decide which objects from the source domain remain constant and which are mapped to new target domain objects.

First all assertions involving the source grid are collected into a list A. Then the set P of physical objects referred to in those assertions is constructed. Then assertions involving those physical objects are added to A.

The target grid is created having the same shape as the source grid. The following is added to the analogy map:

```
source grid => target grid
```

For each physical object in P, if the object is not already in the analogy map, it is added as follows:

```
object => new instance of object
```

Certain types of assertions which should not be mapped to the target domain (such as `polity-of`) are removed from A. Then for each assertion P in A, the analogy map is used to map P to P': Each object in P which is in the left-hand side of the analogy map is mapped to the object which is in the corresponding right-hand side of the analogy map. P' is asserted in the context.

Then the `polity-of` the grid is asserted based on the nationality of the actor: If the actor is French, the grid is set in Paris; if the actor is American, the grid is set in New York; and so on.

Now that the target grid and assertions have been created, a target object which is an instance of the class of object originally sought by the planning agent is obtained by consulting the analogy map. It will be present since a source grid known to contain the class of object was previously selected.

Once the target object of the desired class is found, the actor is *transported* to that object: Instead of planning and executing a path from the actor's current location to the object, the actor is simply plopped down near the object since (1) the actor's current location may not be known, and (2) the new target grid is not integrated into the existing network of grids and wormholes, so it is impossible to get there anyway.

The target object of the desired class is returned to the planning agent that invoked FINDO. Planning should now succeed provided it does not stray from the target grid.

Toward a story understanding program

We now have a set of mechanisms that should enable us to address that hardest of AI problems: story understanding. Leo Perutz's thriller *Zwischen neun und neun* (Perutz, 1918/1988) was chosen for some initial experiments.

A simplified English translation of the first few sentences and some questions are processed by ThoughtTreasure as follows:

```
>>>>> Mrs. Jeanne Püchl was a grocer.
> Is Jeanne Püchl a cat?
No, but a cat and her are a type of a mammal.
> She is a person?
Yes, Mrs. Jeanne Püchl is in fact human.
> What is her occupation?
She is a grocer.
> Jeanne Püchl does what for a living?
She is a grocer.
> What is her nationality?
Austria is her nationality.
> Why?
Austria is the nationality of Mrs. Jeanne Püchl,
because Austria is the nationality of Püchl.
> Jeanne Püchl was where?
She was in the corner grocery.
> She was in what city?
She was in Vienna.
> She was in what country?
She was in Austria.
> She was on what continent?
She was in Europe.
> She was on what planet?
She was on the earth.
> She was in what solar system?
She was in our solar system.
```

> She was in what galaxy?
She was in the Milky Way.
> She was in what universe?
She was in the universe.
> She was near salami?
Yes, she is in fact near a salami.
> She was near what salamis?
She is near the Danish salami.
> She was near what meats?
She is near the pale lightly salted cooked ham, the
cubes of bacon, the duck pâté, the hot dog, the Danish
salami, the dried sausage, the garlic sausage, and the
smoked salmon.
> She was near what vegetables?
She is near the cery, the chives, the garlic, the
onion, the tomato, the greenhouse lettuce, and the
carrot.
> She was near what electronic devices?
She is near the cash register.
> Jeanne Püchl owns what?
She owns the corner grocery.
> Jeanne Püchl owns a store?
Yes, she in fact owns the corner grocery.
>>>>> At seven am she stepped out into the street.
>>>>> The sky was overcast.
> She stepped out into the street at what time?
She walked to the street from the corner grocery at
seven am.
> Where was her left foot?
Her left foot was in the corner grocery. Her left foot
was on the street.
> How was the weather?
It was overcast.
> Jeanne Püchl was where?
She was in the corner grocery. She was on the street.

The above story and questions are processed as follows: The first sentence parses
to the concept:

@na:na#12|[preterit-indicative [occupation-of Mrs-
Jeanne-P-chl grocer]]
(Mrs. Jeanne Püchl was a grocer.)

(For brevity, we do not discuss all of the alternative parses, each considered in a separate context.) Since the past tense is used, the time understanding agent sets the story time arbitrarily to about a month in the past:

```
UA_Time: Tense input; change 0
   @19960224212846:19960224212846#12 ---3456000-->
<preterit-indicative> -4
   @19960115000000:19960115000000#12
```

The actor understanding agent creates a new actor Mrs. Püchl in the context and starts the sleep and handle proposals planning agents associated with every actor:

```
****START NEW SUBGOAL [handle-proposal Mrs-Jeanne-P-ch1]
****START NEW SUBGOAL [sleep Mrs-Jeanne-P-ch1]
```

The above concept is passed to the relation understanding agent, which asserts it into the context:

```
****ASSERTED @na:na#12|[occupation-of *Mrs-Jeanne-P-ch1
*grocer]
```

(In general, the relation understanding agent is responsible for maintaining the consistency of relations across time: For example, if Morita was known to be the chair of Sony since 1960 and it is then asserted that Kimba is the chair of Sony in 1994, the relation understanding agent will update the first assertion so that Morita was the chair of Sony between 1960 and 1994.)

The above concept is then passed to the occupation understanding agent, which looks for an active grocer subgoal (planning agent instance) on behalf of the actor Mrs. Püchl. One is not found, so it creates a new grocer planning agent and instructs it to spin to state 100 (ready to handle customers):

```
****START NEW SUBGOAL [grocer Mrs-Jeanne-P-ch1]
19960224212854: PA_SpinTo <grocer> <100>
```

The grocer planning agent starts by trying to find the employee's side of the counter so the grocer can walk there to handle customers. The FINDO routine is called, which is unable to locate Mrs. Püchl or the counter, so it invokes the analogy understanding agent:

```
GRID ANALOGY MAP <Mrs-Jeanne-P-ch1>
employee-side-of-counter760 --> Mrs-Jeanne-P-ch1-employee-side-of-counter
customer-side-of-counter761 --> Mrs-Jeanne-P-ch1-customer-side-of-counter
sidewalk762 --> Mrs-Jeanne-P-ch1-sidewalk
```

```
rue-de-Provence --> Mrs-Jeanne-P-chl-STREET
side-chair763 --> Mrs-Jeanne-P-chl-side-chair
store-refrigerator767 --> Mrs-Jeanne-P-chl-store-refrigerator
Coke769 --> Mrs-Jeanne-P-chl-Coke
Orangina771 --> Mrs-Jeanne-P-chl-Orangina
carrot774 --> Mrs-Jeanne-P-chl-carrot
greenhouse-lettuce775 --> Mrs-Jeanne-P-chl-greenhouse-lettuce
tomato776 --> Mrs-Jeanne-P-chl-tomato
onion777 --> Mrs-Jeanne-P-chl-onion
wall800 --> Mrs-Jeanne-P-chl-wall2368
wall801 --> Mrs-Jeanne-P-chl-wall
Danette802 --> Mrs-Jeanne-P-chl-Danette
Yoplait803 --> Mrs-Jeanne-P-chl-Yoplait
yogurt-Danone804 --> Mrs-Jeanne-P-chl-yogurt-Danone
Fjord805 --> Mrs-Jeanne-P-chl-Fjord
Ovaltine806 --> Mrs-Jeanne-P-chl-Ovaltine
lait-Lactel807 --> Mrs-Jeanne-P-chl-lait-Lactel
biscotte-Heudebert808 --> Mrs-Jeanne-P-chl-biscotte-Heudebert
small-city-food-store1 --> Mrs-Jeanne-P-chl-small-city-food-store
grid-small-city-food-store1 --> Mrs-Jeanne-P-chl-grid-small-city-food-store1
Henri-Bidault --> Mrs-Jeanne-P-chl-human
Florence-Bidault --> Mrs-Jeanne-P-chl

...
```

A small grocery store off rue de Provence in Paris had been entered into the database. The following was entered: a grid, the grid's contents (including the store's walls, door, groceries, cash register), and its fictitious owners Florence and Henri Bidault. A new grid and its contents are created by analogy to this existing grid:

```
****ASSERTED @na:na#12|[owner-of Mrs-Jeanne-P-chl-small-city-food-store
                       Mrs-Jeanne-P-chl-human]
****ASSERTED @na:na#12|[owner-of Mrs-Jeanne-P-chl-small-city-food-store
                       Mrs-Jeanne-P-chl]
****ASSERTED @na:na#12|[at-grid Mrs-Jeanne-P-chl-employee-side-of-counter
                       Mrs-Jeanne-P-chl-grid-small-city-food-store1
                       <gridsubspace 7 11>]
****ASSERTED @na:na#12|[at-grid Mrs-Jeanne-P-chl-customer-side-of-counter
                       Mrs-Jeanne-P-chl-grid-small-city-food-store1
                       <gridsubspace 6 15>]
****ASSERTED @na:na#12|[at-grid Mrs-Jeanne-P-chl-sidewalk
                       Mrs-Jeanne-P-chl-grid-small-city-food-store1
                       <gridsubspace length 41: 0 5>]
****ASSERTED @na:na#12|[at-grid Mrs-Jeanne-P-chl-STREET
                       Mrs-Jeanne-P-chl-grid-small-city-food-store1
                       <gridsubspace length 70: 0 0>]

...
```

Mrs. Püchl is Austrian, so the grid is placed in Vienna:

```
****ASSERTED @na:na#12|
[polity-of Mrs-Jeanne-P-chl-grid-small-city-food-store1 Vienna]
```

(Mrs. Püchl's nationality was added to the database by the anaphoric parser when attempting to resolve the name *Mrs. Jeanne Püchl* into a person. No such person was found in the context, so a new human was created. Since the last name Püchl is marked in the database as Austrian, she was assumed to be of Austrian nationality.)

Mrs. Püchl is then transported to the new store:

```
****ASSERTED @19960115000000:inf#12|
[at-grid Mrs-Jeanne-P-chl
Mrs-Jeanne-P-chl-grid-small-city-food-store1 <gridsubspace 7 11>]
```

and the object:

```
Mrs-Jeanne-P-chl-employee-side-of-counter
```

is returned by FINDO to the grocer planning agent as originally requested.

The grocer planning agent then initiates a subgoal for Mrs. Püchl to be near this object:

```
****START NEW SUBGOAL [near-reachable Mrs-Jeanne-P-chl
                        Mrs-Jeanne-P-chl-employee-side-of-counter]
```

This subgoal succeeds immediately since the analogy understanding agent had already transported her to this object.

The grocer planning agent has therefore reached state 100 and it stops spinning:

```
-----subgoal <Mrs-Jeanne-P-chl> [grocer Mrs-Jeanne-P-chl]
   100 was WAITING
19960224212854: PA_Grocer
FINISHED SPINNING
   UA_Occupation returns relev 1.000000 sense 1.000000
   novelty 1.000000
   UA_Statement returns 1.000000
UnderstandUtterance3 returns 1.000000
19960224212854: **** UNDERSTANDING AGENCY END ****
```

The first sentence of the story has been processed, and now the user proceeds to ask several basic questions to test the program's understanding. The first two questions are answered by the ISA question answering agent:

```
19960224212900: QUESTION <UA_QuestionISA> <Yes-No-question>
@na:na#122|[isa *Mrs-Jeanne-P-chl *cat]
19960224212900: INPUT TEXT <Is Jeanne Püchl a cat?>
19960224212900: ANSWER sense 0.1
[sentence-adverb-of-negation [but [isa [and cat Mrs-Jeanne-P-chl] mammal]]]
(No, but a cat and her are a type of a mammal.)
...
19960224212907: QUESTION <UA_QuestionISA> <Yes-No-question>
```

```
@na:na#1222|[isa *Mrs-Jeanne-P-chl *human]
19960224212907: INPUT TEXT <She is a person?>
19960224212907: ANSWER sense 1
[adverb-of-affirmation [isa Mrs-Jeanne-P-chl human]]
(Yes, Mrs. Jeanne Püchl is in fact human.)
```

In the first question, Mrs. Püchl is not a kind of cat, but Mrs. Püchl and the cat have a common ancestor in the class hierarchy: the mammal. (Here the pronoun *her* is generated with the wrong case. See however the discussion of Pinker, 1994, pp. 390-392.)

The next two questions are answered by the pronoun question answering agent:

```
19960224212914: QUESTION <UA_QuestionPronoun>
<question-word-question>
@na:na#12224|
[*occupation-of *Mrs-Jeanne-P-chl object-interrogative-pronoun]
19960224212914: INPUT TEXT <What is her occupation?>
19960224212914: ANSWER sense 1
@na:na#12224|[occupation-of Mrs-Jeanne-P-chl grocer]
(She is a grocer.)
...
19960224212917: QUESTION <UA_QuestionPronoun>
<question-word-question>
@na:na#122242|
[occupation-of *Mrs-Jeanne-P-chl *object-interrogative-pronoun]
19960224212917: INPUT TEXT <Jeanne Püchl does what for a living?>
19960224212917: ANSWER sense 1
@na:na#122242|[occupation-of Mrs-Jeanne-P-chl grocer]
(She is a grocer.)
```

This agent attempts to prove the pattern given by the question—that some occupation is Mrs. Püchl's occupation. The answer is the pattern instantiated with the bindings from the proof (which bind the variable to the occupation previously asserted into the context).

The next question is also answered by the pronoun question answering agent:

```
19960224212921: QUESTION <UA_QuestionPronoun>
<question-word-question>
@na:na#1222423|
[*nationality-of *Mrs-Jeanne-P-chl object-interrogative-pronoun]
19960224212921: INPUT TEXT <What is her nationality?>
19960224212921: ANSWER sense 1
[nationality-of Mrs-Jeanne-P-chl Austria]
(Austria is her nationality.)
```

The next question asks for an explanation of the previous answer:

```
19960224212923: QUESTION <UA_QuestionCanned>
```

```
<question-word-question>
explanation-request
19960224212923: INPUT TEXT <Why?>
19960224212923: ANSWER sense 1
[since [nationality-of ausn-Puchl Austria]
       [nationality-of Mrs-Jeanne-P-chl Austria]]
(Austria is the nationality of Mrs. Jeanne Püchl, because Austria is
the nationality of Püchl.)
```

When the anaphoric parser asserted into the context that Mrs. Püchl is Austrian, it attached a justification to that assertion—that the last name Püchl is Austrian. The explanation question answering agent simply feeds back this justification attached to the answer to the previous question.

The next question is answered by the location pronoun question answering agent:

```
19960224212934: QUESTION <UA_QuestionLocationPronoun>
<question-word-question>
@na:na#122242323|
[location-of *Mrs-Jeanne-P-chl *location-interrogative-pronoun]
19960224212934: INPUT TEXT
<Jeanne Püchl was where?>
19960224212934: ANSWER sense 0.666667
@19960115000000:inf#122242323|
[location-of Mrs-Jeanne-P-chl Mrs-Jeanne-P-chl-small-city-food-store]
(She was in the corner grocery.)
```

This agent invokes spatial code which finds a room (or, in general, an apartment, building, road, city, and so on) containing Mrs. Püchl which can be used to describe her location to the user. (Locations are stored internally as points or regions of grids.)

A similar agent and process are used to answer a series of questions requesting particular types of containing entities:

```
19960224212947: QUESTION <UA_QuestionLocation>
<question-word-question>
@na:na#1222423233|[location-of
 *Mrs-Jeanne-P-chl
 *[question-element city interrogative-identification-determiner]]
19960224212947: INPUT TEXT <She was in what city?>
19960224212947: ANSWER sense 1
@19960115000000:inf#1222423233|[location-of Mrs-Jeanne-P-chl Vienna]
(She was in Vienna.)
...
19960224213025: QUESTION <UA_QuestionLocation>
<question-word-question>
@na:na#-1768531817|[location-of
 *Mrs-Jeanne-P-chl
 *[question-element universe
```

```
         interrogative-identification-determiner]]
19960224213025: INPUT TEXT <She was in what universe?>
19960224213025: ANSWER sense 1
@19960115000000:inf#-1768531817|
[location-of Mrs-Jeanne-P-chl our-universe]
(She was in the universe.)
```

The next question is answered by the Yes-No question answering agent, which attempts to prove the questioned assertion:

```
19960224213030: QUESTION <UA_QuestionYesNo2> <Yes-No-question>
@na:na#-505448985|[near *Mrs-Jeanne-P-chl *salami]
19960224213030: INPUT TEXT <She was near salami?>
19960224213030: ANSWER sense 1
[adverb-of-affirmation @na:na#-505448985|
[near Mrs-Jeanne-P-chl salami]]
(Yes, she is in fact near a salami.)
```

The near concept is not stored in the context, so spatial code must be invoked by the prover in order to determine the grid locations of the two objects and measure their distance.

The next series of questions is answered by the near question answering agent which invokes spatial code to look for physical objects of a specified type near a specified object:

```
19960224213038: QUESTION <UA_QuestionNear>
<question-word-question>
@na:na#-759522553|[near
 *Mrs-Jeanne-P-chl
 *[question-element salami interrogative-identification-determiner]]
19960224213038: INPUT TEXT <She was near what salamis?>
19960224213038: ANSWER sense 0.666667
@na:na#-759522553|
[near Mrs-Jeanne-P-chl Mrs-Jeanne-P-chl-salami-danois]
(She is near the Danish salami.)
...
19960224213044: QUESTION <UA_QuestionNear> <question-word-question>
@na:na#994709063|[near
 *Mrs-Jeanne-P-chl
 *[question-element meat interrogative-identification-determiner]]
19960224213044: INPUT TEXT <She was near what meats?>
19960224213044: ANSWER sense 0.666667
@na:na#994709063|
[near Mrs-Jeanne-P-chl Mrs-Jeanne-P-chl-jambon-de-Paris]
@na:na#994709063|[near Mrs-Jeanne-P-chl Mrs-Jeanne-P-chl-lardons]
@na:na#994709063|
[near Mrs-Jeanne-P-chl Mrs-Jeanne-P-chl-pate-de-canard]
@na:na#994709063|
[near Mrs-Jeanne-P-chl Mrs-Jeanne-P-chl-saucisse-de-Francfort]
```

```
@na:na#994709063|
[near Mrs-Jeanne-P-ch1 Mrs-Jeanne-P-ch1-salami-danois]
@na:na#994709063|
[near Mrs-Jeanne-P-ch1 Mrs-Jeanne-P-ch1-saucisson-sec]
@na:na#994709063|
[near Mrs-Jeanne-P-ch1 Mrs-Jeanne-P-ch1-saucisson-a-l-ail]
@na:na#994709063|[near Mrs-Jeanne-P-ch1 Mrs-Jeanne-P-ch1-saumon-fume]
(She is near the pale lightly salted cooked ham, the cubes of bacon,
the duck pâté, the hot dog, the Danish salami, the dried sausage, the
garlic sausage, and the smoked salmon.)
...
```

Stylistic discourse-level transformations are used in the generator to merge the assertions into a single sentence.

The next two questions are answered by the pronoun question answering agent and the Yes-No question answering agent:

```
19960224213102: QUESTION <UA_QuestionPronoun>
<question-word-question>
@na:na#-1723349560|
[owner-of *object-interrogative-pronoun *Mrs-Jeanne-P-ch1]
19960224213102: INPUT TEXT <Jeanne Püchl owns what?>
19960224213102: ANSWER sense 0.666667
@na:na#-1723349560|
[owner-of Mrs-Jeanne-P-ch1-small-city-food-store Mrs-Jeanne-P-ch1]
(She owns the corner grocery.)
...
19960224213105: QUESTION <UA_QuestionYesNo2> <Yes-No-question>
@na:na#-53626415|[owner-of *store *Mrs-Jeanne-P-ch1]
19960224213105: INPUT TEXT <Jeanne Püchl owns a store?>
19960224213105: ANSWER sense 0.833333
[adverb-of-affirmation @na:na#-53626415|[owner-of
  Mrs-Jeanne-P-ch1-small-city-food-store Mrs-Jeanne-P-ch1]]
(Yes, she in fact owns the corner grocery.)
```

Next the second sentence of the story is entered and parsed into the concept:

```
@na:na#-536264148|[preterit-indicative
  @19960115070000#-53626415:19960115070000#-53626415|
[ptrans-walk Mrs-Jeanne-P-ch1 na Mrs-Jeanne-P-ch1-STREET]]
(At seven am she stepped out into the street.)
```

The anaphoric parser resolved *the street* into the nearby street: objects of the specified class in the same grid as actors in the context are considered.

The time understanding agent sets the story time to the time of day explicitly provided in the input:

```
UA_Time: TsRange input -4
```

```
@19960115000000:19960115000001#-536264148 ------> -4
@19960115070000:19960115070000#-536264148
```

The space understanding agent starts a new planning agent on behalf of Mrs. Püchl with the goal to be in the street and instructs it to spin to the success state:

```
****START NEW SUBGOAL
[near-reachable Mrs-Jeanne-P-chl Mrs-Jeanne-P-chl-STREET]
...
19960224213109: PA_SpinTo <near-reachable> <-5>
```

Trip planning is invoked to find a path from Mrs. Püchl's current location to the street:

```
19960224213109: finding path from <Mrs-Jeanne-P-chl> 7 11 to
                <Mrs-Jeanne-P-chl-STREET> 0 0
<gridsubspace grid-small-city-food-store1>
&&&&&&&&&&&&&&&&&&&&&&&&&&&&&&&&&&&&&&&&&&&&&&&&&&&&&&&&&&&&&
&**        wwwwwwwwwwwwwwwwwwwwwwwwwwwwwwwwwwwwwwwwwwwwwwwwW&
&  **     w                                           scssw&
&   ***                                               ssssw&
&     **                                              sFssw&
&     w*                                              ssssw&
&     w*  ttt         ssssSssss                       ssssw&
&     w * tttc   ssssssssssssssssssssssssssss         ssssw&
&     w s*ctt    ssssssssssssssssssssssssssss         sCssw&
&     w   ttt            C         l                  ssssw&
&     w                                               swssw&
&     w                                               ssssw&
&     w                                               ssssw&
&     w                                               ssssw&
&        wwwwwwwwwwwwwwwwwwwwwwwwwwwwwwwwwwwwwwwwwwwwwwwwwwW&
&&&&&&&&&&&&&&&&&&&&&&&&&&&&&&&&&&&&&&&&&&&&&&&&&&&&&&&&&&&&&
19960224213109: dist 3.18862 speed 1 dur 3
* grid-walk Mrs-Jeanne Mrs-Jeanne-P-chl-gri Mrs-Jeanne-P-chl
Mrs-Jeanne-P-chl-STR path 19960115070000#-536264148
19960115070003#-536264148
```

A trip using walking with a duration of three seconds is found and carried out, the planning agent terminates successfully, and spinning is completed:

```
990->SUCCESS <Mrs-Jeanne-P-chl>
  [near-reachable Mrs-Jeanne-P-chl Mrs-Jeanne-P-chl-STREET]
...
FINISHED SPINNING
  UA_Space returns relev 1.000000 sense 0.750000 novelty 1.000000
    UA_Statement returns 0.750000
UnderstandUtterance3 returns 0.750000
```

```
19960224213111: **** UNDERSTANDING AGENCY END ****
```

The next story sentence is parsed into the concept:

```
@na:na#-1067674182|[preterit-indicative [overcast-sky sky]]
(The sky was overcast.)
```

This concept is processed by the weather understanding agent, which asserts the weather condition of the grid into the context:

```
****ASSERTED @19960115070003:inf#-1067674182|[overcast-sky
   Mrs-Jeanne-P-chl-grid-small-city-food-store1]
      UA_Weather returns relev 1.000000 sense 1.000000
      novelty 1.000000
   UA_Statement returns 1.000000
UnderstandUtterance3 returns 1.000000
19960224213111: **** UNDERSTANDING AGENCY END ****
```

Now some more questions are asked by the user and answered by the program:

```
19960224213136: QUESTION <UA_QuestionTimeAdverb> <question-
word-question>
@na:na#-2086807227|[time-of-day-interrogative-adverb
  [ptrans-walk *Mrs-Jeanne-P-chl na *Mrs-Jeanne-P-chl-STREET]]
19960224213136: INPUT TEXT
<She stepped out into the street at what time?>
19960224213136: ANSWER sense 0.714286
@19960115070002:19960115070003#-2086807227|[grid-walk Mrs-
Jeanne-P-chl
   Mrs-Jeanne-P-chl-grid-small-city-food-store1
   NUMBER:u:7 NUMBER:u:11 NUMBER:u:0 NUMBER:u:0]
(She walked to the street from the corner grocery at seven
am.)
```

The prover is invoked, which converts the concept `ptrans-walk` used in natural language into the concept `grid-walk` used by the spatial code in the program. A `grid-walk` is retrieved as the answer which contains the detailed walk information. The generator converts this back into a `ptrans-walk` which refers to containing objects (street and corner grocery) instead of to grid coordinates (<7, 11> and <0, 0>). (That concept is built inside the generator and not shown above.) In the next question, spatial code is invoked to find containing objects of Mrs. Püchl's left foot:

```
19960224213258: QUESTION <UA_QuestionLocationPronoun>
<question-word-question>
```

```
@na:na#606764216|[location-of *location-interrogative-pronoun
  *Mrs-Jeanne-P-chl-left-foot]
19960224213258: INPUT TEXT <Where was her left foot?>
19960224213258: ANSWER sense 0.333333
@19960115000000:19960115070003#606764216|[location-of
  Mrs-Jeanne-P-chl-left-foot
  Mrs-Jeanne-P-chl-small-city-food-store]
@19960115070003:inf#606764216|[location-of
  Mrs-Jeanne-P-chl-left-foot Mrs-Jeanne-P-chl-STREET]
(Her left foot was in the corner grocery. Her left foot was
on the street.)
```

If the spatial code cannot locate an object, it attempts to locate objects of which that object is a part.

The next question is answered by the weather question answering agent, which retrieves weather assertions on grids containing actors in the context:

```
19960224213305: QUESTION <UA_QuestionWeather2>
<question-word-question>
@na:na#1772674866|
[standard-copula manner-interrogative-pronoun weather]
19960224213305: INPUT TEXT <How was the weather?>
19960224213305: ANSWER sense 1
@19960115070003:inf#1772674866|
[overcast-sky pronoun-it-expletive]
(It was overcast.)
```

Finally Mrs. Püchl's location is queried:

```
19960224213321: QUESTION <UA_QuestionLocationPronoun>
<question-word-question>
@na:na#546879479|[location-of *Mrs-Jeanne-P-chl *location-
interrogative-pronoun]
19960224213321: INPUT TEXT <Jeanne Püchl was where?>
19960224213321: ANSWER sense 0.666667
@19960115000000:19960115070003#546879479|[location-of
  Mrs-Jeanne-P-chl Mrs-Jeanne-P-chl-small-city-food-store]
@19960115070003:inf#546879479|
[location-of Mrs-Jeanne-P-chl Mrs-Jeanne-P-chl-STREET]
(She was in the corner grocery. She was on the street.)
```

Exercises

1. Add an understanding agent analogous to the relation understanding agent, which handles personality and object trait attributes such as *passionate* and *lovely*.

Modify the program to be able to answer the following questions given the movie review presented in the previous chapter:

```
> How is the film?
It is passionate.
> How is Gwyneth Paltrow?
She is lovely.
```

2. Modify the above understanding agent to assign a make sense rating to input attributes based on whether they make sense given attributes previously learned by the agent. For example, if the agent is told that a movie is interesting, it would later not make sense to be told the movie was boring.

3. Modify the program to make use of the rating communicon and to answer the question:

```
> How good is the film?
Excellent.
```

4. Add an understanding agent which bases the make sense rating of an input concept on the MPAA ratings:

```
G        all ages OK
PG       some material may not be suitable for children
PG-13    < age 13 discouraged
R        < age 17 requires accompanying parent
NC-17    < age 17 not OK
```

For example, this would enable disambiguation of *A 10-year old went to see Bambi*, where one movie called Bambi is rated G and another also called Bambi is rated R.

5. Extend the emotion understanding agent to generate or infer emotions in more situations. Go through the emotion ontology to find missing cases.

6. Extend the friend understanding agent to handle more of the complex rules needed to describe when *tu* or *vous* is used in France and elsewhere.

7. Modify the sleep understanding agent to handle sleeping in a hotel room bed. The agent currently locates a bed owned by the actor.

8. Improve the setting and adjustment of story time in the program.

9. Make use of the fact that the Leo Perutz's novel was published in 1918. (Don't set story time to 1996.)

10. Extend the program to ask the user *Which Jim do you mean?*, if there are two Jims in the context, and an input sentence refers to *Jim*, and the high sense ratings of the two interpretations are similar. The question asking agent can be used to implement part of this. Note however that the processing which must be performed here is different from existing mechanisms — the answer to the question is used to select among the alternative contexts.

11. Extend the program to integrate a new grid into the network of the town or city it is supposed to be contained in, when creating new grids by analogy to existing ones. Create streets and other supporting grids as necessary.

Chapter 9: Learning in ThoughtTreasure

ThoughtTreasure performs various types of learning, summarized in the following table:

description	target	method	source	result	M	
product	product	TA_Product	text input	db file	Y	*
media object	media object	TA_MediaObject	text input	db file	Y	*
human name	human name	TA_Name	text input	db file	Y	*
human	human object	anaphor parse	text input	db file	Y	*
table-based	arbitrary	TA_Table	text input	db file	Y	
data extraction	arbitrary	NL parsing	text input	db file	Y	*
word formation	words	deriv morph	text input	db file	Y	
analogic morph	inflections	induction	lexicon	infl file	Y	
data mining	various	various	lexicon/db	file	N	
gender valid	gender feat	induction	corpus	file	N	*

The type of information learned, such as ThoughtTreasure objects, assertions, lexical entries, or inflections, is shown in the *target* field. Learning is performed by various *methods* such as scanning of text by text agents, full natural language parsing, derivational morphology, or simple methods for induction. Learning takes input from some *source*, such as short natural language texts, from large natural language corpora, or from ThoughtTreasure's own lexicon and database. The *results* of learning is written to one or more files intended (1) to be read in again by ThoughtTreasure the next time the program is started and/or (2) to be examined by a human in order to make manual changes to the ThoughtTreasure database or code. Database and inflection files produced by learning are in the standard formats. Learning optionally makes *modifications* (shown as *M* above) to the state of the running program such as creating new objects, creating new lexical entries and inflections, and making database assertions. An asterisk ("*") at the end denotes a type of learning addressed in other chapters.

Learning from tables in text

Given the input text:

```
Here are some country code modifications
to be added:
    Australia   this         61
```

```
Cameroon    is              237
Canada      another           1
Guyana      field           592
India       with             91
Italy       nothing         390
Jordan      of              959
Kenya       real            254
Mars        use            9999
Monaco      inside           33
Oman        this            968
Peru        very            510
Zaire       field           243
```

That is all for now.

ThoughtTreasure senses the presence of a table with 13 lines and 3 fields, determines that the fields are for country, unknown, and phone prefix, and learns the following modifications to its database:

```
|@19960224150123:na|
[phone-prefix-of Italy STRING:phone-prefix:"390"]|
[phone-prefix-of Jordan STRING:phone-prefix:"959"]|
===country//
===*Mars2411//Mars.z/
|@19960224150123:na|
phone-prefix-of=STRING:phone-prefix:"9999"|
[phone-prefix-of Monaco STRING:phone-prefix:"33"]|
[phone-prefix-of Peru STRING:phone-prefix:"510"]|
```

(The modifications are made in memory and dumped to the file outlrn.txt.) New phone prefixes of Italy, Jordan, Monaco, and Peru are learned, and a new country called *Mars* is learned along with its phone prefix. The phone prefixes of the other countries were already known to ThoughtTreasure.

Sensing the presence of a table

In the first phase of parsing, various text agents scan the input text in order to locate words and phrases and generate parse nodes for them. A special type of text agent called the *table text agent* scans the input text for tables.

At the beginning of each line in the input, the table text agent attempts to sense the presence of a new table. It does this by keeping a 1-dimensional bitmap of character positions, scanning successive lines, and setting those character positions occupied by nonwhite characters.

For example, the agent attempts to locate a table starting with the first line in the input text:

```
Here are some country code modifications
```

Having started with an empty bitmap, it now sets bits occupied by nonwhite characters:

```
**** *** **** ******* **** *************
```

The second line is read and more bits are set:

```
to be added:
************* ******* **** *************
```

The third line is a blank line, which is one of the ways tables are terminated. Tables are also terminated by separator lines or when all the bits in the first 40 characters of the bitmap would become set if the next line were to be included. The separator line text agent recognizes various separator lines such as those consisting of dashes or "CUT HERE." 2 table lines and 4 table fields have been sensed. In order for a table to be sensed, at least 5 table lines and from 2 to 5 fields must have been found. (These constants may be modified.) An insufficient number of table lines have been found, so a table is not sensed at this point.

The table text agent then attempts to locate a table starting with the second line. Only 1 line is found this time, which is insufficient for a table.

Starting at the fourth line, the table text agent attempts to locate a table and updates the bitmap as follows:

```
Australia  this           61
********   ****           **
Cameroon   is            237
********   ****           ***
Canada     another         1
********   *******        ***
...
Mars       use          9999
********   *******        ****
...
```

After hitting the end of the table, a blank line, it has found 13 lines and 3 fields. This is an acceptable number of lines and fields, so a table is sensed and this is reported in the log file:

```
19960224151509: TA_Table: table sensed:
   ********  ******    ****
   Australia  this           61
   Cameroon   is            237
   Canada     another         1
   Guyana     field         592
   India      with           91
   Italy      nothing       390
   Jordan     ...
[TABLE
FIELD #0 2-10 <> ?
FIELD #1 13-19 <> ?
FIELD #2 25-28 <> ?
 55-452:<  Australia   this           61 >]
```

A table parse node is added containing the character position ranges of the sensed fields, and the beginning and ending positions of the table in the input text. Later in the log, the beginning and ending positions of the table are indicated with square brackets:

```
TABLE:
Here are some country code modifications
to be added:

[[  Australia  this           61
    Cameroon   is            237
    Canada     another         1
    Guyana     field         592
    India      with           91
    Italy      nothing       390
    Jordan     of            959
    Kenya      real          254
    Mars       use          9999
    Monaco     inside         33
    Oman       this          968
    Peru       very          510
    Zaire      field         243
]]
That is all for now.
```

The table text agent will then attempt to sense further tables starting with the first line not in the previous table.

Parsing the sensed table

So far, the existence of the table has been sensed, but its contents have not been parsed. The table parser is later invoked from within the semantic parser. Parsing is accomplished as follows: A vertical slice corresponding to each table field is stripped out of the input text. A list of strings is produced for each field, where each string has leading and trailing blanks removed. Each string is then parsed into one or more concepts by looking them up in the lexicon. For the first field, the following concepts are found in the French lexicon:

```
Oman cracker-Monaco Monaco Mars March Kenya
aamgn-Jordan indium Guyana Canada
```

Monaco is both a country and a brand of cracker. Mars is both a planet and a month of the year. In French, India is the plural of the chemical element indium— or so the program believes. (The French word for India is *Inde*.) The following concepts are found in the English lexicon:

```
Zaire Peru Oman Monaco Mars Kenya aamgn-Jordan Jordan
Italy India Guyana Canada Cameroon Australia
```

Jordan is both a name and a country in English. The parents (in the hierarchy) of the above concepts are collected and the number of occurrences of each is tallied:

```
1 Crackers-Belin
1 planet
1 month-of-the-year
1 Anglo-American-male-given-name
1 atom
5 country
```

```
1 planet
1 Anglo-American-male-given-name
12 country
```

The parent concept with the highest count determines the class and language of the field. Here the highest count is for `country` in English. Given this information, all the strings are reparsed into single concepts, using the class `country` and language English to restrict interpretations. (Any remaining ambiguities are resolved at random.) Strings which cannot be parsed given the restriction (such as the country Mars) are temporarily assigned an interpretation of `na`. Thus for the first field we have parsed the following concepts:

```
Australia Cameroon Canada Guyana India Italy Jordan
Kenya na Monaco Oman Peru Zaire
```

The same process is performed for the second and third fields. The second field does not contain useful information; it is parsed into the following concepts:

```
na location-of na na na na na na na na na na na
```

The third field is first parsed into the following concepts:

```
"243" Levi-s-510-jeans "510" "968" Alfa-Romeo-33 "33"
"9999" "254" "959" "390" "91" "592" F49 1XB "1" "237"
"61"
```

The parent counts are then:

```
1 Levi-s-jeans
1 unknown-car-type
1 grammatical-person
1 crossbar-switch
1 local-switch
13 string
```

The class is thus determined to be `string` and the concepts are reparsed as:

```
"61" "237" "1" "592" "91" "390" "959" "254"
"9999" "33" "968" "510" "243"
```

Next, the table parser attempts to determine what relations hold between pairs of fields. Each pair of fields where f1 is not equal to f2 is considered. Assertions of the form:

```
[?relation f1 f2]
```

are looked up in the database. For each pair, the number of relations of each type are tallied. Between the first and third fields, the relation `phone-prefix-of` is found to occur 8 times:

```
8 phone-prefix-of
```

It is therefore selected as the table's relation between the first and third fields:

```
FIELD #0 2-10 <country> z relations
      #2:<phone-prefix-of>
```

Learning from the parsed table

Now that the table has been parsed into a list of concepts for each field, a class for each field, and a list of relations between fields, it is time to do the actual learning. Each `na` concept is created as a new instance of the class of the field it occurs in. Thus a new country Mars is created in memory and dumped to the `outlrn.txt` file. For each relation between fields n and m, each pair of concepts from fields n and m corresponding to a line of the table is considered. If the relation is already asserted between the first concept and the second concept, nothing is done. Otherwise, the new relation between these concepts is learned by asserting it into the database and dumping it out to the `outlrn.txt` file.

Learning inflectional morphology

At first the inflections of words were entered into ThoughtTreasure by hand, with a manual cross check against existing paper dictionaries. Checking was performed not only for difficult French verbs, but for many English nouns as well—there are more alternate spellings and subtle points in forming the plural than one would suspect. Here are a few examples from ThoughtTreasure's EnglishInflection file:

```
bus.S/buses.P/busses.ÀP/
duck.S/ducks.P/duck.qP/
thorax.S/thoraxes.P/thoraces.P/
triceps.S/triceps.P/tricepses.qP/
proscenium.S/prosceniums.P/proscenia.P/
iris.S/irises.P/irides.P/
manteau.S/manteaus.P/manteaux.P/
NYC.S/NYCs.P/
CIS.S/CIS's.P/
Waverly.S/Waverlys.P/
orchestrator.S/orchestrators.P/orchestrater.S/
orchestraters.P/
velour.S/velours.S/velours.P/
vicuña.S/vicuñas.P/vicuña.qP/
preppy.S/preppies.P/preppie.S/
story.ÀS/stories.ÀP/storey.gS/storeys.gP/
preterit.S/preterits.P/preterite.S/preterites.P/
when.S/whens.P/
somewhere.S/somewheres.îS/somewheres.P/
sherry.S/sherries.P/sherris.oS/sherrises.oS/
```

```
filet.ÀS/filets.ÀP/fillet.gS/fillets.gP/
crossroad.S/crossroads.S/crossroads.P/
violoncello.S/cello.ÍS/violoncellos.P/cellos.ÍP/
violoncelli.P/celli.ÍP/
allegretto.S/allegrettos.P/
Reuter.S/Reuters.S/Reuters.P/
Kitts.S/Kittses.P/
Johannes.S/Johannes.P/
Mr.S/Messrs.P/
linguistics.S/linguistics.P/
helix.S/helices.P/helixes.P/
genesis.S/geneses.P/
knowledge.S/knowledges.P/
Sears.S/Sears.P/
Cheerio.qS/Cheerios.S/Cheerios.P/
```

Algorithmic morphology

Then an *algorithmic morphology* module was written, which has hardcoded into it:

- 10 common French verb conjugation paradigms (from Battye and Hintze, 1992, pp. 165-173),
- 8 French noun/adjective paradigms (from Battye and Hintze, 1992, pp. 156-160), and
- basic English noun and verb inflection rules (from Collins, 1987, pp. 850-852).

As the database files are read in, any words whose inflections have not been previously defined in the inflections files are passed to the algorithmic morphology module. The inflections generated by this module are added to memory and also written out to a suggested inflections file (`outeinfl.txt` and `outfinfl.txt`). These files can then later be examined and possibly modified by a human and appended to the verified inflections files (`eninfl.txt` and `frinfl.txt`).

The algorithmic morphology module may also be employed directly by typing `algmorph` at the ThoughtTreasure shell prompt:

```
* algmorph
Welcome to the algorithmic morphology tool.
Enter language (y/z): y
Enter part of speech (V/A/N): V
Enter french infinitive: usenetter
usenetter.f/
```

```
usenette.pG1S/usenettes.pG2S/usenette.pG3S/usenettons.pG1P/
usenettez.pG2P/
usenettent.pG3P/
usenettais.iG1S/usenettais.iG2S/usenettait.iG3S/
usenettions.iG1P/usenettiez.iG2P/usenettaient.iG3P/
usenettai.sG1S/usenettas.sG2S/usenetta.sG3S/usenettâmes.sG1P/
usenettâtes.sG2P/usenettèrent.sG3P/
usenetterai.uG1S/usenetteras.uG2S/usenettera.uG3S/
usenetterons.uG1P/usenetterez.uG2P/usenetteront.uG3P/
usenetterais.cG1S/usenetterais.cG2S/usenetterait.cG3S/
usenetterions.cG1P/usenetteriez.cG2P/usenetteraient.cG3P/
usenette.pJ1S/usenettes.pJ2S/usenette.pJ3S/usenettions.pJ1P/
usenettiez.pJ2P/usenettent.pJ3P/
usenettasse.iJ1S/usenettasses.iJ2S/usenettât.iJ3S/
usenettassions.iJ1P/usenettassiez.iJ2P/usenettassent.iJ3P/
usenetté.dSM/usenettée.dSF/usenettés.dPM/usenettées.dPF/
usenette.pI2S/usenettons.pI1P/usenettez.pI2P/
usenettant.e/
|
Enter french infinitive: usenettir
usenettir.f/
usenettis.pG1S/usenettis.pG2S/usenettit.pG3S/
usenettissons.pG1P/usenettissez.pG2P/usenettissent.pG3P/
usenettissais.iG1S/usenettissais.iG2S/usenettissait.iG3S/
usenettissions.iG1P/usenettissiez.iG2P/usenettissaient.iG3P/
usenettis.sG1S/usenettis.sG2S/usenettit.sG3S/
usenettîmes.sG1P/usenettîtes.sG2P/usenettirent.sG3P/
usenettirai.uG1S/usenettiras.uG2S/usenettira.uG3S/
usenettirons.uG1P/usenettirez.uG2P/usenettiront.uG3P/
usenettirais.cG1S/usenettirais.cG2S/usenettirait.cG3S/
usenettirions.cG1P/usenettiriez.cG2P/usenettiraient.cG3P/
usenettisse.pJ1S/usenettisses.pJ2S/usenettisse.pJ3S/
usenettissions.pJ1P/usenettissiez.pJ2P/usenettissent.pJ3P/
usenettisse.iJ1S/usenettisses.iJ2S/usenettît.iJ3S/
usenettissions.iJ1P/usenettissiez.iJ2P/usenettissent.iJ3P/
usenetti.dSM/usenettie.dSF/usenettis.dPM/usenetties.dPF/
usenettis.pI2S/usenettissons.pI1P/usenettissez.pI2P/
usenettissant.e/
|
```

Analogical morphology

Even with the algorithmic morphology module there were a number of words that did not fit any of the coded paradigms and much editing of the guessed inflections was required. So then an *analogical morphology* module was written, which inflects words by analogy to previously entered words. Through this mechanism the system can learn a paradigm by exposure to as little as one example of the paradigm. This allows us to bootstrap a database of inflected words much more quickly.

The *analogical morphology* module contains two parts: training with known inflections and application to words with unknown inflections.

Training

The lexical entries having verified inflections are used for training. Only adjectives (in French), nouns, and verbs are dealt with. For each verified lexical entry, prefixes of increasing length L are generated: First $L = 0$, then $L = 1$, until the first L characters are not identical in all inflections. For a given L, a list of suffixes is built corresponding to the inflections in the training word. (The prefix concatenated with the suffix yield the inflection.) For example, for $L = 4$ and the training example:

```
cutaway.S/cutaways.S/
```

the following list of suffixes is built:

```
way.S/ways.P/
```

This list of suffixes is then compared with previously stored lists of suffixes in order to find an equivalent one — a list with the exact same entries and which is for the same language, gender, and part of speech. If such a list is found, its `count` is incremented. Otherwise the new list is added with a `count` of 1 and each suffix in the list is used to index this list in a hash table. Each stored list of suffixes is called an *analogical morphology class*, or class for short.

Application

Inflection of a new word proceeds as follows: Each length-L prefix of the new word is considered as in training. The corresponding suffix is looked up in the hash table and each class containing that suffix is considered. (Note that the same suffix could in principle be, say, the plural noun form of one class and the second person singular verb form of another.) For example, given the word *breakaway* and $L = 6$, the following class is retrieved from the hash table using the suffix *way* as an index:

```
way.S/ways.P/
```

If any class is found for a given L, then the class having the highest `count` is used as the answer—how to inflect the new word. The length-L prefix of the new word (*breaka* in our example) is concatenated with each suffix in the class to produce the inflections of the word:

```
breakaway.S/breakaways.P/
```

Any classes above incompatible with known features—such as language, gender, and part of speech—of the new word are of course discarded. Note however that when features of a word are unknown, this algorithm can be used to fill them in. For example, having trained on a French inflection corpus but without having seen the word *usenettîmes*, analogical morphology will tell you that this is a first person plural passé simple.

According to this algorithm, the most specific (longest suffix) example locks out less specific (shorter suffix) ones. An example having a count of 1 will even be preferred over a shorter example having a count of 100. (Though it may be better to use other heuristics such as a minimum threshold on the count.)

Analogical morphology replaces the algorithmic morphology module. Like that module, it generates inflections in memory and writes them out to a suggestions file for human verification. But it incurs a modest space and time penalty over algorithmic morphology, so the latter is retained as an option. They are plug compatible.

The analogical morphology module may be employed directly by typing `anamorph` at the ThoughtTreasure shell prompt.

Induced morphological paradigms

To see what paradigms analogical morphology is generating, you can request a dump of the analogical morphology classes by typing `report` and then `anam` into the ThoughtTreasure shell. The class with the highest count (2807) is the one for English nouns having a plural in -s, followed by the class for French masculine nouns with plural -s, and then French feminine nouns:

```
2807 ENG N    NA     s.P/.S/
 918 FR  N    M      s.MP/.MS/
 725 FR  N    F      s.FP/.FS/
```

Later, a paradigm for French verbs with infinitive in -er appears:

```
101 FR   V    NA
ez.pP2I/ons.pP1I/e.pS2I/assent.iP3J/assiez.iP2J/assions.iP1J/
ât.iS3J/asses.iS2J/asse.iS1J/ent.pP3J/iez.pP2J/ions.pP1J/
e.pS3J/es.pS2J/e.pS1J/ant.e/ées.dFP/ée.dFS/és.dMP/é.dMS/
eraient.cP3G/eriez.cP2G/erions.cP1G/erait.cS3G/erais.cS2G/
erais.cS1G/eront.uP3G/erez.uP2G/erons.uP1G/era.uS3G/
eras.uS2G/erai.uS1G/èrent.sP3G/âtes.sP2G/âmes.sP1G/a.sS3G/
as.sS2G/ai.sS1G/aient.iP3G/iez.iP2G/ions.iP1G/ait.iS3G/
ais.iS2G/ais.iS1G/ent.pP3G/ez.pP2G/ons.pP1G/e.pS3G/es.pS2G/
e.pS1G/er.f/
```

and a paradigm for English verbs:

```
80 ENG V    NA      ing.e/ed.d/ed.i/.pP/s.pS3/.pS1/.f/
```

Some other highlights:

```
56 FR   N    NA      istes.FP/iste.FS/istes.MP/iste.MS/
54 FR   ADJ  NA      ales.FP/ale.FS/aux.MP/al.MS/
29 FR   ADJ  NA      ennes.FP/enne.FS/ens.MP/en.MS/
28 FR   ADJ  NA      tives.FP/tive.FS/tifs.MP/tif.MS/
26 FR   N    NA      trices.FP/trice.FS/teurs.MP/
                     teur.MS/
 5 ENG  N    NA      ors.PÀ/ours.Pg/or.SÀ/our.Sg/
 4 ENG  N    NA      iums.P/ia.P/ium.S/
 4 ENG  N    NA      's.P/.S/
```

Learning new words via derivational morphology

Humans are naturally creative with language, and one aspect of this is the creation of new words. Some words are created on the fly in a conversation and never used again, as when you cannot think of a word (or when a needed word does not exist) and are forced to invent one. Other new words become popular only within a group of friends, while others are used in the mass media or on the net (tracked in the "Among the New Words" section in each issue of *American Speech* or William Safire's column in the *New York Times Magazine*).

ThoughtTreasure must be able to cope with new words, since words not in its lexicon will always crop up. (Researchers working with corpora have noted that no matter how large a corpus they use to build a lexicon, if they then process new text they will encounter words not in that lexicon.) How should ThoughtTreasure cope with unknown words? It could ignore them, it could ask the user to define them, or it could attempt to understand them on its own. The last possibility, attempting to understand, has been implemented in the program for one class of new words, those formed by adding prefixes and suffixes.

152 English affixes (29 prefixes and 123 suffixes) are defined in ThoughtTreasure's database. A total of 38 distinct derivational rules are defined (several affixes may be associated with a single derivational rule).

Here is an example of ThoughtTreasure's ability to interpret new words:

```
> What is an intelligentphobe?
An intelligentphobe is a type of human. Intelligentphobes
hate geniuses.

> What is a workstationphobe?
A workstationphobe is a type of human. Workstationphobes hate
workstations.

> What is a Magyarphone?
A Magyarphone is a type of human. A Magyarphone speaks
Hungarian fluently.

> What is a dogette?
A dogette is a type of dog. Dogettes are small.

> What is a minicat?
A minicat is a type of cat. Minicats are small.

> What is a SPARCstationfest?
A SPARCstationfest is a type of script. A SPARCstationfest
involves a SPARCstation.

> What is a xylophonephile?
A xylophonephile is a type of human. Xylophonephiles like
xylophones.

> What is a phonophobe?
A phonophobe is a type of human. Phonophobes hate sounds.

> What is a Pentiumologist?
A Pentiumologist is a type of human. A Pentiumologist is
knowledgeable about a Pentium.

> What is an IRCathon?
An IRCathon is a type of script. An IRCathon involves
Internet Relay Chat.
```

Derivational rules

A derivational rule transforms a word and an affix (the left-hand side or *lhs* of the rule) into another word (the right-hand side or *rhs*). Derivation rules such as the following are defined in the `affix` hierarchy:

```
====suffix-Adj-to-N-hate//phobe.»z/
|lhs-class-of=concept|lhs-pos-of=F65|rhs-pos-of=F78|
rhs-class-of=human|[rhs-assertion-of suffix-Adj-to-N-hate
[like rhs-obj lhs-obj -1.0u]]|
```

This rule states that the suffix *phobe* can be used to transform an adjective (F65) into a noun (F78) which means a human who does not like the (concept linked to the) adjective.

The following rules enable affixes to be entered in the database under `attribute` and `adverb-of-absolute-degree`:

```
===affix-attribute//|lhs-class-of=r1|lhs-pos-of=F78|
rhs-pos-of=F78|[rhs-assertion-of affix-attribute [affix-obj
rhs-obj affix-weight]]|
===affix-intensifier-adj//
|lhs-class-of=attribute|lhs-pos-of=F65|
rhs-class-of=rhs-class-synonym|
===affix-intensifier-adv//
|lhs-class-of=attribute|lhs-pos-of=F66|
rhs-class-of=rhs-class-synonym|
```

Then:

```
====big.Az//hyper,maxi,mega,super,ultra.«z/
[-Inf⁻-.1]/small.¹Az/mini,micro.«z/ette,let,ling.»z/

====adverb-of-average-degree//somewhat.¹Bz/quasi,semi.«z/
ish.»z/
```

Here is a description of the relations defined on each `affix` object:

lhs-class-of

The class which the left-hand-side concept must be a kind of. If not defined, any left-hand-side concept will match. There is a special case for handling attributes: if this is `r1`, the selectional restriction of the object the affix was associated with (such as `big`) is instead used.

lhs-pos-of

The part-of-speech of the left-hand-side word. If not defined, any left-hand-side part-of-speech will match.

rhs-class-of

If not defined, the meaning of the new right-hand-side word will be a new object having the left-hand-side concept as parent. Otherwise if this is `rhs-class-synonym`, the new right-hand-side word will have as its concept the same object as the left-hand-side word-this is used to define a synonym such as an adjective which refers to the same concept as a noun. Otherwise, this specifies what class the new right-hand-side word will be a kind of.

rhs-pos-of

The part-of-speech of the new right-hand-side word. If not defined, the new word will have the same part-of-speech as the left-hand-side word.

rhs-assertion-of

An assertion on the new right-hand-side word concept. This assertion may contain `lhs-obj` which is substituted with the left-hand-side concept, `rhs-obj` which is substituted with the right-hand-side concept, or `affix-obj` which is substituted with the concept with which the affix is associated (useful in the case of `attributes`).

Processing new words

When ThoughtTreasure encounters a word (but not a phrase) that is not in its lexicon (such as *intelligentphobe*), it invokes word formation.

For every plausible part of speech, ThoughtTreasure invokes algorithmic or analogical morphology to generate a new lexical entry consisting of a root form and inflections for the unknown word (such as the root *intelligentphobe* with singular *intelligentphobe* and plural *intelligentphobes*). The use of morphology in this step is particularly important in French, where heavily inflected forms (such as *téléphonassions*) must be converted back to their root form (*téléphoner*) before derivational rules can be applied.

Some facts about the French language described by Guillet (1990) are exploited to restrict the investigated parts of speech. (See also Brill, 1994.)

Then the program attempts to derive each lexical entry from known words: For each suffix matching the tail of the root form (prefix matching the head of the word), it attempts to find a lexical entry which matches the head (tail) of the root form and has the part of speech `rhs-pos-of`. (So, for example, the suffix *phobe* matches the tail of *intelligentphobe* and the program looks for and finds an adjective lexical entry matching the head *intelligent*.)

Looking for a head (tail) lexical entry is permitted to recurse through word formation, so that multiple levels of derivation are handled (as in *intelligentphobephile*—one who likes those who hate intelligence).

The head (tail) of the word is optionally subject to certain orthographic transformations commonly employed in English word derivation:

```
Change final i to y before suffix starting with
consonant:
  dirti -> dirty (as in dirtily)

Delete s if suffix is ville:
  dulls -> dull (as in dullsville)

Reduce double final consonant before suffix starting
with vowel:
  redd -> red (as in redden)

Reduce double consonant plus vowel before suffix
starting with consonant:
  yummo -> yum (as in yummorama)

Delete vowel before suffix starting with consonant:
  chompa -> chomp (as in chomparama)

Add e after final consonant preceded by vowel before
suffix starting with vowel:
  molecul -> molecule (as in molecular)

Add e after vowel preceded by consonant before suffix
starting with vowel:
  tru -> true (as in truize)

Add first letter of suffix starting with consonant:
  flavo -> flavor (as in flavorama)
```

Then for each concept associated with each head (tail) lexical entry, ThoughtTreasure attempts to apply the derivational rule: If the class of the concept satisfies the restriction `lhs-class-of` and the part of speech of the head (tail) lexical entry satisfies the restriction `lhs-pos-of`, then the rule is applied: A new lexical entry is learned, with a meaning as specified by `rhs-class-of` and `rhs-assertion-of`. (So, for example, the new lexical entry *intelligentphobe* is associated with an object `intelligentphobe`, which is a kind of `human` asserted to hate the attribute `intelligent`.)

The new lexical entry adopts features specified in the affix. So, for example, words formed with the suffix *rama* are marked as informal or those formed with *ess* are marked as pejorative.

Output of learning

When ThoughtTreasure processes a new word, it outputs the learned information to a file in database file format. The contents of the file can then be reviewed by a human and added to the regular database files, or the file can be read automatically by ThoughtTreasure the next time it is restarted.

The learning output from the `wordform1` test suite is as follows:

```
===human//
====intelligentphobe//intelligentphobe.z/
|[like intelligentphobe intelligent NUMBER:u:-1]|
====workstationphobe//workstationphobe.z/
|[like workstationphobe workstation NUMBER:u:-1]|
====Magyarphone//Magyarphone.z/|fluent-language-of=hongrois|
====xylophonephile//xylophonephile.z/|like=xylophone|
====phonophobe//phonophobe.z/|
[like phonophobe sound NUMBER:u:-1]|
====Pentiumologist//Pentiumologist.z/
|specialty-of=Intel-Pentium|
===dog//
====dogette//dogette.z/|fanciful=NUMBER:u:0.55|
====dogette2443//dogette.z/|big=NUMBER:u:-0.55|
====dogette2444//dogette.z/|female|
===cat//
====minicat//minicat.z/|big=NUMBER:u:-0.55|
===script//
====SPARCstationfest//SPARCstationfest.z/|
association-of=SPARCstation|
===langue//
====Rooseveltspeak//Rooseveltspeak.zT/|
official-language-of¤Roosevelt|
===script//
====IRCathon//IRCathon.z/|association-of=online-chat|
===object-trait//
====interesting//[-1⁻-0.1]/boringsville.z/
===personality-trait//
```

```
====intelligent//[-1ˉ-0.1]/stupidster.zþ/
===electronic-appliance//
====phone//telephoneness.zî/
===common-stock//
====stock-T//telephoneness.zî/
===attribute-taste//
====delicious//yumarama.UzT/
===color//
====orange//orangeridden.Az/
===personality-trait//
====courageous//gutsily.Bz/
====intelligent//smartify.Vzéê/
===color//
====yellow//yellowize.Vzéê/
===fabric//
====twill//twillen.Vzéê/twillen.Vzê/twillen.Az/
===computer-company//
====Intel//Intelesque.Az/Intelfashion.Bz/
===occupation//
====performing-arts-professional//businessite.zþ/
businessite.Azþ/
====businessperson//businessite.zþ/businessite.Azþ/
===computer//
====server//serverize.Vzéê/serverize.Vzê/
===interpersonal-script//
====conversation//talkancy.zî/talkancy.zT/talkancy.Az/
talkee.zá/
===online-communication//
====online-chat//talkancy.zî/talkancy.zT/talkancy.Az/
talkee.zá/
```

Word formation tool

Besides allowing new words to be used in any text, ThoughtTreasure also has a tool for testing out its word formation facility. The following ThoughtTreasure shell commands are provided:

```
wf2e -file FILENAME (for English)
wf2f -file FILENAME (for French)
```

The input file should contain a list of words, one per line. The trace goes into the log and the learning output into the various out*.txt files.

Learning derivational rules

Derivational rules are manually coded. But an experiment was performed to learn new derivational rules automatically from the existing lexicon. One type of derivational rule is learned: the synonym rule in which a new word pointing to a concept is derived from an existing word. The new word may differ in part of speech, language, and other features from the existing word.

These rules are found as follows: Every pair of words associated with every concept in the database is used as a training example. Borrowed (foreign) words, infrequent words, and phrases are excluded. For each training example, prefixes of increasing length L are considered, starting with L = 3, until the first L characters of W1 and W2 are not identical. For each L, a derivational rule is constructed:

```
·head(W1, L).features -> head(W2, L).features
```

(Actually, the rules can be applied in either direction.) Then either this rule is added to a list of rules with a count of 1, or an identical rule already in the list has its count incremented by 1.

Here are some single-language rules found using this method:

number	suffix			suffix			exemplar	exemplar
265		N ENG			ADJ ENG		multinational	multinational
51		ADJ ENG	ly		ADV ENG		semitonal	semitonally
32	ism	N ENG		ist	N ENG	PER	pluralism	pluralist
26	ist	N ENG	PER	ist	ADJ ENG	PER	subjectivist	subjectivist
21	e	N ENG		e	V ENG		love	love

Here are some cross-language rules found using this method:

number	suffix			suffix			exemplar	exemplar
491		M N FR			N ENG		premium	premium
245		F N FR			N ENG		altitude	altitude
77	e	M N FR			N ENG		paragraphe	paragraph
35	me	M N FR		m	N ENG		minimalisme	minimalism
31	iste	N FR	PER	ist	N ENG	PER	pluraliste	pluralist
31	if	M N FR		ive	N ENG		progressif	progressive
31	ation	F N FR		ation	N ENG		variation	variation
24	que	ADJ FR		c	ADJ ENG		diatonique	diatonic

The learned rules can then be used to derive the meaning of an unknown word: each applicable rule is applied to an unknown word to derive synonyms, and the concepts, if any, associated with those synonyms then become associated with the unknown word.

The learned rules can also be used to run through ThoughtTreasure's lexicon and suggest meanings of lexical entries not connected to any concepts. (This can arise when a word is used inside a phrase and not defined separately.) Only rules with a count greater than 20 are applied. Some of the better results of such a run were as follows:

```
51 .Az -> ly.Bz         ====different//differently.Bz/
51 .Az -> ly.Bz         ====important//importantly.Bz/
51 .Az -> ly.Bz         ====cold//crisply.Bz/
22 ve.Nz -> ve.Az       ====ergative//ergative.Az/
22 ve.Nz -> ve.Az       ====birth-control-device//contraceptive.Az/
67 ion.Nz -> ion.FNy    ====logical-extension//extension.FNy/
44 t.MNy -> t.Nz        ====battle//combat.Nz/
45 n.Nz -> n.Az         ====hongrois//Hungarian.Az/
21 al.Ay -> al.Az       ====attribute-novel//original.Az/
53 e.Nz -> e.Az         ====variable//variable.Az/
44 t.MNy -> t.Nz        ====accent-mark//accent.Nz/
```

But the run also suggested some (at least partially) faux amis:

```
80 e.MNy -> e.Nz            ====news-magazine//magazine.Nz/
31 ation.FNy -> ation.Nz ====categorize//classification.Nz/
31 ation.FNy -> ation.Nz ====increase//augmentation.Nz/
54 tion.FNy -> tion.Nz    ====decrease//diminution.Nz/
```

And a number of incorrect suggestions were made:

```
151 e.FNy -> e.Nz          ====music//musique.Nz/
51  .Az -> ly.Bz           ====love//madly.Bz/
21  e.Vz -> e.Nz           ====fear//fore.Nz/
53  e.Nz -> e.Az           ====phone//telephone.Az/
22  tte.FNy -> tte.Nz      ====cap//casquette.Nz/
21  e.Vz -> e.Nz           ====advise//urge.Nz/
53  e.Nz -> e.Az           ====France//France.Az/
```

The suggestions can be reviewed by a human and then added manually back into the database files. Or the learned derivational rules can be used only on a demand basis.

ThoughtTreasure data mining

The database and lexicon of ThoughtTreasure can be mined, enabling various studies to be carried out.

French gender rules

In French class one is taught heuristics such as that words ending in *age* and *ment* are masculine, and those ending in *té* are feminine. By typing `suffgender` into the ThoughtTreasure shell, you can test such theories in the program's dictionary. (This can also be used to find coding errors.) Here are some results:

suffix	counts			minority items
-age	57 M	3	F	cage image plage
-ance	0 M	34	F	
-e	694 M	1325	F	(numerous)
-eau	47 M	2	F	eau peau
-ée	2 M	36	F	coryphée lycée
-ence	1 M	33	F	silence
-er	93 M	2	F	mer lager
-esse	0 M	13	F	
-eur	80 M	17	F	largeur longueur hauteur distributeur torpeur douleur fadeur peur erreur rumeur saveur faveur fleur liqueur valeur couleur chaleur
-euse	0 M	12	F	
-ier	52 M	0	F	
-ière	2 M	24	F	cimetière derrière
-in	93 M	2	F	main fin
-isme	75 M	0	F	
-me	149 M	25	F	(numerous)
-ment	89 M	0	F	
-oir	18 M	0	F	
-on	150 M	239	F	(numerous)
-ot	29 M	1	F	boot
-que	21 M	59	F	(numerous)
-sion	0 M	37	F	
-te	41 M	206	F	(numerous)
-té	8 M	80	F	décolleté été doigté feuilleté côté sauté pâté comté
-tion	1 M	187	F	himation
-ve	3 M	21	F	rêve mauve fleuve

Standard and inverse alphabetical dictionaries

An *inverse alphabetical dictionary* (Courtois, 1990) is a list of inflections sorted by last letter, next to last letter, and so on. This brings out similarities in word or phrase endings:

```
Reuters Marketfeed 2000
SPARCcenter 2000
1973 Alfa Romeo GTV 2000
```

```
...
chukka
polka
yarmulka
Lanka
Sri Lanka
Bazooka
shapka
parka
ska
Dayka
...
suspension
intension
extension
version
aversion
diversion
inversion
passion
concession
...
```

A similar inverse dictionary of human names is as follows:

```
Baker
Fenstermaker
Handsaker
Becker
Stalnecker
Stricker
Walker
Drooker
Parker
Starker
Bibler
Badler
Schmeidler
Mandler
Hendler
...
```

Phrasal derivation

In English, compound nouns are commonly formed by juxtaposing two nouns:

```
antenna + jack -> antenna jack
```

In French, the corresponding structure is usually noun *de* noun:

```
prise + de + antenne -> prise d'antenne
```

However, in recent years, apparently under the influence of English, the *de* is sometimes dropped in French as well. (There have always been noun-noun combinations in French when the two nouns are coordinated, as in *robe-manteau* [coat dress]. In this case a hyphen is usually used.)

The following statistics on phrase derivation were obtained from ThoughtTreasure's lexicon:

```
ENG N       4290 N N
ENG N       2298 ADJ N
FR  N       1389 N ADJ
FR  N       1021 N PREP N
ENG N        821 N N N
ENG N        783 ADJ N N
FR  N        678 N N
FR  N        331 ADJ N
ENG N        283 N N N N
ENG N        247 N PREP N
ENG N        208 ADJ ADJ N
FR  N        181 N N N
ENG ADJ      118 ADJ PREP
FR  N        102 N PREP N ADJ
ENG N        101 N ELEMENT N
FR  N         98 N ADJ ADJ
FR  N         96 N PREP DET N
ENG N         95 ADJ N N N
ENG EXPL      86 DET N
ENG N         73 N ADJ N
ENG N         73 N N N N N
FR  N         69 N ADJ PREP N
FR  N         67 N PREP ADJ N
FR  N         63 N N N N
FR  EXPL      62 DET N
...
```

Faux amis

Faux amis are "pairs of words in French and English which have a common origin, whose homonymy misleadingly suggests synonymy." (Van Roey, Granger, and

Swallow, 1991, p. xviii). A list of potential faux amis in ThoughtTreasure can be obtained by typing `report` into the ThoughtTreasure shell followed by `faux`:

```
expression figée N (phrase) FR = phrase N ENG
 phrase N (sentence) FR = sentence N ENG
avoué plaidant N (pleading) FR = agent N ENG
 agent N (broker) FR = broker N ENG
focus N ENG = foyer N FR
 foyer N ENG = hall N FR
combinaison jupon N (chemise) FR = slip N ENG
 slip N (bikini) FR = bikini N ENG
...
```

Anagrams and palindromes

A report of anagrams across English and French, ignoring case and accentuation, can be obtained by typing `report` into the ThoughtTreasure shell followed by `anag`. 4685 anagram equivalence classes are found:

```
longer ADJ ENG; grêlon N FR M SING;
clairon N FR M SING; Locrian ADJ ENG;
novelist N ENG SING; violents ADJ FR M PL;
hows N ENG PL; show V ENG PRES PL; Whos N ENG PL;
Maureens N ENG PL; username N ENG SING;
tièdes ADJ FR F PL; édités V FR PP M PL;
brosse N FR F SING; sobres ADJ FR F PL; sobers V ENG PRES
SING 3;
salvations N ENG PL; valoissant V FR PRESP;
won V ENG PRES ELISION MODAL; now INTERJ ENG; own ADV ENG;
Lenats N ENG PL; telnas V FR SIMPP SING 2 INDIC;
nonpareils N ENG PL; planerions V FR CONDIT PL 1 INDIC;
oriental ADJ FR M SING; relation N ENG SING;
skin N ENG SING; inks N ENG PL; sink V ENG PRES PL;
organs N ENG PL; sarong N ENG SING; granos N FR M PL; argons
N FR M PL;
existés V FR PP M PL; sexiste ADJ FR F SING;
Salina N ENG SING; Alains N ENG PL; Alanis N FR M PL;
Ovaltine N ENG SING; volaient V FR PAST PL 3 INDIC;
Lindas N ENG PL; Island N FR PL; Ladins N ENG PL;
...
```

A report of palindromes can be obtained by typing `report` into the ThoughtTreasure shell followed by `pali`.

Exercises

1. Use all available text agents for parsing table strings, instead of just looking them up in the lexicon. Perhaps even invoke the entire parser recursively.

2. Recognize that *minicat* is possibly another word for *kitten*.

3. Learn new words by definition in a text, as in *this process is called creolization*. The word being defined is often set in italics.

4. The program does not yet handle metalinguistic parsing and generation properly. For example, even though it has learned *yumarama* as a new interjection, and *gutsily* as a new adverb, it does not describe them very well:

```
> What is 'yumarama'?
Delicious is a type of taste.

> What is 'gutsily'?
Courage is a type of personality trait.
```

Fix the program to output *'Yumarama' is an interjection meaning delicious*.

5. Fix these problems with relations:

```
> What is 'orangeridden'?
"pulls De Fursac" are barely orange. "cravates en soies
numéro 21 d'Ermenegildo Zegna" are barely orange.
Nicole Miller ties are barely orange. Rykiel ties are a
little bit orange.

> What is 'smartify'?
Insects are stupid.
```

6. Some of the learned filter features of new words such as roles, attachments, isms, and the *become feature* ("ê") are not yet properly incorporated into parsing and generation, so we get:

```
> What is 'yellowize'?
Browns are some yellow. Yellow roses are yellow. Gotcha
trunks are a little bit yellow. "costumes droits en
laine De Fursac" are nearly yellow. "vestes droites
```

De Fursac" are nearly yellow. Sole shirts are yellow.
"T-shirts de Galfa Club" are a little bit yellow. "T-
shirts de Oxbow" are a little bit yellow. UCLA Bruins
shorts are barely yellow. "pantalons jaunes en laine De
Fursac" are nearly yellow. "cravates De Fursac"
yellowize 0.05. "cravates De Fursac" are barely yellow.

Fix the program to output *'Yellowize' means to make something yellow*.

7. Fix the program to output *'Telephoneness' is the quality that telephones have*:

```
> What is telephoneness?
A phone is a type of electronic appliance.
```

8. Fix the following problems:

```
> What is 'talkancy'?
A conversation is a type of interpersonal script.

> What is a 'talkee'?
A conversation is a type of interpersonal script.

> What is 'Intelfashion'?
Intel is a computer company.
```

9. Fix ThoughtTreasure to deal properly with description questions involving
negative weight attributes. Its current behavior is:

```
> What is boringsville?
ENG interesting ADJ; FR intéressant ADJ;
ANT: ENG boringsville, boringsville, dullsville INFML;
boring ADJ, FR ennuyeux
ADJ, ENG old ADJ INFML, tiresome ADJ, tedious ADJ, dull
ADJ; FR chiant ADJ SL,
emmerdant ADJ INFML;

> What is a stupidster?
A genius is a type of personality trait.
```

This is because a list is required to store a weight, and the list is reduced to a
symbol at some point in the parsing causing the weight to be lost.

10. Implement the following word formation processes:

- All gradable adjectives can become nouns:
  ```
  I want cold.
  We're comforting the comfortable.
  ```

- All nouns can become verbs:
  ```
  Zipcode the letter.
  (= Include a zip code on the front of the letter.)
  ```

- Derivation of prepositions from other prepositions:
  ```
  nearish the theater
  ```

- Clipping:
  ```
  bro (from brother)
  resto (in French, from restaurant)
  ```

- Abbreviation:
  ```
  cholest
  cholest.
  ```

- Splicing:
  ```
  triticale (from triticum + secale)
  ```

- Juxtaposition:
  ```
  Maryanne
  ```

11. Use derivational morphology to invent new words when *lexical gaps* are encountered. For example, if an adjective is required for an object, but only a noun is in the database, use an adjectival suffix to convert the noun into an adjective. See the source code for the required orthographic transformations (such as consonant doubling). See also the function WordFormGenerate which generates lexical gaps for automatically learned derivational rules.

12. Implement processes for *phrase formation*. First of all, many of the word-level derivational rules apply as well to what are technically phrases in ThoughtTreasure (anything with a separator in it):

```
non-ADJECTIVE -> ADJECTIVE
  non-conventional
French: non ADJECTIVE -> ADJECTIVE
  non conventionnel
```

```
super-ADJECTIVE -> ADJECTIVE
  super-rich
out-VERB -> VERB
  out-argue
```

13. Implement the following additional phrase formation rules for parsing and generation:

```
in a ADJECTIVE way -> ADVERB
  "in a silly way"
French: de façon/manière ADJECTIVE -> ADVERB
French: de NOUN -> ADJECTIVE
to out NAME NAME -> VERB
  "to out Einstein Einstein"
to pull a NAME -> VERB
  "to pull a Chomsky"
French: attribute ADJECTIVE -> person (þ) NOUN
  "chanceux" "lucky"/"lucky person"
```

14. Investigate how phrases map between languages. For example, what percentage of noun-noun combinations in English map to noun-adjective combinations in French?

Chapter 10: Applications of ThoughtTreasure

The applications of ThoughtTreasure are:

```
  Chatterbot/conversation
* Calendar book
* Emotion and interpersonal relationship understanding
  Data extraction
* Identifying names/companies/products in text
* Learning from tables
* Story understanding
  Interlingual and transfer-based translation
* Simulation/story generation/daydreaming
  Associative thought stream generation
* Dictionary
* Linguistic studies
  Internet content indexing
```

Applications preceded by an asterisk ("*") are presented in other chapters.

Chatterbot

ThoughtTreasure may be used as a chatterbot (Mauldin, 1994)—a program which carries on a conversation with the user. The chatterbot is started with the chateng (for English) or chatfr (for French) commands in the ThoughtTreasure shell:

```
chateng
chatfr
chateng -speaker Jim -listener TT
chatfr -speaker Jim -listener TT
```

Several lines of input text may be typed, containing one or more sentences. End of input is indicated by a blank line. (Alternatively, the parse shell command can be used to process text contained in a file.)

For example, the user types:

```
> Hi there.
>
Hello.
> How are you?
>
Very well, thank you.
```

Stimulus-response rules generate the above canned responses to canned questions. The program's generator also has the capability of producing time-dependent greetings such as *good morning*.

```
> What is your name?
Thomas.
```

The top of the deictic stack consists of the speaker Jim Garnier and the listener ThoughtTreasure. *your* refers to the listener. The English word *name* refers to the relations `first-name-of` and `last-name-of` (among others). Thus the input sentence can be interpreted as meaning *What is ThoughtTreasure's first name?* as well as *What is ThoughtTreasure's last name?*. Both interpretations make sense, since both can be answered by doing a lookup: the database contains the assertions that ThoughtTreasure's first name is Thomas and that ThoughtTreasure's last name is Tiberius. The first interpretation is selected (at random, since both interpretations make equal sense), and the corresponding retrieved answer is generated.

```
> What is your address?
"Thomas_Tiberius@email.francenet.fr" was my email
address between April 1994 and Monday October 23, 1995.
"tt at panix.com" is my email address since Monday
October 23, 1995.
```

The English word *address* refers to the relations `residence-of`, `mailing-address-of`, and `email-address-of`. Thus the input sentence has (at least) three corresponding interpretations. A database retrieval of the third interpretation turns up two assertions, giving the (currently fictitious) email address of the program over two different time intervals. The first assertion holds over a time interval in the past, so it is generated using the past tense. The second assertion is true in the present and therefore generated using the present tense. (Actually, in English, the present perfect *has been* should instead be used here since the time interval runs from the past up until the present moment [and beyond].)

```
> How big are you?
4738120 bytes is my storage size. 0.1 meters is the
width of a human. 0.3 meters is the length of a human.
1.7 meters is the height of a human.
```

A set of assertions relate attributes such as `big` to relations such as `width-of`, `length-of`, `height-of`, and `uncompressed-size-of`. The size in bytes of the program is retrieved, as well as the average dimensions of a human. According to its database, the ThoughtTreasure program is an instance of a human —without this, pronouns referring to the program would not be parsed or generated properly, and verbs involving the program would not parse or generate properly when they are restricted (via selectional restrictions) to humans. The retrieved assertions on ThoughtTreasure and on ThoughtTreasure's ancestor `human` are all generated as an answer. In the database, all measurements are stored in standard units such as meters.

```
> What is my name?
Jim is your first name.
```

This is similar to *What is your name* except that it refers to the speaker, Jim Garnier. The reader might have noticed that here a complete sentence is generated as the answer, while above a single word was generated. This is because there are actually two question answering agents who know how to answer this question: One agent (the top-level question element question answering agent) resolves the intension given by the question—"a name N such that N is the first name of Jim Garnier"—into the extension "Jim". The other agent (the pronoun question answering agent) attempts to prove the pattern given by the question—that some variable is a name of Jim Garnier. It then instantiates the pattern with the bindings from the proof, and generates the result. Both agents are doing essentially the same thing, and for this type of a question, they both produce answers. Neither agent is favored—they both produce the same make sense rating—so the output of one of them is selected at random.

```
> What is my first surname?
Garnier is your first family name.
```

Here a more specific English expression is used, which refers only to the relation `first-surname-of`. When the result is generated, the expression *family name* is used rather than *surname*, since the output channel's dialect is set to American English. (The dialect, style, and language can be set independently for each input and output channel. A running interlingual translation of a session can be produced in multiple dialects, styles, and languages.) ThoughtTreasure has the relations `first-surname-of` and `second-surname-of` in order to enable the representation of family names which consist of multiple names, such as hyphenated family names.

```
> How tall am I?
You are of average height.
```

An assertion relates the `tall` attribute to the `height-of` relation, specifying what values of `height-of` correspond to what values of `tall`. Attributes have values along a scale from -1.0 to 1.0. When generating an attribute, an appropriate adjective is selected based on the value. In the case of *tall*, -1.0 is generated as *short*, 0.0 as *of average height*, and +1.0 as *tall*.

```
> Why?
You are of average height, because 1.7 meters is your
height.
```

An explanation is stored along with each question answer, which is only generated if requested.

```
> Exactly how tall am I?
1.7 meters is your height.
```

The *exactly* here disables the adjective generation described above and forces generation of a value.

```
> What is my height?
1.7 meters is your height.
```

Here the word *height* is used, which refers directly to the relation `height-of` instead of having to proceed via the `tall` attribute.

```
> What is today's date?
It is Friday March 22, 1996.
> What time is it?
It is quarter past ten am.
```

The current date or time is generated in response to these canned requests.

```
> Is bread food?
Yes, bread is in fact a type of food.
```

This question causes the program to check its hierarchy of concepts to see whether bread is a kind of food, to which the answer is yes.

```
> Is food bread?
Bread is a type of food.
```

In this case, food is not a type of bread, but the program notices that bread is a type of food, and generates that as the answer.

```
> Is Irish soda bread a drink?
No, but a beverage and Irish soda bread are a type of
food.
```

This question is answered by finding a common ancestor of the two concepts.

```
> What is bread?
ENG bread U; FR pain M;
Bread is a type of food. Types of bread: challah, corn
bread, matzo, soda bread, the "pain de fantaisie", the
biscuit, the English muffin, the long loaf of bread,
the pita, the pretzel, the round loaf of bread, the
slice of bread, and the small bread. Other types of
food: cereal, fruit, meat, pastries, seafood, the
beverage, the condiment, the confection, the dairy
product, the egg, the sandwich, the spice, and the
vegetable.
```

Asked *What is ...*, ThoughtTreasure responds with dictionary-like information. It provides related words in both English and French (synonyms in this case, but also antonyms, stronger forms, and weaker forms in the case of attributes). Children of the concept are listed, as well as other children of the concept's parents. If the program does not have an English word for a concept but it does have a French word—as is the case for *pain de fantaisie*—the French word is generated in quotes.

```
> How many breads are there?
There is 53 breads.
> How many foods are there?
There is 1444 foods.
```

Here ThoughtTreasure provides a count of the number of descendant concepts of bread and food.

```
> Are elephants purple?
No, they are not purple. Elephants are gray.
```

In order to answer a Yes-No question, the program attempts to prove the questioned assertion. If the proof fails, as in this case, the response is no. For attributes, when the answer is no, the program also ascends the hierarchy to find other assertions which might be related—in this case, any color assertion on elephant. The generator uses the pronoun *they* to refer to the previously mentioned *elephants*.

```
> Are elephants gray?
Yes, they are in fact gray.
```

This is similar to the above except that the answer this time is yes.

```
> What color are elephants?
They are gray.
```

Here the value of the color assertion on elephant is retrieved.

```
> Are elephants dumb?
No, they are not stupid. Elephants are gray.
> How tall are elephants?
They are extremely tall.
> Why?
An elephant is extremely tall, because 3 meters is the
height of an elephant.
> How big are elephants?
3 meters is the height of an elephant.
> Are ants intelligent?
No, they are not intelligent.
> Are human beings intelligent?
Yes, humans are in fact intelligent.
> What is the most dense atom?
Lawrencium.
> What is the least dense atom?
Hydrogen.
```

The program runs through all descendants of atom, finding the one maximizing (or minimizing) the value of the atomic-weight-of relation (which is related by an assertion to the dense attribute).

```
> What is the circumference of the Earth?
```

```
40003236 meters is its circumference.
```
The program looks up the value of the `circumference-of` relation on the Earth.

```
> What is the capital of New Jersey?
Trenton is its capital.
> Who assassinated Henri IV?
François Ravaillac assassinated him.
> Who created Bugs Bunny?
Tex Avery created Bugs Bunny.
```

The program looks up the actor of the `create` action with object Bugs Bunny.

```
> Who painted _Le Déjeuner sur l'herbe_?
Édouard Manet painted "Le Déjeuner sur l'herbe".
> Who is the President of the United States?
John Fitzgerald Kennedy and Lyndon Baines Johnson were its
presidents. Richard Milhous Nixon was its president. Gerald
Ford was its president between 1974 and Thursday January 20,
1977. Jimmy Carter was the president of the United States
between Thursday January 20, 1977 and Tuesday January 20,
1981. Ronald Reagan was its president between Tuesday January
20, 1981 and Friday January 20, 1989. George Bush was the
president of the United States between Friday January 20,
1989 and Wednesday January 20, 1993. Bill Clinton is its
president since Wednesday January 20, 1993.
> Who is the President of France?
De Gaulle, Félix Gouin, Georges Bidault, Léon Blum, Vincent
Auriol, and René Coty were its presidents. Georges Pompidouth
was its president. Giscard d'Estaing was its president
between 1974 and 1981. François Mitterrand was the president
of France between 1981 and May 1995. Jacques Chirac is its
president since May 1995.
> What is the country code of the UK?
Country code "44" is its dialing prefix.
```

Various assertions are retrieved from the database.

```
> What are jeans?
ENG jeans PL C; FR jean M; ENG denims PL RARE C;
Jeans are a type of pants. Types of jeans: black jeans, blue
jeans, Guess jeans, Lee's jeans, Levi's jeans, Sasson jeans,
stonewashed jeans, and Wrangler jeans. Other types of pants:
clam diggers, drawers, ducks, flannels, gabardines,
galligaskins, high-water pants, hip-huggers, hot pants,
kerseys, knee breeches, knee pants, long pants, long
trousers, moleskins, pantalets, peg pants, pegtops, plus-
```

fours, riding pants, sacks, smallclothes, stretch pants, the
shintiyan, toreador pants, trews, trouserettes, trunks,
tweeds, whites, and others. Jeans are blue.

The program generates other assertions regarding the concept, namely that jeans
are blue.

```
> What is amaretto?
ENG amaretto U; FR amaretto M;
Amaretto is a type of liqueur. Types of amaretto: the Amaretto di
Saronno. Other types of liqueurs: anisette, banana liqueur,
Benedictine, blackcurrant liqueur, Calvados, chartreuse, Cointreau,
curaçao, fruit brandy, kümmel, lemon liqueur, maraschino, raspberry
liqueur, the "anis", the peppermint cordial, the rakee, the ratafia,
and Triple Sec.
> Who is Noam Chomsky?
ENG Noam Chomsky GENONLY; FR Noam Chomsky M GENONLY;
Noam Chomsky is the author of Syntactic Structures, "Structures
syntaxiques", Aspects of the Theory of Syntax, "Aspects de la théorie
syntaxique", Lectures on Government and Binding, Some Concepts and
Consequences of the Theory of Government and Binding, and "La
nouvelle syntaxe". Noam is his first name. Chomsky is his first
family name. He is male. Noam Chomsky invented generative grammar, an
early transformational theory, and the standard theory. He invented
government-binding theory in 1981. He invented X-bar theory in 1970.
                              creation
```

	19691231190002	the standard theory early transformational theory
19700101000000	19700101000001	X-bar theory
19810101000000	19810101000001	government-binding theory

Assertions are generated in a tabular format when there are several with the same
predicate.

```
> Who is Jacques Chirac?
ENG Jacques Chirac GENONLY; FR Jacques Chirac M GENONLY; A Jacques
Chirac is a human. Jacques Chirac is the president of France since
May 1995. Jacques is his first name. Chirac is his first family name.
He is male. Jacques Chirac is French.
> Are you sad?
No, I am not sad. I was motivated. I am motivated. I want me to
handle proposals, and me to speak online. I want to speak online. I
am American. 4738120 bytes is my storage size.
> What is the meaning of life?
A life is a type of script.
Human being is a R1 of a life.
> Why do radios flay?
No, I do not do a radio.
> Why do radios fly?
No, a radio station does not do the flies.
```

```
> What is EMPL?
EMPL is a type of APL.
I use tu with Erik Thomas Mueller. He created EMPL.
> You are actually quite funny, you know?
No, a lot, I am not humorous and I do not know.
No, a lot, I am not humorous.
No, I do not know.
>Bye.
Goodbye.
```

Data extraction

ThoughtTreasure can be used to extract database records from natural language text via the `parse` shell command. For example, the program reads the following Usenet ad:

```
Article 26827 of rec.autos.marketplace:
Path: panix!news.eecs.umich.edu!newsxfer.itd.umich.edu!
tank.news.pipex.net!pipex!usenet.eel.ufl.edu!
quapaw.astate.edu!quapaw.astate.edu!toddspi
From: toddspi@quapaw.astate.edu (Todd Spires)
Newsgroups: rec.autos.marketplace
Subject: FS:  1978 Fiat 124 Spyder (Ark)
Date: 28 Sep 1995 13:11:48 -0500
Organization: Arkansas State University
Lines: 6
Message-ID:
NNTP-Posting-Host: quapaw.astate.edu

1978 Fiat 124 Spyder, 75k miles, lost of new and
improved pieces, new clear-coat paint (original red),
new top, shocks, battery.  Has alloy rims (Chromadora).
Asking $3000  E-mail for more details.
toddspi@quapaw.astate.edu
```

and learns the following assertions:

```
[isa Todd-Spires human]
[first-name-of Todd-Spires aamgn-Todd]
[first-surname-of Todd-Spires aasn-Spires]
[male Todd-Spires]
[nationality-of Todd-Spires United-States]
[email-address-of Todd-Spires
STRING:email-address:"toddspi@quapaw.astate.edu"]
@19950928131148|
```

```
[for-sale 1978-Fiat-124
          NUMBER:USD:3000
          Todd-Spires
          na
          na
STRING:email-address:"toddspi@quapaw.astate.edu"
STRING:Usenet-newsgroup:"rec.autos.marketplace"
STRING:message-ID:"toddspi.812311772@quapaw.astate.edu"
          na]
```

(ThoughtTreasure was unable to fill the phone number, location, and URL slots of the `for-sale` template-na is used as a placeholder. The program does not yet parse mileage, type of shocks, and so forth.)

The user may then query the program using natural language (or also by browsing the database):

```
> I want to buy a Fiat Spyder.
There is twenty possibilities.
A 124, a 2000, or a 1800?
> What?
You want to buy a 124, a 2000, or a 1800?
> A 124.
A 1978 Fiat 124 was for sale for 3000 dollars by Todd
Spire at "toddspi@quapaw.astate.edu" in Usenet
newsgroup "rec.autos.marketplace" in message ID
"toddspi.812311772@quapaw.astate.edu".
```

How ThoughtTreasure parses a Usenet ad

First, text agents scan the text and produce parse nodes of various types. A parse node is generated for every recognized word, phrase, and entity in the input text:

```
[EMAILHEADER <standard-email-header>
<string-message-ID><na>FROM<Todd-Spires>
<toddspi@quapaw.astate.edu>
SUBJ<FS:  1978 Fiat 124 Spyder (Ark)>
NEWSGROUP<rec.autos.marketplace>
0-473:<Article 26827 of rec.autos.mar>]
[NAME:N <Todd Spires>:<>G<Todd:> <:><:>S<Spires:> <:>P<>
217-229:<Todd Spires)\n>]
[A <FS.Az><:  > 273-277:<FS:  >]
[TSRANGE:B @19780101000000:19780101000000 278-282:<1978 >]
[PRODUCT:N 1978-Fiat-124 277-299:< 1978 Fiat 124 Spyder (>]
[TSRANGE:B @19950928000000:19950928000000
```

```
311-322:<28 Sep 1995 >]
[PRODUCT:N 1978-Fiat-124 474-496:<\n1978 Fiat 124 Spyder, >]
[V <paint.p1SVz>< (> 556-562:<paint (>]
[N <paint.SNz ,>< (> 556-562:<paint (>]
[NUMBER:N NUMBER:USD:3000 642-646:<$3000>]
```

(Only a few of the parse nodes are shown above. Several parse nodes may be generated for a given chunk of text if it is ambiguous. Parsed chunks may overlap arbitrarily.)

Second, the *product trade text agent* looks at the parse nodes created in the previous step. It attempts to find the following within a single email message: a product, a price, and a lexical entry having a meaning of `for-sale` or `wanted-to-buy`. Once found, these and other optional items are used to create and fill an appropriate template. (This method fails on messages containing more than one ad.)

Third, the new template and related information are added to memory. The information is also dumped to a file for future use.

Translation

Two types of translation are possible in ThoughtTreasure:

- interlingual translation, and
- transfer-based translation.

Translation may be requested using options of the `parse` shell command.

Interlingual translation

Interlingual translation uses the full power of ThoughtTreasure: An input sentence in the source language is converted into the single ThoughtTreasure concept that makes the most sense—the output of the understanding agency. This concept is then generated in the target language. Because the program's coverage is limited, so is the coverage of this method.

Interlingual translations are produced whenever output is requested in a language different from the input language. A shell command such as the following produces an interlingual French translation of English input:

```
parse -lang z -dialect À -dcin int.txt -dcout outte.txt
-lang y -dialect ? -parain 1 -echoin 0 -dcout outtf.txt
```

Here is an example interlingual translation from English to French of the tutoyer test suite:

```
) Jacques est un ennemi de François.
) Il déteste François.
Effectivement, Jacques est son ennemi.
) Jacques tutoie François.
Mais je croyais que Jacques était un ennemi de
François.
) Lionel est un ennemi de Jacques.
) Il tutoie Jacques.
Effectivement, Lionel est titulaire d'une promotion
Stendhal de l'École nationale d'administration et il
est titulaire d'une promotion Vauban de l'École
nationale d'administration.
) Jacques réussit à être le président de la France.
) Il est heureux.
Effectivement, Jacques réussit à être le président de
la France.
) Lionel en veut à Jacques.
Effectivement, Jacques réussit à être le président de
la France et Lionel est un ennemi de Jacques.
) François est heureux pour Jacques.
Oui, Jacques réussit à être le président de la France.
Mais je croyais que Jacques était un ennemi de
François.
```

Note that both user inputs and program outputs are translated. Actually most program outputs do not have to be translated since they exist already as ThoughtTreasure concepts; they only have to be generated in the target language. (A few outputs of the program are generated directly into the target language for convenience in the dictionary tool.)

Transfer-based translation

The beginnings of a *transfer-based translation* mechanism have been coded. Eventually this could be made into a broad-coverage translator for translating sentences ThoughtTreasure cannot understand. A transfer-based translation is produced whenever the -translate option of the parse shell command is set to 1. This translator takes a parse tree in the source language as input, and produces one or more parse trees in the target language as output.

The argument structure of a verb is translated, for every concept associated with the verb lexical entry. Subject, object, and indirect objects may occur in different orders, and prepositions may be added, deleted, or modified. Thus *Jim likes rain* maps to *La pluie plaît à Jim* (rain pleases to Jim).

The following database file entry:

```
===like.Véz//plaire* à+.Vúy/|r1=human|r2=nonhuman|
```

gets expanded to:

```
<like>.<·Vz¸> <¹> <like>
    1:    subj                        human
    2:    obj                         nonhuman

<plaire>.<Vy¸> <¹> <like>
    1:    iobj            à. Ry¸       human
    2:    subj                        nonhuman
```

The numbers 1 and 2 are the indices of theta roles in the concept `like`. Thus *Jim likes rain* is represented as:

```
[like Jim rain]
```

To do transfer-based translation, the indices are used to generate a structural mapping from one language to another:

```
like:
english     french
subj    -> iobj (à)
obj     -> subj
```

The results of semantic parsing of the parse tree (which makes use of selectional restrictions) are used to prune possible senses of each word. Output from transfer-based translation is post-edited by transformational rules.

The transfer-based translation of the `tutoyer` test suite input is as follows:

```
Jacques est un « enemy » de François.
Jacques est un ennemi moins François.
```

```
He déteste François.
Il déteste François.
```

```
He tutoie François.
Il tutoie François.
```

```
Lionel est un « enemy » de Jacques.
Lionel est un ennemi moins Jacques.
```

```
He tutoie Jacques.
Il tutoie Jacques.
```

```
Jacques réussissait à « being » « elected President » moins France.
Jacques réussi à « being » « elected President » moins France.
Jacques réussi à étant « elected President » moins France.
Jacques réussissait à étant « elected President » moins France.
Jacques réussi à être « elected President » moins France.
Jacques réussissait à être « elected President » moins France.
```

```
He est heureux.
He veut heureux.
He demeure heureux.
Il est heureux.
Il veut heureux.
Il demeure heureux.
```

```
Lionel est pleins de ressentiment à l'égard vers Jacques.
Lionel veut pleins de ressentiment à l'égard vers Jacques.
Lionel demeure pleins de ressentiment à l'égard vers Jacques.
```

```
François est heureux pour Jacques.
François veut heureux pour Jacques.
François demeure heureux pour Jacques.
```

He may appear to be the English pronoun appearing unquoted in the French translation, but actually this is the chemical symbol for helium: *Helium hates François* is a possible reading of the sentence without semantics to prune it away. There are numerous other problems in the above.

Associative thought stream generation

When ThoughtTreasure is not in Turing mode, an associative stream of thought is included in the output of the dictionary tool. This tool can be obtained by typing dict into the ThoughtTreasure shell.

Two types of associative streams of thought are produced: In an *object-based* thought stream, a stream of objects is generated by transitioning from object to object across random database relations and hierarchical links. In an *assertion-based* thought stream, a stream of database assertions is generated by randomly transitioning from assertion to assertion, each of which has an object in common with the preceding. Hierarchical links are not traversed. A given object or assertion is not allowed to occur more than once in a stream.

Here are some sample associative thought streams:

```
OBJECT-BASED, IN RESPONSE TO 'Bellcore':
Bellcore. Bell Atlantic. BEL. USD. AT. AirTouch
Communications. Paul White. White. Vana White. A Wheel of
Fortune. WABC-TV. The Joker Is Wild. Nancy Kovack. Nancy.
Anna. Anna Freud. Austria. Vienna. The city. A location. A
room.

OBJECT-BASED, IN RESPONSE TO 'Intel':
Intel. A 4004. A 4-bit microprocessor. A CISC processor.
Motorola. A 68030. A 33-MHz 68030. A 3/480. A rackmount. A
3/180. A 68881. A 3/260. A VME bus. A 3/150. A 3/160. A
deskside chassis. A 4/360. A 25-MHz CY7C601. A SPARCserver
390. A sun4. A 4/280. A 4/260. A Sun-4. A SunOS. A Sun-2. A
170. A 68010.

ASSERTION-BASED, IN RESPONSE TO 'NYNEX':
Ivan Seidenberg heads up NYNEX. Seidenberg is his first name.
He is a member of the board of directors of NYNEX. Raymond
Burke is an executive vice president of NYNEX. Burke is his
first name. Burke is the first family name of Walter Burke.
Walter Burke and Alex Arcy are some actors of some Fine
Feathered Finks. Arcy is the first name of Alex Arcy.

ASSERTION-BASED, IN RESPONSE TO 'Brazil':
Country code "55" is its dialing prefix. Postal code "55" is
a zip code of "Meuse". "Bar-le-Duc" is the capital of
"Meuse". "Meuse" consists of "Bar-le-Duc". "Lorraine"
consists of "Meuse". "Metz" is the capital of "Lorraine".
"Moselle" consists of "Metz". Postal code "57" is a zip code
```

```
of "Moselle". Country code "57" is the dialing prefix of
Colombia. Spanish is an official language of there and
Paraguay. South America consists of there and Jamaica.
English is an official language of Jamaica and Uganda.

ASSERTION-BASED, IN RESPONSE TO 'Noam Chomsky':
He is the author of Some Concepts and Consequences of the
Theory of Government and Binding. "La nouvelle syntaxe" is a
translation of Some Concepts and Consequences of the Theory
of Government and Binding. Lélia Picabia is the translator of
"La nouvelle syntaxe". Picabia is her first family name.
```

Associative thought streams can be used to spot check the coding of lexical entries and database assertions.

Ontologies for Internet context indexing

The ThoughtTreasure ontology could serve as an index to Internet content, allowing the user to zero in on a specific concept of interest. Suppose you wanted to search the net for information about TSPS, the Western Electric telephone operator services switching system. If you typed "TSPS" into a keyword-based search engine, you would likely get back a lot of recipes mentioning "tsps" (teaspoons). You could then attempt to narrow your search using an expression such as:

```
[and TSPS [or telephone operator switching]]
```

In contrast, each of the meanings of TSPS is already disambiguated in the ThoughtTreasure ontology. So if you requested information on TSPS, the following objects would be displayed:

```
TSPS busy verification tone (busy verification tone)
TSPS operator (toll operator)
TSPS position (Traffic Service Position)
TSPS switching system (electronic switch)
teaspoon (liter)
```

To implement this, URI references would have to be added to every ThoughtTreasure concept, and concepts would have to be added to fill in gaps in the current database. Actually, the indexing service Yahoo! has already been constructing a hierarchical database of the Internet since April 1994. One problem with this type of index is that as it grows, it gets more and more messy. As David

Judson Haykin put it in 1943 regarding the Library of Congress headings ontology:

```
The failures in logic and consistency are, of course, due to
the fact that headings were adopted in turn as needed, and
that many minds participated in the choice and establishment
of headings.
(Library of Congress, 1987, p. viii)
```

A better index of Internet content would take this one step further by disambiguating the meaning of each and every word of every Internet resource— called a *semantic concordance* by (Miller, 1995a). Then content could be retrieved via specific senses of words, rather than simply on words. (Texts encoded as semantic concordances would have other benefits: spelling could be adjusted automatically according to the dialect [British/American English] of the reader.)

An even better index of Internet content would make use of ThoughtTreasure assertions, not just atomic objects. Suppose you want to search the net for all Sun workstations available for less than $5000. Currently, there are many computer classified ad services and no uniform way to search them all. You have to go to each service one by one.

A ThoughtTreasure representation added to the end of each ad would enable more users to find the ad more quickly:

```
From: tim@chibble.com
Date: 18 Jul 1996 16:14:51 -0400
Subject: FS: SPARCstation 10
Newsgroups: misc.forsale.computers.workstation

Sun Microsystems SPARCstation 10 - Model 30
S10GX-30-64-P45
 19-inch Trinitron Monitor
 30 Processor
 64-Mbytes
 424-Mbyte Internal SCSI Disk

$ 4,100

-Tim

Ph#: 555-357-1943
```

```
<ttel>
[define W1] [isa W1 10-30]
[model-number-of W1 "S10GX-30-64-P45"]
[define M1] [isa M1 19-inch-color-monitor]
[define T1] [isa T1 Sony-Trinitron-CRT]
[cpart-of T1 M1]
[cpart-of M1 W1]
[RAM-of W1 64Mbyte]
[define D1] [isa D1 internal-hard-disk-drive]
[isa D1 SCSI-device]
[storage-size-of D1 424Mbyte]
[cpart-of D1 W1]
@19960718161451|[ap W1 NUMBER:USD:4100]
[define H1] [isa H1 human]
[first-name-of H1 aamgn-Tim]
[email-address-of H1 STRING:email-address:"tim@chibble.com"]
[phone-number-of H1 STRING:pstn:"15553571943"]
[owner-of W1 H1]
</ttel>
```

The ads could then be picked up by various spiders and search engines and made available to users for easy querying.

How many assertions appear in the ad depends on how much is already in the ThoughtTreasure ontology. For example, if a 19-inch-color-monitor were not already defined, the advertiser would instead use:

```
[define M1] [isa M1 color-monitor]
[diagonal-length-of M1 19in]
```

Similarly, if a 10-30 were not already defined, the advertiser would use:

```
[define W1] [isa W1 SPARCstation-10]
[processor-of W1 36-MHz-superSPARC]
[SPECint92-of W1 45.2u]
[SPECfp92-of W1 54.0u]
```

The ThoughtTreasure shell

The user interface to ThoughtTreasure is via the *ThoughtTreasure shell*, which is entered once the program finishes loading. The shell prompts with an asterisk "*". A complete list of ThoughtTreasure shell commands is provided in Appendix A.

The `parse` command is used to initiate parsing of a file containing natural language text. A list of arguments to this command is provided in Appendix A. The command:

```
parse -lang z -dialect À -dcin int.txt -dcout outte.txt
-lang y -dialect ? -parain 1 -echoin 0 -dcout outtf.txt
```

causes ThoughtTreasure to parse the American English input file `int.txt`, placing output in the American English file `outte.txt` and French file `outtf.txt`, with French paraphrases and no verbatim English echoing. Other shell commands are discussed in appropriate sections of this book.

Statistics on ThoughtTreasure lexical entries

The lexical entries of ThoughtTreasure break down as follows:

Lexical entries:

fea	type	n	%	objs	/le	0	1	>=2	poly	infls	i/le
yN	word	10294	20.5	9364	0.9	19.2	73.1	7.7	9.5	21511	2.1
yN	phrase	5199	10.4	5327	1.0	0.0	98.0	2.0	2.0	10722	2.1
yN		15493	30.9	14691	0.9	12.8	81.4	5.8	6.6	32233	2.1
yA	word	2562	5.1	1485	0.6	52.4	40.2	7.5	15.7	8586	3.4
yA	phrase	256	0.5	278	1.1	0.0	92.2	7.8	7.8	1024	4.0
yA		2818	5.6	1763	0.6	47.6	44.9	7.5	14.3	9610	3.4
yV	word	402	0.8	421	1.0	25.1	62.4	12.4	16.6	20243	50.4
yV	phrase	107	0.2	270	2.5	0.0	65.4	34.6	34.6	5510	51.5
yV		509	1.0	691	1.4	19.8	63.1	17.1	21.3	25753	50.6
y	word	13765	27.5	11728	0.9	26.0	66.0	8.0	10.8	51033	3.7
y	phrase	6247	12.5	6446	1.0	2.5	94.2	3.2	3.3	17972	2.9
y		20012	39.9	18174	0.9	18.7	74.8	6.5	8.0	69005	3.4
y,	word	3897	7.8	3808	1.0	26.8	57.2	16.0	21.8	18645	4.8
zN	word	12781	25.5	11601	0.9	21.6	69.4	9.0	11.5	26062	2.0
zN	phrase	10549	21.0	10746	1.0	0.0	98.3	1.7	1.7	21033	2.0
zN		23330	46.5	22347	1.0	11.8	82.5	5.7	6.5	47095	2.0
zA	word	3353	6.7	1821	0.5	50.8	45.0	4.2	8.5	3469	1.0
zA	phrase	481	1.0	514	1.1	0.0	93.1	6.9	6.9	481	1.0
zA		3834	7.6	2335	0.6	44.4	51.0	4.5	8.1	3950	1.0
zV	word	575	1.1	679	1.2	23.8	66.4	9.7	12.8	4115	7.2
zV	phrase	127	0.3	343	2.7	0.0	49.6	50.4	50.4	916	7.2
zV		702	1.4	1022	1.5	19.5	63.4	17.1	21.2	5031	7.2
z	word	17692	35.3	14859	0.8	28.2	63.7	8.1	11.3	34741	2.0
z	phrase	12429	24.8	12706	1.0	1.6	96.0	2.5	2.5	23702	1.9
z		30121	60.1	27565	0.9	17.2	77.0	5.8	7.0	58443	1.9
z,	word	7135	14.2	6935	1.0	24.8	61.7	13.5	17.9	14157	2.0
	word	31457	62.7	26587	0.8	27.2	64.7	8.1	11.1	85774	2.7
	phrase	18676	37.3	19152	1.0	1.9	95.4	2.7	2.8	41674	2.2
		50133	100.0	45739	0.9	17.8	76.1	6.1	7.4	127448	2.5

The meaning of each field in the above report is as follows:

fea

Set of features used to select lexical entries. The lexical entry must contain all of the listed features in order to be selected.

type

Whether words, phrases, or both are selected. Phrases are those lexical entries which contain white space or whose theta roles include expletive elements. Expletive elements are not considered part of the lexical entry's identity. Thus, for example, *take on* and *take off* are both stored under the single lexical entry *take*.

n

The number of selected lexical entries.

%

The number of selected lexical entries as a percentage of the total number of lexical entries in the system.

objs

The number of unique lexical-entry-to-object links: Sometimes a lexical entry is linked to a given object more than once, as when the links contain different usage features. Here only each unique link between lexical entry and object is counted. If all the links were counted, the numbers would be slightly higher.

/le

The average number of unique objects linked to a selected lexical entry.

0

The number of lexical entries linked to zero objects, as a percentage of the number of selected lexical entries. These arise when words whose meanings in isolation are not defined are used inside phrases.

1

The number of lexical entries linked to one object, as a percentage of the number of selected lexical entries. These are lexical entries with one meaning.

>=2

The number of lexical entries linked to two or more objects, as a percentage of the number of selected lexical entries. These are polysemous lexical entries.

poly

The number of lexical entries linked to two or more objects, as a percentage of the number of lexical entries linked to one or more objects. This is the percentage of polysemous lexical entries excluding those lexical entries not linked to any concept.

infls

The number of inflections linked to the selected lexical entries. There may be several inflections consisting of the same character string, but with different features: For example, "lived" occurs both as a simple past and past participle and is therefore counted as two inflections.

i/le

The average number of inflections linked to a selected lexical entry.

Most of the lexical entries are nouns. French lexical entries appear to be about a percentage point more polysemous than English lexical entries.

Statistics on ThoughtTreasure objects

The objects of ThoughtTreasure break down as follows:

class	n	%	les	/o	0	1	2	3	4	asser	ISA
object	19334	89.8	40181	2.1	12.7	25.3	41.7	8.1	12.2	13439	21335
abstract-object	9897	46.0	23948	2.4	5.2	21.1	51.7	7.8	14.3	7950	11022
media-object	2343	10.9	6509	2.8	7.3	30.7	29.1	11.5	21.5	1988	2784
theory	1366	6.3	4710	3.4	11.3	16.1	29.1	12.4	31.2	556	1678
computer-program	867	4.0	2092	2.4	10.7	36.8	25.4	11.2	15.9	254	957
operating-system	239	1.1	372	1.6	0.0	67.4	15.1	15.1	2.5	26	253
human-name	3133	14.6	6071	1.9	3.2	0.2	96.6	0.0	0.1	1620	3212
surname	1696	7.9	3350	2.0	1.4	0.1	98.5	0.0	0.1	542	1720
given-name	1409	6.5	2716	1.9	3.7	0.1	96.1	0.0	0.1	1056	1463
polity	818	3.8	1695	2.1	2.4	49.8	27.4	6.5	13.9	2202	904
country	193	0.9	595	3.1	0.0	4.1	58.5	19.2	18.1	1072	199
country-subdivisi	127	0.6	314	2.5	0.0	36.2	36.2	7.9	19.7	470	150
city	272	1.3	352	1.3	7.4	73.2	14.0	1.1	4.4	717	304
political-system	165	0.8	641	3.9	0.6	27.9	36.4	8.5	26.7	64	188
occupation	434	2.0	1394	3.2	3.0	13.6	32.5	23.3	27.6	121	458
financial-instrum	182	0.8	367	2.0	30.2	9.3	27.5	18.1	14.8	187	188
data-structure	4228	19.6	9495	2.2	6.3	5.9	77.9	2.6	7.3	2185	4476
knowledge-structu	4136	19.2	9289	2.2	6.5	5.2	78.8	2.4	7.1	2143	4382
number	174	0.8	449	2.6	0.0	23.0	42.5	16.7	17.8	211	192
value-name	163	0.8	571	3.5	0.0	3.7	35.0	14.1	47.2	117	180
linguistic-concep	5250	24.4	12230	2.3	6.0	10.1	69.9	4.1	9.9	2800	5711
concept-cliche	159	0.7	138	0.9	47.8	30.8	14.5	3.1	3.8	54	174
langue	404	1.9	649	1.6	0.2	59.7	30.7	5.2	4.2	268	446
adverb	238	1.1	1278	5.4	2.5	13.9	24.4	10.9	48.3	85	275
pronoun	122	0.6	318	2.6	14.8	9.8	34.4	16.4	24.6	18	203
preposition	118	0.5	284	2.4	17.8	16.1	36.4	12.7	16.9	20	199
atom	122	0.6	474	3.9	0.0	0.8	8.2	0.8	90.2	126	123
clothing	990	4.6	2141	2.2	16.7	42.7	18.7	8.6	13.3	990	1132
organization	1651	7.7	3580	2.2	1.3	45.9	29.8	7.8	15.3	3483	2006
company	500	2.3	887	1.8	0.0	55.2	29.6	6.6	8.6	1142	737
music	368	1.7	750	2.0	5.2	40.5	31.0	9.0	14.4	154	411
physical-object	8713	40.5	14187	1.6	22.6	29.3	31.6	8.6	7.9	7936	9498
building	297	1.4	315	1.1	38.7	35.7	14.8	7.4	3.4	603	309
exterior-area	947	4.4	833	0.9	28.7	63.9	3.4	1.4	2.6	381	957
roadway	721	3.4	735	1.0	11.0	83.4	2.9	0.7	2.1	166	728
street	665	3.1	612	0.9	11.0	87.4	0.9	0.6	0.2	139	666
room	133	0.6	225	1.7	30.8	18.8	34.6	5.3	10.5	91	136
furniture	510	2.4	218	0.4	80.4	2.9	11.8	3.5	1.4	432	528
musical-instrumen	134	0.6	336	2.5	2.2	3.7	59.0	20.1	14.9	51	151
personal-article	1320	6.1	2724	2.1	17.0	35.8	25.6	10.5	11.1	1114	1479
material	392	1.8	473	1.2	11.7	64.8	17.3	4.3	1.8	67	397
transportation-ve	284	1.3	496	1.7	4.6	45.8	32.7	10.6	6.3	260	304
car	212	1.0	339	1.6	6.1	50.9	31.6	6.1	5.2	189	225
electronic-device	1301	6.0	2513	1.9	14.2	30.7	29.3	14.1	11.6	1446	1673
computer-equipmen	296	1.4	560	1.9	0.0	48.3	31.1	10.1	10.5	655	330
phone	200	0.9	429	2.1	4.0	15.5	62.5	12.5	5.5	72	452

food	1300	6.0	2598	2.0	6.1	22.9	50.5	12.5	7.9	140	1354
beverage	300	1.4	503	1.7	18.3	30.7	32.3	11.3	7.3	42	318
drug	225	1.0	367	1.6	16.9	33.8	31.6	10.7	7.1	43	245
celestial-object	269	1.2	420	1.6	1.9	58.7	32.0	1.9	5.6	69	272
satellite	168	0.8	200	1.2	3.0	76.8	19.0	0.6	0.6	50	169
living-thing	1237	5.7	2488	2.0	11.7	9.7	62.5	7.0	9.1	2992	1314
part-of-human	263	1.2	615	2.3	1.1	3.4	75.3	12.5	7.6	108	309
human	520	2.4	1197	2.3	3.8	1.9	78.8	2.9	12.5	2617	536
state	2491	11.6	8365	3.4	15.3	24.7	24.8	7.0	28.2	784	2819
relation	894	4.2	2502	2.8	20.8	22.9	29.6	6.8	19.8	445	1046
human-relation	136	0.6	718	5.3	6.6	35.3	27.9	5.9	24.3	104	201
attribute	1337	6.2	5722	4.3	4.2	27.5	24.4	7.3	36.6	376	1534
personality-trait	106	0.5	983	9.3	0.0	2.8	16.0	13.2	67.9	16	111
object-trait	136	0.6	13831	0.2	2.2	8.8	19.1	7.4	62.5	62	139
broadcast-station	125	0.6	261	2.1	0.0	43.2	35.2	8.0	13.6	574	175
broadcast	200	0.9	311	1.6	2.0	67.0	22.0	5.5	3.5	878	218
enum	335	1.6	507	1.5	42.4	24.2	11.0	6.3	16.1	42	382
action	884	4.1	2819	3.2	18.2	17.1	23.3	10.9	30.5	530	985
primitive-action	501	2.3	1626	3.2	18.4	19.6	23.2	11.4	27.5	283	549
mtrans	368	1.7	1153	3.1	22.0	23.4	17.9	9.5	27.2	97	410
script	372	1.7	1154	3.1	18.5	13.7	23.4	9.9	34.4	240	423
particle	161	0.7	328	2.0	0.0	53.4	23.6	9.3	13.7	192	195
force	317	1.5	698	2.2	12.6	42.3	17.0	6.0	22.1	174	360
concept	21521	100.0	46437	2.2	14.8	24.3	39.7	7.9	13.2	13827	23335

The meaning of each field in the above report is as follows:

class

The class of object used to select lexical entries. A given object is counted under a number of classes in the report.

n

The number of selected objects.

%

The number of selected object entries as a percentage of the total number of atomic (non-list) objects in the system.

les

The number of all object-to-lex-entry links.

/o

The average number of lexical entries linked to a selected object.

0

The number of objects linked to zero lexical entries, as a percentage of the number of selected objects. These are objects used internally in ThoughtTreasure which are not parsed or generated (or they are objects for which lexical entries need to be added).

1

The number of objects linked to one lexical entry, as a percentage of the number of selected objects. These are objects that only have a lexical entry in one language. In most cases, this is because a translation has not yet been entered. There are however a few cases in which a word for an object does not exist in one of the languages.

2

The number of objects linked to two lexical entries, as a percentage of the number of selected objects.

3

The number of objects linked to three lexical entries, as a percentage of the number of selected objects.

4

The number of objects linked to four lexical entries, as a percentage of the number of selected objects.

asser

The number of database assertions involving the selected objects.

ISA

The number of hierarchical links involving the selected objects. (A link from a parent to a child plus a link from child to a parent are counted as one link.)

Chapter 11: Experiences and unexpected results

Though a computer can only "do whatever we know how to order it to perform" (Lady Lovelace, quoted in McCorduck, 1979, p. 27), it often does things which the programmer would never have expected. There were a number of examples of this in the development and testing of ThoughtTreasure.

Unexpected question answers

What is my name? was once parsed as *What is the name that I own?*: this is merely a case of ambiguity of the genitive, which is used for a variety of purposes:

- Equative role: *Joyce is Jim's mother*.
- Argument to a nominalized verb: *John's walk*
- Ownership: *Karen's calendar book*
- Part-whole relationship: *Lincoln's left foot*
- Pseudoownership: *Hilary's rental apartment*, *Hilary's living room*, *Grice's book* (authorship), and so forth.

Because of a bug, the program was unable to resolve the anaphora in *What did she do?*. Instead of throwing out the sentence altogether it substituted the placeholder na ("not available") for *she*. Due to another bug, *what* was lost and the result of the parse was *Did NA do?*, a Yes-No question instead of the question-word question it should have been. The Yes-No question answering agent then looked in the database for an assertion matching the question, where na matches anything, and found quite a few two-place assertions:

```
> What did she do?
SEMANTICS CONCEPTS:
0.90000:[do-past
 [action subject-pronoun]]
ANAPHORA CONCEPT:
[do-past
 [action na]]
UNDERSTANDING SYNTAX:
[Z
 [X [Pro What]]
 [W
  [W
```

```
   [W [V did]]
   [H she]]
   [V do]]]
```

UNDERSTANDING CONCEPT:
@na:na#4256721|[do-past [action na]]
Yes, something in fact discoverred an upsilon particle. Yes,
something in fact discoverred a J family. Yes, something in
fact discoverred a bottom quark. Yes, something in fact
discoverred a top quark. Yes, something in fact discoverred a
strange quark. Yes, something in fact discoverred a charm
quark. Yes, something in fact discoverred a down quark. Yes,
something in fact discoverred an up quark. Yes, something in
fact discoverred an electron. Yes, something in fact created
an A1. Yes, something in fact created a 50AL. Yes, something
in fact created a 1021. Yes, something in fact created a 10.
Yes, something in fact created a 9. Yes, something in fact
created a 3. Yes, something in fact created a 2. Yes,
something in fact created a "telephone de Gower". Yes,
something in fact created a Hunnings Transmitter. Yes,
something in fact created a Blake Transmitter. Yes, something
in fact created an Usenet newsgroup. Yes, something in fact
created a FTP. Yes, something in fact created the "maison de
Radio France". Yes, something in fact created Opera Bastille.
Yes, something in fact created Opera Garnier. Yes, something
in fact created an Amaretto di Saronno. Yes, Roget's 1911
Thesaurus was in fact published. Yes, Roget's Thesaurus 1852
Edition was in fact published.

A seemingly simple question leads to a host of unanticipated parses: Given *Who is
the President of the United States?*, in addition to the correct interpretations,
ThoughtTreasure came up with:

```
Context 12 sense 0.101245 MODE_STOPPED
@19951025135110:19951025135110#12
Sprout concept [present-indicative [President-of United-
States rock-group-the-Who]]
Answer    sense 0.1
[President-of United-States rock-group-the-Who]
0.00000:[sentence-adverb-of-negation
 [not
  [President-of United-States rock-group-the-Who]]]

Context 53 sense 0.101035 MODE_STOPPED
@19951025135110:19951025135110#53
Sprout concept [present-indicative [isa rock-group-the-Who
Kennedy]]
Answer    sense 0.1
[isa rock-group-the-Who Kennedy]
```

```
0.00000:[sentence-adverb-of-negation
 [but
  [ako
   [and Kennedy rock-group-the-Who]
   human]]]
```

That is, it interpreted the question as meaning (1) *Is the rock group the Who the President of the United States?* to which it suggested the answer *No*, and (2) *Is John Kennedy a type of the Who, the rock group?* (with the intension *the President of the United States* evaluating to one of its extensions) to which it suggested the answer *No, but the Who and John Kennedy are both humans.*

As a partial solution to this problem, code was added to assign scores based on known article collocations: For example, *Who* meaning *the rock group the Who* is coded as normally being preceded by a definite article. Other examples in ThoughtTreasure's database:

empty article	definite article
France	the Antarctic
Bell Atlantic	the Baby Bells
MIT	the Massachusetts Institute of Technology
UCLA	the University of California, Los Angeles
Roxy Music	the Stones
U2	the B-52's
NBC	the WB
	the Dow
	the Internet
	the KGB

But these are soft restrictions (consider *I like my Stones album* and *Which band is the Roxy Music of the 90's?*), so ThoughtTreasure still has to wade through a number of alternatives.

During the debugging of Usenet ad parsing, ThoughtTreasure output the following:

```
> Asking $3000  E-mail for more details.
> toddspi@quapaw.astate.edu
Humans are not very conscious.
> 80,000 mi.  20,000 since complete engine rebuild and
paint. Humans are not very conscious.
> Please respond to:
Humans are not very conscious.
```

Humans are not very conscious is simply one of ThoughtTreasure's canned responses (after Minsky) to the *Computers can never be conscious* objection to AI cliché. (ThoughtTreasure contains an ontology of philosophical and cognitive science clichés.) A bug in the canned question/request agent was generating this on every input concept.

Non sequiturs are produced by ThoughtTreasure:

```
> Tex Avery created Bugs Bunny.
) Did he?
No, a concept does not do.

> Where was Napoleon born?
) Where is him?
I do not know that s he is not born, but I was going to
know something.
```

(A greater than sign precedes user input; a right parenthesis precedes ThoughtTreasure's paraphrase of the input; other text is ThoughtTreasure's output.)

```
> What is my address?
You live in your rented apartment.
```

Here the question was interpreted as meaning *What do you reside in?* (the relation `residence-of`) instead of *What is your mailing address?* (the relation `mailing-address-of`).

One time, *the love of Jim for New York City* was bizarrely being parsed as *the love of Jim for Paris*. This was because the prepositional phrase *for New York City* was being ignored due to a bug, and *the love of Jim* was resolving to *Paris* as had been previously learned.

Here is one incorrect paraphrase of a French question:

```
> Quelle est la circonférence de la Terre ?
) She is a girth of the Earth?
```

It should be *What is the circumference of the Earth?*

The `description` question answering agent recognizes questions of the form *What is nonhuman?* (as in *What are jeans?*) and *Who is human?* (as in *Who is Noam Chomsky?*). Given the hypothetical word *intelligentphobe*, ThoughtTreasure infers a new type of human, one that does not like intelligence. When asked *What is an intelligentphobe?*, the question answering agent did not respond, because *What is* `human`*?* was not a legal combination. In fact this usage is quite common for roles as in *What is a dentist?* and *What is she?* (= *What does she do?*). Should `intelligentphobe` be a role rather than a human? The answer is not clear. In the meantime *What is* `human`*?* has been added as a legal combination.

Unexpected syntactic parses

The expected parse of *The American who is Jim's sister ate* is:

```
[[The American [who is [Jim's sister]]] ate.]
```

But ThoughtTreasure also came up with:

```
[[[The American [who is Jim]]'s sister] ate.]
```

which could be rephrased as *The sister of the American who is Jim ate*. Now, it happened in this case that Jim and his sister are both American, so the two parses resolved to the same extension, namely that Jim's sister ate. But in other examples this might cause a problem.

The solution is not to rule out long arguments to the genitive *'s*, since sentences such as *The woman who I was visiting last night's sister ate* are acceptable, if a bit awkward. Rather, it appears that *NP's NP* prefer to be grouped together. Preferences can be modeled by assigning scores and using these scores to prioritize processing. The syntactic component would thus parse *The woman who is a democrat's sister* as:

```
[[The woman who is a [democrat's sister]] ate.]
```
    with higher score
```
[[[The woman who is a democrat]'s sister] ate.]
```
    with lower score

Cases in which the lower score parse turns out to be the correct interpretation (as in *Peter is teaching the schoolchildren who are his sister's bike riding*) should nonetheless be correctly interpreted by the understanding agency. Since *the schoolchildren who are his sister's bike riding* does not make any sense in the context, the understanding agency goes on to examine the lower *syntactic parse score* alternative which in the end is assigned a higher *make sense score*. ThoughtTreasure was unable to parse *Is an elephant intelligent?* because the `intelligent` attribute was coded with a `human` selectional restriction. What is needed are soft constraints: for many attributes applied to humans, they can sometimes be applied to animals as well. Perhaps we should adopt Lyons (1977) suggestion to distinguish `person` from `human`, with personified animals (such as those of fairy tales) counting as persons.

Unexpected semantic parses

```
> What is the capital of New Jersey?
Trenton is a city.
```

Here ThoughtTreasure resolves the intension *the capital of New Jersey* into the extension *Trenton*, getting *What is Trenton?*, for which the answer is *Trenton is a city*. To solve this problem, the *make sense score* assigned to description questions by the description question answering agent was reduced, so that if the other agents that answer interrogative pronoun questions succeed, their answers will have a higher score. Now ThoughtTreasure produces:

```
> What is my first name?
Jim is your first name.
```

instead of:

```
> What is my first name?
Jim is an Anglo-American male given name.
```

Some Gricean or other constraints on what questions a user is likely to ask are in order here.

The number of parses for a simple sentence can be mind boggling. At one point, before a number of constraints were added, ThoughtTreasure produced 276 semantic parses for *Où étais mon pied gauche ?* (*Where was my left foot?*). Strangely, the 6th parse was the correct one.

When parsing a sentence of the French translation of *Zwischen neun und neun* which begins:

```
Pierre, qui était en train de préparer la carriole dans
la cour ...
```

two lexical entries for *Pierre* were retrieved, doubling the number of parses. This is because Pierre is the capital of South Dakota and that possibility has to be considered.

One meaning of *à* in French is possession. ThoughtTreasure came up with an odd interpretation of *J'étais à Paris* (*I was in Paris*), namely *Paris owned me*:

```
[imperfect-indicative [owner-of Jim Paris]]
```

Unexpected spellings

The analogical morphology agent of ThoughtTreasure guesses the spelling of new words by analogy to existing words. Here are some of the unexpected results (sometimes exposing inconsistencies in the English spelling system relative to the words it already knew):

The British English spelling of *craftsman* was incorrectly guessed to be *craughtsman*, by analogy to *draftsman* in American English and *draughtsman* in British English.

The British English spelling of *minor* was incorrectly guessed to be *minour*, by analogy to *color* in American English and *colour* in British English.

The American English spelling of the noun *sour* (as in *whisky sour*), was incorrectly guessed to be *sor*, by analogy to *labour* in British English and *labor* in American English.

An alternative plural of *rum* was guessed to be *ra*, by analogy to *spectrum* and *spectra*.

An alternative plural of *genius* was guessed to be *genii*, by analogy to *nucleus* and *nuclei*.

tied was correctly interpreted as a preterit, but the resulting conjugation, by analogy to the verb *to pretty (up)* and *prettied (up)* contained one incorrect form:

```
*I ty (present)
he ties (present)
he tied (preterit)
he is tying (present progressive)
```

(*tying* and *tieing* are both acceptable spellings.)

telephone was interpreted as the past participle of a hypothetical verb *telepho*, by analogy to *done* and *do*. Thus this verb *telepho* was conjugated as:

```
*I telepho (present)
*he telephoes (present)
*he telephid (preterit)
*he has telephone (present perfect)
*he is telephoing (present progressive)
```

This type of problem becomes less frequent as the system has more examples to work from.

Unexpected text agent parses

Given *SUN-ROOF, Cruise Control, 2.0 Liter Engine*, part of a car ad on Usenet, ThoughtTreasure's product text agent proposed the following database addition:

```
===ROOF//
====Sun# Microsystems#P ROOF#.z//
|product-of¤Sun-Microsystems
```

First of all, the lexical entry *sun roof* should be added to the database, but that begs the question. What ThoughtTreasure needs to know is that it is unlikely that a roof is a product of the computer manufacturer Sun Microsystems, though it could be. (Here there is the additional complication that the item appears entirely in capital letters.) Perhaps the `manufacturer-of` relation on companies could be employed.

Unexpected generation output

The question *Who is Jim Garnier?* was being paraphrased by ThoughtTreasure as:

```
) Karen Garnier's brother's boss was who?
```

This may seem like an error, but technically it was correct: Karen is Jim's sister and the system had been told that Jim was his own boss. This roundabout way of referring to Jim resulted from a bug in name generation: When name generation failed, ThoughtTreasure fell back on another strategy which generates a reference to a person whose name is unknown, using other known relations.

```
> Is a bordeaux bread?
Yes some foodstuffs are in fact of some bread a kind.
```

This was before the generation of expletive phrasal elements (such as *the bucket* in *kick the bucket*) had been properly ordered. There are some other problems as well. ThoughtTreasure did however use the subjunctive in the French version of the answer to a similar question:

```
> Is beer bread?
Non quoiqu'elle et le pain soient d'un aliment une
sorte.
```

(This should be *une sorte d'aliment*.)

ThoughtTreasure generated:

```
De Gaulle was the president of the Fifth Republic
between November 1945 and Sunday January 20 1946.
```

The Fifth Republic is a synonym for France in the database, but in 1945-1946 de Gaulle was leading the provisional government after the Liberation, prior to the formation of the Fourth Republic. ThoughtTreasure lexical entries do not have timestamp ranges associated with them, but it appears they should. (However, human name changes are already handled properly: all human names involve relations such as first-name-of and first-surname-of which apply over certain timestamp ranges.)

At one point ThoughtTreasure was going a bit overboard with contractions in French:

```
J't'en suis.
```

I'm not sure what it was trying to say. Similarly:

```
Elle était à Hightstown High School entr'août 1975 et
août 1979.
```

An attempt at transfer-based translation was producing quite a few translations of *et comment il déconstruit l'idée de la mémoire là-dedans*:

```
of a memory there inside / and how he deconstructs the topic
of a memory there inside / and how he deconstructs the topic
of a memory there inside and how he deconstructing the topic
```

```
of a memory inside / and how he deconstructing the topic of a
memory there inside / and how he deconstructing the topic of
a memory there inside / and how he deconstructing large topic
of a memory there inside / and how he deconstructs large
topic of the memory there inside / and how he deconstructs
the topic of the memory there inside / and how he
deconstructing large topic of the memory there inside / and
how he deconstructing large topic of a memory there inside /
and how he deconstructs the topic of a memory there inside /
and how he deconstructs the topic of a memory there inside
and how he deconstructing the topic of a memory there
inside / and how he deconstructing the topic of a memory
there inside / and how he deconstructing large topic of a
memory there inside / and how he deconstructs large topic of
the memory there inside / and how he deconstructs the topic
of the memory there inside / and how he deconstructing large
topic of the memory there inside / and how he deconstructing
large topic of a memory there inside / and how he
deconstructs the topic of a memory there inside / and how he
deconstructs the
```

Deconstruction, indeed.

Unexpected planning results

In a planning sequence in which a mother was going to drive her child somewhere, the mother picked up the child and put her in the car. This was because the car is a container and the plan for putting an object into a container was used: go to the object, move grasper to it, grasp it, go to the container, move grasper into the container, and release. The inside planning agent was adjusted to use a different plan for placing animate objects in large containers, namely for the animate object to go itself inside the container. (This is just a temporary patch, as many more issues are potentially involved here—speech acts, goals, and so on.)

The online chat planning agent was coded and a selectional restriction was added that the participants of an online-chat are human. A wrapper was then written so that this same agent could be used for ThoughtTreasure to participate in an online chat with a human. When it was first run, it printed the warning:

```
@@@@@@@@@ START NEW SUBGOAL [online-chat &ThoughtTrésor &Jim]
guide: NULL
19941212152127: !!!! <ThoughtTrésor> is not <human>:
[online-chat &ThoughtTrésor &Jim]
```

Because of this and other problems (such as the parsing and generation of pronouns referring to ThoughtTreasure), ThoughtTreasure was made a human in the database.

Chapter 12: Conclusions and future work

The beginnings of a computer that can understand natural language have been constructed in the form of the ThoughtTreasure program. Now the program needs to be scaled up: planning and understanding agents need to be added for all aspects of human experience which are able to cope with the many possible state transitions and ways of expressing these state transitions in natural language. This kind of work is slow going and requires much persistence, but the hope is that if we keep plugging away, we will finally arrive at a machine that understands. Let's do it!

I will now close with some speculations about how artificial intelligence will come into existence.

Will symbolic AI or automated methods succeed?

Since around 1986, when the books on parallel distributed processing (PDP) (Rumelhart et al., 1986), were published, we have seen an explosion of work in bottom-up models such as neural nets, decision tree learning, statistical and corpus-based natural language processing, genetic algorithms, cellular automata, and artificial life. This work generally grew out of a frustration with symbolic AI, which seemed to require so much manual coding for so little results. In contrast, bottom-up approaches seek to build a mechanism that can evolve useful systems *by itself*.

Statistical language models can now perform many tasks once thought to require manually constructed rules, such as word-sense disambiguation (Zernik, 1991; Yarowsky, 1995). Automatically constructed models have the potential to provide a much more accurate cognitive model than manually constructed ones. Using speech corpora it is now possible (Tajchman, Jurafsky, and Fosler, 1995) to update Chomsky and Halle's (1968) manually constructed phonology, described in their book *Sound Pattern of English*, with a model that not only runs on a computer and is free of ambiguities but fits the data more accurately.

At the same time, work in symbolic AI has continued. In business, many symbolic expert systems have been deployed (such as my own ExperTik program used by a Wall Street firm to hypothesize and track the state of specialist's book of outstanding orders on the New York Stock Exchange). In academia, a symbolic paradigm called lexical semantics has recently emerged among computational linguists. (Though in many ways this is a rediscovery of the approaches taken by researchers in the 1970's such as Schank [Schank and Abelson, 1977] or the generative semanticists [Green, 1974].)

In 1986, Minsky published a book-length account of his society of mind theory (Minsky, 1977, 1981, 1986), in which he wrote:

> What magical trick makes us intelligent? *The trick is that there is no trick.* (emphasis in original) The power of intelligence stems from our vast diversity, not from any single, perfect principle. Our species has evolved many effective although imperfect methods, and each of us individually develops more on our own. Eventually, very few of our actions and decisions come to depend on any single mechanism. Instead, they emerge from conflicts and negotiations among societies of processes that constantly challenge one another. (Minsky, 1986, p. 308)

Earlier, in 1983, Douglas Lenat and a team of researchers had begun a major symbolic AI project (Lenat et al., 1983) along Minsky's lines, not to find the magical trick that many were hoping for, but to painstakingly build the massive database of commonsense knowledge presumably needed by any intelligent computer program. Their philosophy was perhaps best summarized when they wrote:

> [W]e believe that many of the recent trendy paradigm shifts in AI are due to laziness—researchers with "physics envy" insisting that there must be some elegant "free lunch" approach to achieving machine intelligence. They work on natural language understanding, or representation theory, or whatever, for a few years; if it doesn't "work" after a little effort, they try another field, like automated discovery; if that doesn't "work" after a few years, they switch approaches again and try memory organization, automatic indexing, neural nets, fuzzy logic, knowledge-free computing, or (if they have tenure) philosophizing. Many of the smartest folk in AI have fallen into that sad track. Our belief was—and still is—that what's needed is not a new paradigm but rather a few order of magnitude more elbow grease applied to one project within *any* of those paradigms. (Guha and Lenat, 1993, pp. 166-167)

Work on the project, called Cyc, began at the Microelectronics and Computer Technology Corporation (MCC) in 1984 (Lenat and Guha, 1990) and continued there until 1995 when work shifted to the development of business applications at a newly-formed company called Cycorp (Lenat, 1995). Guha moved to Apple Computers and was quoted in Fortune Magazine as saying that "the goal of creating a system that would exhibit real common sense failed" (Stipp, 1995).

To some, Cyc was the last hope for symbolic AI. Lenat and his group have certainly put in much effort: 100 person-years worth (Lenat, 1995), quite a bit more than the 2 person-years spent on ThoughtTreasure. Despite this work, the Cyc program still cannot understand natural language. (Surprisingly, Lenat claims natural language is "a red herring, though one we cannot ignore forever because most people use it so heavily to communicate" [p. 48].)

Has symbolic AI failed? Well, we have only been attempting to construct symbolic AI programs for only four decades — a minuscule period viewed from the time scale of human evolution. Symbolic AI may still succeed if more effort is put into it. Still, it is clear that several cognitive and management obstacles need to be overcome if this is to happen.

Find ways of managing the complexity. Writing a symbolic AI program can be mind blowing. There are so many possibilities and so many wrong paths the program takes which need to be repaired and so many new situations which always remain to be added. It is difficult to maintain one's concentration in the face of a seemingly infinite list of future tasks.

Finding ways of staying focussed. As Arno Penzias puts it, it is easy to find oneself "getting more and more fascinated about less and less" (Farnham, 1996, p. 46). This happens easily when attempting to capture human knowledge, which is fractal in the sense that no matter how deep you go, there are always more details to represent.

Finding the time to do the work. There are many distractions from working on the program.

The brand of symbolic AI in which rules are coded manually may very well be at a dead end, or may simply be too cumbersome. Though it may be possible to achieve symbolic AI in theory, unless we can overcome the above hurdles and write all the necessary code, symbolic AI will not succeed. Symbolic AI should therefore be bootstrapped, where possible, through the use of automated learning techniques. Such techniques have already been successful in the lexical component for learning part-of-speech tagging rules (Brill, 1994), and somewhat successful in the semantic component for learning selectional restrictions (Hindle and Rooth, 1993) and verb argument structure (Brent, 1993). Recently, we have begun to see the first inkling of research on learning within the understanding agency: primitive methods have been described for learning make-sense rules (Knight and Hatzivassiloglou, 1995) and for learning scripts (Miikkulainen, 1993; Reithinger and Maier, 1995).

The closer we get to the understanding agency, the more training data and processing power we need in order to learn rules automatically. Thus, for English part-of-speech tagging, all the rules have basically been learned automatically. For verb argument structure, only a subset of the actual subcategorization frames have so far been learned using automated techniques. Almost none of the standard human scripts have as yet been learned through automated techniques. But as available data and processing power increase, we may in fact be able to learn all human scripts automatically.

The limits of automated learning methods will depend on how clever those programs have to be. In a sense, automated methods just bump the AI problem up to a meta level: instead of writing a program that is intelligent, we write a program that can write a program that is intelligent. So the methods are not really automatic — much human labor still goes into figuring out how to write the learning program. But if that program itself has to be intelligent in order to work, we are in a Catch-22 situation. One thing is for sure: once we have one intelligent computer, creating more will be easy. (Or will intelligent computers find it just as difficult as humans to write AI programs?)

The most likely scenario is that we will succeed in bootstrapping AI through an iterative process combining techniques at multiple levels — by thinking about what symbolic rules should look like, by writing programs to discover rules automatically, and by augmenting automatically generated rules with manually entered ones.

When we now look back at the early attempts at AI, we see how futile they were. The computers and software tools available at the time were simply not up to the task. A similar observation will surely be made by people looking back at the state of AI in 1998.

AI will continue to progress.

The evolution of a new cyberspatial intelligence

The human world without computers is very complex. But with computers, we seem to be heading toward a new level of complexity. The recent evolution of telephone switching systems is a case in point: An electromechanical No. 5 crossbar switching system, introduced in the 1940's, handles the phone calls of a suburban community and fills a medium-sized building. Its complete operating manual fits in several notebooks (Western Electric Company, 1963). A 5ESS digital switch, introduced in the 1980's, configured to handle the same volume of phone calls, only takes up a small corner of the same building, and has many, many more capabilities. Its documentation fills hundreds of notebooks (AT&T, 1990).

We may be coding for the past when we attempt to build programs which can understand the computerless human world. After all, the human world is in the process of being rebuilt and redefined in cyberspace. Business transactions — such as "vehicle baying order," "report of injury or illness," "product registration," and "request for student educational record" — are already codified as X12 transaction sets. The World Wide Web Consortium and other organizations are in the process of defining digital protocols for everything from "micropayments" to "PICS content labels." When cyberspace becomes the place where most things happen, the focus of artificial intelligence will shift to that world (if it hasn't already).

Cyberspace is its own simulation. Well, this is not entirely true, since there are humans adding new code and interacting in it. But much of it already exists as computer code, so artificial intelligence will be a lot easier to achieve in cyberspace. In fact, it could be that simply by building applications in cyberspace, we will naturally arrive at artificial intelligence (see Etzioni, 1993).

Talbott (1995) argues in his book *The future does not compute* that through the ages our intelligence has become more and more rigid, deterministic, and mechanical, culminating in modern science with its view of a "clockwork universe" (p. 31, quantum physics notwithstanding) and more recently, computers and cyberspace. He assumes we will achieve artificial intelligence, but only by making ourselves into artificial intelligences, by "descending to the machine's level" (dust jacket).

Indeed, one aspect of intelligence which seems to have become more rigid over the years is language: Compare the writing style of Kant (1787/1991) with that of Dennett (1984). Kant's sentences are much longer and free-flowing, and his book as a whole appears less structured than Dennett's. The writing style in vogue now is that of the executive summary with lots of bullets. (Microsoft PowerPoint makes it easy to create these.) Partly as a result of deliberate invention and rationalization — for example the work of grammarians such as the Académie française (Institut de France, 1994) — a more relaxed use of language (free word order, orthography, idiosyncratic constructions) has given way to a more structured use, to the point where a Noam Chomsky can now convincingly argue (Chomsky, 1975) that these structures are innate and universal. Which universe and in what stage of its development?, I wonder. But this is only the beginning.

Language appears to be headed for a whole new level of codification: As we develop more and more languages like X12, we will start to think in those languages. As increasing use is made of knowledge representation languages such as CycL (Lenat and Guha, 1990), a greater portion of our lives will be conducted using them. If we do not adopt these new languages, then intelligent programs certainly will. As intelligence evolves in cyberspace, will it want to use human language to communicate? Why not use a language, call it a "cyberlanguage" or "e-language", which is more efficient and less ambiguous?

Talbott is concerned that we are becoming more mechanical, more like the Stepford Wives, more brain-dead. But the rigidity Talbott has pointed out is what you will always see if you view evolution from a fixed vantage point. If you focus on a certain way of doing things X (such as a language or mode of artistic expression), you are going to find it becoming more rigid over time. You have developed all the variations of X, know what they are, so you stop retreading that same ground. X then appears to be static. Put another way: X might be a vague and open-ended concept. But with time it becomes less so, because you start to figure it out, to codify it. Then X seems more rigid. The mistake is trying to preserve X. You cannot preserve X, since, as Barlow (1994) puts it, "information wants to change." Instead, it is time to invent a new vague and open-ended concept Y which is more interesting. I think this is what we are all trying to do in cyberspace.

Human language might be the X which has become rigid, and the future e-language of cyberspace might be the new and free-flowing Y. We do not know what that new language will look like, because the universe it will exist in has not yet evolved. But one can imagine the possibilities for richness of a language existing in a completely new space, with a new set of transactions, and many types of interacting agents instead of just one (humans).

Our universe would be the physical support for another universe. What would it look like from within? The physicists in cyberspace would inhabit a world not of 3-dimensional space plus time, but of communications channels, virtual circuits, data packets, programs, resources, URIs, and IP addresses. (Is a particle a packet or a processor? Perhaps bosons are packets and fermions are processors?) Cyberphysicists would have the luxury of working with a universe built out of a very simple thing: the bit. But they might not see it that way: Distance in their space would be a very odd thing, determined by various propagation delays for transmitting and receiving packets. They would have to model the program entities in their world, and modeling programs is a hard problem (Lewis and Papadimitriou, 1981). There would be hardware errors from time to time, causing anomalous experimental outcomes—there would simply be no explanation at their level for what had happened. If a computer broke, a part of their universe would vanish.

Will intelligence evolve in cyberspace as distinct agents, as assumed above? Or as intelligent combinations of human and software agents? Or as a net which is intelligent taken in its entirety?

We have probably been looking at the artificial intelligence problem in the wrong way. Because "intelligence" is a static word, we have misled ourselves into thinking it is a static entity. We have then tried (and so far failed) to write computer programs which would embody it. But the intelligence that is useful to humans now might not be the same as the intelligence that will be useful to humans and computers in the future. Intelligence is relative to the context in which it is embedded. If we were to succeed at creating a program that is intelligent in the real world, then that same program might be clueless in cyberspace. So instead of attempting to write an intelligent program for the real world—which is an alien context to computers anyway—perhaps we should work on intelligent programs in the natural medium for programs, cyberspace.

Exercises

1. Write routines in Java (Gosling, Joy, and Steele, 1996) to parse and dump ThoughtTreasure objects. For example, the parse routine should be able to convert the following text string into an object:

```
[appointment Pam Susan Susan-office
 [conversation Pam Susan IPO1]
 @1996072211]
```

and convert that object back into the above string.

2. Write routines in Java to transmit and receive ThoughtTreasure objects over network sockets (`java.net.Socket`).

3. Work on evolving cyberspatial intelligence as described in this chapter: Develop an intelligent agent in Java which uses the ThoughtTreasure representation language to negotiate appointments. The agent should handle the various cases which arise in human negotiation and keep track of the current status of all appointments. For example, the conversational sequence:

```
Pam: Can we meet to discuss the IPO? Perhaps Monday or
Tuesday?
Susan: How about Monday at 11 am
Pam: Sounds good. Shall we meet in my office or yours?
Susan: Mine.
Pam: OK. I'll see you Monday at 11 am in your office.
```

can be modeled as the exchange of the following ThoughtTreasure objects between two Java agents over a socket connection:

```
[propose Pam Susan
 [appointment Pam Susan na [conversation Pam Susan IPO1]
  [or Monday Tuesday]]]

[propose Susan Pam
 [appointment Pam Susan na [conversation Pam Susan IPO1]
  @1996072211]]

[propose Pam Susan
 [appointment Pam Susan [or Pam-office Susan-office]
  [conversation Pam Susan IPO1]
  @1996072211]]

[propose Susan Pam
 [appointment Pam Susan Susan-office
  [conversation Pam Susan IPO1] @1996072211]]

[confirm Pam Susan
 [appointment Pam Susan Susan-office
  [conversation Pam Susan IPO1] @1996072211]]
```

Model other interactions such as the following:

```
I'm afraid I'm going to have to cancel our Monday meeting.
[reject Susan Pam
 [appointment Pam Susan Susan-office
  [conversation Pam Susan IPO1] @1996072211]]

Can we reschedule it for later in the week?
[propose Susan Pam
```

```
    [appointment Pam Susan Susan-office
     [conversation Pam Susan IPO1] @19960723:19960726]]

Wednesday is bad for me.
[reject Pam Susan
 [appointment Pam Susan Susan-office
  [conversation Pam Susan IPO1] Wednesday]]

When would you like to meet?
[propose Susan Pam
 [appointment Pam Susan Susan-office
  [conversation Pam Susan IPO1] question-element]]

What was the topic of this meeting?
[ask Susan Pam
 [appointment Pam Susan Susan-office question-element na]]
```

Appendices

Appendix A: ThoughtTreasure shell commands

```
adverbial -dir dirname
adverbial -file filename
  Find potential adverbials.
algmorph
  Run algorithmic morphology tool.
anamorph
  Run analogical morphology tool.
cfe -w word
  Find in English corpus.
cff -w word
  Find in French corpus.
chateng
chateng -speaker Jim -listener TT
  Run English chatterbot. Indicate end of input with a
  blank line. Indicate end of chat session with 'quit'.
chatfr
  Run French chatterbot.
corpusfind
  Find in corpus.
corpusload/cl -lang z -dir dirname
  Load corpus.
corpusvalagainst
  Validate against corpus.
covcheckeng
  Check English coverage.
covcheckfr
  Check French coverage.
covcheckengm
  Check English coverage and print missing.
covcheckfrm
  Check French coverage and print missing.
daydream
  Run daydreamer.
db
  Run database tool.
```

```
dbg -flags syn/sem/synsem/all -level off/bad/ok/detail
  hyper
    Set the debugging flags and level. Affects log file
    output. Default is "all" flags and "detail" level.
dict/dict0
    Run dictionary tool.
exit
    Exit ThoughtTreasure.
filtfeat
    Run filter tool.
genhtml
help
    Print this list of commands.
html
inflscan
    Run inflection scanner.
learnnames
    Learn names.
legal
    Print legal notice.
lexentry
    Run lexical entry tool.
lexentryjuxt
    Run lexical entry juxtaposition tool.
lexentryscan
    Run lexical entry scanner.
logclear/lc
    Truncate the log file.
obj
    Run object tool.
objhref
parse -dcin infn -outsyn 1 -outsem 1 -outana 1
  -outund 1 -dcout outfn
    Parse a file. (See the detailed description of the
    arguments below.)
polysem
    Print polysemous lexical entries.
pop
    Pop up a level.
posambig
    Print entries with ambiguous part of speech.
prover
    Run theorem prover tool.
quit
    Exit ThoughtTreasure or pop up a level.
```

report
  Run report tool.
simul
  Run sample simulations.
sortbyline
  Sort by line.
sortbytree
  Sort by tree (note last line must be === */).
stop
  Call the function Debugger(). When running
ThoughtTreasure from
  a debugger, a breakpoint should be set on this
  function, so that the stop command will cause the
  program to break in the debugger.
suffgender
  Study French gender suffixes.
test
  Take ThoughtTreasure shell commands from
  ../examples/test.tts.
testcomptense
  Test generation of compound tenses.
testgenattr
  Test generation of attributes.
testgenrel
  Test generation of relations.
testgentemp
testgentempdb
  Test generation of temporal relations.
testsa
  Test generation of speech acts.
testtrip
  Test trip finding.
testts
  Test timestamp range generation.
tt -file filename
  Invoke the ThoughtTreasure shell recursively on the
  specified filename.
up
  Pop up a level.
validate -old filename -new filename
  Run Unix diff to compare two files and report whether
  they differ. Used to validate test suite runs against
  previous runs.
wflfill
  Fill in words.

wf1train
  Train word formation.
wf2e
  Test English word formation.
wf2f
  Test French word formation.
!!
  Rerun the last command (not including stop).

Command arguments

-dcin filename
  Filename of the input channel. Its language is
  specified by -lang.
-dcout filename
  Filename of an output channel, of which there may be
  several. Attributes of the channel are specified by
  -lang, -dialect, -style, -parain, -echoin, -outsyn,
  -outsem, -outana, and -outund.
-dialect À/g/ç/î/o
  Dialect of the input or output channel:
    À = American (default)
    g = British
    ç = Canadian
    î = other
    o = old.
-dir DIRNAME
-echoin 1/0
  Whether to echo the input verbatim to the output.
  (Echo output is indicated by "" at the start of each
  line.) Default is 1.
-file/-f FILENAME
-flags syn/sem/synsem/all
-lang z/y
  Language of the input or output channel:
    z = English (default)
    y = French.
  The -lang, -dialect, -style, -parain, -echoin,
  -outsyn, -outsem, -outana, and -outund options apply
  to later -dcout (and -dcin) options until modified by
  another occurrence of -lang, -dialect, and so on.
-level off/bad/ok/detail/hyper
-listener object
  The listener ThoughtTreasure object to be pushed onto

the deictic stack before starting to parse the input
file (or participate in a chat). Default is TT
(ThoughtTreasure).

-new

-obj/-o

-old

-outana 0/1
Whether to output all anaphoric parse list objects to
the file. Default is 0.

-outsem 0/1
Whether to output all semantic parse list objects to
the file. Default is 0.

-outsyn 0/1
Whether to output all syntactic parse trees to the
file. Default is 0.

-outund 0/1
Whether to output the single best syntactic parse
tree and semantic parse list object as determined by
the understanding agency. Default is 0.

-parain 0/1
Whether to regenerate a paraphrase of the input on
the output channel. This may be used to produce an
interlingual translation of the input. (Paraphrase
output is indicated by ")" at the start of each
line.) Default is 0.

-runana 1/0
Whether to run the anaphoric parser. If the anaphoric
parser is not run, then the understanding agency is
not run. Default is 1.

-runsem 1/0
Whether to run the semantic parser. If the semantic
parser is not run, then anaphoric parser, and
understanding agency are not run. Default is 1.

-runsyn 1/0
Whether to run the syntactic parser. If the syntactic
parser is not run, then the text agency is run and
the semantic parser, anaphoric parser, and
understanding agency are not run. "1/0" indicates
that either 1 or 0 may be specified. Default is 1.

-runund 1/0
Whether to run the understanding agency. Default is
1.

-speaker object
The speaker ThoughtTreasure object to be pushed onto
the deictic stack before starting to parse the input

file (or participate in a chat). Default is Jim.
-style ?/t/T/a
  Style of the input or output channel:
    ? = standard (default)
    t = literary, technical
    T = informal
    a = slang
-translate 0/1
  Whether to produce a transfer-based translation of
  the input to the file outtrans.txt. The translation
  is French if the input is English and vice versa.
  Default is 0.
-word/-w

Appendix B: ThoughtTreasure manual page

```
tt(1)                        User Commands                        tt(1)

NAME
     tt - run ThoughtTreasure

SYNOPSIS
     tt [-l] [-c cmd] [-f file]

OPTIONS
     -l      Do not load the ThoughtTreasure database.

     -c cmd  After the database is loaded (if it is loaded),
             execute the ThoughtTreasure shell command cmd.

     -f file After the database is loaded (if it is loaded),
             execute ThoughtTreasure shell commands in file.

FILES
     ./log         Program trace and debugging log.
     ./in*.txt     Program input files.
     ./out*.txt    Program output files.
     ttlegal.txt   Copyright and other legal information.
     help.txt      List of ThoughtTreasure shell commands.
     src/*         Source code.
     db/*          Database.
     htm/*         Documentation in HTML format.
     examples/*    Example program input and output.
     bin/*         Executables.

ENVIRONMENT VARIABLES
     TTROOT        Location of root of ThoughtTreasure tree.
```

The output files of ThoughtTreasure are as follows:

```
outadv.txt                English adverbial
outdicte.txt              English dictionary tool output
outdictf.txt              French dictionary tool output
outeinfl.txt              learned English inflections
outfinfl.txt              learned French inflections
outfname.txt              learned given names
outhuman.txt              learned humans
outtrans.txt              output from transfer-based
                          translation
outlrn.txt                various learning output
outlname.txt              learned family names
```

Appendix C: ThoughtTreasure feature characters

Feature	Abbreviation	Description	Type
%		to be entered	other feature
?	NA	empty feature	other feature
@	TODO	unattested	other feature
_	OPT	optional	other feature
˓	CHECKED	inflections checked	other feature
¿	ZBZ	ZBZ block	rule block
+	REQ	mandatory	other feature
±	+PRESP	present participle	subcategorization
«	PRE	prefix	part of speech
»	SUFF	suffix	part of speech
×	VOUVOIEMENT	vouvoiement	mode of address
÷	+INDIC	indicative taker	subcategorization
§		masculine,feminine	instruction
©	COORD	coordinator	rule block
®	TDMK	brand name	noun
°	BZZ	block	rule block
μ	MODAL	modal auxiliary	grammatical modal
¶		no inflection	instruction
·	REALLY	true inflection	other feature
0	EXPL	expletive	part of speech
¾	TRANSONLY	translation only	frequency
1	1	first person	person
¹	FREQ	frequent word	frequency
2	2	second person	person
²	TUTOIEMENT	tutoiement	mode of address
3	3	third person	person
6	POSITIVE	positive degree	absolute degree
7	COMPAR	comparative degree	relative degree
8	SUPERL	superlative degree	relative degree
9	ELEMENT	element	part of speech
A	ADJ	adjective	part of speech
a	SL	slang	language style
ª	GENONLY	generate only	frequency
Á	ELISION	elision	alternative form
á	ROLE2	role name at I=2	parallel universe
à	ROLE1	role name at I=1	parallel universe
À	US	American English	dialect
Ä	PREVOWEL	pre-vowel form	alternative form
ä	ROLE3	role name at I=3	parallel universe
Æ	BEE	BEE block	rule block
B	ADV	adverb	part of speech
b	PREPOSED	preposed adjective	other grammatical
C	NEUT	neuter	gender
c	CONDIT	conditional tense	inflection tense
ç	CAN	Canadian	dialect
d	PP	past participle	inflection tense
D	DET	determiner	part of speech
ð	WBW	WBW block	rule block
e	PRESP	gerund	inflection tense
E	ADJP	adjective phrase	constituent
é		object at I=2	object location
É	ZEROART	zero article taker	other grammatical
è		object at I=1	object location
È	ASP	aspirated	phonetic feature
ê		state-change verb	subcategorization
ë		object at I=3	object location
F	F	feminine	gender
f	INF	infinitive	inflection tense
g	GB	British English	dialect
G	INDIC	indicative mood	grammatical mood
H	PRON	pronoun	part of speech
h	DEROG	derogatory word	connotation
I	IMPER	imperative mood	grammatical mood

i	PAST	simple past	inflection tense
í	CONTRACTION	contraction	alternative form
ì	VOC	vocalic	phonetic feature
î	REGION	regional	dialect
î̃	ISM	abstract quality	parallel universe
ï	+INF	infinitive taker	subcategorization
ï	C	common inflection	other grammatical
J	SUBJ	subjunctive mood	grammatical mood
j	BORR	borrowing	other feature
K	CONJ	conjunction	part of speech
k	DEFART	definite article	other grammatical
l	ETRE	être taker	other grammatical
L	ADVP	adverb phrase	constituent
m	U	non-count noun	other grammatical
M	M	masculine	gender
N	N	noun	part of speech
ñ	HUMOR	humorous word	connotation
o	OLD FASH	dated word	dialect
O	+SUBJ	subjunctive taker	subcategorization
ǫ		multilingual name	instruction
ó	EPITH	attributive	rule block
ô	NR	no reordering	other grammatical
Ô	NOTPROGR	no progressive	other grammatical
ö		iobj at I=3+	iobj location
õ		iobj at I=4+	iobj location
p	PRES	present tense	inflection tense
P	PL	plural	number
q	RARE	infrequent word	frequency
Q	QUES	interrogative	sentence
R	PREP	preposition	part of speech
s	SIMPP	passé simple	inflection tense
S	SING	singular	number
ß	INV	invariant word	instruction
t	FML	technical word	language style
T	INFML	informal word	language style
Ð	BWW	BWW block	rule block
þ	ATTACH	attachment	parallel universe
U	INTERJ	interjection	part of speech
u	FUT	future	inflection tense
Ú	PRED	predicative	rule block
ú		subject at I=2	subject location
ù		subject at I=1,2	subject location
ü		subject at I=3	subject location
v	PROV	proverb	other feature
V	V	verb	part of speech
w	COORD	coordinator	conjunction
W	VP	verb phrase	constituent
x	SENTENCE	sentence	part of speech
X	NP	noun phrase	constituent
y	FR	French	language
Y	PP	prepositional phrase	constituent
ÿ	FUS	fused	instruction
z	ENG	English	language
z	S	sentence	constituent

Appendix D: ThoughtTreasure database file format

```
atomic-object-definition -
  ==...==lexentry0/parent,parent,.../lexentry/lexentry/.../
  |item|item|...|
```

```
indent ISA format       polity format
====== ========== ==================
   =         ISA           cpart-of
   *    concrete            capital
   -    contrast multilevel polity
```

```
polity format:
=continent
==country
===U.S. state, France region, territories
====U.S. county, France département
=====city
======U.S. borough, France arrondissement
=======city-subsubdivision (neighborhood)
========city-subsubsubdivision
=========city-subsubsubsubdivision
==========city-subsubsubsubsubdivision)
```

```
lexentry0 - lexentry OR atomic-object
```

```
item - @tsrange,tsrange,... OR
       atomic-object OR                    (predicate)
       atomic-object=value,value,... OR    (relation)
       atomic-object¤value,value,... OR    (relation)
       list-object OR                      (assertion)
       GS=griddef
```

```
tsrange - ts{:ts{:days{:tod{:dur}}}}{Ð}
  {} indicate optional
```

```
ts - tsnumber timezone-stem OR na
tsnumber - yyyy OR yyyymm OR yyyymmdd OR yyyymmddhh OR
              yyyymmddhhmm OR yyyymmddhhmmss OR -inf OR +inf
timezone-stem - pt OR et OR gt OR ts OR EMPTY
days - day+day+... OR day¯day OR na
day - mon OR tue OR wed OR thu OR fri OR sat OR sun OR
      lun OR mar OR mer OR jeu OR ven OR sam OR dim
tod - todnumber timezone-stem OR na
todnumber - hh OR hhmm OR hhmmss
dur - number dur-stem OR na
dur-stem - hrs OR min OR sec OR hhmm OR hhmmss
```

```
value - atomic-object OR
        #atomic-object OR    (create instance)
        constant-object OR
        quick-object

list-object - [list-object1 list-object1 ...]
list-object1 - value OR list-object

griddef - gridsnap gridkey
gridsnap - character character ...
gridkey - gridkey1 OR gridkey1 gridkey
gridkey1 - character {. character character ...} :
            {&} atomic-object
  {} indicate optional

constant-object - "string" OR
                    string misc-stem OR
                    number stem OR
                    STRING:atomic-object:"string" OR
                    NUMBER:atomic-object:number

stem - unitless-stem OR length-stem OR
       velocity-stem OR frequency-stem OR
       mass-stem OR bytes-stem OR
       currency-stem OR timezone-stem

unitless-stem - u OR pc
length-stem - m OR km OR ft OR mi
velocity-stem - mps OR mph OR kmph
frequency-stem - hz OR khz OR mhz OR ghz OR ang
mass-stem - g OR lbs
bytes-stem - byte OR Kbyte OR Mbyte OR Gbyte OR Tbyte
currency-stem - $ OR F
misc-stem - usch OR frch OR usca OR frca OR dbw OR
            coor OR km2 OR mi2

quick-object -
  HUMAN:lexentry
  MALE:lexentry
  FEMALE:lexentry
  GROUP:lexentry
  BUILDING:lexentry:street-number:street-name:postal-code:
    city:state:country
  FLOOR:lexentry:level:street-number:street-name:postal-code:
    city:state:country
  APARTMENT:lexentry:apt:level:street-number:street-name:
    postal-code:city:state:country
  ROOM:lexentry:room:apt:level:street-number:street-name:
    postal-code:city:state:country
```

```
PLAY:lexentry:playwright:composer
OPERA:lexentry:composer:librettist
DANCE:lexentry:choreographer:composer
MUSIC:lexentry:composer
```

Bibliography

AAAI, ACM, et al. (1995). *The AI directory*. Menlo Park, CA: American Association for Artificial Intelligence.

Abbott, E. A. (1991). *Flatland*. Princeton, NJ: Princeton University Press. (Original work published 1884)

Abelson, R. P. (1981). Constraint, construal, and cognitive science. In *Proceedings of the Third Annual Conference of the Cognitive Science Society* (pp. 1-9), Berkeley, CA.

Alexander, L. G. (1988). *Longman English grammar*. London: Longman.

Allen, J. (1983). Maintaining knowledge about temporal intervals. *Communications of the ACM, 26,* 832-843.

Allen, J. (1995). *Natural language understanding*. Redwood City, CA: Benjamin/ Cummings.

Armstrong, S. (Ed). (1993). *Using large corpora*. Cambridge, MA: MIT Press.

Asch, T., and Chagnon, N. (1976). *Moonblood: A Yanomamo creation myth as told by Dedeheiwa*. 16mm, 14 min. Distributed by Documentary Educational Resources.

AT&T. (1990). *5ESS Switch Documentation Description and Ordering Guide* (Publication 235-001-001 Issue 6.00). Winston-Salem, NC: AT&T.

Austin, J. L. (1962). *How to do things with words*. Oxford: Clarendon Press.

Baker, C. L. (1978). *Introduction to generative-transformational grammar*. Englewood Cliffs, NJ: Prentice-Hall.

Barger, J. (1995). Comp.ai.imho FAQ: A short course in AI with net pointers (Version 1.5). Posted to comp.ai.

Barlow, J. P. (1994). The economy of ideas. *Wired, 2.03*.

Barrow, J. D., and Tipler, F. J. (1986). *The anthropic cosmological principle*. Oxford: Oxford University Press.

Bates, J., Loyall, A. B., and Reilly, W. S. (1992). Integrating reactivity, goals, and emotion in a broad agent. In *Proceedings of the Fourteenth Annual Conference of the Cognitive Science Society*, Bloomington, Indiana.

Battye, A., and Hintze, M.-A. (1992). *The French language today*. London: Routledge.

Binsted, K., and Ritchie, G. (1994). An implemented model of punning riddles. In *Proceedings of the Twelfth National Conference on Artificial Intelligence*. pp. 633-638. Menlo Park, CA: AAAI Press and Cambridge, MA: MIT Press.

Boulle, J. (1978). Evolution des langues et théorie du langage (Mars 1978). Paris: Université de Paris VII.

Boulle, J. (1988). Théorie aspectuelle (Document 4, I49, Avril 1988). Paris: Université de Paris VII.

Boulle, J. (1992). Théorie aspectuelle (Novembre 1992). Paris: Université de Paris VII.

Brent, M. R. (1993). From grammar to lexicon: Unsupervised learning of lexical syntax. In S. Armstrong (Ed.), *Using large corpora*. pp. 203-222. Cambridge, MA: MIT Press.

Bresnan, J. (1978). A realistic transformational grammar. In M. Halle, J. Bresnan, and G. A. Miller (Eds.), *Linguistic theory and psychological reality*. pp. 1-59. Cambridge, MA: MIT Press.

Brill, E. (1994). Some advances in transformation-based part of speech tagging. In *Proceedings of the Twelfth National Conference on Artificial Intelligence*. pp. 722-727. Menlo Park, CA: AAAI Press and Cambridge, MA: MIT Press.

Brunot, F., and Bruneau, C. (1969). *Précis de grammaire historique de la langue française*. Paris: Masson et Cie.

Cambridge University Press. (1994). *Cambridge word routes*. Cambridge: Cambridge University Press.

Carlut, C., and Meiden, W. (1976). *French for oral and written review*. New York: Holt, Rinehart, and Winston.

Chapman, R. L. (Ed.) (1992). *Roget's international thesaurus* (Fifth edition). New York: HarperCollins.

Charniak, E., Riesbeck, C. K., and McDermott, D. V. (1980). *Artificial intelligence programming*. Hillsdale, NJ: Lawrence Erlbaum.

Chomsky, N. (1957). *Syntactic structures*. The Hague: Mouton.

Chomsky, N. (1965). *Aspects of the theory of syntax*. Cambridge, MA: MIT Press.

Chomsky, N. (1970). Remarks on nominalization. In R. A. Jacobs and P. S. Rosenbaum (Eds.), *Readings in English transformational grammar*. Waltham, MA: Ginn and Company.

Chomsky, N. (1975). *Reflections on language*. New York: Pantheon Books.

Chomsky, N. (1982). *Some concepts and consequences of the theory of government and binding*. (Linguistic Inquiry monograph 6). Cambridge, MA: MIT Press.

Chomsky, N. (1987). *La nouvelle syntaxe* (French translation of *Some concepts and consequences of the theory of government and binding* by Lélia Picabia with additional commentary by Alain Rouveret). Paris: Éditions du seuil. (Original work published 1982)

Chomsky, N. (1986). *Barriers*. (Linguistic Inquiry monograph 13). Cambridge, MA: MIT Press.

Chomsky, N., and Halle, M. (1968). *The sound pattern of English*. New York: Harper and Row.

Chuquet, H., and Paillard, M. (1989). *Approche linguistique des problèmes de traduction anglais-français* (Edition révisée). Paris: Ophrys.

Churchland, P. M. (1984). *Matter and consciousness: A contemporary introduction to the philosophy of mind*. Cambridge, MA: MIT Press.

Clancey, W. J., Smoliar, S. W., and Stefik, M. J. (Eds.) (1994). *Contemplating minds: A forum for artificial intelligence*. Cambridge, MA: MIT Press.

Clocksin, W. F., and Mellish, C. S. (1981). *Programming in Prolog*. Berlin: Springer-Verlag.

Colby, K. M. (1975). *Artificial paranoia: A computer simulation of paranoid processes*. New York: Pergamon Press.

Collins. (1987). *Robert-Collins French-English English-French dictionary* (Second Edition). London: Collins.

Corbeil, J.-C., and Archambault, A. (1992). *Le Visuel: Dictionnaire thématique*. Québec: Éditions Québec-Amérique.

Corréard, M.-H., and Grundy, V. (Eds.) (1994). *The Oxford-Hachette French Dictionary*. Oxford: Oxford University Press.

Courtois, B., and Silberztein, M. (Eds.) (1990). Dictionnaires électroniques du français. *Langue française, 87*, 1-127.

Courtois, B. (1990). Un système de dictionnaires électroniques pour les mots simples du français. *Langue française, 87*, 11-22.

Craik, K. (1943). *The nature of explanation*. Cambridge: Cambridge University Press.

Crouch, R. S., and Pulman, S. G. (1993). Time and modality in a natural language interface to a planning system. *Artificial Intelligence, 63*, 265-304. Elsevier.

Davis, E. (1990). *Representations of commonsense knowledge*. San Mateo, CA: Morgan Kaufmann.

Dennett, D. C. (1984). *Elbow room: The varieties of free will worth wanting*. Cambridge, MA: MIT Press.

Dewdney, A. K. (1984). *The Planiverse: Computer contact with a two-dimensional world*. New York: Poseidon.

Dyer, M. G. (1983). *In-depth understanding*. Cambridge, MA: MIT Press.

Eco, U. (1992). *The limits of interpretation* (English translation of *I limiti dell'interpretazióne*). Indiana University Press. (Original work published 1990)

Eco, U. (1995). *The search for the perfect language*. Blackwell.

Etzioni, O. (1993). Intelligence without robots: A reply to Brooks. *AI Magazine, 14*(4), 7-13.

Farnham, A. (1996). Are you smart enough to keep your job? *Fortune*, January, 15, 1996, pp. 34-48.

Feyerabend, P. (1975). *Against method*. London: New Left.

Fillmore, C. J. (1968). The case for case. In E. Bach and R. T. Harms (Eds.), *Universals in linguistic theory*. New York: Holt, Rinehart, and Winston.

Foley, J. D., van Dam, A., Feiner, S. K., and Hughes, J. F. (1990). *Computer graphics*. Reading, MA: Addison-Wesley.

Gagnon, M., and Lapalme, G. (1996). From conceptual time to linguistic time. *Computational linguistics*, *22*(1), 91-127.

Genesereth, M. R., and Fikes, R. E. (Eds.) (1992). *Knowledge interchange format, Version 3.0 reference manual* (Technical report Logic-92-1). Stanford University, Computer Science Department.

Girodet, J. (1988). *Pièges et difficultés de la langue française*. Paris: Bordas.

Gosling, J., Joy, B., and Steele, G. (1996). *The Java language specification*. Reading, MA: Addison-Wesley.

Green, G. (1974). *Semantics and syntactic irregularity*. Bloomington: Indiana University Press.

Greenbaum, S., and Quirk, R. (1990). *A student's grammar of the English language*. London: Longman.

Grevisse, M. (1986). *Le bon usage* (12th edition, revised by A. Goosse). Paris: Duculot.

Gruber, T. R. (1993). A translation approach to portable ontology specifications. *Knowledge acquisition*, *5*(2), 199-220.

Guha, R. V., and Lenat, D. B. (1993). Response to book review. *Artificial Intelligence*, *61*, 151-173. Elsevier.

Guillet, A. (1990). Reconnaissance des formes verbales avec un dictionnaire minimal. *Langue française*, *87*, 52-58.

Gutowitz, H. (Ed.) (1990). *Cellular automata*. Cambridge, MA: MIT Press.

Heider, F. (1958). *The psychology of interpersonal relations*. Hillsdale, NJ: Lawrence Erlbaum.

Hindle, D., and Rooth, M. (1993). Structural ambiguity and lexical relations. In S. Armstrong (Ed.), *Using large corpora*. pp. 103-120. Cambridge, MA: MIT Press.

Hobbs, J. R., Stickel, M. E., Appelt, D. E., and Martin, P. (1993). Interpretation as abduction. *Artificial Intelligence, 63*, 69-142. Elsevier.

Huls, C., Bos, E., and Claassen, W. (1995). Automatic referent resolution of deictic and anaphoric expressions. *Computational linguistics, 21*(1), 59-79.

Hutcheson, G. D., and Hutcheson, J. D. (1996). Technology and economics in the semiconductor industry. *Scientific American, 274*(1), 54-62.

Institut de France. (1994). *Le dictionnaire de l'académie française 1694-1994: sa naissance et son actualité*. Paris: Institut de France.

Jackendoff, R. S. (1972). *Semantic interpretation in generative grammar*. Cambridge, MA: MIT Press.

Jackendoff, R. S. (1977). *X' Syntax: A study of phrase structure*. (Linguistic Inquiry monograph 2). Cambridge, MA: MIT Press.

Johnson-Laird, P. N. (1983). *Mental models: Towards a cognitive science of language, inference, and consciousness*. Cambridge, MA: Harvard University Press.

Kant, E. (1991). *Critique of pure reason*. London: J. M. Dent. (Original work published 1787)

Katz, J. J., and Fodor, J. A. (1963). The structure of a semantic theory. *Language, 39*(11), 170-210.

Kernighan, B. W., and Ritchie, D. M. (1988). *The C programming language* (Second edition). Englewood Cliffs, NJ: Prentice-Hall.

Knight, K., and Hatzivassiloglou, V. (1995). Two-level, many-paths generation. In *33rd annual meeting of the Association for Computational Linguistics*. pp. 252-260. San Francisco: Morgan Kaufmann.

Lakoff, G. (1971). On generative semantics. In D. D. Steinberg and L. A. Jakobovits (Eds.), *Semantics: An interdisciplinary reader in philosophy, linguistics, and psychology*. Cambridge: Cambridge University Press.

Langton, C. (Ed.) (1995). *Artificial life*. Cambridge, MA: MIT Press.

Lasnik, H. (1976). Remarks on coreference. *Linguistic Analysis*, 2.

Lehmann, F. (1995). Combining ontologies, thesauri, and standards. *Workshop on basic ontological issues in knowledge sharing*, August 19-20, 1995, Montreal.

Lenat, D. B. (1995). CYC: A large-scale investment in knowledge infrastructure. *Communications of the ACM*, *38*(11), 33-48.

Lenat, D. B., and Guha, R. V. (1990). *Building large knowledge-based systems*. Reading, MA: Addison-Wesley.

Lenat, D. B., Borning, A., McDonald, D., Taylor, C., and Weyer, S. (1983). Knoesphere: Building expert systems with encyclopedic knowledge. In *Proceedings of the Eighth International Joint Conference on Artificial Intelligence*. Los Altos, CA: Morgan Kaufmann.

Levinson, S. C. (1983). *Pragmatics*. Cambridge: Cambridge University Press.

Lewis, H. R., and Papadimitriou, C. H. (1981). *Elements of the theory of computation*. Englewood Cliffs, NJ: Prentice-Hall.

Library of Congress. (1987). *Subject headings* (Eleventh edition). Washington, DC: Library of Congress.

Longman. (1992). *Longman dictionary of English language and culture*. London: Longman.

Longman. (1993). *Longman language activator*. London: Longman.

Lyons, J. (1977). *Semantics*. (Volumes I and II). Cambridge: Cambridge University Press.

Marcus, M., Santorini, B., and Marcinkiewicz, M. (1993). Building a large annotated corpus of English: The Penn treebank. *Computational linguistics*, 19(2).

Mauldin, M. L. (1994). ChatterBots, TinyMUDs, and the Turing Test: Entering the Loebner Prize competition. In *Proceedings of the Twelfth National Conference on Artificial Intelligence*. pp. 16-21. Menlo Park, CA: AAAI Press and Cambridge, MA: MIT Press.

McCorduck, P. (1979). *Machines who think*. San Francisco: W. H. Freeman.

Meehan, J. (1976). *The metanovel: Writing stories by computer* (Research Report 74). New Haven, CT: Yale University, Computer Science Department.

Mellish, C. (1995). *Proceedings of the Fourteenth International Joint Conference on Artificial Intelligence*. San Mateo, CA: Morgan Kaufmann.

Miikkulainen, R. (1993). *Subsymbolic natural language processing: An integrated model of scripts, lexicon, and memory*. Cambridge, MA: MIT Press.

Miller, G. A. (Ed.) (1990). WordNet: An on-line lexical database. *International Journal of Lexicography*, *3*, 235-312.

Miller, G. A. (1995a). Building semantic concordances: Disambiguation vs. annotation. In *Representation and acquisition of lexical knowledge: Polysemy, ambiguity, and generativity* (Technical Report SS-95-01). Menlo Park, CA: AAAI Press.

Miller, G. A. (1995b). WordNet: A lexical database for English. *Communications of the ACM*, *38*(11), 39-48.

Minsky, M. L. (1977). Plain talk about neurodevelopmental epistemology. In *Proceedings of the Fifth International Joint Conference on Artificial Intelligence*, pp. 1083-1092. Los Altos, CA: Morgan Kaufmann.

Minsky, M. L. (1981). K-lines: A theory of memory. In D. A. Norman (Ed.), *Perspectives on cognitive science*, pp. 87-104. Norwood, NJ: Ablex.

Minsky, M. (1986). *The society of mind*. New York: Simon and Schuster.

Moeschler, J., and Reboul, A. (1994). *Dictionnaire encyclopédique de pragmatique*. Paris: Seuil.

Montague, R. (1974). *Formal philosophy*. New Haven, CT: Yale University Press.

Mueller, E. T. (1990). *Daydreaming in humans and machines*. Norwood, NJ: Ablex.

Mueller, R. E. (1967). *The science of art: The cybernetics of creative communication*. New York: John Day.

Newell, A., and Simon, H. A. (1972). *Human problem solving*. Englewood Cliffs, NJ: Prentice-Hall.

Newmark, P. (1993). *Paragraphs on translation*. Clevedon: Multilingual Matters.

Neufeldt, V. (Ed.) (1994). *Webster's New World Dictionary* (Third College Edition). New York: Prentice Hall.

O'Rorke, P., and Ortony, A. (1994). Explaining emotions. *Cognitive science*, *18*(2), 283-323.

Ortony, A., Clore, G. L., and Collins, A. (1988). *The cognitive structure of emotions*. New York: Cambridge University Press.

Perrin, M. (1995). Personal communication, March 1995.

Perutz, L. (1988). *Le tour du cadran* (French translation of *Zwischen neun und neun* by Jean-Jacques Pollet). Paris: Christian Bourgois. (Original work published 1918)

Pfeifer, R. (1982). *Cognition and emotion: An information processing approach* (CIP Working Paper 436). Pittsburgh, PA: Carnegie-Mellon University, Department of Psychology.

Picoche, J. (1995). Définitions actancielles. *Cahiers de lexicologie*, *66*(1), 67-76.

Pinker, S. (1994). *The language instinct*. London: Penguin Books.

Pratt, V. (1994). *Cyc report*. Published on the web April 20, 1994.

Prieditis, A., and Russell, S. (Eds.) (1995). *Machine learning: Proceedings of the Twelfth International Conference on Machine Learning*. San Francisco: Morgan Kaufmann.

Reithinger, N., and Maier, E. (1995). Utilizing statistical dialogue act processing in Verbmobil. In *33rd annual meeting of the Association for Computational Linguistics*. pp. 116-121. San Francisco: Morgan Kaufmann.

Rey-Debove, J., and Rey A. (1993). *Le Petit Robert*. Paris: Dictionnaires Le Robert.

Ringle, M. D. (Ed.) (1993) *Cognitive science* (Special issue on situated action), *17*(1).

Rulifson, J., Derksen, J., and Waldinger, R. (1972). *QA4: A procedural calculus for intuitive reasoning* (Technical Note 73). Stanford, CA: Stanford Research Institute, Artificial Intelligence Center.

Rumelhart, D. E., McClelland, J. L., and PDP Research Group (Eds.). (1986). *Parallel distributed processing: Explorations in the microstructure of cognition* (Volumes 1 and 2). Cambridge, MA: MIT Press.

Schank, R. C. (1975). *Conceptual information processing*. New York: North-Holland.

Schank, R. C., and Abelson, R. P. (1977). *Scripts, plans, goals, and understanding*. Hillsdale, NJ: Lawrence Erlbaum.

Searle, J. R. (1969). *Speech acts*. Cambridge: Cambridge University Press.

Simon, H. (1967). Motivational and emotional controls of cognition. *Psychological Review*, *74*(1), 29-39.

Small, S., and Rieger, C. (1982). Parsing and comprehending with word experts (a theory and its realization). In W. G. Lehnert and M. H. Ringle (Eds.), *Strategies for natural language processing*. Hillsdale, NJ: Lawrence Erlbaum.

Steinberg, S. G. (1996). Seek and ye shall find (maybe). *Wired, 4.05*.

Stipp, D. (1995). 2001 is just around the corner. Where's HAL? *Fortune*.

SunSoft. (1994). *Solaris for PowerPC Porting Guide*. Mountain View, CA: Sun Microsystems.

Tajchman, G., Jurafsky, D., and Fosler, E. (1995). Learning phonological rule probabilities from speech corpora with exploratory computational phonology. In

33rd annual meeting of the Association for Computational Linguistics. pp. 1-8. San Francisco: Morgan Kaufmann.

Talbott, S. L. (1995). *The future does not compute*. Sebastopol, CA: O'Reilly and Associates.

ter Meulen, A. G. B. (1995). *Representing time in natural language*. Cambridge, MA: MIT Press.

Tesnière, L. (1966). *Éléments de syntaxe structurale* (2nd edition). Paris: Klincksieck.

Turkle, S. (1995). *Life on the screen*. New York: Simon and Schuster.

Van Roey, J., Granger, S., and Swallow, H. (1991). *Dictionary of faux amis*. Paris: Duculot.

Walter, H. (1994). *L'aventure des langues en occident*. Paris: Robert Laffont.

Western Electric Company. (1963). *No. 5 Crossbar Switching System, Volume 1: Equipment Applications*. Western Electric Company.

Whitten, D. (1995). The unofficial, unauthorized CYC frequently asked questions information sheet (Version 2.0). Posted to comp.ai.

Winograd, T. (1972). *Understanding natural language*. New York: Academic Press.

Winograd, T., and Flores, F. (1986). *Understanding computers and cognition*. Norwood, New Jersey: Ablex.

Winston, P. H. (1977). *Artificial intelligence*. Reading, MA: Addison-Wesley.

Wittgenstein, L. (1961). *Tractatus logico-philosophicus* (English translation by D. F. Pears and B. F. McGuiness). London: Routledge & Kegan Paul. (Original work published 1921)

Wittgenstein, L. (1953). *Philosophical investigations*. Oxford: Basil Blackwell and New York: Macmillan.

Yaguello, M. (1984). *Les fous du langage*. Paris: Seuil.

Yarowsky, D. (1995). Unsupervised word sense disambiguation rivaling supervised methods. In *33rd annual meeting of the Association for Computational Linguistics*. pp. 189-196. San Francisco: Morgan Kaufmann.

Yokoi, T. (1995). The EDR electronic dictionary. *Communications of the ACM*, *38*(11), 42-48.

Zernik, U. (Ed). (1991). *Lexical acquisition*. Hillsdale, NJ: Lawrence Erlbaum.